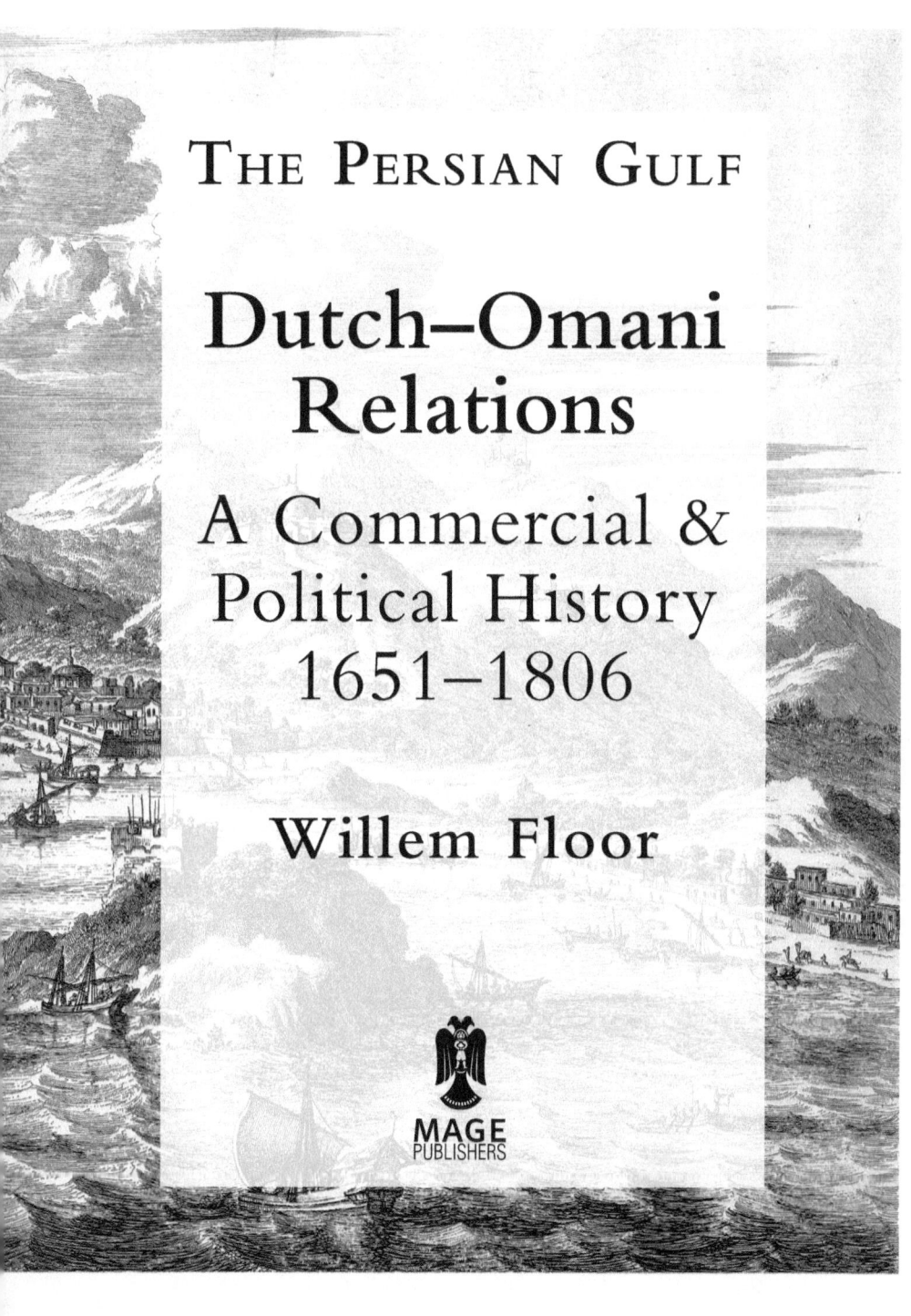

THE PERSIAN GULF

Dutch–Omani Relations

A Commercial & Political History 1651–1806

Willem Floor

MAGE
PUBLISHERS

Copyright © 2014 Willem Floor

"Wood, Horses and Friendship: The Arabic Letters from Muscat to the
Dutch in Kochi (1779) and Batavia (1798–1806)"
© 2013 Jan Just Witkam

All rights reserved.
No part of this book may be reproduced
or retransmitted in any manner whatsoever,
except in the form of a review, without the
written permission of the publisher.

Library of Congress Cataloging-in-Publication Data
Available in detail at the Library of Congress

ISBN Hardcover
1-933823-68-2
978-1-933823-68-3

Paperback
1-933823-69-0
978-1-933823-69-0

Printed and Manufactured in the United States

Mage Publishers
Washington DC
202-342-1642 • as@mage.com
Visit Mage Publishers online at
www.mage.com

CONTENTS

FOREWORD
AMBASSADOR OF THE SULTANATE OF OMAN TO THE NETHERLANDS . . . xiii

FOREWORD
AMBASSADOR OF THE KINGDOM OF THE NETHERLANDS TO OMAN . . . xvi

FOREWORD
NETHERLANDS OMAN FOUNDATION. xix

PREFACE xxi

CHAPTER ONE
DUTCH AND MUSCATI RELATIONS DURING THE
 PORTUGUESE OCCUPATION, 1624–1650. 1
  INTRODUCTION 1
  VOC ORGANIZATION. 6
  DEVELOPMENTS AFTER THE FALL OF HORMUZ 7
  DUTCH REFUSE NAVAL SUPPORT FOR A PERSIAN INVASION OF OMAN . . . 10
  A DUTCH-ENGLISH FLEET BATTLES THE PORTUGUESE FLEET 11
  DUTCH OFFER NAVAL HELP TO PERSIA. 17
  THE END OF PORTUGUESE RULE IN OMAN 19

CHAPTER TWO
THE FIRST PERIOD OF DUTCH-OMANI CONTACTS 1651-1719. . . . 21
  THE DEVELOPMENT OF MUSCAT AS A PORT-OF-CALL 21
  THE BEGINNING OF PORTUGUESE ATTACKS (1652) 23
  THE PERSIANS ASK FOR DUTCH SUPPORT TO
   INVADE MUSCAT (1664). 28
  NEW ROUND OF HOSTILITIES WITH
   PORTUGAL (1666-1674) 37

· v ·

THE DUTCH ESTABLISH A FACTORY AT MUSCAT (1672-1675) 39
  PORTUGUESE-OMANI TRUCE (1672) 55
  WHY THE DUTCH WITHDREW FROM MUSCAT (1675). 58
  A CHANGE OF POLICY IN MUSCAT.. 74
  THE SAFAVIDS WANT AN ANTI-OMANI ALLIANCE (1695-1719) 76
  OMAN ATTACKS AND CONQUERS BAHRAIN (1717) 92

CHAPTER THREE
YA`ARIBA MUSCAT (1650-1725). 101
  POPULATION. 101
  THE HARBOR 105
  BUILDINGS AND WALLS 107
  RELIGION 111
  FOOD SUPPLIES 113
  TRADES AND CRAFTS 116
  SYSTEM OF GOVERNMENT 118
  CONCLUSION 134

CHAPTER FOUR
THE SECOND PERIOD OF DUTCH-OMANI CONTACTS 1755-1806 . . . 139
  INTRODUCTION 139
  PROPOSAL FOR ANNUAL MUSCAT VOYAGES 141
  THE FIST MUSCAT VOYAGE 144
  THE SECOND MUSCAT VOYAGE 148
  VOC DECIDES TO DISCONTINUE MUSCAT VOYAGES 155
  RESUMPTION OF ANNUAL MUSCAT VOYAGES 159
  CONCLUSION 167

ANNEX 1
A REPORT ON THE DISCOVERY OF THE COAST OF OMAN IN 1666 . . . 169

ANNEX 2
THE TRADE OF MUSCAT IN 1673 185

ANNEX 3
PRICES IN MUSCAT, 1672–1675 211

ANNEX 4

THE *AMSTELVEEN* SHIPWRECK, 1763 215
   INTRODUCTION 215
FATEFUL VICISSITUDES 223

ANNEX 5

LETTERS FROM MUSCAT TO BATAVIA, 1798-1806 267
   YA'ARIBA DYNASTY 267
   AL BU SA'ID DYNASTY 268
   GOVERNORS-GENERAL OF THE VOC (1610-1796) 268
   GOVERNORS-GENERAL OF THE DUTCH
      EAST-INDIES (1796-1811) 269
   VOC DIRECTORS IN THE PERSIAN GULF
      (BASED AT BANDAR ABBAS) 270

ANNEX 6

**WOOD, HORSES AND FRIENDSHIP: THE ARABIC LETTERS FROM MUSCAT
TO THE DUTCH IN KOCHI (1779) AND BATAVIA (1798–1806)** . . 272

BIBLIOGRAPHY 305

INDEX . . . .

TABLES

Table 3.1: Weights used in Muscat (1673) 127
Table 3.2: Customs duties charged at Muscat in 1673 130
Table 4.1 List of all goods offered for sale in Muscat in 1757
   and the usual prices obtained 150
Table 4.2: Profit and Loss Account of the *Marienbosch*
   (in Dutch guilders) 154
Table 4.3 Proposed cargos for continued voyages to Muscat . . 156
Table 4.4: Dutch ships sailing to Muscat, 1777-1793 160

Maps & Illustrations

Cover Image: Map of the Bay of Muskette, Dirk van der Velden,
   1696, Library of the University of Leiden: COLLBN 006-14-007
Title Page Image: Lithograph of Oman, Rijksmuseum, Amsterdam
Coastal Oman x
Mouth of the Persian Gulf and the Bay of Muscat xi
Muscat, 1670, Rijksmuseum, Amsterdam xv
Replica of East Indiaman *Amsterdam*,
   Scheepvaartmuseum, Amsterdam xviii
Former Town Hall of Batavia, in today's Jakarta, Indonesia,
   Photo: Kai van Hasselt xx
Shah Abbas I 3
Bay of Diba (Dobi) (1645) 9
Cape of Jask; View of the Cape (1645) 25
Goa Island and Cape Musandam;
   Omani Coast at Cape Musandam (1645) 39
The Coast of Oman 172
Bay of Muscat 173
The Mouth of the Persian Gulf and the Strait of Hormuz . . 173

All maps from inside the book courtesy of:
   Nationaal Archief, The Hague

Dutch Coinage

1 gulden = 20 stuivers = 320 penningen

1 stuiver = 16 penningen

1 stuiver = 8 duiten

1 rijksdaalder = 2.5 guilders = 50 stuivers

1 reaal van acht = 8 schellingen = 48 stuivers

1 schelling = 6 stuivers

Persian Coinage

1 tuman = 100 mahmudis
50 abbasis
1 lari
10,000 dinar

Weights

The common Persian weight was the *man*, which had no fixed weight. The most common weight was the *Tabriz man* of 2.96 kg and the *Shah man* of 5.9 kg. All other weights or measures are explained in a footnote when they are mentioned in the text. For more information, see Willem Floor, "Weights and Measures in Qajar Iran" *Studia Iranica* 37/1 (2008), pp. 57-115.

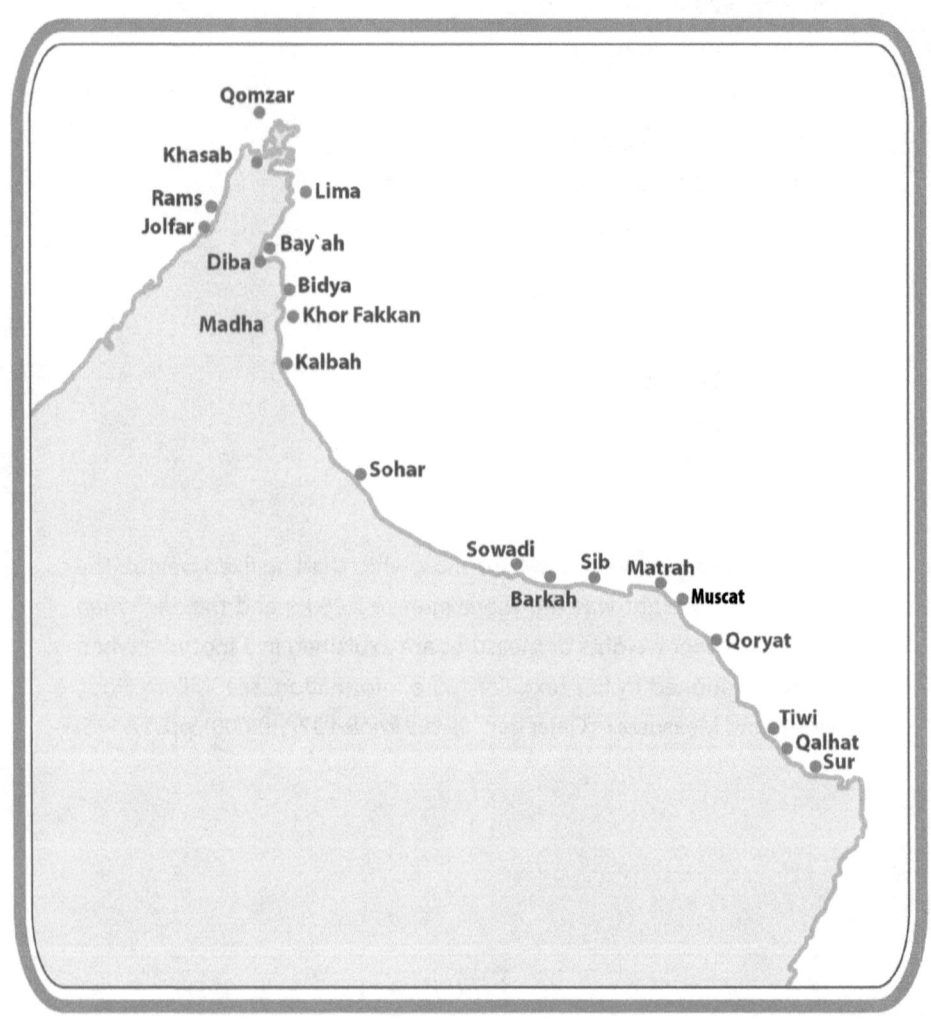

Coastal Oman

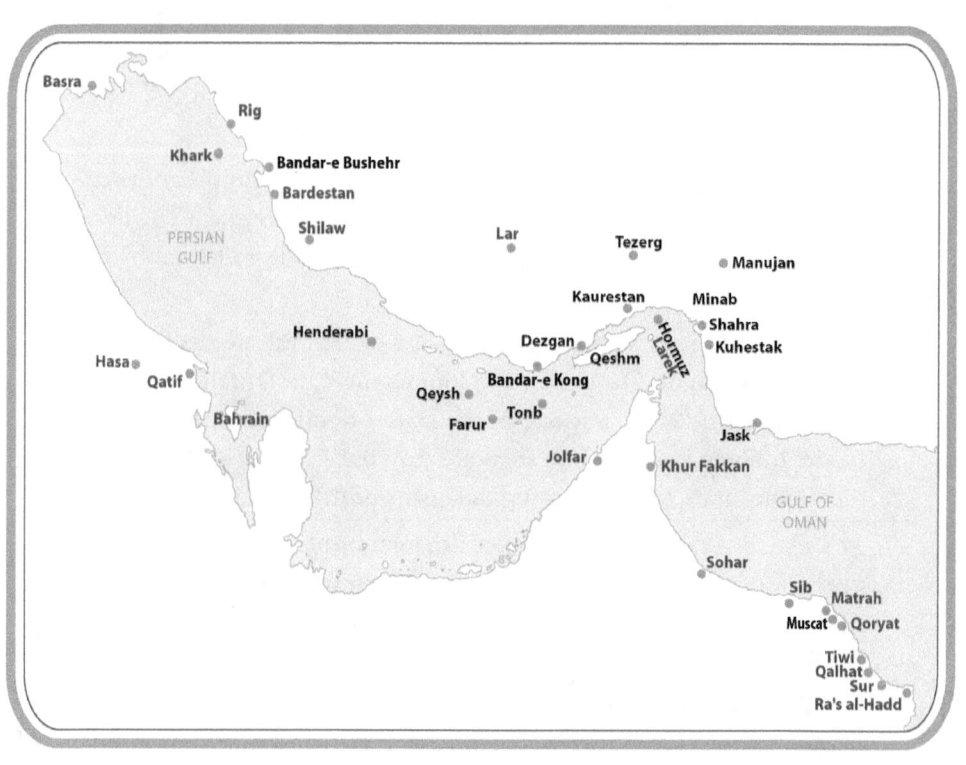

Mouth of the Persian Gulf and the Bay of Muscat

FOREWORD

Ambassador of the Sultanate of Oman to the Netherlands

A major task of the historian is to capture events, as much as possible, as they actually were. Willem Floor's book explores the historical facts and figures of the Dutch-Omani relationship from political and commercial perspectives.

Chronologically the author covers the period from the mid-seventeenth century to the early part of the nineteenth century. The book is divided into four main chapters and a conclusion followed by the annexes.

The author draws upon a wide range of archival sources from the VOC—Verenigde Oostindische Compagnie (the Dutch East-India Company). The VOC was one of the largest trading companies in the world. It owned hundreds of ships and had trade offices in the ports of the Netherlands, as well as along the coasts of Africa and Asia.

The historical overview of the bilateral relationship, which makes up the bulk of the study, consists largely of descriptive narratives providing sufficient thematic cohesiveness to convey a greater understanding of the dynamics of the historical context of the periods covered.

The book begins with VOC agents and representatives seeking trade relations with the Al 'Yariba rulers who were successful in forcing out the Portuguese invaders from Oman in the mid-seventeenth century. During the following century, commercial relations and contacts continued with the Al Bu Said dynasty who had driven out the Persian invaders.

With a broad, ambitious sweep, the author takes the reader through Dutch commercial and political history in the Persian Gulf from the height Portugal's dominance to its eventual demise. The author provides rich details of the growing importance of Oman as a seafaring nation determined to take back some of its own coastal territory from the European occupier and to challenge Portugal's hegemony by taking control of its colonial possessions in India and Africa.

Portuguese settlements and trading posts on the Indian and African coasts were frequently raided and plundered by the Omanis. The Omani successes alarmed the Persians, English, Indians and Dutch. Alliances were formed in an effort to contain the Omanis' unprecedented dominances of the seas in the area. The author offers interesting insights and perspectives, in particular about Persian attempts to launch an anti-Oman alliance with the promise of increased commercial opportunities for the Dutch, as well as for their English and French rivals. However, owing to conflicting commercial and political priorities and interests these alliances could not be sustained.

The chapters focus on the complex relationship between VOC agents and the rulers of Persia and Oman and their respective representatives. The author's conclusion that VOC's decision to leave Oman was driven by economics is well supported by the reports prepared by the Company's agents.

I am confident that this book will fulfill its objective of being not only easy to read but accurate and as thorough as possible on the subject of the history of the commercial and political relations between the Netherlands and Oman from the mid-seventeenth century to the early nineteenth century.

Muhammed Harub Al Said
Ambassador of the Sultanate of Oman
to the Kingdom of the Netherlands
9 April 2014

Muscat, 1670, Rijksmuseum, Amsterdam

Foreword

Ambassador of the Kingdom of the Netherlands to Oman

The development of historical knowledge, the study and documentation of archives and the access to cultural heritage helps our understanding of the past; understand how the present situation came about and how the future may develop. Reading about history gives us a sense of humanity's progress (and sometimes regress); it makes us think sensibly about our world and our place in it.

Today, the world has become the integrated, highly connected network that dawned at the end of the sixteenth century in Europe. At the turn of that century Dutch ships sailed for the first time around the world. They were not the first to have achieved this milestone. After the successes in the Baltic and later the trade within Europe, the trade with the East highlighted the rise of the Dutch Republic in becoming the leading global transport and logistics powerhouse. Trade and finance had always been key ingredients to the Dutch success as the insightful publication you are now holding in your hands shows. And they still are.

When the Dutch mate Cornelis Eyks of the Dutch East India Company sailed to the East Indies in the eighteenth century, Oman's strategic long coastline was already recognized as having ideal conditions for international trade. Consequently trade relations between Oman and the Netherlands flourished as currently witnessed in the prominent cooperation between the Omani Port of Sohar and the Dutch Port of Rotterdam. This has resulted in a powerful transport and logistics hub in Oman

The two countries' quest for trade and their joint efforts towards global entrepreneurship has intertwined and blossomed ever since they shared part of this history together. Many Dutch families currently (and throughout these years) have lived in Oman; some moved on after a while and returned to the Netherlands. But Oman is still in their hearts. A large number of them travel to Oman, from time to time, to meet old friends and to develop new ones.

The cooperation between the two countries goes beyond trade and logistics. Dutch and Omani companies are continuously venturing together in many fields. And more is yet to come.

Documenting history helps nourish the existing long-term commitment to this relationship and recognizes the historical and cultural ties between the two countries up to the present. The great significance of this relationship was exemplified during the state visit of H.M. Queen Beatrix to the Sultanate of Oman.

It makes us proud and humble to see how these old ties have developed into the present bond between us. Whereas we share the appetite for globalization, we also cherish the friendship between our nations and peoples.

Barbara Joziasse

The Ambassador of the Kingdom of the Netherlands
to the Sultanate of Oman

24 March 2014

Replica of East Indiaman *Amsterdam*, courtesy Scheepvaartmuseum Amsterdam. The *Amsterdam* was a sister ship of the *Amstelveen*, that wrecked off the coast of Oman in 1763.

FOREWORD

NETHERLANDS OMAN FOUNDATION

In 2013, the Foundation financed the creation of the documentary film *Expedition Oman* and supervised the maritime archaeological survey of the wreck of the Dutch East Indiaman *Amstelveen*. Two fascinating projects executed under the patronage of the Omani Ministry of Heritage and Culture that were realized with the help of Dutch and Omani business partners.

These two projects underpinned the observation that there was great interest among Omani scholars for a comprehensive overview of Omani relations with European nations from the early beginnings until about 1900.

Four of these nations are of particular importance when studying Omani history. The Portuguese, Dutch, English and French all had ties and interactions with the Imam, his court and traders for many years and they kept records of these contacts.

To some extent, these records have been systematically investigated. However, from the Dutch side, no comprehensive academic overview has been available until the publication of this book.

The Foundation is honored and proud to have been able to take up the challenge of the publication of this book with the help of business partners. Their involvement shows that private companies do understand the need for investments in cultural projects. Showing genuine interest in countries and cultures where companies do their business is a way to connect with them, and it lowers business risk at the same time.

Therefore, we thank our sponsors for their support of this publication: Peter Kelder and Teun van Schijndel of Royal HaskoningDHV, the renowned engineering and consultancy company that does various projects in Oman and the Middle East as well as Liesbeth van der Pol of Dok Architecten, an Amsterdam-based leader in architecture and urban consultancy.

We thank as well Professor Dr. J.J. Witkam (emeritus) of Leiden University for his contribution to this document and Professor Dr. M. al Muqadam of Sultan Qaboos University for his suggestions.

We would like to especially thank both the Omani Embassy in The Hague and the Dutch Embassy in Muscat for their ongoing support of the Foundation's projects.

Peter van Ees, Chairman
Stichting Netherlands Oman Foundation,
Amsterdam, 20 March 2014

Former Town Hall of Batavia, in today's Jakarta, Indonesia. Photo: Kai van Hasselt

Preface

Despite the fact that Dutch-Omani relations span some 150 years, this relationship was of a varying nature and intensity and hence its description, as offered here, may be perceived by some as somewhat fragmentary. This is because the two periods when these relations were of some substance were rather short and were some 75 years apart. That did not mean that prior, in between and after these two periods of substantial relations there were no meaningful contacts, as is clear from this study. Nevertheless, there was a hiatus at certain times, which is also reflected in this study.

Dutch relations with Muscat and Oman date from 1651, when on 23 October 1651, the flute *Concordia* arrived in Muscat to assess market opportunities. However, chief merchant Elias Boudaens considered the market of Muscat not sufficiently interesting. Its annual turnover was too small to even cover the operating cost of a VOC factory. At that time the VOC had a factory in Gamron (Bandar Abbas) and Isfahan (from 1623), and another intermittent one at Basra (from 1645). Ships coming from Batavia usually sailed via Colombo (Sri Lanka) to Bandar Abbas and took the same route back. VOC ships only called on Muscat, either coming from Bandar Abbas or Batavia, to take on fresh water, food supplies and firewood.

The VOC's negative attitude towards Muscat's trade prospects did not change in the following years, although trade conditions in Muscat improved over time. By the 1670s, its trade was mostly with Sind, Gujarat, the Canarese and the Malabar Coast, Mokha, Aden, Malindi (East Africa) and the Maldives. It was only in 1666, when trading conditions in Bandar Abbas worsened that the VOC considered establishing relations with Muscat, where trade was on the rise and customs rates were much lower. Therefore, in April 1665, chief merchant van Wijck, the head of the Bandar Abbas factory, sent a Banyan to the Imam of Muscat. The Banyan returned in June with a letter from the Imam in which he requested the VOC to come and trade because "we always have been friends." Nevertheless, Batavia decided not start any new activities in Muscat, because in 1666, van Wijck wrote that the situation in Bandar Abbas had improved greatly, whereas that of Muscat had deteriorated.

The governor-general changed his mind in 1670, and ordered Bandar Abbas to send a junior-merchant to Muscat. This change of attitude had been caused by the growing difficulties in Safavid Persia with the court as well as a decrease of sales in that country. In early December 1671, the *Masulipatnam*, with junior merchant Georgius Hartsing, who had been on a trade reconnaissance mission to Basra, arrived in Muscat. The Imam was desirous to have the Dutch come and trade in Muscat and promised them exemption from paying customs and other imposts. Batavia was very pleased about this information and ordered Rijcklof van Goens, the governor of Ceylon, to examine the possibilities of a trade agreement.

Chief merchant Padbrugge left Colombo on 17 February 1672 and arrived in Muscat on 5 May 1672. The Dutch were well received, but because the Imam was not in Muscat, Padbrugge decided to continue to Bandar Abbas, where he arrived on 17 May 1672. Padbrugge's mission was discussed by the VOC policy council of Bandar Abbas, which decided to send Padbrugge to Muscat together with junior merchant Wilmson. They were charged to try and conclude a commercial treaty with the Imam of Muscat.

On 11 June 1672, Padbrugge arrived in Muscat, but he left soon after it became clear that the Imam was unwilling to grant trading privileges. Wilmson remained behind and continued to receive a rather neutral treatment. Despite the disappointing result of Padbrugge's mission, Batavia nevertheless concluded that the VOC had obtained the right to maintain a residency in Muscat and instructed the Bandar Abbas factory to thoroughly examine the trade of Muscat. On 3 June 1673, the VOC council at Bandar Abbas instructed Wilmson to broach the subject of the commercial treaty with the Imam. After having received a neutral reply, Wilmson was ordered to return to Bandar Abbas. Batavia wanted to withdraw its staff from Muscat, but in view of the war with Britain, it kept a resident there to warn arriving Dutch ships about the eventual presence of enemy ships in the Persian Gulf. The VOC factory was finally closed in 1675, and thus ended Dutch relations with Muscat, which would not be renewed for quite some time. Thereafter, Dutch ships would continue to call on Muscat to take on fresh water, food supplies and firewood, whether coming from Batavia or from Bandar Abbas.

This situation continued until 1756 when the VOC extended its trade to Muscat. By that time, the VOC factories in the Persian Gulf were operating at a loss. Batavia even considered withdrawing from the Gulf in 1748, but in 1753 it decided to open a new factory on the island of Khark, while closing those at Basra and Bushire. One of the main reasons for this change was the need to sell as much Java sugar as possible to boost Batavia's economy. Jacob Schoonderwoerd, the VOC chief at Bandar Abbas, on his return to Batavia, sailed to Muscat where he arrived on 7 January 1756. The Imam of Muscat, Ahmad b. Sa'id (1744-1783) told Schoonderwoerd that it would please him if the VOC established a factory in Muscat. Meanwhile, Batavia had decided to send to Muscat the *Marienbosch* with a cargo of various goods, but mainly sugar, instead of Khark, to be followed later by a second ship. On 8 June 1756, Batavia decided that the second ship, *'tPasgeld*, would travel to Diewil-Sind if trade prospects in Muscat were unfavorable.

On 19 July 1756, the *Marienbosch* and *'tPasgeld* left Batavia and arrived in Muscat respectively on 27 August 1756 and 19 September 1756. *'tPasgeld* left Muscat on 26 October 1756 for Sind, because of the dim prospects of selling a second cargo of merchandise. Nevertheless, in 1757, although the profits from this voyage were not encouraging, Batavia decided to send another ship, the *Barbara Theodora*, to Muscat in the hope of better results. Not only did the council wish to get rid of surplus stocks of sugar, but the mere eight-month voyage to and from Muscat was considered promising. The *Barbara Theodora* left Batavia on 27 July 1757 and arrived in Muscat on 21 September 1757. After an uneventful voyage it returned to Batavia on 8 March 1758.

Because the chief of the Khark factory, Tido von Kniphausen, complained that Muscat's profit was Khark's loss, Batavia decided to discontinue all voyages to Muscat. As far as Batavia was concerned, Java sugar could just as well be sold in Khark, which already had a VOC factory and therefore, had to show a profit. Von Kniphausen was instructed to inform the Imam of Muscat that no VOC ships would call in 1758. Thus, the VOC flirtation with Muscat had no real commercial basis, and only served to rid Batavia of its surplus stocks of Java sugar. The speedy abandonment of Muscat by the VOC bears this out.

However, this decision did not signal the end of relations between the VOC and Muscat and friendly relations were maintained. This is clear from the aftermath of the shipwreck of the *Amstelveen* en route to Khark on the coast of Oman on 5 August 1763 near Cape Mataraqa (Materace) with the loss of its cargo and of the 105 men crew, 75 drowned. On 11 September, eight survivors, after a hellish journey of 31 days, finally reached Muscat, where they found assistance. Later another 14 survivors arrived. The Dutch were still very much in favor with the Imam of Muscat. In January 1766, when Khark, the VOC's last factory in the Persian Gulf was conquered by a local Persian chief, survivors of the Khark debacle were warmly welcomed in Muscat; when in the same year, a Dutch ship sent from Surat came to see what could be salvaged, the Imam even offered naval and military assistance to help the Dutch retake Khark.

Shipping from Batavia to Muscat was resumed only in July 1777, when the High Government allowed merchant Willem van Hogendorp to buy 1,500 canisters of sugar from the VOC stocks, on the condition that he also purchase and export 150 *leggers*[1] of arak and transport these with his own private ship to Muscat. Van Hogendorp's initiative set an example and soon it was followed by other private Dutch merchants. By 1780 two ships per year were sailing to Muscat. Batavia allowed them to do so, provided they sold 30 *picol*s of cloves on the account of the VOC and invest half of the proceeds of the voyages in VOC letters of credit. Dutch voyages from Batavia to Muscat were discontinued in 1796, due to the Napoleonic war in Europe. However, the Imam of Muscat valued the commercial relationship with Indonesia. Therefore, in 1798 he sent a ship to Batavia to find out why Dutch ships were no longer coming to his country and to buy sugar and spices. This first successful voyage of an Omani ship to Indonesia established a pattern of regular annual voyages from Muscat to Batavia. Although we only have solid evidence that these voyages still took place in 1806, there is no reason to assume that thereafter they were discontinued. The Dutch from their side resumed annual voyages to Muscat as of 1824 until 1831. This seems to have been the last year in which such direct maritime contacts between Oman and Indonesia took place.

---

1. A barrel with a capacity of 400 or 563 liters

CHAPTER ONE

Dutch and Muscati Relations During the Portuguese Occupation, 1624–1650

Introduction

Until the early seventeenth century the Dutch knew little about the countries adjacent to the Persian Gulf. However, the publication of the *Voyage* of Jan van Linschoten (1563-1611), a Dutchman in the service of the Portuguese in Goa, changed that. His account of Asia and of the Persian Gulf was influential throughout Europe and raised North-Western European interest in direct trade with Asia and Persia. Van Linschoten had detailed both the riches that could be gained as well as the weakness of the Portuguese in Asia that could be overcome and thus whetted Dutch and English commercial appetites.[1] Until 1594 direct maritime voyages from Europe to Asia were a Portuguese enforced monopoly. This monopoly was breached in that year by Dutch and English commercial voyages. In 1602, the Dutch United East-India Company (*Verenigde Oost-Indische Compagnie* or VOC) was created through the merger of six small companies to provide financial and political strength and cohesion to Dutch commercial efforts to compete with other Europeans for Asian commodities. Its primary objective was to gain control over the Spice Islands in S. E. Asia. It was only after the Dutch had firmly established themselves there that they began to develop

---

1. J.H. van Linschoten, *The voyage of Jan Huygen van Linschoten to the East Indies* ed. and tr. A.C. Burnell and P.A. Tiele, 2 vols. (London, 1885).

their commercial network in other parts of Asia. The Dutch were quite aware of the existence of the integrated Indian Ocean market and its close commercial ties with West Asia and South-East Asia. This realization meant that their next logical step was to advance into the Indian Ocean area. But before the VOC could extend its commercial relations to the Persian Gulf it first had to establish itself in S. Asia, where it faced fierce competition from the Portuguese and the English East India Company (EIC). Persia and the Persian Gulf, therefore, were not as yet on the horizon of Dutch policy makers.

The reverse was true for Persian policy makers, for Shah Abbas I (r. 1587-1629) sent Zeyn al-Abedin Khan Beg, his ambassador to the European courts (1604-1609), also to the Netherlands in 1608 to ask for technical and military assistance. The Dutch government was not willing to provide such assistance, given its friendly relations with the Ottomans, against whom it would be used. The Dutch were, however, ready to start commercial operations in Persia. For the VOC directors received (be it incorrect) information in 1608 that the king of Hormuz had risen against the Portuguese. They wrote to their admirals in India that "if this be true, you will try to conclude an alliance with this king so that we may secure the trade of Persia. You will also try to get a substantial cargo of raw silk from Persia, if this possible, as well as other many goods which may be profitable here."[2] From this report it is clear that the Dutch were especially interested in Persian silk, because by that time Amsterdam had become a major center of the European silk industry. Although the VOC decided not to develop trade relations with Persia as yet, several project makers, amongst whom Robert Sherley and Dutch entrepreneurs who wanted to circumvent the VOC monopoly of trade with Asia, tried to promote Dutch silk trade with Persia via Russia in the years thereafter. It was not, because the VOC had lost interest in Persian silk, on the contrary, for it needed silk for the European market. The Chinese silk that it bought at Pattani (Thailand) since 1609 was entirely

---

2. NA, VOC 478 (Amsterdam, 11 April, 1608).

Shah Abbas I

needed for the trade with Japan.³ The VOC, however, did not make a decision to start trading in an area based on a single commodity, but rather how this commodity fit in its inter-Asian trading network. Also, the Portuguese were still too strong in the Indian Ocean area and the VOC therefore first had to build up its military and financial strength. Slowly it spread its trading stations over South Asia, in fierce competition with the English and Portuguese, and from that safe base the VOC moved into the western Indian Ocean. Thus, the history of the Dutch and English Companies in the East was, with regard to their use of force, always something of a mixed bag and during their first thirty years the Companies' very existence in the East depended upon their ability to defend themselves aggressively.⁴

Once the VOC's position had been soundly established in these parts it indeed turned its attention to the Persian Gulf. Hormuz was both commercially and strategically the obstacle that had to be conquered, if access to Persian silk was to be obtained. Because the English, who had preceded the Dutch in opening trade relations with Persia (since 1617), were struggling with what a modern manager might call 'start up' problems in their Persia trade, they believed that, despite their fierce competition elsewhere, they might more easily overcome these problems by joining forces with the Dutch. In 1620, therefore, the EIC proposed the VOC to jointly develop the Persian silk trade. Neither party felt strong enough, financially and militarily, to do this on its own. It was decided that a joint fleet would do battle with the Portuguese and the silk trade would be jointly financed, with the VOC having a majority share.⁵ Because

---

3. On the silk trade and the various project makers, see Willem Floor, "The Dutch and the Persian Silk Trade," in Charles Melville ed. *Safavid Persia* (London, 1996), pp. 323-68 and Rudi Matthee, *The Politics of Trade in Safavid Iran*. (Cambridge, 1999).
4. The problem of this mixture of policies has been studied in detail by Niels Steensgaard, *Carracks, Caravans and Companies. The structural crisis in the European-Asian trade in the early 17th century* (Copenhagen, 1973).
5. H. Dunlop, *Bronnen tot de geschiedenis der Oostindische Compagnie in Perzië* (The Hague, 1930), p. 6; R. W. Ferrier, *British-Persian Relations in the 17th Century*, unpublished dissertation (Cambridge University 1970), p. 53, note 131.

the VOC managing directors were in favor of this cooperation, a Dutch fleet of nine ships was assembled in Batavia (now Jakarta) under the command of Admiral Jacob Dedel and on 2 September 1621, it was ordered to sail into the Indian Ocean where it was to cooperate with the already present English against the Portuguese. Moreover, the admiral was instructed to promote the VOC trade in India, Surat, the Red Sea, and Persia.[6] Admiral Dedel was ordered to investigate its possibilities, but because funds were limited, not to open up the Persian market. Moreover, the governor-general clearly viewed the expedition as a probe of the entire Portuguese sphere of influence in the western Indian Ocean, where Dutch experience was at best spotty.

Although one general objective of Dedel's fleet was to gather trade information, it also had a more specific purpose. Neither Company was prepared to go to the expense of mounting a major expedition merely to inform itself of trade possibilities. There was also hope of profit. The combined Dutch-English fleet had to destroy the Portuguese carracks and galleons. More specifically the Dutch fleet was to stand off the Malabar coast with the specific purpose of intercepting any Portuguese ships destined for Goa and then, in April 1622 they were to sail to Mozambique and the islands off south-east Africa. They were to be back at Goa in time to intercept the Portuguese fleet, which would arrive before the end of that year. Thus, the actions of the Dutch fleet complemented the action of the English fleet in the Persian Gulf, where on 23 April 1622 the English and Persians joined forces to take the Portuguese fort of Hormuz. However, Dedel's fleet did not arrive at Surat until 4 October 1622. When it arrived, the VOC chief of the Surat factory, van den Broecke wanted to send a ship to Persia as soon as possible, but Dedel claimed that he could not spare one from his fleet.[7] It was only in June 1623 that one Dutch ship, the *Heusden* arrived at Bandar Abbas to explore market possibilities in Persia. The leader of the Dutch

---

6. H. T. Colenbrander and W. Ph. Coolhaas eds. *Bescheiden Jan Pietersz. Coen* 7 vols. (The Hague, 1919-52), vol. 3, p. 210.
7. Dunlop, *Bronnen*, p. 14, 16; Colenbrander-Coolhaas, *Bescheiden*, vol. 1, p. 760.

commercial mission, Huybert Visnich, traveled to Isfahan and concluded a commercial treaty with Shah Abbas I (r. 1587-1629), which formed the foundation for future Dutch trade with Persia.[8]

VOC Organization.

Before continuing with the developments in the Persian Gulf and the Dutch role therein it is necessary to know how the VOC was managed and what its organization was in Persia. The VOC was a joint-stock company managed by a board of 17 directors, who were known as the *Heeren Zeventien* (the Seventeen Gentlemen) or in short the *XVII*. This board delegated daily management of its operations in Asia to a governor-general and his council, which were based in Batavia in Indonesia. This body took decisions by majority vote. Operations in Asia were organized along the lines of the so-called Directorates. The so-called Persian Directorate included not only Persia, but also Basra, and other activities that the VOC might carry on in the Persian Gulf such as in Muscat. The director of the Persian Directorate was based in Bandar Abbas. Like the governor-general he was assisted by a council, which consisted of the leading VOC commercial staff. The military, who were only based there in time of insecurity, had no voice in the management of the directorate. When needed, one or more officers would be invited to voice their opinion. The commanding military officers could only be a member of the policy council (*raad van politie*), but never of the trade council (*negotie raad*). When the ships' captains were included in the deliberations the council was referred to as the broad council (*breede raad*). A council could override a director and did so at many occasions. The collegial way of management proved to be both flexible and effective in the absence of rapid means of communications with Batavia and/or the XVII. The same council system also existed at the trading stations that depended on Bandar Abbas such as Isfahan and Basra.

---

8. For the text of Visnich's instructions see H. Terpstra, *De Opkomst der Westerkwartieren der Oost-Indische Compagnie (Suratte, Arabië, Perzië* (The Hague, 1918), pp. 288-90; for the text of the Dutch and English treaties see Dunlop, *Bronnen*, p. 765ff.

The VOC had the following system of hierarchy for its commercial staff in its directorates. The highest ranking official (director, *gezaghebber*, or *resident*) usually held the rank of chief merchant (*opperkoopman*). The next in rank was a merchant (*koopman*), followed by a junior merchant (*onderkoopman*), a book-keeper (*boekhouder*), and finally an assistant (*assistent*); the latter might be a member of the council in a small factory. Other lower-ranking staff were not members of the council.[9] The total staff of the VOC in the Persian directorate was limited. Around 1700, in total some 25 people would stay in Persia, most of whom, about 20, in Bandar Abbas.

To promote its trade, the VOC established a factory or trading station in Bandar Abbas (1623-1759) and Isfahan (1623-1745) as well as rest-houses in Lar and Shiraz for its caravans traveling between Isfahan and Bandar Abbas. In Shiraz, the VOC had a winemaker, usually an Armenian, to ensure the necessary supply of Shiraz wine for export. As of 1659 it had trading post in Kerman (1659-1738) and as of 1734 one in Bushehr (1734-1749). As of 1645, the Dutch had a factory in Basra, which, with long intervals of being closed, operated until 1753. The VOC withdrew its last factory from Persia's mainland in 1758, when it closed its factory in Bandar Abbas. However, as of 1753, it continued trading with Bushehr, Basra and other ports in the Persian Gulf from a newly built factory on the island of Khark until the end of 1765.

Developments after the fall of Hormuz

Despite the fact that in April 1622 the English had helped the Persians to conquer Hormuz, the Portuguese still reigned supreme in the Persian Gulf. For, although they had lost Hormuz, the Portuguese were still strong in the Indian Ocean and the Persian Gulf where they had effective bases in Muscat and Sohar and other ports on the Omani coast. Given the Portuguese threat, the Dutch and the English agreed henceforth to sail with combined fleets to Surat and the Persian Gulf. After

---

9. Pieter van Dam, *Beschrijvinge van de Oost Indische Compagnie*, ed. F. W. Stapel, Rijks Geschied-kundige Publicatiën 83, The Hague, 1939.

the loss of Hormuz, the Portuguese needed a solid and secure base for their continued commercial operations in the Persian Gulf. Without such a base they just would not have lost the battle for Hormuz, but in fact the war for the Persian Gulf. This meant that they not only had to try and crush the new upstarts (the Dutch and the English) who were trying to oust them from their positions all over Asia, but also to contain the Safavid threat against Muscat, as well as (after 1625) the Ya`ariba threat from the interior of Oman against the Portuguese forts on the Omani coast. The first danger required vigorous naval warfare, while the second only needed enough force to dislodge Safavid troops from some coastal towns and to deter the Safavids from sending an invasion force to Oman as well as to make them come to a political settlement with the Portuguese. The third danger required sowing dissent among the Imamite forces combined with strong vigorous and targeted offensive and defensive military operations. The Portuguese failed in the first and third, but succeeded in the second objective.

Despite the loss of Hormuz, the Portuguese were not as yet defeated. They still were a power to reckon with and had both a considerable naval force in the Persian Gulf and land-based military defenses on the Arab littoral. Shah Abbas I therefore, wanted to take the war to the Portuguese, in particular against Muscat, their second major base in the Persian Gulf after Hormuz, to annihilate any future threat from their side. Therefore, in 1622-23, Bandar Abbas looked very much like an army camp and the town was brimful of soldiers. Because the Safavids claimed to be the heirs of the Hormuz kingdom they also considered themselves overlords of some ports on the Batinah coast. This, as well as their enmity to the Portuguese, may explain why in 1622-23 the population of some forts near Muscat, as well as those of Khur Fakkan, Diba, Lima, Khasab, Rams, and Jolfar rebelled against the Portuguese and submitted to Safavid rule. In February 1623, Safavid troops were sent to the Omani coast to assist the local population in their revolt and to deny the Portuguese access to any of these ports. Shah Abbas I would have liked the English to assist him in the Muscat operation, but both Dutch and English sources state that they did not do so.[10] The Safavid offensive

---

10. Dunlop, *Bronnen*, p. 17 (16/03/1623); Foster, William ed. *The English Factories in India 1618-1669*. 13 vols. (London, 1906-27), 1622-1623, pp. 166, 181, 186, 189, 201, 339, 344.

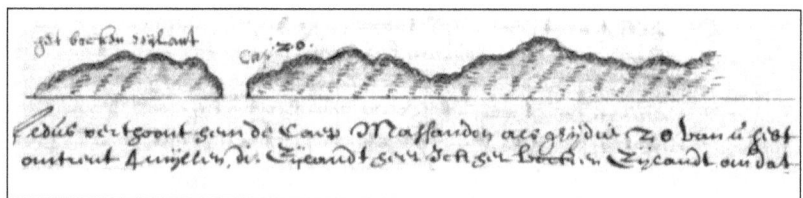

Bay of Diba (Dobi) in Oman with depths in fathoms (1645),
Journael van Claes Jansen Speelman, Nationaal Archief, The Hague

came to a halt in the Persian Gulf after having suffered a defeat at Basra due to Portuguese support of the local ruler of that city.[11] Eleven large and medium ships were sent to execute this campaign accompanied by 100 *terradas*.[12] When the Safavid expeditionary Omani force asked for reinforcements to launch their offensive it was recalled. The Safavid army was ordered to withdraw to Jolfar, which was considered safer against Portuguese naval attacks.

Rui Freire de Andrade, the Portuguese military commander in the Persian Gulf with a force of 20 *galeotas* and 20 *terranquins*[13] then moved on to Khor Fakkan, where he found one of his loyal Arab henchmen, Ali Jamal (Hali Camal), in charge. He obtained the allegiance of the locals and then moved to Diba, which declared for Portugal and ousted the 800 Safavid troops. This saved them from being massacred, but those of Lima were not so lucky, because the entire population was massacred and its fort destroyed; thereafter all other ports submitted to the Portuguese.[14] Having secured the Arabian coast, Rui Freire turned to the task of retaking Hormuz. Despite a three-month blockade and the

---

11. Foster, *English Factories* 1624-1629, pp. 42-43.
12. A *terrada* (properly *tarradah*) was a one-masted light sailing and oared cargo vessel that often was used for naval warfare; it was also often called *tranki*. Nowadays it means a fast motorized glassfiber boat.
13. *Terranquin* or *tranki*, see previous note.
14. C.R. Boxer, tr. *Commentaries of Ruy Freyre de Andrada* (London, 1930), pp. 185-92; Luciano Cordeiro, *Questões Histórico-Colonais* 3 vols. (Lisbon, 1936), pp. 324-25; J. G. Lorimer, *Gazetteer of the Persian Gulf* (Calcutta, 1915 [1970]), p. 399; João Manuel de Almeida Teles y Cunha, *Economia de um império. Economia política do Estado da Índia em torno do mar Arábico e golfo Pérsico. Elementos conjuncturais: 1595-1635.* (Universidade Nova de Lisboa, 1995), pp. 46-49.

inability of the Safavids to supply the island, as well as attacks all along the Safavid Persian coast, the Portuguese had to withdraw from Hormuz not having achieved their objective. The need for European naval assistance against the Portuguese became very urgent after the failed Safavid operation to occupy and hold on to coastal forts on the Arabian coast, and in particular after Rui Freire's attacks on the Safavid Persian littoral against which the Safavids had no defense. The Safavids expected such help from the Dutch and English.

Dutch Refuse Naval Support for a Persian Invasion of Oman

Shah Abbas I had previously contacted the Dutch with a request for naval support. His ambassador to the Netherlands, Musa Beg, who was in The Hague in 1624, offered Safavid military support if the Dutch would be willing to take the fortresses of Muscat, Larek and others that he said were detrimental to Dutch interests.[15] In reply to Shah Abbas I's request for assistance against Muscat, the States-General of the Dutch Republic wrote that they would send an ambassador to discuss the matter with him. On the basis of this outcome of that discussion a decision would be taken.[16] According to the Dutch ambassador's (Jan Smidt) instructions, he had to discuss the Muscat request with Shah Abbas I. By the time that Smidt arrived in Isfahan Shah Abbas I was dead and Safi I, his successor, did not raise the Muscat operation. Anyway, Jan Pieterszoon Coen, governor-general of the VOC, had instructed Smidt not to make any agreement regarding Muscat as the VOC did not have sufficient forces to be engaged in such an operation.[17]

---

15. Dunlop, *Bronnen*, p. 694.
16. Dunlop, *Bronnen*, pp. 707-08.
17. Dunlop, *Bronnen*, pp. 751-52, "Instructie voor Willem Janssen, admiral of the fleet to the Gulf (03/08/1627)," who had to reconnoiter Muscat carefully, and to find out what would be the best time to make advantageous use of that knowledge. If need be he might assist the Persians in reinforcing their fort at Bandar Abbas. Dunlop, *Bronnen*, p. 786, n.1.

Apart from the high cost, one of the reasons that the Dutch and English were reluctant, if not unwilling, to provide naval assistance for the Safavid plans to take Muscat, was because Portuguese naval power was still considerable. Rui Freire continued hostilities in the Persian Gulf and the Gulf of Oman. He retook and destroyed coastal settlements on the Arabian coast and destroyed Safavid Persian settlements between Jask and Bandar-e Kong. Further, he harassed Safavid shipping and blockaded Hormuz. Fortunately, for the Safavids, Rui Freire de Andrade did not have the means to sustain a long blockade or an assault of the fort and thus he had to abort his operation.[18] Nevertheless, so uncertain was the situation that around August 1623, the Dutch received information that the Portuguese had taken Hormuz again, and that their ships were cruising around the island. Also four galleons were expected from Goa to Muscat. Therefore, the Dutch in Bandar Abbas consulted the English about a coordinated naval action against the Portuguese.[19] Rui Freire de Andrade's operations continued in 1624 and they sufficiently annoyed the Dutch who decided to cut off the Portuguese commercial base that financed these activities. In July 1624, the Dutch at Gamron informed Batavia that to "better secure our trade we have to prevent Portuguese voyages from India to Muscat and from Muscat to Basra."[20]

---

18. Boxer, *Commentaries*, pp. 47-58; Ibid., "Anglo-Portuguese rivalry in the Persian Gulf," in E. Prestage ed. *Chapters in Anglo-Portuguese Relations* (Watford, 1935), p. 90. The Portuguese committed many atrocities among the coastal population, of which Thevenot gives a disgusting example, and in particular Rui Freire was a "name to this day [1665] so terrible unto them, that they use it to still their little Children when they cry, threatening them with Lowis de Fereyra." J. de. Thevenot, *The Travels of M. de Thevenot into the Levant* (London, 1686 [1971]), vol. 2, p. 173. The same reputation is reported in Portuguese sources; see Boxer, *Commentaries*, p. 198; Manuel Godinho, *Relação do novo caminho que fêz por terra e mar vindo da Índia para Portugal, no ano de 1663 o Padre Manuel Godingo* (Lisbon, 1944), p. 101.
19. Dunlop, *Bronnen*, p. 24 (29/10/1623). According to Anonymous, *A Chronicle of the Carmelites in Persia and the Papal mission of the seventeenth and eighteenth centuries*, 2 vols. (London, 1939), vol. 1, p. 275, in January 1625, "there is a report that Hurmuz is surrounded by the Portuguese, who prevent any supplies whatever from reaching it."
20. Dunlop, *Bronnen*, p. 59 (24/07/1624).

A Dutch-English Fleet Battles the Portuguese Fleet

Consequently, the Dutch and English agreed to join forces in the Persian Gulf with a view to provide sufficient counterforce. This strategy paid off, for when the two fleets met on 7 December 1625 the Portuguese fleet (8 galleons and 16 frigates) withdrew after having engaged in a battle with the combined Dutch-English fleet of eight ships; they did not pursue the Portuguese fleet due to lack of ammunition.[21] The Italian traveler, Pietro della Valle saw Rui Freire de Andrade after the battle, probably at Khur Qoway. The Portuguese had suffered 400 wounded and more than 350 dead, according to the Dutch.[22] Although both sides claimed victory, the battle was inconclusive and the Portuguese were still strong in the Persian Gulf. However, for the first time their supremacy had been seriously challenged. The Portuguese fleet suffered so much damage that it did not sail to Goa in early 1626, but remained at Muscat. Therefore, after repairs the Portuguese had to decide what to do with their still redoubtable fleet. There were two options: (i) cruise the West coast of India in September to catch the outgoing Dutch and English ships off Swally; or (ii) support Rui Freire to recapture Hormuz. The council at Goa could not agree and left the decision to Rui Freire de Andrade and Nuno Àlvares Botelho in Muscat, who chose the first option. They

---

21. Boxer, "Anglo-Portuguese Rivalry," pp. 93-100; Dunlop, *Bronnen*, p. 152 (07/12/1624; 16/03/1625); Lorimer, *Gazetteer*, p. 28. Pietro della Valle, *Les Fameux Voyages* 4 vols. (Paris: Gervais Clouzier, 1664), vol. 4, p. 417 remarked on the low level of discipline on Portuguese vessels as well as their need for sailors. For the Portuguese view of these events see Boxer, *Commentaries*, pp. 200-03, 233-42; Botelho de Sousa, A. *Nuno Àlvares Botelho* (Lisbon, 1940), pp. 95-111 (*relaçao sumaria*); Anonymous, *Relacion verdadera en la qval se da cvente como la armada de su Magestad, que trae a su cargo Nuño Albarez Botello … con las Armadas de Olanda, y de Inglaterra, en el estrecho de Ormuz. De que vino auiso en 20. de Febrero de 1626* (Cordova, 1626); Anonymous, *Relacion Cierta y Verdadera* (Madrid: Esteuan Liberos, 1625); Matos, *Das relações*, p. 299 (citing yet another *Relacion*).
22. Dunlop, *Bronnen*, p. 156 (22/04/1625); della Valle, *Voyages*, vol. 4, p. 423; Lorimer, *Gazetteer*, p. 29 (estimated the Portuguese losses much lower).

rightly argued that if they were able to destroy the Dutch and English ships then the recapture of Hormuz could take place thereafter, without hindrance from these competitors. Botelho sailed to Goa and engaged three English ships in October 1626. Although much damaged, the English ships were able to escape. One of them, the *Lion*, 'limped' back to Gamron, where it was captured by Rui Freire de Andrade. He massacred everybody on board, except the cook who had treated him well during his English captivity, despite the fact that he had offered quarter to the crew, if they surrendered. Meanwhile, Botelho was faced with an overwhelming Anglo-Dutch combined fleet of 15 ships so that he, having only seven galleons, avoided battle. Therefore, he sailed to the Red Sea in the hope of better luck and easier victims. The Anglo-Dutch fleet sailed together to the Persian Gulf in December 1626 to ensure that if they had to face Botelho they would be able to give a good, if not victorious, account of themselves. The same fleet sailed back to Swally Roads in March 1627, after having rejected the annual Safavid proposal to jointly attack Muscat.[23]

The Dutch knew that Botelho's ships had been destroyed or were heavily damaged, for they were lying without masts and allegedly beyond repair at Muscat.[24] As a result, rather than leaving together, the Dutch and English fleet left separately. Contrariwise, Rui Freire fearing an attack against Muscat recalled D. Gonçalo de Silveira, his deputy who was engaged in the Qatif area. Together with Botelho's remaining repaired four galleons, the Portuguese had a strong enough force to face such an attack, which however failed to materialize. Neither the Dutch nor the English were interested in endangering their capital and ships to advance Safavid interests. They left in February 1628, and were followed by Botelho a few weeks later, once the Portuguese were sure the Anglo-Dutch danger was really gone. Because the Dutch and English did not know that Botelho had returned to Goa they still sailed

---

23. Boxer, "Anglo-Portuguese Rivalry," pp. 100-08. "The destruction of the Lion in Gombroon Road was a disastrous blow." Ferrier, *British-Persian Relations*, p. 51, n. 126.
24. Dunlop, *Bronnen*, p. 232 (04/08/1627- 06/1628).

jointly in the Persian Gulf in 1629, but there was no Portuguese fleet to challenge them.

By that time, the Dutch and English had concluded that the Portuguese had weakened to such an extent that they felt confident about the outcome of their conflict. However, until 1631, Portuguese power was still sufficiently strong that they felt the continued need to sail in combined fleets for security reasons. In December 1629, for example, the Dutch learnt that eight Portuguese ships and 20 frigates had sailed to Muscat.[25] English naval squadrons also were instructed to "keep company with the Dutch, and if they meet the Portuguese galleons to 'applie your utmost indevours to effect their finale ruine.'"[26]

Despite the failure of the Muscat expedition materializing after 1623, Shah Abbas I had not abandoned the plan to take the war to the Portuguese on the Arabian side of the Persian Gulf. This issue was raised regularly with the Dutch and English whenever their ships arrived in Bandar Abbas. In December 1626, the English instructed their staff that if a joint attack on Muscat were agreed upon, they had to insist that "the English are to be allowed the sole possession of the castle after its capture, leaving the rest to the Persians; but the attempt seems too hazardous until the Portuguese galleons have been destroyed." The Dutch were to be kept out of such a joint operation, because they would claim a share of the profits.[27] Dutch naval supremacy in the Persian Gulf was clearly recognized by Shah Safi I when, at the end of 1629, he wrote to Prince Frederik Hendrik, Stadtholder of the province of Holland, that he assumed that the latter "would [continue] to keep the sea clear of the Portuguese and that none of his subjects, would be expected to open the road to all voyagers."[28]

---

25. Dunlop, *Bronnen*, p. 282 (25/12/1628 - 03/01/1629).
26. Foster, *English Factories* 1624-1629, p. 164. Two English ships had in fact gone to Socotra instead of Bandar Abbas, because "they feared to find the Portuguese in force at Ormus." Ibid., p. 163.
27. Foster, *English Factories* 1624-1629, p. 164.
28. Dunlop, *Bronnen*, pp. 157-59 (24/04/1625).

The invasion plan disappeared from the correspondence such that in early 1631, the English reported that, "the taking of Muscatt to our knowledge hath not hitherto bin spoken of; nor, [wee] thinke, was ever intended by the King or Chon."[29] However, in 1632 the Portuguese once again feared an attack by the governor of Shiraz on Muscat and the presence of a large Dutch-English fleet at Bandar Abbas fed this fear, because it was believed that this fleet would help the Safavid attack. Immediately, the viceroy sent a fleet of 12 ships from Goa, but the fear had been caused by a plan that never materialized. For, at the end of 1631, Emam Qoli Khan, the governor-general of Fars, had sent the Dutch and English a formal request to support his planned operation against the Portuguese in Muscat and to take their fort. The English factors asked for instructions and pointed out the danger to their trade if the EIC would refuse to help, for "the Dutch have offered their service against Muscatt, so we might not be joined in the action; but are refused until we give our absolute aunswer."[30]

Emam Qoli Khan had indeed asked the Dutch to assist him in this endeavor for which he had already assembled troops. He had offered the Dutch the dilapidated Portuguese frigates taken at Hormuz in 1621.[31] Philips Lucassen, the visiting VOC inspector, reported that in 1632, Emam Qoli Khan had discussed in secret the request with Heynes the EIC director but he did not know the result. For this reason the Dutch had not believed that their help was needed, because they assumed that the English would supply it. Meanwhile, in 1630-31, the governor of Bandar Abbas had eight good ships at his disposal equipped to attack the Portuguese positions. However, Emam Qoli Khan was unhappy,

---

29. Foster, *English Factories* 1630-1634, p. 141.
30. António Bocarro, *Livro das plantas de todas as fortalezas, cidades e povoações do estado da India Oriental*. 3 vols, (Lisbon, 1992), pp. 92-93; Foster, *English Factories* 1630-1634, p. 1208. Lorimer, *Gazetteer*, p. 37. Nevertheless, they were pleased when the plan was shelved due to Emam Qoli Khan's execution. Anonymous, *Chronicle*, vol. 1, p. 312.
31. Boxer, "Anglo-Portuguese Rivalry," pp. 114-18; Foster, *English Factories*, 1630-33, p. 295; Hendrick Hagenaer, "Scheep-vaert naar Oost-Indien," in Izaäk Commelin, *Begin ende Voortgangh* 2 vols. (Amsterdam, 1645), p. 39 (01/12/1632).

because he had never heard anything from the Dutch about support, although he had raised the issue in three separate letters. Faced with the Dutch-English unwillingness to supply naval support, Emam Qoli Khan finally made an agreement with Rui Freire de Andrade and granted the Portuguese access to Bandar-e Kong and half of its customs. Therefore, in 1631 the visiting VOC inspector Philips Lucassen somewhat disingenuously argued, it was hard to believe that Emam Qoli Khan wanted Dutch help; moreover, the Dutch ships that were in Bandar Abbas at that time only served to protect the VOC silk transport.[32]

In the second half of 1632, Emam Qoli Khan was raising an army to take Muscat. Because the Dutch allegedly had offered their assistance, the English factors recommended promoting EIC commercial interests by offering their assistance as well. "Ytt is generally thought to bee a very easie warr, and that the place cannot hold out ten dayes, in regard their water may be cut off without anie difficultie, and the irresitable armie the Duke meanes to send. As for the Portugals, they are not like to have anie helpe from Goa, where they want men to furnish their shipinge."[33] The Dutch, however, declined the Safavid request to assist in an attack on Muscat, and even Emam Qoli Khan dropped the idea after having observed that only three Dutch ships arrived in Bandar Abbas in October 1632. Two months later he was executed at Shah Safi I's orders and with him the driving force behind the Muscat conquest died as well. His great antagonist Rui Freire de Andrade died shortly thereafter in December 1632. It was a case of bad timing, for an English flotilla of four ships arrived in February 1633 ready to assist Emam Qoli Khan to take Muscat.[34] After Rui Freire de Andrade's death, the Portuguese at Muscat expected a new governor from Goa with reinforcements,

---

32. Dunlop, *Bronnen*, pp. 404-05 (06/01/1633 Lucasz instruction); Foster, *English Factories* 1630-33, pp. 256, 278.
33. Foster, *English Factories* 1630-1634, pp. 240, 256 ("To wyn Muscatt, the Dutch do offer their assistance to the Duke, to do it aloane."), 278 (Dutch allegedly offered their help).
34. Boxer, "Anglo-Portuguese Rivalry," pp. 114-18; Foster, *English Factories*, 1630-33, p. 247 (what terms the English had to ask for their help), 279 (the Duke had been ordered to use his troops against an insurrection in Georgia, therefore, "if the fleet is not wanted for the siege of Muskat."), 295 ("the death of Rufrere in December [1632]"); Ibid., *English Factories* 1634-1636, p. 62 (24/03/1633); Hagenaer, "Journael," p. 39 (01/12/1632).

for they still expected a Safavid attack.³⁵ However, it did not happen for the Safavids were totally absorbed by the war with the Ottomans. On the other hand, Portuguese caution was warranted. For in 1634, the Safavids again discussed naval protection, and even an attack of Muscat, with the Dutch.³⁶

Dutch Offer Naval Help to Persia

By 1634, the Dutch no longer considered the Portuguese a real danger in the Persian Gulf. Allegedly, they still had 24 frigates and five to six galliots at Goa, but they did nothing with them.³⁷ In 1635, following the instructions of Batavia as part of the overall VOC Asian strategy that aimed to weaken the Portuguese, Nicolaes Overschie, the then chief of VOC trade in Persia, informed the Safavid grand vizier that the VOC was ready to send a fleet to the Persian Gulf to help the shah take Muscat. If adequate incentives were offered, the promised fleet would be of the same size as the English had sent to take Hormuz. Overschie was at pains not to make a definite commitment, but to make it conditional on the shah taking concrete steps up-front.³⁸ Where possible, VOC ships captured Portuguese shipping, such as in 1635, when goods were sold, which had been taken as booty from a Portuguese vessel in the Persian Gulf.³⁹ Therefore, it was not entirely an exaggeration when the VOC director Wollebrandt Geleynsen argued in 1641 that the Dutch were protecting Safavid Persia's southern border against the Portuguese, and that the grand vizier, Mirza Taqi, should take this service into account when assessing the benefits of Safavid Persia's relations with the Dutch.⁴⁰

Whereas the Dutch remained at war with Portugal (then still ruled by the king of Spain, the arch-enemy of the Netherlands at that time),

---

35. Dunlop, *Bronnen*, p. 471 (28/03/1634).
36. Dunlop, *Bronnen*, p. 500 (15/08/1634).
37. Dunlop, *Bronnen*, p. 527 (15/03/1635).
38. Dunlop, *Bronnen*, p. 548 (15/12/1635).
39. Dunlop, *Bronnen*, p. 558 (January 1636).
40. NA, VOC 1149, Westerwolt to Batavia (28/04/1739), f. 1249; Idem, (06/04/1639), f. 1283; NA, VOC 1156, Geleynsen to Batavia (21/05/1640), f. 802; NA, VOC 1160, Geleynsen to Batavia (25/10/1641), f. 275.

England concluded a peace treaty with Portugal in January 1636.[41] To blacken the English reputation, Overschie immediately told the Safavid grand vizier that the English had made peace with the Portuguese and were discussing plans to retake Hormuz and to make Bandar Abbas an English port. On that occasion, the grand vizier told Overschie with regard to the Dutch offer to jointly take Muscat that he had asked the *shahbandar* to investigate the matter.[42] Allegedly a royal order had been sent to the governor and *shahbandar* of Bandar Abbas to ready troops if the Dutch wanted to take Muscat. Overschie told both officials that it was too late, because the Dutch fleet had already departed; he would write to Batavia about it and he hoped for the arrival of an adequate fleet next year.[43] He also informed Batavia that there were few military forces in Muscat, according to Portuguese prisoners.[44] The English even reported in December 1636 that a Dutch fleet had gone with the intention (it was supposed) of capturing Muscat.[45] The plans, if that is what they were, came to naught, because the *Heeren XVII*, i.e. the managing directors of the VOC, did not want to attack Muscat; their motto was: no war, but trade.[46] This position coincided with a lack of interest in the scheme at the Safavid court that now considered Muscat too far away.[47] It did not mean that that the Dutch were less hostile to the Portuguese in the Persian Gulf. In 1638, for example, the Dutch took a Portuguese vessel sailing from Sind to Muscat with textiles and food supplies such as wheat, rice, and flour. It was taken to Bandar Abbas. The *shahbandar* claimed its cargo, because it belonged to Banyans[48] and these goods

---

41. Boxer, "Anglo-Portuguese Rivalry," pp. 119-20; English ships then also started to call on Muscat, see Foster, *English Factories* 1634-1636, pp. 120, 147, 186, 283; Lorimer, *Gazetteer*, p. 38 (there was already an end to hostilities as of 1634).
42. Dunlop, *Bronnen*, p. 566 (25/03/1636).
43. Dunlop, *Bronnen*, p. 569 (25/03/1636).
44. Dunlop, *Bronnen*, p. 578 (06/04/1636).
45. Foster, *English Factories* 1634-1636, p. 329.
46. Dunlop, *Bronnen*, pp. 597 (24/11/1636), 600.
47. Dunlop, *Bronnen*, p. 615 (25/03/1637).
48. *Banya*, a Gujarati word meaning 'trader.' The Portuguese used this word, in the form of Banyan, to refer to any Indian trader, and this appellation was

had to be unloaded at Bandar-e Kong where the shah had 50% of the customs revenues.[49] The Dutch and Portuguese finally reached a truce for the Indian Ocean area in December 1642.[50] The truce was valid only for ten years and war would flare up again in 1652 as a result of conflicting interests in the Indian Ocean area.

The End of Portuguese Rule in Oman

In addition to the need to contain, if not eliminate, the danger of Dutch, English, and Safavid operations in the Persian Gulf, the Portuguese also needed to cover their backs, i.e. to contain if not control the increasing attacks by the growing Ya`ariba forces on Muscat and other fortified ports on the Batinah coast. The power vacuum was filled by Sheikh Naser b. Morshed al-Ya`ariba who was elected as Imam of the Ibadi sect in 1624. His first aim was to 'convince' those who did not accept him as Imam, to which end he used guile, brute force and assassination. His second aim was to oust the Portuguese from Oman. He made his center of operations at Nizwa. From there he launched his attacks against the Portuguese and dissenter tribes.

The Dutch, based on discussions with people in Muscat, reported:

> Having pacified the interior reasonably well, the Portuguese were the remaining foremost obstacle. They had possession

---

later adopted by other Europeans as well as the Omanis, because during the Portuguese control over Muscat and other Omani ports, Banyans were also living there, as they continued to do after the Portuguese ouster from Oman in 1650.

49. Dunlop, *Bronnen*, pp. 650 (20/04/1638), 655 (10/08/1638). The Dutch also took a Portuguese ship coming from Sind going to Muscat; it was sold at Bandar Abbas and a present was given to the grand-vizier and *shahbandar*. W. Ph. Coolhaas ed., *Generale Missieven van Gouverneurs-Generaal en Raden aan Heren XVII der Verenigde Oostindische Compagnie*, 6 vols. (The Hague, 1960-1980), vol. 2, p. 35 (18/12/1639); J.A. von Mandelslo, *Journal und Observation (1637-1640)* ed. M. Refslund-Klemann (Copenhagen, 1942), p. 10 (20/03/1638).

50. *As Gavetas da Torre do Tombo, Gavetas I-XXIII* (henceforth *Gavetas*) 12 vols., edited by A. Silva Rego (Lisbon: Centro de Estudos Históricos Ultramarinos, 1960-77), *Gavetas* XVIII-4286, pp. 17-30 (02/06/1641; peace treaty text), 120-50 (armistice agreement text); Anonymous, *Chronicle*, vol. 1, p. 358.

of the principal sea-ports and caused much trouble together with the dissenting [Arabs]. The Imam realized that he would never have a peaceful country for as long as these [Portuguese] had strongholds in that country. He therefore aimed all his might at their expulsion. He attacked them at such moments when they were unable to put up large-scale resistance. In this way he first took the small seaports, some of which he found to have been deserted due to weakness of [their] force. He finally attacked Muscat at a certain moment, when they [the Portuguese] had divested themselves of all supplies on the advice of a certain Banyan and took possession of it with very little trouble.[51]

On August 8, 1640 Naser b. Morshed died. That same day his second-cousin Sultan b. Seyf (r. 1640-1679) succeeded him as Imam.[52] He pursued his predecessor's aggressive and anti-Portuguese policy and slowly but surely all ports on the Omani coast fell into his hands. Finally, the last port, Muscat fell on December 2, 1649 followed by the surrender of the impregnable forts on January 20, 1650 in exchange for the garrison's freedom.

---

51. Willem Floor, "A Description of Muscat and Oman anno 1673/1084 H," *Moyen Orient & Océan Indien* 2 (1985), p. 33. Anonymous. *Relãçao das plantas e descripções de todas as fortelezas, cidades e povoações que os Portugueses tĕm no Estado da India* ed. A. Botelho da Cousa Veiga (Lisbon, 1936), p. 12, which states that the Sheikhs close to Muscat kept the peace with the Imam by paying him off.
52. E.C. Ross ed. *Annals of Oman from Early Times to the Year 1728 AD* (Cambridge: Oleander Press, 1984), p. 55. For the origin and rise of the Ya`ariba dynasty see Bathhurst, R.D. *The Ya`rubi Dynasty of Oman* (unpublished dissertation Oxford University, 1967); Wilkinson, J. *Water and Tribal Settlement in South-East Arabia* (Oxford, 1977) and idem, *Imamate Tradition*; A.A. al-Ashban, "The Foundation of the Omani Trading Empire under the Ya`arubah Dynasty 1642-1719," *Arab Studies Quarterly* I/4 (1979), pp. 354-71; Bathhurst, R. "Maritime Trade and Imamite Government: Two Principal Themes in the History of Oman to 1729," in: D. Hopwood, *The Arab Peninsula. Society and Politics* (London, 1972), pp. 89-106.

CHAPTER TWO
===

THE FIRST PERIOD OF DUTCH-OMANI CONTACTS 1651-1719

THE DEVELOPMENT OF MUSCAT AS A PORT-OF-CALL

The new regime in Muscat took immediate measures to secure its commercial viability. A long-term first step was to make Muscat an attractive distributive emporium for Indian and Red Sea commodities. The competitors of the Portuguese were not only happy with their ouster from Muscat, they also wanted to explore whether they might be able to do some profitable business there.[1] On 23 October 1651, the VOC sent the flute *Concordia* to the coast of Arabia to assess market opportunities.[2] Chief merchant Elias Boudaens reported, amongst other things, that after the capture of Muscat, the Imam had not yet levied any customs. The Imam told him that the port was open for anyone who wanted to trade there. He also offered the Dutch a house as a present. However,

---

1. Coolhaas, *Generale Missieven*, vol. 2, p. 417 (10/12/1650).
2. NA, KA 1072 bis, Instructie ende ordre voor den oppercoopman Elias Boudaen (06/03/1651), f. 839-42; Idem, NA, KA 1086, Sarcerius to Batavia (27/11/1651), f. 778.

Boudaens considered the market of Muscat not interesting enough. Its main imports, according to leading Banyan merchants, consisted of rice, pepper, black sugar, and coarse textiles with an annual turnover of only Dfl. 20,000-25,000. This was too small an operation to even cover the operating cost of a Dutch factory, hence Boudaens advised against starting trading at Muscat. The population was also poor; they only owned the coarse fabrics in which they were dressed, while trade was mostly in barter.[3] When an English ship called on Muscat that year the Imam also invited the East India Company (EIC) to come and trade there.[4]

Although the Dutch were not interested in the Muscat trade Asian merchants were. Boudaens observed that Moslem and other Asian merchants traded there in decrepit vessels.[5] This division between Asian and European merchants with regard to the attractiveness of the port persisted throughout the Safavid period. Muscat had only a few export goods, which in the first two decades of the eighteenth century consisted of: horses, dates, fine brimstone, some coffee but inferior to that from Mokha, some madder, and some pearls. There was a little manufacturing of coarse cotton linen and camelins.[6] The horse trade could be substantial, although it varied from year-to-year. For example, in 1680, 400 horses had been ordered from Muscat for Cananore, but these were unavailable.[7] Often vessels coming from India, but bound for Bandar Abbas, would first call at Muscat for two reasons. First, to avoid paying

---

3. NA, VOC 1188, Boudaens "Schriftelick relaes," f. 546r-vs; NA, KA 1072 bis, Boudaens to XVII (05/10/1651), f. 824vs. On the poor hinterland see Floor, "A description," pp. 30-32; Della Valle, *Voyages*, vol. 4, p. 412 (the bay of Qalbu was settled by Arab fishermen and some Baluchis); Bocarro, *Livro das plantas*, p. 66; see also Annex 1. The land route allegedly offered to the Dutch in 1651 (S.B. Miles, *The Countries and Tribes of the Persian Gulf* (London, 1969), pp. 211) is a nice story, but is not based in historical fact.
4. Foster, *English Factories* 1651-1654, p. 73.
5. NA, VOC 1188, Boudaens, "Schriftelijck relaes," (Surat 29/11/1651), f. 546vs.
6. Alexander Hamilton, *A New Account of the East Indies* 2 vols. (London, 1930), vol. 1, p. 47.
7 Coolhaas, *Generale Missieven*, vol. 4, p. 457 (29/04/1681).

customs duties twice (first at Bandar Abbas and then at Muscat) by disembarking those goods destined for Muscat, and secondly, to order horses to be kept ready for their return journey.[8] It is of interest to note that Hamilton no longer listed sugar as an export product of Muscat.

In view of the hostile actions by the Portuguese, the low level of commercial activities and the influx of now unemployed soldiers in Muscat, the Imam had to respond. Therefore, many of the Arabs living in Muscat earned their living as raiders, looking for Portuguese ships and vessels. They were interested in anything they could lay their hands on, but slaves were certainly one of their objectives. Bathhurst is therefore right in concluding that the Omanis "reacted to the European-controlled trading system and European and native piracy, by resorting to buccaneering themselves."[9]

The Beginning of Portuguese Attacks (1652)

It was, therefore, risky to develop trade relations with Muscat at that time. Following the fall of Muscat in 1650, the Omanis started harassing Portuguese merchantmen as well as warships in the Persian Gulf. The main objective of the Omanis was Portuguese ships, both to destroy Portuguese power as well as to take booty. On 22 January 1651, news arrived in Bandar Abbas that at Jask the Omanis had captured a Portuguese private vessel fully laden with rice and fabrics coming from Goa en route to Basra, "who now have two small ships and five frigates in the Gulf where they dominate. It was said from a reliable source that this was on purpose rather than chance and the Banyans in Goa collected in bottomry twice as much as the value of the cargo."[10] On 3 October 1651, according to the Dutch, a bloody or rather a silly battle (*bloedich*

---

8. Godinho, *Relação*, p. 75.
9. Bathhurst, "Maritime Trade," p. 102.
10. NA, KA 1077bis, Sarcerius to Batavia (25/03/1651), f. 582vs; Coolhaas, *Generale Missieven*, vol. 2, p. 554 (19/12/1651). The term bottomry refers to a contract whereby the owner or master of a ship borrows money for a voyage at interest or premium, pledging the ship as security (if the ship is lost, the lender loses his money).

of liever bloodigh) was fought between the Omanis and the Portuguese at Bandar-e Kong. The Omanis had raided Bandar-e Kong and taken three Portuguese vessels, besides attacking a "Cáfila" or convoy bound for Basra coming from Sind, which was escorted by seven small Portuguese warships, of which one was set ablaze by them. The remaining six had to return to Goa because they were no match for the Omani fleet. The Omanis became more and more daring and successful with regard to the Portuguese. The Omani fleet had also grown since the beginning of 1651, and counted five small ships with respectively 24, 20, 16, 12 and 9 cannons, 8-10 frigates and several barques by the end of 1651. The Omanis also captured a Portuguese vessel at Ra's al-Hadd, en route to Basra, laden with coffee from Mokha belonging to Armenian merchants. The Portuguese and Banyan crew who refused to become Moslems were killed.[11]

The English reported that the Portuguese fleet "so awes the Arabs that none of their vessels dares to put out from Muskat; against which place the generall spent some shott, but no great hurt was done to either side."[12] However, such awe is not evident from Omani actions. Despite the presence of a strong Portuguese fleet the Omanis were also active at sea. A Moslem yacht with goods, owned by Mondas Naan, was pursued by the Omanis near Jask and told to strike its sails. Fortunately, the ship was crewed by VOC sailors, who told the Omanis that they were Dutch

---

11. NA, KA 1086, Sarcerius to Batavia (27/11/1651), f. 778; *Assentos do Conselho do Estado 1618-1750 (Proceedings of the State Council at Goa)*, edited by Panduronga S. S. Pissurlencar/ Vithal T. Gune, 5 vols. (Bastorá/Goa: Rangel, 1953-57), henceforth cited as *ACE*, vol. 3-105, p. 189 (12/12/1651).
12. Foster, *English Factories* 1651-1654, p. 128. The Portuguese king, João IV, was very pleased with the success of António de Sousa Coutinho in Muscat against the Imam. *Boletim da Filmoteca Ultramarina Portuguesa* 50 vols. (Lisbon, Centro de Estudos Históricos Ultramarinos, 1955-1989), henceforth cited as *BFUP* 24, no. 126, p. 227 (18/03/1654). One year later he urged the viceroy to well prepare the next fleet for operations in the Straits of Hormuz, although no fleet came that year. For due to the wars against the Dutch in Ceylon and Canara the Portuguese were unable to send any ship to the Persian Gulf. *BFUP* 24, no. 12, p. 261 (08/03/1655); *BFUP* 23, no. 101, p. 133 (08/03/1655).

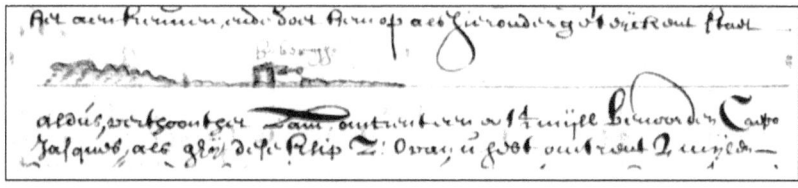
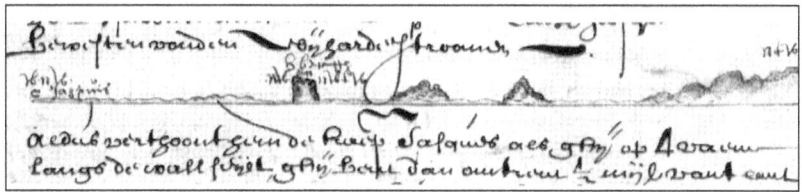

Top: Cape of Jask as seen from c. 11 km out at sea; *Below*: View of the Cape when sailing past at a distance of of 3.5 km (1645), Journael van Claes Jansen Speelman, Nationaal Archief, The Hague

so were allowed to continue their voyage.[13] Of interest in this context is that the English and Tavernier reported the alleged Dutch-Omani contacts at that time. Tavernier reported that the Emir of Vodona, an Arab Prince offered to show the Dutch an easy road from Muscat to Basra, but the Dutch did not want to upset their relationship with Safavid Persia.[14] In 1653, the English also reported that the Dutch were believed to have designs on Muscat. In fact already, the Imam was said to have offered that port as "their cheife residence for all their affaires in these partes." Also, his agents were said to have visited the Dutch factory at Bandar

---

13. NA, KA 1079 A, Joan Cuneaus/Shiraz to XVII (03/07/1652), f. 285r.
14. Jean-Baptiste Tavernier, *The Six Voyages* translated by John Phillips 2 vols. (London: R.L. and M. Pitt, 1678), vol. 1, p. 94. Vodena, also called Moyesur, is a place near Jolfar that is found on many old maps. It also occurred as Dadena, which possibly is the same as Daion in Balbi, *Viaggio*, p. 121, the modern day Dihan near Jolfar. See B.J. Slot, `*Arab al-Khalij, 1602-1784: fi daw' masadir Sharikat al-Hind al-Sharqiyah al-Hulandiyah* (Abu Dhabi, 1995), p. 394. Dan Potter has suggested that if Vodona is a copyist's error for Dadena then there can be no doubt that it is Dadna (emirate of Fujairah) rather than Dihan near Jolfar. Dadna has old remains; there are two settlements, Rul Dadnah and Syh Dadna, both with forts. Ziolkowski, *The historical archaeology*, pp. 135-140 (sites 19-29); cf. also Brass, L. and Britton, G. "An archaeological survey of northern Fujairah." *Arabian Archaeology & Epigraphy* 15 (2004), pp. 191-194 (sites 63-65).

Abbas on a daily basis, after the English had left.[15] Dutch sources mention nothing of this kind and, in fact in 1651, the Dutch had already decided that trade with Muscat was of no interest to them. What all this 'noise' implies is that the Imam of Muscat had serious internal problems and apparently was casting about for any help, even from outside sources. This may explain why the Imam, to ensure his position, had awarded governorships to political enemies, such as Sheikh Omar or Omeyr (Vali Ommer), who became governor of Muscat.[16]

That much trade would be drawn to Muscat was to a certain extent fortuitous for in fact this was already happening. Apart from the initially tax-free trade policy at Muscat, later changed to a 2.5% customs duty, there was the pleasant welcome accorded to merchants, which stood in contrast to the harassment and higher customs rates at Bandar Abbas. As a result there was a diversion of trade from Bandar Abbas to Muscat.[17] By the early 1660s, Muscat had become a major port-of-call for ships coming from India. In 1664, 125-150 ships did business at Muscat. Ships paid 2.5% *ad valorem* compared to 10-12% in Bandar Abbas and 9% in Bandar-e Kong.[18] Especially the trade from Konkan and Malabar came to Muscat.[19]

The commercial success went hand in hand with military success, for the Imam carried out a series of attacks on Portuguese possessions all over the Indian Ocean basin. In 1660, Muscat with a considerable force conquered Malindi, Mombasa and some other Portuguese settlements. Many Portuguese women and children were captured and much booty was taken. On their return voyage the Muscat force captured three rich Portuguese ships. Also goods imported from Oman were sold at Bandar-e

---

15. Foster, *English Factories* 1651-1654, pp. 195 (27/09/1653), 203, 209.
16. See Floor, "A description," p. 56. According to Rüdiger Klein, *Trade in the Safavid Port City Bandar Abbas and the Persian Gulf Area (ca. 1600-1680). A Study of Selected Aspects* (School of Oriental and African Studies, 1993/94), p. 127, n. 133 Vali Ommer probably was a leading member of the very important al-Omayri tribe, which seems correct to me.
17. NA, VOC 1242, Gamron to XVII (20/06/1664), f. 1091.
18. NA, VOC 1252, van Wijck to Batavia (19/01/1665), f. 716-17.
19. Floor, "A description," pp. 42-44; see also Annex 2.

Kong that had been pirated from Safavid merchantmen. However, according to the Dutch mate Cornelis, serving on a Masulipatnam ship, these were Portuguese goods.[20] After 1652, the Portuguese had been almost absent from the Persian Gulf as they needed all their resources for the war with the Dutch in Malabar and Ceylon, which lasted until 1664, when they signed a peace accord. In 1662, some 70-80 frigates arrived unhindered at Muscat with pepper, ginger, curcuma (turmeric), coconuts and *dungarees*[21] from Malabar. They sold these goods at prices that were sufficiently competitive with VOC prices, so that van Wijck observed that his colleagues at Malabar had to be more attentive.[22] The Portuguese factor in Bandar-e Kong told his Dutch colleague at Bandar Abbas that a fleet was being prepared in Goa to fight the Omanis and harass the Safavid Persians because of the affronts suffered. In November 1663, when the Arabs heard that two Portuguese vessels were sailing to Basra they launched a fleet of eight ships, small vessels as well as rowing frigates, and captured the two ships on their return from Basra. The Dutch therefore remarked that it would be difficult for the Portuguese to trade with Safavid Persia as long as the Arabs were their enemies.[23]

The argument that 'piracy paid' also held true for Muscat, for it too prospered as a result of warfare in the 1660s.[24] This allowed the Imam to build a large fortress at Nizwa to assert his power over the unruly hinterland. The Ya`ariba Imams themselves had become more involved in commercial matters. The second Ya`aribi Imam Sultan b. Seyf "had agents who were known to buy and sell on his account."[25] Seyf b. Sultan

---

20. NA, VOC 1236, van Wijck to Batavia (03/09/1661), f, 784.
21. *Dungaree* or *dongry* (in Dutch), was a kind of coarse and inferior cotton cloth
22. NA, VOC 1240, van Wijck to Batavia (13/05/1662), f. 690.
23. NA, KA 1131, van Tuynen to Batavia (15/02/1664), f. 581.
24. Ross, *Annals*, p. 55 ("taking many towns and ships and enriched himself with much booty taken from them"). The Omanis and the Portuguese were not the only pirates in the W. Indian Ocean. The Sanganians (the *Nautaques* of the Portuguese), were very infamous. There also were Malabar pirates, one of whose vessels the Dutch captured near Muscat in 1667, which they sold for 8,000 *mahmudis*. Coolhaas, *Generale Missieven*, vol. 3, p. 611 (06/12/1667).
25. Ross, *Annals*, p. 55.

I (r. 1692-1708) owned 24 large ships, 28 barques, and 1,700 slaves.[26] He also invested, as did his admirals, in sugarcane plantations run with slave labor and hired workers to dig new irrigation channels. The production of sugar expanded rapidly from 400,000 lbs. in 1672 to 760,000 lbs. at the end of the seventeenth century.[27] Seyf b. Sultan I built on his predecessor's work by extending the irrigation works outside Muscat.[28] Allegedly, he financed the planting of 20,000 date and 6,000 coconut palms, and in general boosted agricultural production.[29]

The Persians ask for Dutch Support to Invade Muscat (1664)

In the 1620s and early 1630s, Safavid authorities tried to draw the Dutch into their plan to conquer Muscat as was discussed above. In 1664, Safavid authorities once again asked the Dutch for naval support to attack Muscat. This request set a number of actions into motion, which led to the first formal bilateral relations between the Netherlands and Muscat.[30] In 1664, Morteza Qoli Beg, the *shahbandar* of Bandar Abbas, proposed to van Wijck, the VOC director in Bandar Abbas, in name of the shah that the VOC lend some ships to blockade the bay of Muscat, while barques would ferry Safavid troops so as to take Muscat from the landside. Van Wijck did not commit himself, but promised that he would inform the governor-general about the proposal, which he did on April 26, 1664. He suggested that if Batavia (Jakarta) wanted to go

---

26. Bathhurst, "Maritime Trade," p. 103; Ross, *Annals*, p. 56; Miles, *Tribes*, pp. 225-26.
27. Floor, "A Description," p. 31; NA, VOC 1480 (16/03/1692); Ross, *Annals*, pp. 55-56; Bathhurst, "Imamate Trade", p. 48; Wilkinson, *Imamate Tradition*, pp. 220-23; G.P. Badger tr., *History of the Imams and Seyyids of 'Oman by Salil Ibn Razik from AD 661-1856* 2 vols. (London, 1871), p. 56.
28. Bathhurst, "Maritime Trade," p. 102.
29. Ross, *Annals*, pp. 55-56; Bathhurst, "Maritime Trade," p. 103.
30. Chief merchant Elias Boudaens had already visited Muscat in 1651; also Armenian servants of the VOC had 'hidden' themselves among the servants of the *shahbandar* of Bandar Abbas who was said to have regular contacts with his counterpart in Muscat. Dunlop, *Bronnen*, p. 566 (25/03/1636). For contacts in the 1640s see *ANTT*, DRI LV, f. 7-r-vs.

ahead with the proposal it should: (i) demand freedom of trade in Safavid Persia and half of the customs revenues of Muscat; (ii) stipulate that if the English declared war on Safavid Persia the VOC had equal moiety rights so that the English could not make any claim on the VOC as to payment of Bandar Abbas customs duties; (iii) consider leasing the ships, as the Dutch Republic did in Europe, because the VOC had no reason to make war on Muscat. The VOC might later, after the end of the operation, make the shah a present of the lease money; and (iv) ensure that the naval action against Muscat might be easily executed with two ships having 28 to 30 cannon each and two fast light yachts with 8 to 10 pieces each, for Arab ships could not stand against the better-armed European vessels. He further reported that people in Bandar Abbas who did regular business with Muscat had told him that the people of Muscat would welcome a Dutch protectorate, because they feared attacks by both the English and Portuguese. Moreover, van Wijck pointed out some of the negative points of the request. Collecting customs duties at Muscat required a considerable financial outlay, while the possibility of ships to go to cheaper Safavid Persian ports might harm the welfare of Muscat. Moreover, Safavid officials would be much better at this than the Dutch, implying that their 'moiety' value would be larger. Finally, van Wijck had no confidence in the outcome of the military undertaking. He was convinced that the Safavid troops, who were peasants from the southern province of Fars with no military experience, would be unable to stand the climate, while the inhabitants of Muscat would withdraw into the desert with all their goods and food supplies, leaving poisoned water-wells behind. Moreover, the defenses of Muscat were very strong and garrisoned by battle-hardened soldiers. Nevertheless, van Wijck also reported that the Omanis recently had suffered a loss of 500 men in Sind when they tried to do something about the pirates there. The governor of Lar had asked van Wijck to come to Lar during the hot season to discuss these matters. Because he was too weak due to illness, van Wijck intended to handle the matter by mail, and if that was not satisfactory he would send van Bosem, his deputy.³¹

Batavia instructed van Wijck to do nothing with regard to the *shahbandar*'s proposal. A decision on this issue would only be taken after it had received a formal written request from the shah.³² Such a request was never made. Meanwhile, local Safavid officials sent some persons knowledgeable about Muscat to the royal court for more information about the shah's intentions. They were not received at court, but were told after a six-months' wait, to depart, thus wasting their own time and money. Van Wijck ascribed the court's non-responsive attitude to the fact that Abbas II (r. 1642-66) was unpredictable. He only amused himself and did not care about matters of state. As an example, he referred to the recent attack by the Uzbegs on Mashhad and Herat, where they took much booty (people and cattle). The shah had not even sent army, for he was not interested in new conquests. The governor of Lar meanwhile had made a similar request as the *shahbandar*. He only asked for a promise of assistance by VOC ships if Safavid troops were to occupy Muscat. The governor also wanted to know when it would be the best time to attack Muscat.³³

The *Heeren XVII*, i.e. the managing directors of the VOC, took more interest in the proposal than the governor-general had. They wrote to Batavia that they would be willing to cooperate in this project, provided profitable privileges might be obtained, and if it became clear that the Portuguese and the English would undertake a military action against Muscat.³⁴ Since the *Heeren XVII* normally were hardly ever in favor of military operations in the Persian Gulf this change of attitude may be explained by the fact that at that time (1665) the Netherlands were at

---

31. NA, VOC 1242, van Wijck to XVII (21/06/1664), f. 1091-92; NA, VOC 1245, van Wijck to XVII (09/01/1665), f. 364. For the customs at Bandar-e Rig and its temporary closure see NA, VOC 1251, van Wijck to XVII (06/04/1666), f. 1325.
32. NA, VOC 888 Maetsuycker to Gamron (02/09/1664), f. 395. One year later the governor-general wrote that he hoped that the Shah would not return to the subject. NA, VOC 889, Governor-general to van Wijck (13/09/1665), f. 517.
33. NA, VOC 1252, van Wijck to Batavia (19/01/1665), f. 707.
34. Coolhaas, *Generale Missieven*, vol. 3, p. 570 (25/01/1667).

war with both Portugal and England. Inflicting defeat on the enemy, while at the same time obtaining commercial advantages must have appeared attractive to the VOC directors, an opportunity they could not afford to let pass.[35] Although less enthusiastic than his principals, the governor-general suggested to van Wijck that he could send an agent to Muscat to see what might be done in the commercial field, for he understood that Muscat and Bandar-e Kong both had attracted an increasing volume of trade.[36]

Van Wijck replied that indeed both ports attracted more trade, for Shah Abbas II did not care about the welfare of his own seaports. During the 1663-1664 trading season more ships than ever had gone to Bandar-e Rig, both for imports and exports. Above all English ships from Basra navigating to India with freight sailed from Bandar-e Rig. He predicted that this would hurt Bandar Abbas, because these merchants did not pay customs there and were given a polite welcome, while at Bandar Abbas there were many difficulties and instead of the normal customs rate of 10% some 11% and even 12% or more was collected. However, Van Wijck was not very keen to move to Muscat unless trade worsened at Bandar Abbas than at present. He submitted that the entire Malabar trade and part of the Vengurla trade had all concentrated in Muscat in 1664, although sometimes two to three frigates came to Bandar Abbas via Muscat. In 1664 apparently 125 ships and frigates and, according to some, even 150 called at Muscat where they paid little (2¼ % customs duties but in Bandar Abbas 10% plus presents). Nevertheless, all these goods landed at Muscat were destined for Safavid Persia and were imported via Bandar-e Rig and other ports where the shah did not have a customs-house and where merchants could land those goods by giving a present to the local sheikh or *mir*. However,

---

35. See, for example, Willem Floor and Mohammad Faghfoory, *The First Dutch-Iranian Commercial Conflict* (Costa Mesa: Mazda, 2004), pp. 156-60, annex 5; see also Steensgaard, *Carracks*, p. 134.

36. Because of the decline of the port of Bandar Abbas the governor-general considered the option of moving the VOC factory to Muscat, which van Wijck opposed. NA, VOC 1245, van Wijck to XVII (09/01/1665), f. 369; NA, VOC 1252, van Wijck to Batavia (19/01/1665), f. 716.

van Wijck pointed out that the VOC did not pay any customs duties at Bandar Abbas. Also, the VOC should not be involved in retail trade, because goods from Malabar and many other places would always yield more in Bandar Abbas than in Muscat. To obtain cargo for their return voyage merchants went to Bandar-e Rig. Therefore, van Wijck argued it would be harmful if the VOC adopted a different policy. If Batavia wanted to test the commercial waters he suggested the following: horses were difficult to get at Bandar Abbas and therefore, the VOC might try to buy them at Muscat. To test the market, the VOC could send: 800-1,000 lbs. of cloves; 1,000 lbs. of *rompen*; 200-300 lbs. of Ceylon cinnamon; 500-600 lbs. of Japanese camphor; 1,000-1,200 lbs. of tin; 1,000-1,200 lbs. of copper rods; 500-600 lbs. of sappanwood; and 2 pieces of cloth because Muscat and the Arab coast were supplied with these goods from Bandar Abbas. After some time, the VOC could increase the volume of these goods depending on trade results. For export the VOC might try to buy pearls at Sohar or Jolfar. Van Wijck further mentioned that Persian official were still considering invading Muscat, because they were convinced that otherwise the English or Portuguese might do so. They realized that Muscat was the key to the Persian Gulf; he who controlled Muscat controlled imports and exports into the Persian Gulf and could therefore enforce payment of customs duties.[37]

All these plans came to naught, for on March 23, 1665 the English Agent in Bandar Abbas told van Wijck that war had broken out between their countries. Although van Wijck had still received no orders from the Netherlands,[38] he intended to have the Dutch ships in the Persian Gulf patrol the area to capture the English ships that were expected

---

37. NA, VOC 1242, van Wijck to XVII (21/06/1664), f. 1091; NA, VOC 1242, van Wijck to XVII (20/06/1664), f. 109; NA, VOC 1245, van Wijck to XVII (09/01/1665), f. 369-vs; NA, VOC 1252, van Wijck to Batavia (19/01/1665), f. 716-18. Van Wijck also pointed out that: "In the past, the Malabar trade was important here. The Portuguese had so much power that if you did not have a pass and had proscribed goods then they confiscated the goods and the vessel. This greatly benefited the Portuguese; it is not a practicable option for the VOC, however," he opined. NA, VOC 1242, van Wijck to XVII (09/04/1664), f. 1055.
38. Van Wijck received orders how to act during the war from the XVII on May 24, 1665, NA, VOC 1253, van Wijck to Batavia (31/05/1665), f. 1531.

from the Coromandel Coast. From Vengurla the Dutch learnt that the Imam would like to do business with the VOC. However, Van Wijck did not consider this the opportune moment. The Dutch were at war with their competitors. It would be different, however, if the English wanted to blockade Bandar Abbas, for then Muscat could be "the spectacles on our nose" as well as a retreat in case of war with the English. Therefore, he decided to send the *Brouwershaven* with a Banyan who spoke Arabic and knew Muscat to go to the Imam in Nizwa (Nosebbae). The Banyan had been instructed to collect information about what the Arabs thought about the English, Portuguese and the Dutch and under whose umbrella they would feel best protected. If the Imam should ask whether the Dutch wanted protection, the Banyan had to reply in the negative and to tell the Imam that he had to write to van Wijck about such matters. The Banyan emissary also had to observe how many ships and of what nature visited Muscat and in general to examine the market and the price levels. Finally, he had to go to the Imam and present him with van Wijck's letter.[39] In this letter van Wijck informed the Imam of Muscat that the Dutch had conquered Cochin, Kananoor and its subject regions. Since the Dutch now ruled that country and because so many ships from the Malabar coast frequented Muscat, it would be a good idea that the Dutch would start trading there, if the Imam agreed to this. He asked the Imam to send his reply with the messenger of the letter, while at the same time informing the Imam that the decision of sending a permanent agent to Muscat would have to be taken by Batavia.[40]

At the last moment van Wijck did not send *de Brouwershaven* to Muscat, for he believed it to be safer to keep this ship ready at Bandar Abbas in view of the state of war that existed with the English. Therefore, on 6 April 1665, he decided to send the Banyan emissary with a local barque to Muscat.[41] Batavia gave its permission for van Wijck's plan to send a mission to the Imam of Muscat, while it also hoped that the

---

39. NA, VOC 1252, van Wijck to Batavia (04/04/1665), f. 687-88.
40. NA, VOC 1245, van Wijck to Imam of Muscat (Seegh Bimhaly free sovereign lord of Eastern Arabia and the sea coast), (04/04/1665), f. 520.
41. NA, VOC 1252, van Wijck to Batavia (04/04/1665), f. 701.

shah would not raise the matter of his plan to attack Muscat. When the Banyan returned two months later he had a letter from the Imam for van Wijck in which he friendly requested the VOC to come and trade because "we always have been friends." Unfortunately, the letter was written in Arabic and the VOC had nobody at Bandar Abbas who could translate it properly.[42] This situation made van Wijck comment that it was a strange matter that Muscat was so near and despite this the Dutch were unable to translate an Arabic letter in Bandar Abbas. This inconvenience was soon remedied, however, by the arrival of Herbert de Jager in Bandar Abbas, who, amongst other things, was an outstanding scholar of Middle Eastern languages.[43]

The Imam's invitation no doubt had been partly influenced by rumors about the Safavid invasion plan, which cannot have escaped the Imam's attention in view of the fact that regular contacts existed between Muscat and Bandar Abbas. Also, the Imam may have had other designs, for he had been trying to enlist the support of other European powers against the Portuguese. The most concrete result of this diplomacy had been the unsuccessful attempt by the English to assist the Imam in 1659. Van Wijck who had hoped that the Imam of Muscat would accept the establishment of a Dutch agent in Muscat was therefore pleased with the result of the first contact with Muscat. He wrote that the climate was better than that of Bandar Abbas, although the Arabs were stricter where religious matters were concerned than the Safavid Persians and the former were less friendly towards Christians due to the treatment

---

42. NA, VOC 1253, van Wijck to Batavia (01/06/1665), f. 1561; Coolhaas, *Generale Missieven*, vol. 3, pp. 502-03 (30/01/1666), 570 (25/01/1667). For the translation of the reply of the Imam see NA, VOC 1251, Imam of the Mohammadans, son of Seif, son of Malick, son of Aboe Larab, Sultan's son to van Wijck (04/04/1665; date of translation), f. 1343.

43. NA, VOC 1259, van Wijck to Batavia (19/11/1665), f. 3303-04. The same letter also reports that there had been heavy storms in the Persian Gulf. Many pearl fishers had died; it was said about 100 at Sohar (Souaar). With this letter van Wijck sent a copy of the Imam's letter to have it translated in Batavia. NA, VOC 1259, van Wijck to Batavia (12/03/1666), f. 3324. Herbert de Jager was a student of Golius and had been earmarked to succeed him.

which they had suffered at the hands of the Portuguese. Van Wijck had already stressed the importance of having a small vessel in Bandar Abbas to cruise the mouth of the Persian Gulf to get advance information on possible English actions, and he believed that having a Dutch agent in Muscat would be even more helpful in this respect. Such an agent could warn and keep Dutch ships there, while communications could be fast by sending a runner overland to Sohar and from there with a barque to Bandar Abbas.[44]

Nevertheless, the governor-general of the VOC decided not to start any new activities in Muscat. It was not only the state of war, which made the Dutch lose interest in Muscat as a trading station, but also the fact that early in 1666 the Imam had raised the customs tariff from 2.5% to 10%, so that van Wijck expected that the merchants would start calling at Bandar Abbas again, because of the comparative advantages which that port had over Muscat now that the tariffs were practically the same. Moreover, the smaller Safavid Persian ports were no longer attractive since they also levied high customs duties after the unification of the customs administration. Because of this, van Wijck expected Bandar Abbas to start flourishing again, especially if the war in Basra continued.[45] In time, the governor-general intended to make use of the friendly attitude of the Imam, but during this period of war with the English it was not considered timely to spread Dutch forces all over the Persian Gulf, while it was also believed in Batavia that the climate was unhealthier than in Bandar Abbas. Moreover, it was not clear from the

---

44. NA, VOC 1259, van Wijck to Batavia (12/03/1666), f. 3324-25. Van Wijck later had pointed out that it would be a good idea, if he had the disposal of a galliot to cruise the Persian Gulf in these warlike times. In this way he would know what happened in the Straits area and "could use it for the discovery of Arabia, where good ports, roadsteads, and places are to be found where provisions and new supplies can be obtained. Van Wijck intended to use the ship *de l loop* for this purpose during that summer." However, the equipment of the ship was too insufficient to hazard the voyage between the cliffs and islands. NA, VOC 1253, van Wijck to Batavia (12/06/1665), f. 1685.
45. This refers to the Ottoman siege of Basra, see Floor, *Five Port Cities*, pp. 557-70.

Imam's letter whether he would give trading privileges to the Dutch. If the Dutch would have to pay customs duties like other merchants Muscat, then it would be of no great importance to the VOC.[46]

Meanwhile, Rijcklof van Goens, the Dutch governor of Ceylon and conqueror of Cochin,[47] decided to send the hooker ship *de Meerkat* to Bandar Abbas, because he considered it important from a military point of view that the VOC suffer no losses inflicted by the English in the Persian Gulf. Since the vessel was perfectly capable of making a trip along the Arab littoral about which little was known van Wijck decided that the Omani coast should be reconnoitered. The *Meerkat* left Bandar Abbas on 25 April 1666 and returned there on 14 June [48] However, the originator of the voyage, van Wijck, did not see the results of his endeavors, since he died on 5 May 1666 just a few days before he was due to return to Batavia on his way home to the Netherlands to fulfill an old wish to see his parents once more.[49]

Although the governor-general was satisfied with the result of the voyage and considered that the information which had been gathered would prove useful for the Dutch, no use was made of it for the time being.[50] Batavia did not want to disperse its forces during the war with England and France (1665-67). Moreover, according to Wouter Roothals, the interim director at Bandar Abbas, trading activities had been stopped in Muscat by the Imam out of fear that other powers

---

46. NA, VOC, van Wijck to Batavia (12/03/1665), f. 3311-12; NA, VOC 889, Batavia to van Wijck (14/11/1665), f. 636; NA, VOC 890, Batavia to Gamron (13/09/1666), f. 605-06.
47. About van Goens see Aalbers, J. *Rijcklof van Goens, commissaris en veldoverste der Oostindische Compagnie, en zijn arbeidsveld, 1653/54 en 1657/58* (Groningen, 1916).
48. NA, VOC 1259, Bosem to Batavia (14/06/1666), f. 3361. For the report of de Meerkat's voyage, see Annex 1.
49. NA, VOC 1259, de Lairesse/Isfahan to Batavia (19/05/1666), f. 3340.
50. NA, VOC 890, Batavia to van Wijck (03/11/1666), f. 693; Coolhaas, *Generale Missieven*, vol. 3, p. 481 (30/01/1665). Batavia was also glad that nothing was heard any more about Safavid plans to attack Muscat. Ibid., vol. 3, p. 503 (30/01/1666).

would cast too covetous an eye on Muscat once it became too affluent. The governor-general, therefore, was glad that he had not yet decided to establish a factory there. The Dutch would remain in Bandar Abbas and Muscat would be sidelined meanwhile.[51] Later Wouter Roothals, who had temporarily replaced van Wijck, reported that this situation had been only temporary, the reason being that intelligence was received that Portuguese supporters in Muscat would betray the city's defenses during an expected attack by the Portuguese fleet. However, when this attack did not materialize, trade was resumed at its former level and again flourished. Roothals commented that it would be worthwhile for the VOC to see and learn the actual situation in Muscat. He intended to send an able young Dutchman and two local servants to Muscat under the pretext of buying horses. They would stay there for one year and find out what profitable trade might be carried on by the VOC in Muscat.[52] The Dutch merchants at Bandar Abbas did not carry out this plan, because Batavia preferred to avoid Muscat in view of the continuing military actions fought between the Portuguese and the Omanis. For at the least rumor about approaching Portuguese, the merchants left Muscat[53] and over the next decade this was a recurring pattern.

New Round of Hostilities with Portugal (1666-1674)

Although the Imam of Muscat had raised the customs duties of his main port to make Muscat a less coveted object for Safavid Persia and other states,[54] this did not constrain his military exploits. In the second half of 1665 the Omanis took four small ships of Shivaji, the Maratha leader,[55] who controlled the West coast of Central India. Its captains were

---

51. Coolhaas, *Generale Missieven*, vol. 3, pp. 597-98 (05/10/1667); NA, VOC 1264, Roothals to Batavia (09/04/1667), f. 663v.
52. NA, VOC 1255, Roothals to XVII (23/09/1667), f. 783v-784.
53. Coolhaas, *Generale Missieven*, vol. 3, p. 650 (01/12/1668).
54. NA, VOC 1259, van Wijck to Batavia (12/03/1666), f. 3311 (The Imam has raised tolls to 10%).
55. Shivaji Bhosale (r. 1674-1680), was the founder of the Maratha Empire, which lasted until 1818, and at its peak covered much of the Indian subcontinent.

arrested and the goods confiscated. According to the Dutch, the Imam had a naval force of four ships with 12-14 frigates, which were ready to attack Shivaji's towns and ships on the Indian coast. But when he learnt that the latter's naval force was more than 100 frigates the Omani force retreated.[56]

Nevertheless, the Imam was right to be concerned, because not only Safavid Persia, but more importantly Portugal again had intentions to take the offensive against Oman. As of 1667 the *Estado* adopted a more aggressive policy to better defend its possessions in India and its interests in the Persian Gulf. This resulted in annual war fleet voyages to collect the Portuguese share in the customs revenues of Bandar-e Kong as well as to engage Omani forces and attack Muscat.[57] The Dutch reported that the Portuguese captain Manuel Mensos, who was at Bandar-e Kong with three ships in 1667, sent a letter to the Imam of Muscat demanding the release of Portuguese prisoners. This the Imam refused. It was then decided that two ships would stay at Sind for the entire year, while Menos returned to Goa.[58]

The Omanis dominated the Gulf of Oman and the Persian Gulf and carried on a serious war against the Portuguese, who had their hands full and suffered losses. Even the position of the Portuguese at Goa was precarious. They were attacked by the Omanis, but did not have the military force to do launch counter attacks. The Omanis also took four of their ships at al-Mokha.[59] By 1669, the Omani fleet had grown so strong that it became a match for the Portuguese. In May 1669, the French merchant François Martin saw the Omani war fleet, which consisted of six ships ranging from 350 to 500 tons. They belonged to Surat merchants. The ships had been en route to Basra and had called on Muscat to take on water. Here the Omanis commandeered the ships, stored their merchandise in warehouses and readied the ships for war.

---

56. NA, VOC 1259, van Wijck to Batavia (19/11/1665), f. 3303.
57. Glenn J. Ames, *Renascent Empire? The House of Braganza and the Quest for Stability in Portuguese Monsoon Asia, ca. 1640-1683* (Amsterdam, 2000), p. 167.
58. NA, VOC 1255, Roothals to XVII (23/09/1667), f. 783vs.
59. Coolhaas, *Generale Missieven*, vol. 3, p. 704 (17/11/1669), 717 (15/12/1669); Ames, *Renascent Empire*, p. 165.

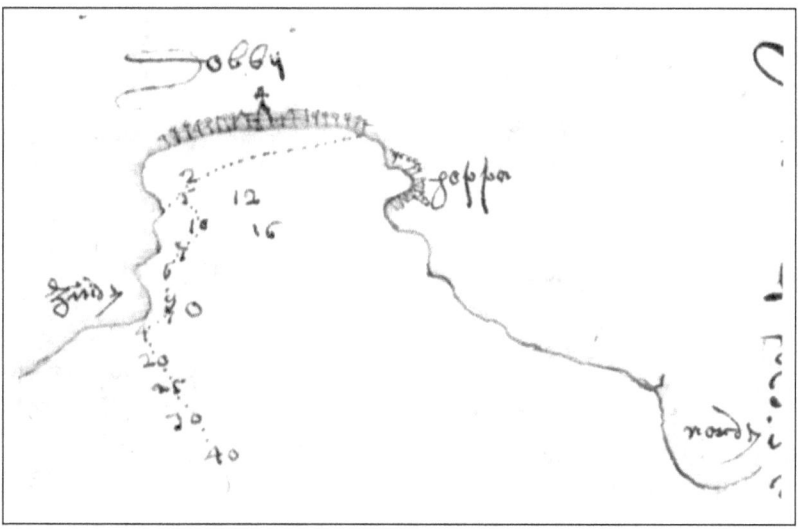

Top: Goa Island and Cape Musandam; *Below*: Omani Coast at Cape Musandam (1645), Journael van Claes Jansen Speelman, Nationaal Archief, The Hague

They also had the service of six to eight other vessels.[60] In 1670, a ship belonging to the king of Siam was sequestered in Muscat and was to be used for some time by the Omanis in their war against the Portuguese. At the insistence of the Dutch, it was released. The Imam of Muscat allowed the Siamese vessel to leave on 8 May 1670. The unfortunate vessel was shipwrecked four days later at Cape Jask.[61]

---

60. Martin, François. *Mémoires de -, fondateur de Pondicherry*, 3 vols. ed. A. Martineau (Paris 1931-34), of which vol. 1 and part of vol. 2 have been translated into English by Aniruddha Ray as *François Martin Mémoires Travels to Africa, Persia & India* (Calcutta, 1990) [cited as Martin, *Travels*], p. 415.
61. NA, VOC 894, Batavia to Gamron (27/08/1670), f. 559.

All these events strengthened Batavia in its decision to postpone trading activities with Muscat.[62] However, for the Omanis it was reason to undertake an even bolder plan, viz. to attack and take Mozambique, but they were defeated suffering heavy losses.[63] This was followed by another crushing defeat near Cape Musandam; although having a weaker force, the Portuguese admiral D. Manoel defeated the Omanis. He sank four of their ships and killed 2,000 men. The rest of the fleet returned to Muscat in need of repairs. The impact was such that: "the natives [on that coast] did not eat fish for many days because of the dead corpses that fouled the seas and beaches [there]."[64] In 1670, such had been the impact that the Portuguese boasted: "The Omanis remain so broken by the encounter they had with our fleet near the island of Queixome, that they gathered the little that remained to them at Maskat, not even sailing this past summer, a great occasion, by which we continued the Straits voyage that promises, not only credit, but also great advantages."[65]

THE DUTCH ESTABLISH A FACTORY AT MUSCAT (1672-1675)

Meanwhile Batavia had taken the decision to assess the commercial potential and advantages of the Muscat trade and ordered Bandar Abbas to send a junior-merchant of their staff to that port.[66] This change of attitude was caused by a number of facts. In the first place there were the growing difficulties with the court in Safavid Persia as well as a decrease of sales. Therefore, Batavia wanted to maneuver itself into a better position *vis à vis* the shah by creating the possibility of another sales

---

62. Coolhaas, *Generale Missieven*, vol. 3, p. 733 (31/01/1670).
63. NA, VOC, Report Harckz, f. 464-65; Ames, *Renascent Empire*, p. 167, n. 78 ("The attack on Mocambique had been deterred by effective defense of the Portuguese and the arrival of the viceregal fleet.").
64. Ames, *Renascent Empire*, p. 166.
65. Ames, *Renascent Empire*, pp. 166-67.
66. NA, VOC 894, Batavia to van der Dussen (17/10/1670), f. 678. Whereas in 1669 Batavia still took the position that Muscat was still too much involved with Portuguese to start trading there. Coolhaas, *Generale Missieven*, vol. 3, p. 733 (31/01/1670).

outlet in the Persian Gulf where the Company might move its factory. Apart from the reconnaissance voyage to Muscat a similar voyage had to be made to Basra.[67] In the second place, Batavia's interest in Muscat had grown as a result of reports it received from other Dutchmen, who called on Muscat and had been very well received. First there was the experience of assistant Jacobus Harckz who had been 'lent' by Batavia to the free merchant Jan Schouten to make a trip to Mokha to explore the nature and volume of trade carried on by Malabar merchants, whose trade was hurting VOC sales. Harckz found that the seafaring people of the Indian west coast were indeed hurting Dutch trade in the Persian Gulf and therefore, he decided to make a voyage to Muscat as well.[68] He arrived on 5 August 1670 with the vessel *tRad van Avontuur*. Having gone ashore, both he and Schouten were very well received by the governor, Vali Omar or Omeyr (Waelie Ommer).[69] The *vali* told the Dutch merchants that if they had merchandise they could sell it quickly in Muscat and he put a house at their disposal. In a fortnight the two Dutchmen sold all their goods at a price about 30% higher than in Mokha. After eight days the *vali* sent for them again and told them that he had received a letter from the Imam, who bade the Dutch welcome and had ordered him to show them friendship and to assist them in selling their goods.[70] Because of the positive results of the voyage, Schouten decided to make a second trip to Muscat, for he came from Sind where he had met with some adverse results. On his arrival in early December 1671, he met another Dutch ship, the *Masulipatnam*, with junior merchant Georgius

---

67. NA, VOC 894, Batavia to van der Dussen (27/08/1670), f. 559.
68. About this voyage see, for example, Coolhaas, *Generale Missieven*, vol. 3, pp. 719-20 (15/12/1669). Nothing is known about Schouten or Harckz. For the latter's report on his voyage to Mokha and Muscat see NA, VOC 1279, Report Harckz, f. 462-68. About the reasons for the voyage to Muscat see Idem, f, 463. Roothals proposed to keep two native barques at Bandar Abbas to be used as lighters and to hunt Malabar vessels to prevent them from bringing pepper into the Persian Gulf. NA, VOC 1268, Roothals to Batavia (26/08/1668), f. 1356vs.
69. I have not been able to find any particulars about this person. Klein, *Trade*, p. 127, n. 313 has suggested that the name should be read Vali Omayr.
70. NA, VOC 1279, Report Harckz, f. 466.

Hartsing, who had been on a trade intelligence mission to Basra. There he had already met Schouten in July or thereabouts, who told him about the good prospects in Muscat. The Imam wanted to send an ambassador to Batavia and asked Schouten for a pilot to navigate one of his own ships. Schouten fearing that Batavia would not like that, said that he could not accommodate the Imam in that respect. Therefore, Hartsing decided to see what he could do in Muscat in the VOC's interest. He arrived on 11 December 1671, where he also met Schouten and Harckz on 7 December. Two other ships accompanying Hartsing arrived in Muscat on 17 December. On 12 December Hartsing went to see the *vali* whom he apprised the purpose of his visit. The *vali* said that he was welcome and would receive his assistance, because for a long time the Imam was desirous to have the Dutch in Muscat. He added that the Dutch would be exempted from paying customs and other imposts. Therefore, he urged Hartsing to return next year, for he could be assured of a friendly welcome and assistance. Hartsing promised to report everything to Batavia. The next day he paid a visit to Mohammad Sheikh Abdallah Soleyman (Mameth Chech Abdul Cheleman)[71] the Imam's representative. The latter repeated what the *vali* had said and on behalf of the Imam formally invited the VOC to come and trade in Muscat. Hartsing asked for a list of best selling goods in Muscat; this was immediately drawn. Hartsing was also successful in selling some goods, which he had been unable to sell in Basra.[72]

At that time, both Omani and Sindi vessels were cruising in the bight of Sind to seize passing merchantmen. The Omani vessels had taken a ship from Surat, the *Salameth Ras*, which belonged to a certain Hajji Qasem. However, its French crew of fifteen men blew up the ship to prevent the pirates taking it. This pirate fleet of twelve vessels, filled to the brim with men, was still on the look out for Basra traders and

---

71. I have not been able to find any particulars about this person.
72. On the roadstead Hartsing found an English vessel, *The Consent*, owned and commanded by Mr. George from Masulipatnam. The latter invited the Dutch to his house ashore where they stayed during the first night. Schouten did not have to pay toll, while the VOC was promised trade with the right of toll-free import and export. NA, VOC 1284, Rapport van 'tRemarcabilste," f. 2246.

therefore, Hartsing decided to wait for the two other smaller vessels, the *Salameth Surat* and the *Sourath*, which had made the voyage with him to Basra. When these arrived, Hartsing left Muscat on 22 December 1671. Before he left, the *vali* asked if there were any complaints about the townsmen's behavior towards the Dutch, if so these people would be tried immediately. Also, whether all merchants had paid for their purchases, if not he would force them to pay at once.[73]

Harckz who had acted as interpreter for Hartsing reported that Schouten had been very pleased about his sales. He also reported that Sheikh Abdallah had asked him whether the VOC would like to have Omani troops to be used against the Portuguese wherever the Company saw fit? Harckz replied that since the Dutch were at peace with the Portuguese there was little need for such an offer, but nevertheless he promised to relay the offer to Batavia. Less satisfied about his welcome was Mr. George, an English merchant, who also decided to sell his goods at Muscat as soon as he learnt that the Dutch had been allowed to sell their goods with exemption from customs duties. However, when Sheikh Abdallah learnt that the king of England was married to a Portuguese princess[74] he became so angry that Mr. George was forced to pay 10% customs duties on his sales as well as 600 *rijksdaalders* for anchorage.[75] The Englishman protested of course and through the good offices of Harckz the affair was settled amiably and Sheikh Abdallah allowed him to depart this time, but he promised that other English ships would neither get water nor would they be allowed to trade in Muscat.[76]

Meanwhile Batavia asked van der Dussen, the VOC director at Bandar Abbas, about the result of the voyage to Muscat by junior

---

73. NA, VOC 1284, "Rapport van 'tremarkabelste soo op onse reyse als in Bassora, Congo, Gamron, en Maskatta is voorgevallen door Georgius Hartsinck," (Surat, no date) [henceforth cited as Hartsing Report], f. 2246vs-2248. Nothing is known about Hartsinck or Hartsing who was a junior merchant at the Surat VOC office, which, on the orders of Batavia, had sent him to investigate the possibilities of the Basra trade in collaboration with the Bandar Abbas office.
74. Charles II had married Catarina de Bragança, princess of Portugal in 1661.
75. One *rijksdaalder*, a unit of account, was equal to 2.5 Dutch guilders.
76. NA, VOC 1279, Report Harckz, f. 466vs-467.

merchant Georg Wilmson.[77] Van der Dussen had intended to send Wilmson in early 1671 to Muscat under the pretext of buying horses to assess the nature of the trade and to sound out the Imam about the nature of the privileges he intended to grant the VOC.[78] Van der Dussen expected that the Imam would at least grant the Dutch exemption of customs duties, because Muscat was mainly a transit-emporium for Indian products and as such did not constitute a profitable market for the VOC. However, van der Dussen instead decided to send Wilmson to Basra with Hartsing and after he returned to Bandar Abbas the intended voyage was again postponed due to news about the French and Portuguese, who were said to be sailing in strength towards the Persian Gulf. Since war with both these countries was imminent, van der Dussen decided to wait and see if the news was true.[79] The relations between the Dutch and the Imam remained very friendly. In July 1670 van der Dussen wrote to the Imam that he was displeased about the seizure of a vessel from Vengurla, which had a Dutch pass. The Imam explained that it had been a mistake and that no harm had been done. In conclusion the Imam assured van der Dussen that they were friends and that his ships were only at sea to seek out enemies and not to harm friends.[80]

Batavia was very pleased about these developments and the reports received so far, the more so since the Imam also had intimated that he wished to enter into an agreement with the Dutch against the Portuguese.[81] Therefore, the governor-general ordered Rijcklof van

---

77. NA, VOC 895, Batavia to van der Dussen (01/09/1671), f. 636.
78. NA, VOC 1284, van der Dussen to Batavia (15/04/1671), f. 2353. This move was approved by the XVII, NA, VOC 319, XVII to Batavia (15/05/1671 and 29/08/1671), unfoliated.
79. NA, VOC 1279, van der Dussen to Batavia (31/01/1672), f. 908 vs. War with Portugal did not come about, although it did with France, England and Germany in 1672.
80. NA, VOC 1274, Imam of Muscat to van der Dussen (no date [1670]) (translation of the original text only), f. 750.
81. Coolhaas, *Generale Missieven*, vol. 3, p. 772, 775 (19/12/1670); NA, VOC 895, Batavia to de Haze (19/11/1671), f. 902-03.

Goens,⁸² the governor of Ceylon, to examine the possibilities of such an agreement. Batavia's interest was mainly of a military nature, for due to developments in Europe war with France, Germany and England, possibly supported by Portugal, loomed large.⁸³ Since the Dutch had extensive possessions along the coast of West India the governor-general considered it of interest to see whether support by a local ruler such as the Imam of Muscat might be of military advantage to the Dutch. Batavia based its expectations on the so far successful military record of the Omanis against the Portuguese as well as on the offers, which had been made to Harckz and Hartsing. Therefore, Batavia decided to send Harckz, who spoke Arabic, to van Goens with orders to send him to Bandar Abbas. Van Goens was authorized to give instructions to van der Dussen in Bandar Abbas about the terms of an agreement with the Imam of Muscat. He also was empowered to send an envoy, possibly Harckz, to Muscat to inform the Imam that the governor-general was not unwilling to conclude such an agreement. If the Imam was interested he had to send a plenipotentiary to Bandar Abbas to do so. Where the military aspect of the agreement were concerned, Batavia stressed that it had to be made clear to the Imam that the Dutch only could support him for as long as the eventual war with Portugal would last. Batavia underlined that this should be crystal clear to the Omanis, for it would not be fair to leave them on their own in such an event. A condition to that effect could be included in the eventual agreement. Van Goens had to be the final arbiter where the need of such a defensive pact was concerned; he had to press the matter only if he thought it would enhance and fit in his defensive strategy for the Indian Ocean area. Batavia also instructed van Goens to try and obtain the privilege of free trade and a permanent residency in Muscat, possibly with the exclusion of all other European

---

82. Rijcklof van Goens had served the VOC in a great many functions in different counties since 1634, when he started at the age of 15 as an assistant. He ended his career with VOC as governor-general (1678-81).
83. On the Portuguese discussions whether to participate in the war against the Dutch in 1672 see Ames, *Renascent Empire*, pp. 174ff. The VOC took the position that to break with Portugal because of Muscat was not responsible. Coolhaas, *Generale Missieven*, vol. 3, p. 820 (31/07/1672).

nations. Furthermore, he had to make a thorough investigation of trade conditions in Muscat in order to see whether the optimistic reports had any basis in reality.[84]

Van Goens decided to see what advantages could be obtained in Muscat without committing the VOC too much. He charged senior merchant Robert Padbrugge[85] with this mission and sent him with Harckz to Bandar Abbas. Padbrugge was instructed to conclude a commercial treaty with the Imam of Muscat which included free and customs-free trade for the VOC. Van Goens did not want to ask for the exclusion of other European nations, since this might cause problems with the English. However, if the Imam wanted to grant this privilege himself, it could be accepted and any English trade in Muscat would be overlooked. Van Goens stressed that the VOC only wanted to show its friendship for the Imam and on no account had Padbrugge to intimate that the VOC was interested in concluding a defensive let alone an offensive treaty. The Dutch were still at peace with Portugal and France and therefore, such a defense treaty could not be concluded. If, however, war broke out with these countries, Padbrugge was authorized to conclude a treaty of mutual military support. But it had to be made clear to the Imam that Dutch support would only be given for as long as the war lasted. Therefore, Padbrugge could promise the delivery of gunners, cannons and other military equipment for the duration of the war. In case the war lasted a long time, van Goens was not unwilling to conclude a defensive and offensive treaty. In that case, he would demand that the

---

84. NA, VOC 1279, Batavia to van Goens (19/11/1671), f. 958; NA, VOC 895, Batavia to de Haze (19/11/1671), f. 907; Coolhaas, *Generale Missieven*, vol. 3, p. 820 (31/07/1672).

85. Robert Pad[t]brugge held a Ph.D. in medicine of the University of Leiden (1663). After his studies he joined the VOC and he served in the rank of merchant in Basra in 1667. He repatriated, but returned in 1670 as chief merchant to Ceylon. After his mission to Muscat he served as governor of the Moluccas (1676-80), as temporary governor of Banda (1680-81), and as governor of Amboina (1882-87). In 1687 he was elevated to the rank of *raad extraordinair* and he repatriated to the Netherlands in November 1688 as commander of the home-bound fleet.

Omanis would engage the Portuguese fleet to force them to spread their forces. If such actions resulted in adverse results for the Omanis, Padbrugge was authorized to promise Dutch naval support. In that connection, Padbrugge was further instructed to examine whether the Imam would be willing to give one of his coastal fortresses to the Dutch as he had intimated to Harckz. Also, the Imam had to give Padbrugge an assessment of the kind of military support he could give to the Dutch. Because Padbrugge's mission was only intended to lay the foundation for further negotiations, van Goens authorized the new VOC director in Bandar Abbas, de Haze, to make the final agreement with the Imam as soon as the expected war with France required such a measure.[86]

Padbrugge left Colombo on 17 February 1672 with three ships, the *Beurs van Amsterdam*, the *Alphen* and the *Muysenbergh*. After a terrible voyage he sailed to Malabar and started his ocean crossing on 23 March from Honawar. Once again, the voyage was dreadful; it turned into an ordeal due to stills and counter winds. In total disarray the *Beurs van Amsterdam* and the *Muysenbergh* arrived in Muscat on 5 May 1672, followed by the *Alphen* one day later. The latter ship had suffered twenty-four dead, while there were only eight healthy crew members left. If the ship would have had to sail another three days, the crew would have been forced to abandon it. The call on Muscat was only made to take on supplies and water and had not been planned.[87] Padbrugge sent Harckz ashore to announce his arrival and the purpose of his mission[88] to the *vali*, Mohammad Sheikh Abdallah Soleyman (Mameth Chech Abdul Cheleman). Harckz first paid a visit to the former *vali*, Sheikh

---

86. NA, VOC 1297, van Goens to Roothals (n.d.), f. 958-958vs. Francois de Haze served as director at Bandar Abbas from 1671 until 1674.
87. NA, VOC 1288, "Rapport gedaan aan van Goens door oppercoopman Padbrugge wegens desselfs verrichtinge in Musquetta ende omtrent den Imam ofte keurvorst vant steenich Arabia." (Colombo 25/10/1672), f. 430-31 [henceforth cited as Report Padbrugge].
88. NA, VOC 1288, "Memorie Padbrugge voor Harckz," Masquette (02/05/1672), f. 975.

Omar[89] before visiting Sheikh Abdallah. Apart from giving alarming rumors about French and Portuguese movements both officials were curious to know whether Harckz had information about the Imam's request? Harckz replied that he had returned with an envoy who was on the roadsteads with three ships. Therefore, Sheikh Abdallah wanted to welcome him in person and invited Padbrugge to come ashore. During the subsequent discussions, Padbrugge pointed out that the French like the Portuguese were idolaters. Furthermore, the Dutch had fought Spain for eighty years, because Spain had wanted to enforce idolatry upon the Dutch, and during that time, Portugal had been in alliance with Spain. Having shown that the Dutch were 'the good guys' Padbrugge asked Sheikh Abdallah whether the Imam had left instructions with regard to his mission. Sheikh Abdallah said he had not, but he had immediately written to the young Imam and expected a reply within three days. Therefore, he asked Padbrugge to wait and not to proceed with his voyage to Bandar Abbas as he had intended. To show his preference for the Dutch, Sheikh Abdallah gave orders to provide the Dutch ships with all kinds of supplies and water first, although an English ship on the roadstead had offered to pay 25% more. Because the Englishman was making preparations to sail for Bandar Abbas and thus might spoil the

---

89. The former *vali* was still greatly loved for his piety and kindness. He was dismissed allegedly because he was not smart enough to handle the financial administration in which Sheikh Abdallah apparently excelled. Omar or Omeyr remained commander of the army, although he was excluded from the state council, according to Harckz, see NA, VOC 1279, Report Harckz, f. 974. Padbrugge relates that Chegh Omer (Sheikh Omar or Omeyr) wanted to pay him a visit during his stay in Muscat in June 1672, which he declined. The reason for this refusal was the fact the Sheikh Omar's family had held sway over Muscat and the area as far as Ra's al-Hadd and had been a supporter of the Portuguese. Padbrugge felt that Sheikh Omar did not like the Imam's control over Muscat and therefore, his visit would raise the Imam's suspicion. The Imam controlled the finances, weigh-bridge and the defense of Muscat and he only used people of his own lineage and that of Sheikh Abdallah to run the administration. Sheikh Abdallah was the governor, one of his brothers was master of the weigh-bridge and the tolls, and another brother was tax collector and in charge of the treasury in Nizwa. NA, VOC 1288, Report Padbrugge, f. 444vs.

market for the Dutch ships, Padbrugge ordered the *Beurs van Amsterdam* and the *Alphen* to make ready to leave. the *Alphen* received fourteen healthy crewmembers from the two other ships, otherwise it would have been impossible even to make the short voyage to Bandar Abbas.

During their stay ashore, the Dutch were lodged by Hajji Khalil[90] the principal counselor of Sheikh Abdallah. His treatment of the Dutch was such that they were overwhelmed. The officers could eat and sleep whenever they wanted, and were freer in his house than "in any of our own factories", Padbrugge reported. Although they offered to pay for the board and lodging, Hajji Khalil refused to accept. After three days the Imam's reply indeed arrived, both from the old and young Imam.[91] They welcomed Padbrugge and invited him to come to their court in Nizwa. Padbrugge made it clear that first he had to go to Bandar Abbas, but they urged him to come as soon as possible, for they wanted to conclude an agreement. Padbrugge commented that the issue of an agreement was mentioned not less than three times in the letter and showed how important the Imams considered his mission to be. Padbrugge had to decline, however, but he assured Sheikh Abdallah that he would return

---

90. Hajji Khalil had a Turkish father and a Bahraini mother. He came from Basra to trade in Muscat where he became the chief counselor of Sheikh Abdallah. Under *vali* Omar he was a leading merchant and had acquired a notorious reputation. The Dutch believed him to be an Ottoman spy. NA, VOC 1288, Report Padbrugge, f. 435vs, 438.

91. Both Padbrugge and Wilmson on several occasions mention the old and young Imams without giving their names. Probably it referred to Sultan b. Seyf as the old Imam and his son, Bel Arab b. Sultan, as the young Imam. The reason for two Imams may have been caused by the serous illness that had befallen Sultan b. Seyf. In June 1672 Padbrugge reported that the old Imam had almost died and was recovering from his illness. NA, VOC 1288, Report Padbrugge, f. 439vs. Wilmson reports (VOC 1304, f. 483) that the Imam did not allow his eldest son to be engaged in foreign trade, which was the main reason for their estrangement. That there can be no doubt about the old and young Imam's identity is borne out by a letter of the [old] Imam "son of Zeef son of Malek from the clan of Yarabie"; see also NA, VOC 1251, f. 688.

soon. The latter accompanied Padbrugge to his ship on 9 May, when he sailed to Bandar Abbas, arriving on 17 May 1672.[92]

Padbrugge's mission, the letters from the governor-general and van Goens were discussed by the policy council of Bandar Abbas on 26 May 1672. The council decided to send Padbrugge to Muscat together with junior merchant Wilmson, who knew Persian and had already experienced dealings with Arabs. Harckz, of course, was also member of the mission and would remain with Wilmson in Muscat after Padbrugge's departure. The council decided that Padbrugge must return to Colombo to inform van Goens about the latest news from Europe. Because the hot season had started in Bandar Abbas, during which time there was little work to do, the council decided to add secretary Jacob Hartman to the mission in order to learn the ropes and how to deal with Arabs, so that he could replace Wilmson in case the council wanted to use the latter elsewhere.

The mission was charged to try and conclude a commercial treaty with the Imam of Muscat. Apart from toll freedom, without which right any treaty would be worthless, it had to ask for certain capitulary rights for the Dutch. Because the Imam had asked the Dutch to come, no presents would be given, but in case an agreement was reached the mission was authorized to give a small present. Because the council did not believe that the Imam would send an envoy to Bandar Abbas (he did not trust the Safavid authorities and knew that Padbrugge had arrived) the mission was instructed to avoid going to Nizwa if possible, for this would take time and money. Because there was no immediate need the mission did not have to rush the negotiations. Mainly, they had to listen to what the Imam wanted and proposed, because as long as trade in Safavid Persia was peaceful, the VOC would forgo the Muscat trade. Its only advantage was that in case of differences with the shah, the Dutch could just abandon their factory in Bandar Abbas and continue their trading operations from Muscat to put pressure on the Safavid government. The council had no intention whatsoever of leaving Bandar Abbas

---

92. NA, VOC 1288, "Memorandum Padbrugge to de Haze," (1 [sic] /05/1672), f. 967; NA, VOC 1279, de Haze to XVII (28/05/1672), f. 952.

for Muscat, for trade in Muscat would only hurt its own sales in Bandar Abbas and Basra. Therefore, Padbrugge should make no commitments; for this, Wilmson would remain behind. The more so, since the council believed that the Imam only wanted to make an agreement with the VOC to seek protection against the Portuguese under a Dutch umbrella. Although the Omanis were brave soldiers, they were bad sailors and had too few experienced sailors to man their fleet. The latter could only fight against frigates and Padbrugge was instructed to make a thorough investigation of the military capability of Muscat and report to van Goens.

Because it was believed that the Imam did not care about a commercial treaty and only wanted to conclude a defensive pact, whilst the Dutch wanted the opposite, the mission was ordered to play down its status and objectives. It had to state that they had come out of friendship and at the Imam's invitation to buy horses and sell some goods. In connection with the latter, Padbrugge had to request from the Imam a residence and a warehouse. Wilmson had to gather detailed information about the nature of trade in Muscat. If the Imam requested Dutch pilots to send one of his ships to Batavia, Padbrugge had to decline this request. If the Imam wanted to send an envoy to Batavia he had to travel on a Dutch ship, in which case Padbrugge would accompany him. With regard to the issue of passes, if raised by the Imam, the mission was instructed not to refuse these outright, but to explain the Imam how the system worked and that these had to be applied for from the Bandar Abbas factory. It was finally decided that de Haze would write a reply to the Imam's letter of July 1671 to thank him for the release of the Vengurla ship and to introduce the two envoys, Robert Padbrugge and Georg Wilmson. Bandar Abbas had withheld this reply, because its director had intended to send it with Wilmson, whose mission had been postponed several times.[93]

On June 5, 1672 the *Beurs van Amsterdam* left with the mission and arrived at Muscat late in the evening of 11 June. The next morning a guard-vessel came to ask who they were and what they wanted.

---

93. NA, VOC 1279, "Instructie de Haze voor Padbrugge en Wilmson," (06/06/1672), f. 1029-30; Idem, Resolutie 26/05/1672, f. 958vs-59.

Padbrugge told them and asked to inform the *vali*. However, nobody came to welcome the mission. For some time, they walked idly on the beach where they ran into Hajji Khalil, who was very friendly and took them to Sheikh Abdallah. The latter, as the Imam's plenipotentiary, opened discussions with the mission. He confirmed that the Imam indeed wanted an alliance against the Portuguese with the purpose of destroying their power and to expel them from India altogether. Padbrugge replied that there was peace between the Netherlands and Portugal, so at the moment such an alliance would be impossible. However, if war broke out between the two countries matters would be different and the director at Bandar Abbas had the authority to conclude such an alliance. This reply chilled the warmth of the welcome considerably, for when Padbrugge asked for a house, Sheikh Abdallah wanted the Dutch to pay rent for it. With regard to the sale of goods and the purchase of horses he said that they would have to pay 2.5% customs duties and could not get exemption. It was clear, Padbrugge commented, that the Imam did not really want the Dutch trade in Muscat. Since he had only been sent to listen to what the Imam wanted, when having heard it, Padbrugge believed it would be better to leave right away after this first cold shower.

The next day Sheikh Abdallah still had not provided the Dutch mission with a house, although they had already brought their merchandise ashore. Because Padbrugge was angered at his reception, which he did not consider to be in accordance with what was due to the VOC, he left the goods on the beach and later had them taken to a house which he himself rented. Sheikh Abdallah was taken aback and asked Padbrugge why he had acted so hastily, for he had already prepared a house for the mission. Padbrugge, in order not to create unnecessary difficulties, accepted Sheikh Abdallah's house. He also presented him with the letter for the Imam. Sheikh Abdallah after having read it objected to the use of certain words, which he claimed sounded offensive to an Arab. He also raised other minor points, but Padbrugge refused to discuss any of these and Sheikh Abdallah gave in without further ado. For ten days no further discussions took place, during which period the Dutch were not treated as welcome friends.

On 22 June 1672 both Sheikh Abdallah and Hajji Khalil opened the discussions and again Sheikh Abdallah said that the Imam wanted to see the mission himself. Padbrugge felt he could not refuse, although his instructions stated that he should not accept such an invitation. However, Sheikh Abdallah raised another problem saying that first he had to announce the coming of the mission which would take time. He used that period to reiterate the Imam's desire for an alliance, to which Padbrugge replied that his very presence was the expression of the same intention on behalf of the VOC. If war with Portugal would break out the Dutch would act as he requested. Sheikh Abdallah then claimed that Padbrugge had not said this before and had in fact stated that the VOC never wanted an alliance with Muscat. These remarks confirmed the Dutch in their opinion that the Imam was only interested in a military alliance and not at all in a commercial treaty. As a result of this meeting their treatment became much politer than before.

The mission finally left for Nizwa, although Wilmson had the idea that it only served to test Dutch willingness to deal with the Imam, for he believed that he heard Sheikh Abdallah say on their departure that they might as well stay, since the Imam would come himself to Muscat. En route, after two days travel, the Dutch mission was passed by the Imam who hurried to Muscat in connection with a report on an approaching Portuguese fleet. He did not stop to speak to the Dutch, who therefore, had to make a turnabout and ride back to Muscat. Here they were received by an ill Imam on 28 June 1672, who gave them a warm welcome. The Imam asked them to conclude an alliance against Portugal to which Padbrugge gave the same reply as he had given to Sheikh Abdallah. He further asked to be allowed to buy horses and to sell goods and that the Dutch would be treated as if they were the Imam's own people. In the days that followed, the Dutch again received the cold shoulder treatment. In the meantime the *Muysenbergh* and the *Alphen* had arrived on the roadstead and Padbrugge had to leave with these ships. Because the Imam also intended to return to Nizwa, Padbrugge asked for a farewell audience and to use that opportunity to discuss the possibility of a commercial treaty with the Imam. Although the audience was granted, it was postponed and later it became known that the Imam had again left.

Padbrugge then received a visit from Sheikh Abdallah, who after much pressure confirmed that he had not taken customs duties from Harckz in 1671 and replied that neither would he take it from Padbrugge, provided a present was given to the Imam. Sheikh Abdallah did not answer any of the questions posed by Padbrugge about the kind of military force the Imam was able to put in the field or at sea, despite the fact that the Imam was only interested in a military alliance. For the Dutch it was clear that the Imam only wanted to use the Dutch military umbrella for Muscat's defense rather than cooperate with them in India against the Portuguese.[94] The Imam needed this support after the reverses he had met against the Portuguese on the African and Indian coast.

That the Imam wanted to keep the Dutch at arm's length was also evident from the fact that no offer was made of a fortress as had been intimated to Harckz. The Omani side did not ask for gunners either and only once for carpenters. However, when they heard how much these people earned they did not raise this matter again. This probably led to a better welcome of the two Englishmen who were staying in Muscat and who had been well received by Sheikh Abdallah. On 15 July 1672 Padbrugge left Muscat totally disappointed, if not disillusioned. He felt that there had been no need for him to have come at all, the more so since Wilmson had already been designated to go to Muscat, who was quite capable to execute that mission, Padbrugge reported. He was so frustrated that he started his report to van Goens with the remark that never before had an envoy been so badly received and badly treated as he had been, and he considered his voyage a waste of time. The Omanis, he submitted, were only interested in furthering their own interests, which, because trade in Muscat was monopolized by Sheikh Abdallah,

---

94. The presence of three Dutch ships on the roadstead of Muscat was almost too much to bear for the Imam. He asked Padbrugge to use them against the Portuguese in the Persian Gulf, which he refused, of course. The Imam then asked whether he could buy, rent or borrow Dutch ships to which Padbrugge said that he would report the Imam's request to the governor-general.

meant that the VOC would be unable to conclude a favorable commercial treaty.⁹⁵

During this stay in Muscat, Padbrugge had not been the only foreign envoy. He met, for example, the envoys from the island of Socotra (now part of Yemen), who had come to Muscat to ask the Imam's support against the Portuguese and from the Imam of Mokha (Yemen), whom they had beaten off recently. They also invited the Dutch to come and trade on their island saying that most of the spices, which were taken to Africa, were bought by rich merchants every year on their island. These merchants traveled as far as the river Gambia, they claimed, where they met other Europeans. Another envoy was from Sind who was on his way back to his country having been on pilgrimage to Mecca. He asked Padbrugge to report to Batavia, that the VOC could hire as many soldiers in his country as it wanted. The third envoy was the one from Shivaji sent to discuss the settlement of the dispute with the Imam. Padbrugge did not meet him, but he had the impression that his mission was not very successful.⁹⁶

After Padbrugge's departure, Wilmson continued to receive a rather neutral treatment. This was not only due to Dutch unwillingness to conclude a military alliance, but also there had been a dispute in the State council about the Dutch presence in Muscat. It is unknown who opposed the Dutch presence and for what reasons. A fact was that the old Imam received the Dutch, and that they were never received by the young Imam, who, according to the Dutch, ruled the country. The

---

95. NA, VOC 1288, Report Padbrugge, f. 430-35vs; NA, VOC 1304, "Rapport wegens 'tvoorgevallene in de commissie omtrent den Ymam staatsvorst van 'trijck Aaman en den handel van Masquetta," (20/02/1674), f. 473-76 [henceforth cited as Report Wilmson].
96. NA, VOC 1288, Report Padbrugge, f. 445. According to Padbrugge, the Shivaji had proposed that each side would keep what it had seized, including the Omani vessels which Shivaji had taken. Together, both forces would attack the Portuguese at Goa. The Imam refused to accept these terms. Finally peace was concluded on the condition that Shivaji would pay an indemnity to the Imam and would return the vessels and goods that he had taken. Coolhaas, *Generale Missieven*, vol. 3, p. 832 (11/12/1672).

situation did not improve when bad intentioned persons said that de Haze had kept the presents sent by Batavia in Bandar Abbas, a story which was believed by many, according to Wilmson.[97]

Despite the disappointing result of Padbrugge's mission, Batavia nevertheless concluded that the VOC had obtained the right to maintain a residency in Muscat and that a conditional exemption of customs duties had been granted in exchange for an annual present for the Imam. Therefore, Batavia instructed de Haze to nurse the friendly relations with the Imam, to thoroughly examine the trade in Muscat, the more so since finally the war with France and England had broken out, with whom Portugal might ally itself. If this happened, and only then Batavia stressed, de Haze might discuss military assistance with the Imam. Since Portugal remained neutral, there was nothing to discuss with the Imam, the more so since from the Omani side the issue of a commercial treaty was not raised either.[98]

PORTUGUESE-OMANI TRUCE (1672)

To oppose the ever-bolder Omani attacks, the Portuguese had to mobilize their forces to send out a fleet strong enough to deal with the Omani threat. On 2 September 1670 "the Portuguese Armada, composed of 25 men-o'-war, arrived of Muscat: and 7 vessels are at Kung, to recover their (Customs) dues from the king of Persia."[99] A fleet of similar strength returned in 1671. With the arrival of the new Portuguese viceroy in Goa, whom the Dutch considered to be "an arrogant piece who calls himself the Restorador," a stronger effort was made to combat the Omanis. He also sent a fleet along the coast of Malabar (Kerala) to show the Portuguese flag, which was not appreciated by the Dutch. They considered hiring Omanis to attack the Portuguese in case these

---

97. NA, VOC 1304, Report Wilmson, f. 477.
98. NA, VOC 896, Batavia to de Haze (03/12/1672), f. 1053.
99. Anonymous, *Chronicle*, vol. 1, p. 426. The Portuguese fleet sent to the Persian Gulf in 1671 consisted of six ships *de alto bordo*. BFUP 33-34, no. 282, p. 553-54 (23/01/1672). Kung is Bandar-e Kong on the Persian coast.

again became their enemy. This was not an academic possibility, because the government in Lisbon was weighing the pros and cons of joining the French and English against the Dutch. But the governor-general in Batavia also considered the possibility that the Portuguese objective was not the Dutch but the Omanis, who were very busy preparing a considerable fleet intimating that they intended to attack Goa.[100] On 20 March 1671 news arrived that "the Armada has reached the Gulf: 14 galleons of which Don Antonio de Mello is the general."[101] According to the Dutch, the Portuguese had sent to the Persian Gulf two galleons, four patches and four frigates with some small vessels to attack the Omanis.[102] In March 1672, according to Portuguese sources, Goa sent a ten-ship fleet (six *de alto bordo* and four *de remo*) under Antonio de Mello de Castro.[103]

The Muscat population was getting weary of the seemingly unending conflict with the Portuguese. One reason was the negative impact on trade, which was quite significant. In 1672, when the Portuguese fleet was in the Persian Gulf it pursued all Arab vessels mercilessly. It was not always easy to get to the small Arab merchant vessels, which stuck close to land, and therefore the Portuguese sent "little galliots, which are small light craft, built rather like galleys, and very suitable for costal expeditions, as they have both sails and oars." The merchantmen defended themselves, and rather sank themselves than to fall into Portuguese hands. Those close to the coast abandoned ship and saved themselves. The Portuguese "refloated the vessels and carried them off." This exploit so terrified the whole Persian Gulf that no vessel, large or small, dared to put out to sea from any port. There was a sort of revolt at Muscat, when this news was brought by those who had escaped.[104]

In 1672, Carré reported "The Arabs in the place, weary of the continual war which hindered their commerce and had brought them only

---

100. Coolhaas, *Generale Missieven*, vol. 3, pp. 771-72 (19/12/1671).
101. Anonymous, *Chronicle*, vol. 1, p. 426.
102. Coolhaas, *Generale Missieven*, vol. 3, p. 819 (31/07/1672).
103. Ames, *Renascent Empire*, p. 167.
104. Abbé Carré, *The travels of Abbé Carré in India and the Near East (1672-74)*, 3 vols. (London: Hakluyt, 1947), vol. 1, p. 115.

ruin and continual losses, made known to the Imam, their king, that they could no longer submit to live in the misery to which they had been reduced for so many years." When in 1672 the Imam made one of his rare visits to Muscat he found that many had left the town out of fear of the Portuguese They had fled into the mountains and the Imam feared that the soldiers would do likewise. The Imam was also worried about food supplies, because with the Portuguese in the Persian Gulf food could not be imported. He made promises and gave presents so that he calmed fears. "By also relaxing the dues and taxes he induced most of the merchants and inhabitants to return to the town, from which they had fled."[105] Shortly before this the Portuguese had destroyed an Omani convoy of trading ships bound for Basra, in retaliation to the many raids the Omanis had carried out against Portuguese ships and settlements.[106] Wilmson also reports the dissatisfaction among the population, which was made worse by a famine in 1672. Half of the population was ready to revolt. The Imam, however, had crushed the old local elite and thus, there were no leaders to start a revolt.[107]

Whether it was a sign of weakness or a ploy to mislead his enemies both at home and abroad is unknown, although it was probably both, the Imam sent a representative by ship to Bandar-e Kong to try and reach a truce. The Portuguese general agreed to the offer, thus violating the Viceroy's instructions.[108] The place agreed upon was the Omani port of Sohar where the Portuguese fleet arrived on 24 September

---

105. Carré, *The Travels*, vol. 1, p. 115-16, 126 (such flight also happened in Sohar when Portuguese sails were sighted). Despite their weariness the Omanis still continued their raiding activities at that time. R.B. Serjeant, "Omani Naval Activities off the Southern Arabian Coast in the late XVIth/XVIIth Century, from Yemeni Chronicles," *Journal of Omani Studies* VI (1983), p. 77-89.
106. NA, VOC 1273, Goske to XVII (28/02/1669), f. 1940; *ACE* III, p. 546.
107. Floor, "A description," pp. 33-34. This had been the Imam's policy from the beginning. The Portuguese mention such purges of the elite since 1639. *ANTT DRI* XLIV, f. 262.
108. Carré, *The Travels*, vol. 1, pp. 117, 119, for the result of the general's disobedience p. 177; Portuguese made agreement with Muscat. Coolhaas, *Generale Missieven*, vol. 3, p. 867 (31/01/1673).

1672, but the Imam was not there. The general then sent a letter and another, being angry that the Imam was not present. Finally the Imam's *vakil* or representative showed up. After a truce had been reached, the Portuguese demanded a port in Oman, which they intended to fortify. They also wanted free access to the interior and the right to sell at their own prices. The Portuguese also made it clear to the *vakil* that the agreement had to be signed by the Imam's son else they would not sign it. The *vakil* refused to grant any privileges to the Portuguese. He was willing to grant exemption of customs, but only on a reciprocal basis.[109] The Portuguese admiral António de Mello de Castro finally accepted an agreement with less specifics.[110] The truce lasted only a few months and did not include commercial relations. Although the Imam had considered the granting of commercial privileges, one faction opposed this, because it was not right.[111] According to de Carré, the negotiations were only a trick to gain the Imam time.[112] However true this may be, the Portuguese were neither really interested at that time to conclude a real peace agreement. In 1673, João Correia de Sá refused Omani proposals because he had received a delegation of 15 sheikhs who were willing to overturn the Ya`ariba dynasty with Portuguese assistance.[113] This was a lost opportunity, for it locked both countries into a seemingly everlasting war of attrition.

Why the Dutch Withdrew from Muscat (1675)

Wilmson used the occasion of the cease-fire concluded between Muscat and Portugal in mid-October 1672 to raise the matter of exemption of

---

109. NA, VOC 1285, Gamron to Batavia (05/12/1672), f. 5-6 (the Portuguese wanted Joerfokoen [Khur Fakkan] and Zetaab [?]).
110. *Collecção de tratados, convenções, contratos e actos publicos celebrados entre a coroa de Portugal e as mais potencais desde 1640 até ao presente*, ed. J.F. Visconte de Borges de Castro 14 vols. (Lisbon, 1856-58), IV, p. 233.
111. NA, VOC 1279, de Haze to Batavia (19/09/1672), f. 1024.
112. Carré, *The Travels*, vol. 1, p. 119.
113. "Letter of João Correia de Sá to the Prince Regent D. Pedro", (Kung, 06/07/1673), in *AHU*, Índia, cx. [29-A] 53, doc. 171.

customs duties. Sheikh Abdallah was unwilling to extend this privilege to the Dutch; he only was willing to grant it in exchange for an annual lump sum payment. He also harassed Wilmson by sending Banyans to demand the rent for his house. When Wilmson complained about this, Sheikh Abdallah replied that the Banyans were like dogs, to whom one had to throw a morsel occasionally. Wilmson replied that if the Imam wanted the Dutch to pay rent he would do so, the more so if he could not look after his guest. This barb struck home and Wilmson was allowed to rent his own house.

Despite the fact that at the end of November 1672 the Imam sent de Haze a letter in which he expressed his friendship with the Dutch, the Omanis acted as if they no longer needed the Dutch. The ceasefire had given them a false sense of security, for they thought it would lead to a peace settlement. However, on 19 April 1673, the Portuguese admiral, D. João Correia de Sá dashed this hope when he appeared with four ships in the bay of Muscat. "The Portuguese fleet remained in the Persian Gulf; he had declared war on the Arabs of Muscat, but warlike operations have as yet begun; the Omanis did not put out to sea, nor did the Portuguese approach the fort to attack it." This would also have been difficult in view of their small number and its strength.[114] Sheikh Abdallah asked for an extension of the cease-fire for sixty days, but the admiral only was willing to accede to a period of forty days. During that time the Omanis could prepare for the coming battle near Bandar-e Kong, and if they did not come, D. João would come and get them himself. However, if the Imam was prepared to negotiate a peace settlement, he had to send an ambassador to Bandar-e Kong within the forty day period. After its expiration, D. João was no longer prepared to discuss the subject of peace. According to Wilmson, the Omanis were so afraid, because they feared that the Portuguese would set their vessels on fire that they tried to bar the bay of Muscat with chains. However, this proved to be impracticable, because the bay was too wide. From Bandar-e Kong D. João wrote a letter to Sheikh Abdallah in which he declared war on Muscat after the expiration of the forty days. Nevertheless, he

---

114. Anonymous, *Chronicle*, vol. 1, p. 426.

held open the door to peace, for D. João added that if the Imam wanted peace he had to send an ambassador to Goa, for which he would provide safe passage. The Omanis meanwhile had prepared their fleet for the expected hostilities, to which end they also pressed five merchantmen into their service. In total they had a fleet of eight to ten large vessels and ten to twelve small ones supported by about forty to fifty barques. Sheikh Abdallah had also asked Wilmson whether the Dutch would be willing to provide naval assistance, if there were ships on the roadstead of Bandar Abbas. He received a negative reply; some time later he asked Wilmson whether the Dutch would be willing to sell or lend four well-equipped men-of-war with forty pieces each. Wilmson referring to the fact that the Dutch were at war and needed the ships themselves again gave a negative reply, although he promised to convey the request to Batavia to keep their relationship at a friendly level. Sheikh Abdallah's worries may have been caused by the fact that the recruitment of troops had not been very successful, moreover, the Omani fleet was in a bad state of repair so that the crews were afraid to go to sea. Meanwhile the Portuguese fleet, consisting of five or six ships and eight to nine rowing frigates, was cruising near Bandar-e Kong and took some passing Indian and Arab barques. Their only opposition was offered by the Arabs from Jolfar, who with twenty-five barques, attacked the roadstead of Bandar-e Kong at night and took a Sindi and a Canarese barque.[115]

On 3 June 1673, the VOC council at Bandar Abbas, instructed Wilmson to broach the matter of the commercial treaty with the Imam. After having received a reply to this request Wilmson was ordered to return to Bandar Abbas. Hartman, who was ill, was allowed to return immediately, and would be relieved by assistant Nicolaes Ritsert, who left for Muscat on 16 July. This delay was caused by the fact that no barques were plying between Muscat and Bandar Abbas out of fear for the Portuguese. On 10 August Hartman returned with the same barque that had taken Ritsert.

---

115   NA, VOC 1285, De Haze to XVII (19/11/1673), f. 406; Ibid., de Haze/Shiraz to XVII (19/10/1673), f. 408vs; Ibid., de Haze to Batavia (02/10/1673), f. 411vs.

As instructed, Wilmson presented Sheikh Abdallah with a proposal for a commercial treaty on August 5, 1673. The VOC requested the following privileges:

> 1. Exemption of customs duties in all ports, exemption of all other imposts, and free trade.
> 2. Exemption of all taxes collected from Omani subjects for VOC staff members and their servants.
> 3. Free trade without being obliged to make use of the services of the auctioneer or anybody else or to be hindered in its trade.
> 4. The right to rent a house for trading purposes.
> 5. The right to import and select its merchandise, without having the customs' farmer inspect or examine their goods.
> 6. The right to weigh their weighable goods on the VOC scales using Dutch weights, while the weigh-bridge farmer would not be entitled to claim any duty.
> 7. The right to select its own broker, who would neither depend on the chief broker nor will have to give an account to the latter about VOC sales.
> 8. The VOC broker would not be required to render services to others.
> 9. Government support to force VOC debtors to pay their debts, in exchange for which the VOC undertook to pay bad debts of VOC personnel or of its broker.
> 10. In case of theft, the judicial authorities would do their best to retrieve and return the stolen VOC property and punish the criminals.
> 11. The right to judge Dutch subjects in accordance with Dutch laws and customs, without interference from Omani judges in case of a dispute between a Dutchman and an Omani subject.
> 12. In case of the death of a Dutch subject, his property will be delivered to the Dutch, and if no Dutchman is present, the property will be stored until an attorney will come.

13. The allotment of a proper burying place.
14. All fugitives, slaves or not, will be searched for and returned to the Dutch and they will not be allowed to convert to Islam.
15. In case of shipwreck on the coast of Oman, all Omani subjects will be obliged to assist in salvage operations.
16. Nobody, judicial personnel or anybody else, will have the right to board VOC vessels or barques.
17. Ships or goods seized by the VOC may be taken to ports in Oman and sold there.
18. Officials will have to pay respect to the Dutch wherever they will be in Oman and will not hinder them in carrying out their trade.
19. Nobody will be allowed to curse or molest a Dutchman in the streets or wherever it may be; if it occurs, such a person will be punished as an example to others.[116]

Wilmson did not bother to raise the matter of the exclusion of other European nations, since their trade with Muscat was insignificant and they, moreover, would have to pay customs duties.[117] He had sounded Omani officials about this matter, who had told him that the Dutch were their friends, and only they would be allowed the free use of their ports. Wilmson had a different impression, however. He felt himself tolerated and had the conviction that the Omanis wished him leave rather than the Malabaris. For the latter group, "brought honey to the bees" and a great deal of money into the treasury. The Malabaris therefore blackened the face of the Dutch, for they feared that once the Dutch had a permanent residency in Muscat it would mean the end of their naviga-

---

116. This proposal shows great resemblance with the first proposal of the commercial treaty submitted to Shah Abbas I of Persia in 1623, see Dunlop, *Bronnen*, p. 677.
117. Four to five small English ships had called on Muscat, mostly laden with rice, while only one French ship had come. Sheikh Abdallah had demanded 5% customs duties, although two of the English vessels had left without paying. The Imam had been displeased about this and had given orders that henceforth the English were to pay 10% customs duties.

tion to Muscat. This belief was not unfounded, for the Dutch had good commercial reasons to make that happen.

After one month, on September 11, 1673 the Imam sent a very short reply to Wilmson. Referring to the precepts of Islam, viz. "not to choose sides and not to divert from the right path" and furthermore "that those who do not follow the religious commandments, are infidel oppressors,"[118] the Imam stated that he would not act against these commandments, implying that Wilmson's request was in contravention with the precepts of Islam. Wilmson had strong indications that the Imam at first had drawn up a polite refusal, but that Sheikh Abdallah had not liked it. He told Wilmson that the Imam's reply had been lost en route. A few days later, the Imam's letter arrived, which dashed all hopes for a commercial treaty. For the Imam had not even bothered to answer Wilmson's points one by one, but only stated in a few sentences that what had been asked was contrary to Islamic law. The Imam only singled out points 10 and 11 about judicial matters, which he would not cede to foreigners. Because of the differences in judicial procedures, Wilmson feared that the Omani authorities might imprison a Dutch resident if he ordered one of his servants to be beaten, because Omani law forbade beatings. In fact such an incident had almost arisen when free merchant Schouten had wanted to punish a sailor aboard his ship, who was protected by Sheikh Abdallah.

Because there was no future in asking for a comprehensive commercial treaty, Wilmson asked Sheikh Abdallah whether the Dutch would be granted exemption of customs duties. Sheikh Abdallah replied that he would let that matter to the discretion of the Dutch. If, however, the Dutch would remain longer in Muscat, he did not know whether freedom of customs would be granted. He added: "We had put our hopes on the VOC, and if the Company would assist us militarily, Muscat would be free and open for the VOC." The Imam was said to have told the State council, that if the VOC did not offer him any assistance, the continued presence of the Dutch would be disadvantageous. Due to illness, Wilmson was not able to do much by the end of 1673, the more

---

118. I have been unable to identify the Qoran verses to which this letter undoubtedly refers to.

so since Jacob Harckz died on 22 November 1673. The Imam and his officials did not change their minds and the presents, which Wilmson gave them had no effect on their relationship.[119]

Batavia meanwhile had come to the conclusion that it had made a mistake in having too great expectations about the Imam's promises. The governor-general concluded that it would appear that the Imam never had the intention of allowing the Dutch to trade in Muscat. Since the nature and volume of trade of Muscat was such that it was of little importance to the VOC, he would prefer to leave Muscat altogether, but in view of the war, Batavia wanted to keep a resident there to warn arriving Dutch ships about the eventual presence of enemy ships in the Persian Gulf.[120]

Towards the end of January 1674 Wilmson announced that he would return to Bandar Abbas and that Jacobus Ritsert would succeed him. Sheikh Abdallah asked Wilmson to report favorably about the Imam and himself, but added in reply to a question by Wilmson that he could give no decision on the matter of the exemption of customs duties. Wilmson then asked him whether he would allow the Dutch to stay in Muscat on the same footing as before. Sheikh Abdallah said neither 'yes' or 'no', but only replied that he would give Wilmson's successor the same welcome he had received himself. Just prior to his departure Wilmson made a final attempt to get a definite answer on the subject of the customs duties, but Sheikh Abdallah only said that the Dutch were friends and not strangers. After an absence of one and a half years Wilmson returned to Bandar Abbas on 14 February 1674 having achieved nothing. He concluded that the Dutch intentions to obtain a commercial treaty would fail, because these clashed with Sheikh Abdallah's private trading interests in which he was supported by Malabari Indian traders.[121]

Ritsert remained behind with provisional assistant Taenmeter. The Omanis still hoped that the Dutch would go to war with the Portuguese.

---

119. NA, VOC 1304, Report Wilmson, f. 477vs-480vs.
120. NA, VOC 897, Batavia to de Haze (30/09/1673), f. 884-86; Coolhaas, *Generale Missieven*, vol. 3, p. 891-2 (13/11/1673).
121. NA, VOC 1304, Report Wilmson, f. 481vs.

If this did not happen de Haze feared that the Omanis would show how unwanted the Dutch really were. For the time being Dutch ships could call on Omani ports, which would give the Portuguese the impression that the Dutch, in case of war, could count on Omani support. For Batavia, however, the only reason for the continued presence of Ritsert was the fact that he could warn Dutch ships about enemy presence in the Persian Gulf.[122] Although the Portuguese fleet had been twice in the Persian Gulf since 1672, both sides had avoided one another and no engagements with the Omanis had taken place. However, this situation changed in 1674. During the first half of October 1673, a Portuguese fleet sailed past Muscat en route to Diu (Gujarat) without making one hostile move. But on 25 January 1674 an Omani fleet consisting of ten ships (the largest ship had sixteen pieces) with 1,800 men sailed away to attack the Portuguese settlement at Bassein (Maharashtra State).

Wilmson had doubts about the outcome of this operation, for he had observed during his stay in Muscat that every time the Portuguese fleet sailed into the Persian Gulf, the Omanis had to take cannons and crews and navigators from the merchandise fleet to man and arm their war fleet.[123] This was an important handicap in mounting operations against the Portuguese, which had been put off many times. For several times the war drum had been sounded, but not enough men had presented themselves. The Muscat war fleet consisted of fifteen to sixteen ships, amongst which three to four were rather large, two of average size, and nine to ten small ones with a total of ninety to ninety-five pieces, mainly of a light caliber. Their crews were inexperienced such as porters, fishermen, boatmen etc. amongst whom were many Baluchis.[124] If prospects for booty looked bright there would be a sufficient number

---

122. NA, VOC 898, Batavia to *Opperhoofd* (chief) at Mascatte (08/07/1674), f. 358-59; NA, VOC 1304, de Haze to XVII (21/03/1674), f. 465vs. Wilmson was promoted to the rank of merchant and appointed Second and *Opperhoofd* of the Isfahan office, where he died on March 6, 1675. NA, VOC 1297, Bent to XVII (01/04/1675).

123. NA, VOC 1304, Report Wilmson, f. 482vs; Ibid., de Haze to XVII (21/03/1674), f. 466.

124. NA, VOC 1304, Report Wilmson, f. 482vs.; Floor, "A description," p. 58, n. 55.

of recruits, but when the enemy fleet was expected to be at sea it was hardly possible to find anyone. Soldiers were recruited from the outlying villages at a pay of 9 to 12 *laris* per month. Their tactics were hit and run rather than of protracted resistance, for the Omani ships soon disengaged when the opposition was fierce. There was little if any discipline among the fleet, and if a crew did not want to fight it just did not partake in the battle. They also lacked a proper commander of the fleet or *sarang*[125] as they called him, while they did not know to handle cannons either. Their gunners were Canarese[126] slaves who had run away from the Portuguese, and six Moors, who knew as little of cannons as the lowest ranking Dutch sailor. Therefore, if something went wrong with their cannons, they had to take them from the Muscati forts.[127]

The Muscat fleet returned on 12 March 1674 after having landed 120 men at Bassein. This fleet was held up by a force of twenty-five Portuguese and twenty-five "blacks" for one whole day. When the Omanis marched on Bassein thirty-five to forty peasants who had been hidden in the sugar cane fields attacked them. The Omani force panicked and fled without finding out how strong the enemy was. In one night they covered the distance, which they had done in three days and left not less than 120 dead behind. On their voyage back home, the Omani fleet encountered a small Portuguese vessel. The Portuguese set fire to their own vessel, being too weak to oppose the Omanis, to prevent it falling into their hands. The Omani fleet finally returned with a Banyan vessel

---

125. Probably *sarhang*, a Persian word meaning 'commander, chief'.
126. Properly 'Canarian', a native a Kanara. The Portuguese called the Indian Christians of their territory 'Canarin' or 'Canarim'. In Portugal the term means a Eurasian. Here it probably is used indiscriminately for Portuguese-Indian subjects. The Omanis were short of experienced sailors; they mainly used Sindi and Surat pilots and sailors. This was the reason why Surat ships avoided Muscat, see NA, VOC 1279, f. 1029.
127. Floor, "A description," p. 17. The Omanis also hired European sailors. Martin, *India*, vol. 2/1, p. 826 (Maltese); R.J. Barendse, *The Arabian Seas. The Indian ocean World of the seventeenth century* (Armonk/London, 2002), p. 80, n. 161 quoting *AHU*, India, cx. 38, 54 (15/01/1696) (English).

laden with rice and cash, the only booty of this disastrous operation.[128] According to Fryer, the Omanis had been successful, however. They had destroyed the cultivated lands around Bassein, set fire to its villages, took men, women and children, butchered the priests, and robbed the churches. "To check these Incursions of the Arabs, the Portugals every Year are at the charge of a lusty Squadron in these Seas, who were no sooner gone, than the Arabs sent their Fleet to do this Mischief here; which now 'tis done, they are again in quest of them, but they fly as often as these pursue."[129]

The result of this disaster was that the Omanis started to treat the Dutch in Muscat much better, and promised that they would continue to do so. The fact that the Omanis had also been unable to buy ships in Surat and also the arrival of Dutch ships in the Persian Gulf contributed to this change of attitude.[130] However, when the departing director

---

128. NA, VOC 1304, de Haze to XVII (24/04/1674), f. 470vs. Apparently the Portuguese crew of the burnt vessel was taken prisoner; there were Portuguese who had been taken prisoners in Bassein, for the Portuguese captain Manuel Mendos, who commanded three ships lying at Bandar-e Kong, wrote a letter to the Imam demanding the release of the Portuguese prisoners. Ritsert did not know what reply the Imam sent, but rumors had it that he was unwilling to set them free. Idem, Bent to Batavia (04/09/1674), f. 516vs. According to Martin, the Omanis had ravaged the entire coastal area at Bassein. Martin, François. *Mémoires de -, fondateur de Pondicherry*, 3 vols. ed. A. Martineau (Paris 1931-34), of which vol. 1 and part of vol. 2 have been translated into English by Aniruddha Ray as *François Martin Mémoires Travels to Africa, Persia & India* (Calcutta, 1990) [cited as Martin, *Travels*] and the remainder of vol. 2 and vol. 3 by Lotika Varadarajan as *India in the 17th Century. Social, Economic and Political (memoirs of François Martin)* 2 vols. in 4 parts (New Delhi, 1981), cited as Martin, *India*, vol. 1/1, p. 414.
129. John Fryer, *A New Account of East India and Persia Being Nine Years' Travels, 1672-1681*, 3 vols. (London, 1909-15), vol. 1, pp. 192-93.
130. Sheikh Abdallah had asked Wilmson for advice where he might best buy ships in Surat, for he intended to send an agent there to buy five ships. Wilmson said that there was no special place and that the VOC factory would not be able to help them either in that respect. NA, VOC 1304, Report Wilmson, f. 476vs-77. In 1674, the agent returned from Surat having achieved nothing. NA, VOC 1304, de Haze to XVII (27/04/1674), f. 740vs.

de Haze visited Muscat on his way to Batavia, he did not receive a clear answer to his request about the prospects of a commercial treaty. Therefore, on 13 June 1674, de Haze instructed Ritsert not to further bother the Omanis about this subject, the more so since the Imam still had not properly replied to Wilmson's written request. He also told him to refer any request for assistance to Bandar Abbas to delay matters.[131] As soon as de Haze left on 21 June the *shahbandar* (harbormaster) came to Ritsert's house to count and weigh the VOC merchandise at the orders of Sheikh Abdallah. Ritsert asked Sheikh Abdallah the purpose of this activity and was told that it was the *shahbandar*'s task to do so. The *shahbandar* also told Ritsert that the VOC broker had to pay customs duties just like the other Banyans. Ritsert believed that this action was aimed at making him leave, so that Sheikh Abdallah did not have to tell him himself.[132] The treatment the Dutch received also became worse. However, it improved again when on 31 August 1674, two Dutch ships called on Muscat. Because the ships did not fly any flag the people of Muscat were afraid that they were Portuguese ships, so that Ritsert could not find anyone who was prepared to go aboard, even when he offered money. The next day, after a night of heavy storm during which many small vessels were destroyed, Ritsert was able to inform both ships that they could continue their voyage to Bandar Abbas, for there were no enemy ships in the Persian Gulf. This better treatment again confirmed the earlier impression that the Omanis were only friendly, when they saw a chance that the Dutch might help them against the Portuguese. They were not interested in discussing commercial matters with the Dutch apart from asking them to buy or transport goods, which was refused.

When the Imam failed to obtain Dutch military support against Portugal he tried to obtain the support of the Hula pirates on the other side of the Persian Gulf. Carré reported that:

---

131. NA, VOC 1304, "Memorie voor de ondercoopman Ritsert door de Haze int schip de Gerechtigheijt te Masquette 13/06/1674," f. 506-506vs.
132. NA, VOC 1304, Bent to Batavia (04/09/1674), f. 514-15.

> Two strange Arabs with a large following wished to see me. Having learnt that they were ambassadors from the Imam-king of Muscat, who had sent them to Kailo, Asalu, and other places on this coast, to ask the Arabs to assist him against the Portuguese. [...They told] We ourselves will never make any peace or treaty with such an arrogant and proud people [as the Portuguese], who wish to rule everywhere and seize rights to which they have no title, without wanting to carry on trade or commerce to the profit of the ports and other places they frequent, as do the other European nations. With the help and good counsel of the Dutch and the intelligent men the latter had lent them, they had been able this year to arm a powerful fleet at Muscat, which they had sent to India against the Portuguese. This fleet had attacked their territories, and had in the last three weeks brought back several Portuguese fidalgos, with their wives and children, in chains as prisoners to Muscat.[133]

When in Baghdad in May 1674, Carré reported that the Imam also considered asking the Ottomans for support for there he:

> found an Indian merchant of my acquaintance, who showed me letters received recently from Bandar Abbas, in which he was informed that the Arab Imam-king of Muscat, weary of the continual wars with the Portuguese in India, and seeing that all business and commerce was so being interrupted and lost, had been sent to Basra to negotiate a treaty with the Pasha to put his town under the protection of the Turks rather than ever allow the Portuguese to retake it. This would be prejudicial to Indian and Persian trade, for if the Turks once became masters of this important town [Muscat], the key of all the Orient, they would rule the whole of the

---

133. Carré, *The Travels*, vol. 3, pp. 830, 862; Foster, *English Factories* 1670-1677, p. 84 (attack on Bassein in February 1674).

Persian Gulf and the Indian Ocean, as the Portuguese did for many years.[134]

In 1674, the Portuguese once again prepared a war fleet against Muscat. The viceroy himself boarded it, but the fleet returned to Goa after eight days due to contrary winds, and thus the plan was abandoned.[135]

Ritsert regularly received some merchandise, the proceeds of which had to be used to cover the expense of the residency and to pay for the supplies of "Dutch ships which called on Muscat." The new director at Bandar Abbas, Bent, feared that when no Dutch ships were in the Persian Gulf, Ritsert would be bothered by Omani officials about these small imports. Although Bent wanted to abandon the Muscat residency, he instructed Ritsert to stay until Batavia gave explicit orders to leave.[136] Bent's fears proved to be true, for when in November 1674 he again sent some goods to Ritsert, the Omani officials claimed 10% customs duties. Ritsert, to show that the VOC did not take any interest in the trade of Muscat, demonstratively sent the goods back. The same officials also had told Ritsert that because he had stayed for quite some time in Muscat and therefore had become familiar with their laws and customs, henceforth he had to live in accordance with Omani laws. This, *inter alia*, meant that he was not allowed to smoke tobacco or to drink wine or other spirits on pain of punishment in case of transgression. Bent had ordered Ritsert to pay not more than 2.5% customs duties, if need be, for merchants from the Canarese and Malabar Coast did not pay more either. However, when Dutch ships again arrived in the Persian Gulf, Sheikh Abdallah changed his whole attitude towards Ritsert and asked him to forget about the whole matter. It had been a mistake, for the Imam had ordered to take 10% from the Europeans, but this order did not hold for the Dutch, of course, because they were friends. They were

---

134. Carré, *Travels*, vol. 3, p. 862.
135. Coolhaas, *Generale Missieven*, vol. 3, p. 949 (17/11/1674).
136. NA, VOC 1297, Bent to Batavia (12/07/1674),f. 1016.

free to give what they deemed to be fair. But this attitude only lasted while the ships were in the Persian Gulf.[137]

Towards the end of 1674 both Ritsert and Taenmeter fell ill, so that they were unable to write. For some time it was feared they would both die. On learning this, Bent immediately sent an assistant to Muscat to manage Dutch affairs in case they really died. For Omani law stated that in case of demise of a foreigner, his property would belong to the Imam as had happened in 1674 in the case of a rich eunuch who had died in Muscat.[138] However, both Dutchmen recovered and in March 1676 Ritsert again broached the matter of the customs duties with Sheikh Abdallah. After much evasive language Sheikh Abdallah finally said that the Banyans paid 7.5%, but because the Dutch were friends and because they imported little he would leave it to Ritsert's discretion. He added, however, that if new goods were imported he would have to refer the matter to the Imam. He concluded that the Imam only wanted to agree to a favorable commercial treaty when Batavia gave a positive reaction to the Imam's request. Ritsert wanted to give only 5%, although he knew that Sheikh Abdallah wanted him to pay 7.5% and he therefore sent him the amount due. Sheikh Abdallah sent it back, however, without saying why. Ritsert paid him a visit the next day and asked him whether he was dissatisfied with the amount. Sheikh Abdallah denied this and said that he did not want to misuse the situation, and added that the Dutch could not count on the same treatment in the future. He had informed the Imam that the Dutch refused to pay 10% customs duties and he had to wait for the Imam's reply. On 21 March 1675, Sheikh Abdallah informed Ritsert that the Imam had stipulated that the Dutch had to pay 5%, because of their mutual friendship, although other foreigners had to pay 7.5%. However, this did not hold for any future goods the Dutch would import. Ritsert sent him the money due and this time Sheikh Abdallah accepted it. Ritsert commented that in his view the Dutch would have to pay not only 10% customs duties, but would have

---

137. NA, VOC 1297, Bent to Batavia (01/04/1675), f. 1014vs. The authorities of Muscat even twice returned a Dutch deserter who had wanted to become a Moslem, if he would be allowed to remain in Muscat, which was a clear sign for the Dutch how desperate the Imam was for naval support.

138. NA, VOC 1279, Bent to Batavia (01/04/1675), f. 1015.

to reckon with an even less friendly treatment. He also believed that Sheikh Abdallah would tell him to leave if the Dutch imported large quantities of goods, because this would hurt his trade interests. This change of attitude Ritsert ascribed to the fact that the Omanis did not expect further assistance from the Dutch.[139]

The uncivil treatment of the Dutch continued as Ritsert had foretold. This time, even when the Dutch ship the *Flaman* arrived at the roadstead of Muscat it had to pay 15 *abbasi*s per water vessel instead of the usual 12 *mahmudi*s. Ritsert refused to pay this higher price knowing that Sheikh Abdallah was behind it and said he had rather let the ship get its water elsewhere. Finally, after orders from the *vali*, a settlement was reached with the water carrier, whereby the Dutch would pay 18 *mahmudi*s per water vessel and 5 *mahmudi*s for bringing it aboard. Sales of the few goods that the VOC had there turned bad. Ritsert believed that this was due to the fact that the officials ordered the merchants and traders to buy only Dutch goods, when these were weighed in the city's weigh-house. Ritsert refused the sale on these grounds after which nothing more was sold. Sheikh Abdallah had gone to Nizwa; Ritsert feared that on his return, new tricks would be played on the Dutch. For the Omanis clearly were willing to be rid of the Dutch, but did not dare to tell them to go, for they had informed them officially that the presence of the Dutch in Muscat was pleasing to them. Therefore, these indirect ways were used to make them go away on their own accord. The rumor mongering of a few English deserters and a Portuguese renegade also contributed to the unpleasant atmosphere. These people told that the Dutch residency was only a reconnaissance point to devise the strategy on how to take Muscat later. They also said that there were no greater cheats than the Dutch and Bent feared that the suspicious Arabs would lend credence to these stories.

Ritsert was ordered not to pay 10% customs on his sales, as he feared Sheikh Abdallah would ask, and to pay not more than 5% like in 1674. If he wanted 10%, which never before had been taken from Europeans, Sheikh Abdallah had to get it by force from the Dutch residency, Bent

---

139. NA, VOC 1297, Ritsert to Bent (18 and 21/03/1675), f. 1019.

added, no doubt believing Abdallah would never dare to do such a thing. In May or thereabouts, Ritsert was relieved of his post in Muscat and promoted to the rank of merchant at his request by Batavia in recompense of his services.[140] He was relieved by assistant Michiel de Mardeville, "who at that time was so ill that in September Bent sent provisional assistant Cornelis de Vos Jobsz to Muscat to help him and take over in case of his death, and to prevent the Muscat authorities taking hold of Dutch property.[141] Bent also wrote to Batavia that by now it was evident that the Omanis were only after their own interests and that their friendship was feigned. The governor-general had been given the complete picture of how matters stood at Muscat and therefore was asked to take a decision what to do with the residency at Muscat and what line should be taken with regard to the Imam. Since June 1673, as ordered by de Haze, no steps had been taken by the Dutch, who only waited for the Imam to reply to Wilmson's request.[142] Because Batavia was totally disillusioned by the situation in Muscat, where none of the privileges that had been promised materialized and where the Imam even claimed the right to order justice over VOC personnel, a thing Batavia would never allow, on 31 August 1675, it therefore ordered Bandar Abbas to abandon Muscat at the first opportunity. Batavia did not want to part enemies and added that it set great store by having friendly relations with local rulers; it therefore ordered Bandar Abbas to give presents in a friendly atmosphere on leaving.[143]

Therefore, on 11 December 1675, Bent sent a barque to Muscat and ordered the VOC personnel to prepare themselves to leave Muscat and to give presents on their departure.[144] De Mardeville went to see Sheikh Abdallah about the customs duties, who was not willing to accept payment of 5%. He said when Ritsert had left he had already made that clear, and on what conditions the Dutch would be allowed to sell their

---

140. NA, VOC 900, Batavia to Bent (18/10/1676), f. 533.
141. NA, VOC 1307, Bent to Batavia (12/09/1675), f. 636vs-37.
142. NA, VOC 1313, Bent to Batavia (02/10/1675), f. 338-38vs.
143. NA, VOC 899, Batavia to Bent (31/08/1675), f. 329-30.
144. For a list of the presents see Floor, "A description," p. 21.

goods. De Mardeville then told him that the Dutch had been ordered to leave and that they had presents for the Imam, the *vali* and himself. Sheikh Abdallah then sang another tune and laughed kindly saying, of course: "I accept 5%." Bent angrily commented that he behaved as if he had granted the VOC a favor by accepting that rate. Sheikh Abdallah promised that after their departure he would continue to assist Dutch ships with supplies and give them a friendly welcome.[145] De Vos returned alone to Bandar Abbas with all VOC property and money. De Mardeville remained behind. The documents do not give the reason for this, so we must assume that he was still seriously ill and could not be moved. He died on 1 March 1676 in Muscat.[146] His death was reported by Sheikh Abdallah in a letter to Bent. At the same time, Sheikh Abdallah affirmed the Imam's friendship with the Dutch and promised that "their ports were those of the Hon. Company, and visiting Dutch ships would be treated as if they were the Imam's own ships."[147] Bent was pleased to observe later that Sheikh Abdallah indeed had kept his word, for the Dutch ships which called on Muscat during 1676 were well received.[148]

In retrospect, Batavia opined that the Muscat factory had only been useful as a listening post and therefore could be discontinued.[149] A further reason to close the Muscat factory was the realization that "the Arabs wanted us for their own profit there, but not to grant us any privileges. They continue their war with the Portuguese. The Arabs have harassed the Portuguese considerably these last four years against which they were unable to do much."[150] Batavia was therefore pleased with the way the residency in Muscat had been closed, a step that was also approved by the VOC directors, the *Heeren XVII*. Batavia did not consider the Muscat experience a negative one, for the Company had

---

145. NA, VOC 1307, Bent to Batavia (09/05/1676), f. 675.
146. NA, VOC 1307, Bent to XVII (28/03/1676), f. 633vs.
147. NA, VOC 1307, Sheikh Abdallah to Bent (n.d.), f. 643 (Dutch translation only).
148. NA, VOC 1307, Bent to Batavia (09/05/1676), f. 675.
149. Coolhaas, *Generale Missieven*, vol. 4, p. 36 (28/02/1675).
150. Coolhaas, *Generale Missieven*, vol. 4, p. 39 (29/08/1675); Ibid., *Generale Missieven*, vol. 3, p. 950 (17/11/1674).

come to know the Omanis and had learnt from that experience, for it would no longer allow them to take advantage of the Company. Thus ended Dutch relations with Muscat; these would not be renewed for many years.[151]

A Change of Policy in Muscat.

Under Imam Bil`arab b. Sultan there was change in Oman, which would be reinforced under his brother Imam Seyf b. Sultan. Whereas in the first half of the 1670s Imami rule had been uncertain, this all changed radically in the second half of that decade, demonstrated by people's weariness of the war, the threat of internal revolt, and fear for Portuguese attacks. The old Imam fearing internal revolt had taken more direct control over Muscat revenues, which meant the dismissal of the old *vali* Omar (or Omeyr) between December 1671 and May 1672; he belonged to a clan that had always been hostile to the Ya`ariba. He was replaced by the Imam's *vakil* or agent, Mohammad Sheikh Abdallah Soleyman, who began to play a more important role in the management of the country's affairs. His lineage was very close to that of the Imam and he may even have been a relative. Sheikh Abdallah's clansmen and men of the Imam's household held all revenue yielding offices in Muscat in 1672. In 1688, Kaempfer reported that the old governor handed his office to his son.[152] In 1672, due to illness of the old Imam, he had delegated the handling of many state matters to the young Imam.[153] Under the old Imam military

---

151. NA, VOC 900, Batavia to Bent (02/09/1676), f. 360; NA, VOC 320, XVII to Batavia (16/05/1676), unfoliated. Even in 1677, the Portuguese were still convinced that the Dutch wanted to get hold of one of the Muscat forts, continue their trading activities there and conclude some kind of confederation with the Imam. *BFUP* 35-36-37, no. 52, p. 154 (23/03/1677); Idem, no. 22, p. 147 (30/03/1677).

152. Floor, "A description," p. 7, n. 31; Engelbert Kaempfer, *Die Reisetagebücher* ed. K. Meier-Lemgo. (Wiesbaden, 1968), p. 149. Ovington reported that the governor was close to the Imam. Ovington, J. *A Voyage to Suratt in the Yeare 1689* (London, 1696), p. 429.

153. Floor, "A description," p. 23; Wilkinson, *The Imamate Tradition*, p. 351, n. 33 submits that this occurred in 1680.

operations relied on local levies, whereby 300-400 men could be raised from villages neighboring Muscat. Wilmson reports that Muscat had a garrison of 100-150 men in its fortresses.[154] The Imam's son wanted to make Muscat more attractive to international trade and also to implement a more aggressive foreign policy in the Western Indian Ocean. He increased military expenditure as soon as he had the reins of power. He further reinforced the defenses of Muscat and improved the outfitting of Omani ships.[155] The result of this new policy was that, according to Fryer, in the 1670s the Omanis had the reputation of "a Fierce and Treacherous People, gaining as much by Fraud as Merchandise."[156]

The main objective of Omani foreign policy was the ouster of the Portuguese from the Indian Ocean area and the establishment of Omani rule over the major ports between Muscat and Kilwa-Zanzibar-Mombasa-Malindi on the African coast. Apart from Portuguese attacks on Omani shipping and settlements, there was also economic warfare. The continuing hit-and-run war between Oman and Portugal was becoming a major problem for trade in the Western Indian Ocean. People leaving Bandar Abbas to Surat were afraid to be enslaved by Omani raiders. According to Gemelli-Careri, there had been a few attempts to make peace, but it always fell apart because the Portuguese insisted on payment of tribute and the erection of a fort near Muscat with a garrison to ensure their peaceful possession thereof.[157] The cost of sustaining the anti-Omani campaign contributed to the decline of Diu and drained the Estado's coffers, which could only continue its warfare in the Gulf of Oman and the Persian Gulf due to the revenues obtained from Bandar-e Kong. The naval operations also helped to keep the Estado's key Indian fortresses safe and secure.[158] In 1692, Martin

---

154. Floor, "A description," p. 32; Kaempfer, Die *Reisetagebucher*, p. 149 as to their readiness.
155. NA, VOC 1285, de Haze to Batavia (13/09/1673), f. 41 r-vs the Omani fleet consisted of 8-10 large and 10-12 small vessels as well as 40-50 small crafts.
156. Fryer, *A New Account*, vol. 2, p. 156.
157. Gio Francesco Gemelli-Careri, *Giro del Mondo* 6 vols. (Napoli: Giuseppe Roselli, 1699), vol. 2, pp. 308-09.
158. Ames, *Renascent Empire*, pp. 167-68; Sanjay Subrahmanyam, *The Portuguese Empire in Asia 1500-1700* (London, 1993), pp. 190-91.

opined "even though the Portuguese are now but a pale reflection of their former selves, they still commanded the respect of the Muslims and Hindus."[159]

THE SAFAVIDS WANT AN ANTI-OMANI ALLIANCE (1695-1719)

As of 1695, the Omanis began their reign of piracy and pillage and tried to establish Oman's supremacy over the Persian Gulf. In January 1695, an Omani squadron of 15 vessels attacked, plundered and laid waste to Bandar-e Kong, under the pretext that they wanted to expel their enemy, the Portuguese. They also captured a richly laden Armenian ship that was in the roads off the town. In total they caused an estimated damage of 60,000 *tuman*s, or according to Gaudereau four millions *écus*, which is highly unlikely.[160] The attack on Bandar-e Kong heralded a wave a piracy in the Persian Gulf and the Gulf of Oman by Omanis and Europeans.[161] At the time of the attack on Bandar-e Kong, the Imam of Muscat had written a letter to Shah Sultan Hoseyn (r. 1694-1722) in which he did not address the shah by name and demanded three things: (i) that the shah deliver all Portuguese and their factors residing in his realm; (ii) that he deliver an Arab merchant whom he suspected to be in league with the Portuguese; and (iii) that the shah gave him the same privileges at Bandar-e Kong as the Portuguese, including the moiety of the customs, in exchange for which the Imam would guarantee with 20 ships, the safety of shipping in the Persian Gulf. The Imam threatened to destroy

---

159. Martin, *India*, vol. 2/1, p. 842.
160. J.Bruce, *Annals of the Honorable East India Company* 3 vols. (London, 1810), vol. 3, p. 169; Lorimer, *Gazetteer*, p. 69; Anne Kroell, *Nouvelles d'Ispahan 1665-1695* (Paris, 1979), p. 72; Coolhaas, *Generale Missieven*, vol. 5, p. 743 (03/11/1695); Martin, *India*, vol. 2/1, pp. 1021-22; Ibid., *India*, vol. 2/2, pp. 1360, 1408.
161. Bruce, *Annals*, vol. 2, p. 657; Anne Kroell, "Louis XIV, la Perse et Mascate," *Le Monde Iranien et l'Islam* 4 (1976-1977), p. 12. Brangwin, the EIC chief at Bandar Abbas, predicted that the Omanis "would prove as great a plague in India, as the Algerines were in Europe." Bruce, *Annals*, vol. 3, p. 198.

Bandar Abbas if his proposal was not accepted. The shah did not bother to send a reply.[162] The Safavid court was in shock.

The Omanis also threatened Bandar Abbas in such a way that the *shahbandar* asked the EIC to delay the departure of their ship *Nassau* [163] so as to provide protection to the town. The shah further demanded that the EIC take offensive action against the Omanis invoking the agreement with Shah Abbas I. The EIC agent Brangwin countered that the same agreement also called for payment of 50% of the customs revenues, which had never taken place. Probably because the Dutch had refused to provide naval assistance,[164] Brangwin was summoned to the royal court in Isfahan. He was told that if the EIC would help transport Safavid troops to Muscat, and would participate with some troops in the capture of Muscat, it would get half of the booty and the same privileges that it enjoyed at Bandar Abbas. Brangwin could, of course, not agree to such a request, even if his ships at Bandar Abbas had been able to perform this task, which they were not.[165] Brangwin was afraid that the Safavids would ask the Dutch to intervene and therefore proposed to his directors that the English should offer their assistance. Bombay, however, vetoed the proposal, because the Omanis had not obstructed English shipping. However, in the years thereafter, Omani ships seized several English private ships and enslaved their crews. Because the English were absorbed by the war with the French (1688-97) no action was taken against Muscat, although it had been decided to do so as soon as the war with France would be over. However, after 1707, after the war with France ended, there was no more mention of acts of piracy by the Omanis against English vessels.[166] For security reasons, Armenians,

---

162. Kroell, *Louis XIV*, p. 11; Ibid., *Nouvelles*, p. 73.
163. Willem III, Stadtholder of the Netherlands, also was king of Great Britain (1688-1702). One of the king's titles was Count of Nassau, hence the German name of an English ship.
164. Coolhaas, *Generale Missieven*, vol. 5, p. 743 (03/11/1695).
165. Bruce, *Annals*, vol. 3, p. 216; Kroell, *Louis XIV*, p. 13; Charles Lockyer, *An Account of British Trade in India* (London, 1711), p. 207; Lockhart, *Fall*, p. 392.
166. Lorimer, *Gazetteer*, p. 79, 405; Bruce, *Annals*, vol. 3, p. 169; Hamilton, *A New Account*, vol. 1, p. 45; Lawrence *The Fall of the Safavi Dynasty* (Cambridge,

Moslem Persians and other merchants henceforth transported their goods with Dutch or English ships whose income increased considerably.[167] According to Martin, there was an understanding between the Dutch and the Omanis, because the latter never accosted or raided Dutch ships.[168]

Only the Portuguese accepted to assist the Safavids, because it coincided with their own interests. After the sack of Bandar-e Kong in 1695, the viceroy of Goa, D. Pedro António de Noronha de Albuquerque, Count de Vile Verde wanted to curb the Omani depredations so as to deter them from attacking Mombasa. Therefore, in 1695, he offered naval protection to Safavid Persia and sent a Portuguese fleet to the Persian Gulf.[169] On 18 March 1695, the Carmelites reported that the Portuguese fleet, "consisting of 6 large and 2 small ships is expected in Kung: and, if they succeed in taking some revenge for the descent, which two months ago the Arabs of Muscat made on Kung, they will easily obtain from this Court whatever they wish."[170] By 17 September, news of a Portuguese-Safavid settlement reached him, which included the promise that that next year the Portuguese fleet would come again and that a Portuguese ambassador would come to the Safavid court to finalize the agreement. Da Silva tried to collect the moiety at Bandar-e Kong, but despite the agreement just concluded, he only received partial payment. On 8 October the flotilla sailed back to India, and on 2 December 1695 it arrived at Goa.[171]

1956), pp. 67-68, 391-92. One of the ships the Omanis captured in 1701 belonged to the EIC President Pitt and had a value of 5,000 *tumans*. Ferrier, *British-Persian Relations*, p. 325 quoting G/40/5, p. 125 (06/08/1701). Outside the Persian Gulf there was continued piracy by the infamous Sanganians, who preyed on ships plying between Indian and Persian Gulf ports.

167. Lockyer, *An account*, p. 218.
168. Kroell, *Louis XIV*, p. 13; Lockyer, *An account*, p. 207.
169. Jean Aubin ed., *L'Ambassade de Gregório Fidalgo à la cour du Châh Soltân-Hoseyn* (Lisbon, 1971), p. 14, notes 4-5; *BFUP* 41-42-43, p. 189.
170. Anonymous, *Chronicle*, vol. 2, p. 1120.
171. *AHU*, Índia, cx. [32-A] 59, doc. 193, "Certidão of D. António de Meneses", (Goa, 25/12/1695). For the discussion in the Council of State in Goa see *ACE* vol. 4-3, pp. 3-8 (31/01/1696), 4-4, pp. 9-10 (23/02/1696).

This renewed Portuguese activity after five years of absence from the Persian Gulf as well as the promise of an embassy, was well received at the Safavid court. Shah Sultan Hoseyn wrote to the viceroy that he sorely missed a Portuguese envoy among the European representatives sent to his court. He further emphasized the friendship and unity that had always existed between the two nations.[172] According to Aubin, with this letter Shah Sultan Hoseyn agreed with the plan for the Luso-Persian alliance. The terms required that Persia mobilized its land forces, while Portugal would supply 20 vessels for the attack against Oman. Also, Portugal would supply six rowing vessels for the defense of Bandar-e Kong. Vessels belonging to merchants of Bandar-e Kong would join the naval force that would be under Portuguese command. Persia would further supply support staff for the fleet as well as 2,000 *tumans* as a subsidy for the annual arrival of the fleet. All ships captured would belong to Portugal, while their cargos would be shared between the allies following Portuguese rules of distribution. All Omani ports captured would belong to Persia except for Muscat, which would be "returned" to Portugal. In all the captured ports Persia would allow Portugal to establish factories with the same charter as that of Bandar-e Kong. Moreover, both parties would not enter into a separate peace treaty with other nations. Furthermore, the shah would ban any nation that had factories in one of his ports from selling gunpowder and ammunition to the Omanis. This article had been inserted because the viceroy believed that the English sold these goods to the Imam of Muscat. Finally, the plan confirmed the equal sharing of the customs of Bandar-e Kong, that the Portuguese factor would receive a building to his liking as his new factory, and that the interpreter was once again allowed to make wine in Shiraz.[173]

---

172. Aubin, *L'Ambassade*, p. 15, notes 1-2; Júlio Firmino Júdice Biker ed., *Collecção de tratados e concertos de pazes que o Estado da India Portuguesa fez com os reis e senhores com que teve relações nas partes da Asia e África Oriental*. 14 vols. (Lisbon, 1881-87), vol. IV, pp. 246-83.
173. Aubin, *L'Ambassade*, p. 15, notes 3-4, 16, note 1; Lorimer, *Gazetteer*, p. 70 (also alleging that Omani vessels were frequently commanded by Englishmen and flew the English flag). For the Portuguese text of the treaty see *BFUP* 41-42-43, pp. 223-226.

In 1695, in reaction to the Portuguese initiative, the Omanis divided their fleet into two squadrons; one of which attacked the East Africa coastal settlements and burnt Mombasa, while the other attacked the Portuguese factory at Mangalore, destroying and plundering it and enslaving many of its population.[174] Even before the embassy arrived in Isfahan the viceroy, who had wanted that the affair be handled in a more diligent manner, realized that the *Estado* did not have the means to actually execute the plan. In the ambassador's instructions it was stated that the Safavid troops had to be ferried in Safavid barques (*terrada*s), but he was allowed to offer numerous vessels for the protection of Bandar-e Kong. Because the viceroy also wanted to retake Hormuz he instructed the ambassador to be very circumspect on this issue and not to give away his intentions on this score.[175]

The viceroy selected Gregório Pereira Fidalgo, a chancellor of the *Estado*, as ambassador from king D. Pedro II. The ambassador left Goa in March 1696, arrived in Bandar-e Kong in June and on 15 October in Isfahan. He left Isfahan on 1 April 1697 and arrived in Goa on 25 October 1697. The ambassador's main interlocutors were the grand vizier, Mirza Taher, whom Gemelli-Careri qualified as "the biggest thief on earth"[176] and his secretary, Mirza Rabi`, who was of the same ilk. The latter's main counselor was Father António de Jesus, who led a desultory life and had his own interests at heart, in particular with regard to the Portuguese half of the customs revenues of Bandar-e Kong.[177] Initially the prospects for the embassy looked bright. The governor of Lar, Abbas Qoli Khan, had already mobilized troops in the coastal area. In October 1696, en route to Isfahan, the ambassador was told by a Safavid officer that he was a member of the planned expeditionary force, while the

---

174. Vahe Baladouni and Margaret Makepeace, *Armenian Merchants of the Seventeenth and Early Eighteenth Centuries. English East India Company Sources* (Philadelphia 1998), p. 177; Lorimer, *Gazetteer*, p. 69. According to Gemelli-Careri, *Giro*, vol. 2, pp. 308-09, at that time [1696] there were 14 warships in the bay of Muscat that had taken Mombasa from the Portuguese.
175. Aubin, *L'Ambassade*, p. 15, note 2, 16, notes 1-2.
176. Aubin, *L'Ambassade*, p. 18; Gemelli-Careri, *Giro*, vol. 2, p. 127.
177. Aubin, *L'Ambassade*, pp. 21-22, 85.

Dutch director, Jacobus Hoogcamer told him that the leader of the force, the *divan-begi*, had already left Isfahan. Fidalgo also saw further military and supply preparations ongoing at Kazerun.[178]

According to the *Dastur-e Shahriyan*, in 1696, Ali Mardan Khan, *beglerbegi* of Kuhgiluy and *divan-begi* had been ordered to march on Bandar Abbas and Bandar-e Kong with 2,000 royal troops, 5,000 of his own troops, troops of his subordinate emirs as well as local levies (*cherik*) from Fars province. Furthermore, Fars province had to furnish supplies for their sustenance, which had to be taken to Bandar Abbas and Bandar-e Kong. However, Fars had suffered a drought and thus, neither supplies nor pack animals were available. Therefore, the execution of the order was postponed to a later date. The Portuguese ambassador was informed of this in November that it was impossible to mobilize Safavid troops that year due to a shortage of food and water supplies.[179] At the end of the fall of 1696 Ali Mardan Khan went to Bandar-e Deylam. He sent for various Arab groups there, to wit: the Khalefat, the Al Zo`ab, the Al Abu Moheyr and gave robes of honor to their chiefs Sheikhs Majd, Khamis, and Amir Mehin to induce them to participate in the military operation. Because many of the Al Zo`ab lived in Muscat, they had written to their chief, Amir Mehin, that, "Now, there is a drought and scarcity in Muscat, so that if supplies were sent here they may be sold at a high price." The chief, at the governor's instructions, replied:

> A general has arrived here from the royal court to take Muscat, to capture and kill its inhabitants and to take revenge for what those rebels had done to the inhabitants of Bandar-e Kong. It was therefore decided, according to his instructions, that not even one *man* of load be transported from here to those parts; thus we cannot send you any food. If they wanted to save themselves they only had to abandon

---

178. Aubin, *L'Ambassade*, pp. 22-24; see also Anonymous, *Chronicle*, vol. 1, p. 477.
179. Mohammad Ebrahim b. Zeyn al-`Abedin Nasiri, *Dastur-e Shahriyan*. ed. Mohammad Nader Nasiri Moqaddam (Tehran, 1373/1995), p. 154; Aubin, *L'Ambassade*, p. 24.

their homeland and flee to these parts for shortly the hoof beats of the army would be multitudinous in that kingdom. Much disturbed, 600 of them came to Bandar-e Rig, and after some time some of them went back to gather their goods and families. Ali Mardan Khan was arranging to bring order to the other ports when the royal order came canceling the expedition.[180]

Apart from the fact that the drought was a real issue, it was aggravated by the dissension among the Safavid courtiers as to the need and wisdom of the Oman expedition.

> The first year because there was no food, and now, the second year, when there is an abundance of food, once again to punish this infidel nothing was given. From this it is clear that there are no relations of friendship between the leaders of the ever-lasting kingdom and the king of Portugal to the detriment of the Portuguese. From these going-ons it is clear that friendly relations between the leaders of the everlasting empire and the king of Portugal were not aimed at, but on the contrary they aimed to offend and disgrace the Portuguese.[181]

The anti-war party thus prevailed and even before the ambassador had returned to Bandar-e Kong news had reached Goa that the Safavids had withdrawn from the alliance, because they did not want to share the Bandar-e Kong customs revenues. Another alleged reason was the fear of Baluchi incursions in southern Safavid Persia, against which the Safavids could do nothing if their troops were in Oman.[182] Shah Sultan Hoseyn sent a letter to the viceroy explaining his inability to carry out the agreed plan. He not only referred to the lack of food supplies and of water in the cisterns, but also to the fact that the promised 20 Portuguese vessels

---

180. Nasiri, *Dastur-e Shahriyan*, p. 154.
181. Nasiri, *Dastur-e Shahriyan*, p. 155.
182. Aubin, *L'Ambassade*, pp. 22-24; see also Anonymous, *Chronicle*, vol. 1, p. 477.

had not come. Because they had not arrived orders had to be given to disband the troops. The grand vizier further refused to pay 1,000 *tumans* for the upkeep of the allied fleet, arguing that he had no money, while the number of ships had been less than stipulated in the agreement. The viceroy had been aware of this and had given his ambassador arguments to explain his inability to adhere to this part of the agreement. He really had tried to raise funds to send more ships, but finally only three frigates (of which one never arrived due to contrary winds), one galliot of 20 pieces, one fire ship and two war barques (*manchuas*) had left Goa for Bandar-e Kong in 1696.[183] However, this flotilla did not amount to much. The Dutch reported that one year after the sack of Bandar-e Kong the Portuguese still had not acted against the Omanis in retaliation for the attack.[184]

Rather than representing Luso-Safavid resolve, the Fidalgo embassy showed the embarrassing inability of both parties to work together and to even live up to the simple physical parts of the agreement (troops, ships, money). These were symptoms of the economic and political weakness of both the Safavid state and the *Estado*. On the face of it, the plan ideally met both parties' objectives, but even the will to make it work was weak on both sides. Officially, the shah only adjourned the plan, thus putting a good face on his inability to deliver, while the viceroy strongly denounced the Safavid point of view, without being able to offer something more concrete either. In the following years there were some sporadic Luso-Safavid operations, but apart from the one in 1718-19 these did not amount to much.[185] The inability to mount a joint Lusano-Persian operation also heralded the decline of a thoroughly devastated Bandar-e Kong; after 1695 no English ships called at this port.[186] To show Portuguese resolve, the viceroy sent another fleet to the Persian Gulf in 1697. D. António de Meneses was promoted to admiral of fleet of the Straits of Hormuz and the Red Sea, with orders similar

---

183. Aubin, *L'Ambassade*, p. 24, note 4, 25, notes 1-5.
184. Coolhaas, *Generale Missieven*, vol. 5, p. 810 (19/01/1697).
185. Aubin, *L'Ambassade*, p. 25, note 6.
186. Lorimer, *Gazetteer*, p. 69.

to those given in 1695. This time he was able to engage six Omani ships coming from Mombasa near Ra's al-Hadd on 11 May 1697. The battle was indecisive, and the Omani ships fled to Muscat with the Portuguese ships in pursuit.[187]

At the same time that the Portuguese ambassador was in Isfahan to discuss a possible joint military operation against Muscat, the Safavid court raised the same issue with the Dutch. The English were very much upset about this possibility. "We believe [the Dutch] will assist the King of Persia against Muscatt designing thereby to get over our heads and make themselves masters of the Gulph of Persia."[188] The fact that the Safavids had been unable to mount such a military operation in 1696 should have made the Dutch wary of the request to support a military expedition against Muscat. The VOC director at Bandar Abbas received a request from shah to assist the newly appointed general Ali Mardan Khan (Alimeerde Chan) to make war on the Omanis, be it by lending VOC ships or something else. New benefits were promised. Jacobus Hoogcamer, the VOC director in Bandar Abbas, was also approached by the grand-vizier in Isfahan about this. The grand vizier promised the cancellation of the 1694 silk contract and total trade freedom without having to pay any imposts, in addition to an annual present of 1,000 *tumans*. Batavia decided on 14 June 1697 to allow VOC ships to protect the vessels that would ferry Safavid troops across, but they were not to help bombard the forts. Also, the VOC would not supply troop support, because it did not have enough manpower. However, if asked the VOC would supply ammunition. Also, Captain Jan Coin, an artillery expert as well as sailors and musketeers expert in the use of artillery might be put at the disposal of the Safavid military. The Dutch fleet duly arrived in the Persian Gulf, but it was unable to do anything because the Safavids had abandoned their plan to attack Muscat.[189] The English could relax

---

187. *AHU*, Índia, cx. [32-A] 59, doc. 193, "Certidão de D. António de Meneses" (Goa, 20/12/1697).
188. Baladouni and Makepeace, *Armenian Merchants*, p. 239 (01/10/1696).
189. Coolhaas, *Generale Missieven*, vol. 5, p. 859-61 (30/11/1697). The Portuguese learnt about Dutch assistance to Safavid Persia from Surat. *BFUP* 41-42-43, p. 279 (31/12/1697).

now, for they feared that the Dutch might secure preferential trading rights in Safavid Persia and thus further undercut the EIC's position.[190]

The announcement of the unexpected death of the Imam of Muscat at the beginning of November 1697 meanwhile stalled any new attacks from either side.[191] The Portuguese believed that this was good news for trade, for the Omanis would be fighting amongst themselves to name the successor.[192] However, the joy was premature, for the Imam lived another 14 years. On 13 May 1698, a squadron of eight Omani vessels, under the command of the governor of Matrah, attacked two Portuguese frigates at Ra's al-Hadd. The Portuguese defeated the Omanis who lost their commander and a large number killed, while the Portuguese only suffered five killed and 11 wounded. However, that was about the only good news, for in 1699 an Omani fleet took Mombasa and killed all Portuguese along the East African coast.[193] After this event, there seems to have been a lull in the attacks on the Portuguese in the Indian Ocean area, but not in the Persian Gulf. For both Omani vessels as well as Danish and other European pirates preyed on Indian shipping to such an extent that by 1700 they had practically annihilated Armenian shipping coming from Hugli (West-Bengal) to the Persian Gulf. Although the Portuguese accused the EIC of giving passes to these pirates, the Company denied it.[194]

---

190. Lorimer, *Gazetteer*, p. 67.
191. Luís Matos ed., *Das relações entre Portugal e a Pérsia 1500-1758. Catálogo bibliográfico da exposição comemorativa do XXV centenário da monarquia no Irão* (Lisbon: Fundação Calouste Gulbenkian, 1972), p. 337 quoting BNL: Pomb. 439, f. 341r. (13/12/1697) (the Imam died 40 days ago).
192. Matos, *Das relações*, p. 341 quoting BNL: Pomb. 439, f. 340r (14/01/1698).
193. Lorimer, *Gazetteer*, p. 70; Matos, *Das relações*, p. 339 (02/01/1698). This news was also brought to the notice of the viceroy by the governor of Surat. There was regular correspondence between the two officials in view of a common interest as the Omanis also preyed on Surat shipping. *FBUP* 35-36—37, p. 360 (06/02/1700).
194. NA, VOC 1582, (15/03/1696), f. 121; Lorimer, *Gazetteer*, p. 70.

In 1698, the shah once again raised the issue of Dutch support for an attack on Muscat. The Dutch replied that it was not the right time to do so; moreover, the ships earmarked for that operation had already left.[195] After the failed attempts to initiate military operations against Muscat with the help of the Portuguese (1696) and the Dutch (1697, 1698) the Safavid court then turned to France with its proposal to attack and capture Muscat at even better terms than offered to the Portuguese. Gaudereau, the French missionary at Isfahan, also promoted French assistance for a Safavid attack on Muscat, to boost the opportunities for French commercial interests. However the French East Indies Company was not enthusiastic about the idea, which was too costly and with no chance for a real net benefit. Gaudeareau continued to push his ideas and he was supported by some officials at court, but not by Portchartrain, the Minister of War.[196] In 1699, the Safavid court not to be left behind, raised the issue of naval and military assistance for an attack on Muscat with the Papal envoy and in 1701, with the French merchant and self-styled Maltese ambassador Jean Billon.[197] The royal court also raised the issue once again with the Dutch envoy, Jacobus Hoogcamer, in 1701. He replied that the VOC might possibly assist the shah for a second time depending on the nature of the privileges the shah would offer. Also, given the considerable expense of such an undertaking, the VOC would at least need a subsidy of 1,600 *tuman*s per year, the moiety of the Muscat customs, and free trade for the Dutch. The Safavids would have to supply all victuals as well as having their own transportation for their troops, with a possible window for the operation in September 1702, all subject to Batavia's approval, of course. Hoogcamer further suggested that because of the cost and difficulties involved whether it would not be better to send an envoy to Muscat to try and conclude a peaceful

---

195. Coolhaas, *Generale Missieven*, vol. 6, p. 42 (06/12/1698).
196. Kroell, *Louis XIV*, p. 14-15; Lockhart, *The Fall*, pp. 434-35.
197. Kroell, *Louis XIV*, p. 38; Idem, "Billon de Cancerille et les rélations Franco-Persanes au début du XVIIIᵉ siècle," *Le Monde Iranien et l'Islam* II (1974), pp. 127-56; Floor, Willem. "The Lost Files of Jean Billon of Cancerilles and French-Persian Relations during the beginning of the eighteenth century," *Eurasian Studies* 2 (2003), pp. 43-94.

settlement of all outstanding issues. The VOC would be willing to send an intermediary to bring about such a settlement, but on condition that the VOC would enjoy total free trade in Safavid Persia and that the payment of the so-called "treaty-goods" in the 1694 silk contract would be abolished. Mirza Rabi`eh, the royal steward (*nazer-e boyutat*), raised the possibility of Dutch protection of Safavid Persian shipping and more transportation of goods belonging to Safavid Persian merchants by Dutch ships. Hoogcamer replied that the Dutch had always transported goods for other merchants, but that there was more demand than space. Safavid Persian ships were free to sail with Dutch ships when they left, but on their own account and responsibility. Also, the Dutch would not wait for any of their ships; they could come and try to keep up with the Dutch ships, but they would be on their own. Finally, the Safavid side had asked that the Dutch keep the seas safe and secure for shipping, to which the answer was, of course, that he would discus it with Batavia. However, he pointed out that contractually this was the responsibility of the English and Portuguese who received the moiety of the customs revenues of Bandar Abbas and Bandar-e Kong respectively.[198]

As a result, the shah lost interest in Dutch support for his Muscat plans, for a time anyway. In 1701, he also had asked the Portuguese for naval assistance, who, unlike the Dutch, had responded favorably. They had been at Bandar-e Kong with six ships at the end of 1702-beginning 1703 to undertake hostile action against Omani interests and Muscat itself. However, the fleet did nothing and its crew starved and many deserted.[199] When some Safavid Persian pilgrims were arrested in Muscat, the shah asked for Dutch intercession to get their release, which the Dutch did.[200] The Omanis got into trouble with the Surat authorities when in 1706 they seized the *Ormus Marsjant*, a private English trader. A

---

198. NA, VOC 1652, f. 641r-42vs, 670vs-681v. (Journal Hoogcamer), f. 719vs-734r. (Appendix 1, requests and replies nr 17-25); 745r-747vs. (Appendix 2, Memorie van Overdracht); Coolhaas, *Generale Missieven*, vol. 6, p. 215 (30/11/1702).
199. *ACE*, vol. 4-38, p. 124 (26/11/1701), 4-130, p. 130 (14/01/1702); Coolhaas, *Generale Missieven*, vol. 6, pp. 234 (04/09/1703).
200. Coolhaas, *Generale Missieven*, vol. 6, pp. 380 (30/11/1705), 458 (30/11/1706).

public conflict arose with Surat, which was not in the economic interest of Muscat, because each year quite a few Omani ships called on that port. This was not lost on the Imam of Muscat either and the conflict was patched up the next year.[201] In December 1707, a Dutch ship called on Muscat to take in water and firewood. On 6 December the *vali* or governor, the chief *vakil* or agent of the Imam (Sheikh Saleh), two of his deputies and four eunuchs came on board to visit the ship. They told the captain that the Dutch were always welcome, but wanted to prevent the ship from departing. The Dutch believed that it was because the Omanis feared an attack by the Portuguese, which would not happen when they saw the Dutch ship in the harbor. However, the Omanis were preparing a naval attack on Goa and did not want this news to leak out. The Imam arrived in Muscat from Matrah with several rowing vessels. A salvo was given by all cannons from the two forts and the ships in the bay. The fleet of 12 vessels with a total crew of 10,000 men sailed on 5 January 1708; six vessels to Goa and six to Mombasa. Apart from the Omani admiral, two of the Imam's loyal slaves, viz. Sheikh Nasir (sjeeg Nassier) and Sheikh Khalil [?] (sjeeg Keel), were also on board as his agents. The Dutch demanded satisfaction for the interference with their ship and the Imam apologized and wrote that he wanted to remain friends with the Dutch. Thereafter, the Omani authorities took excellent care of other Dutch ships that called on Muscat.[202]

Once again in 1707, the shah asked the Dutch for naval assistance against Muscat, and despite their refusal he tried to pressure them.[203] The Safavid court also raised the issue of Muscat with the French ambassador Michel in 1707. The latter, according to the Dutch, offered French assistance against Muscat if the Shah committed himself to expel the Dutch and English from his country, whose place, of course, would be

---

201. Coolhaas, *Generale Missieven*, vol. 6, pp. 376 (30/11/1705), 456 (30/11/1706), 521 (15/01/1708).
202. NA, VOC 1763, Rapport gedaan aan Frans Kastelyn wegens taanhouden van den bodem door de Arabieren op Masquette (27/01/1708), f. 58-63; Coolhaas, *Generale Missieven*, vol. 6, p. 567 (25/11/1708).
203. Coolhaas, *Generale Missieven*, vol. 6, p. 507 (30/11/1707).

taken over by the French. Michel furthermore demanded that merchants would only be allowed to transport their goods in French ships. This proposal was so unrealistic (the French did not even have the ships to realize it) that the Safavid side dropped this issue during the negotiations. Nevertheless, the grand vizier's letter to Louis XIV states that he counted on French military assistance against Muscat. However, France was too weak militarily and economically and too much occupied with its own European problems to follow up even on the commercial opportunities of the treaty, let alone the military ones.[204] After the disappointing French reaction to the Shah's request for military assistance against Muscat, he then turned to the English. John Locke, the EIC agent was said to have promised naval assistance to the Safavid court to transport troops to Oman. The Dutch did not know any details about this alleged English commitment. Maybe in connection with these talks, Mirza Naser (Miersa Nassir) was sent as the Shah's envoy to Bombay to obtain EIC support.[205] In 1709, the governor-general of the VOC made it clear to his director in Bandar Abbas that the VOC would not assist the shah in any way or form against Muscat. For a time it looked as if this question was to become academic, for in March 1709, the Imam of Muscat sent an envoy to Isfahan. He offered to expel the Portuguese from the Persian Gulf altogether on condition of an annual tribute payment. In exchange for this payment the Imam also would keep the Persian Gulf free of pirates. The two Muscat envoys left Isfahan, after having been at the Safavid court for more than seven months, where they were poorly received. In November 1709, they were finally sent to Safi Qoli Khan, the governor of Kuhgilu, who had been instructed to write a reply to the Imam's letter and send an official with it to Muscat. The envoys would have to stay at Kuhgilu until the Safavid official would return

---

204. NA, VOC 1753, Gamron to Batavia (12/01/1709), f. f. 275vs-76 and Ibid., Gamron to XVII (06/07/1709), f. 261-62; Coolhaas, *Generale Missieven*, vol. 6, p. 635 (30/11/1709); Kroell, *Louis XIV*, pp. 38-40.
205. NA, VOC 1790, Isfahan to Gamron (08/12/1710), f. 425; Coolhaas, *Generale Missieven*, vol. 6, pp. 567 (25/11/1708), 635 (30/11/1709).

from his mission to Muscat.[206] The envoys departure was delayed from Kuhgilu and it was even reported that one of them had died. The Dutch wondered what the Imam would do. He sent three ships to Bandar-e Kong in October 1709, but only to ask what the two Portuguese ships had been up to while there during the summer. However, in April 1710 the Imam was said to have been angered about the treatment of his envoys and therefore, he had attacked the island of Qeshm. To defend the coastal settlements, Safi Qoli Khan was said to have raised troops.[207] Nothing came of this diplomatic venture and for some time the Safavid court did not raise the Muscat issue. However, it did not mean that it had been forgotten.

In 1711, Seyf b. Sultan died. His son Sultan b. Seyf continued his aggressive policy towards his neighbors, but even in a more aggressive manner and at a cost that Muscat could ill afford. Despite the Imam's death, there was no pause, just a lull in Omani buccaneering.[208] Maybe in connection with this event, the Safavid court in July 1711 made another half-hearted attempt to obtain Dutch naval assistance. The Dutch agent told Ali Reza Khan, the governor of Bandar Abbas, who had made the request, that it was impossible given the shortage of men-of-war in Europe due to the Spanish succession war (1701-14). He also pointed out that whatever promises Locke, his English counterpart, had made these could not be realized due to the same reason.[209] In the second half of 1711, after the initial lull in Omani naval activities in the Persian Gulf owing to the Imam's death, an Omani force attacked the island of

---

206. NA, VOC 1768, Gamron to XVII (23/12/1709), f. 1872, 2006; Idem, Isfahan to XVII (31/07/1709), f. 1881-vs, 1883vs; Ibid., Isfahan to XVII (26/07/1709), f. 1879vs; NA, VOC 1753, Isfahan to XVII (29/06/1709), f. 285 (the envoys received Dfl. 9.5 per day as defrayment); Coolhaas, *Generale Missieven*, vol. 6, p. 635 (30/11/1709), 706 (29/11/1710).

207. NA, VOC 1790, Gamron to Batavia (12/12/1710), f. 448vs (the Omanis also took two ships coming from Mokha); NA, VOC 1768, Gamron to XVII (23/12/1709), f. 1872-73; Ibid., Isfahan to Gamron (15/05/1710), f. 1917vs.

208. Coolhaas, *Generale Missieven*, vol. 6, pp. 792-93 (30/11/1711).

209. NA, VOC 1790, Isfahan to XVII (January 1712), f. 543.

Larek. It withdrew when reinforcements arrived from the mainland.[210] The Omanis also raided the Indian coast, which led to another conflict with the authorities of Surat, which was patched up in 1713. This did not stop the Omanis attacking the Portuguese on the roadstead of Surat one year later in February 1714. They also attacked Canara,[211] where the Omani prates were much feared.[212] The Omanis further attacked, sacked and burnt the Portuguese factory at Bandar-e Kong that same year and demanded the surrender of the factor, but they were repulsed with a loss.[213]

OMAN ATTACKS AND CONQUERS BAHRAIN (1717)

The Omani threat looked real, certainly taking its naval power into account, which it did not only keep for defense. In 1669, the Omani fleet had about 12-15 ships. Among them were "six from 350 up to 500 tons. These were the ships belonging to the merchants of Surat going

---

210. NA, VOC 1790, Gamron to XVII (17/07/1711), f. 401; Ibid., Gamron to Batavia (26/12/1711), f. 494 vs.
211. The Canara or Kanara coast (Kerala).
212. Coolhaas, *Generale Missieven*, vol. 7, pp. 32 (20/11/1713), 118 (26/11/1714). In November 1711 the viceroy at Goa (D. Rodrigo da Costa) received information that 11 Omani men-of-war had left Muscat. He ordered all ports in the Northern Province to be alerted and asked for more information from the Northern convoy. *BFUP* 6, no. 5, (17/11/1711). A fleet of three frigates under Francisco Pereira da Silva apparently had been able to repulse the Omani fleet and forced it to return to Muscat or seek refuge in other ports. *BFUP* 6, no. 224, p. 380 (07/03/1704). The viceroy, Vasco Fernandes César de Meneses, who was pleased and had no doubt that the enemy ships would be destroyed instructed his admiral to sail to the Persian Gulf via Surat to force any Omani ships to remain there during the winter, so that they would be unable to launch any attack during the next spring. He also informed his admiral that the governor of Surat had given permission to the Portuguese to burn Omani ships that would be in the roadstead of Surat. The admiral further had to hand the factor at Bandar-e Kong the new instructions on passes as well as the present for the shah. *BFUP* 6, no. 224, p. 372 (06/02/1714); Ibid., no. 232, p. 375 (13/02/1714).
213. Lorimer, *Gazetteer*, p. 70; Matos, *Das relações*, p. 349 quoting BA: 51-IX-33[46], f. 220 r (1715).

to Basra. They had anchored before Muscat to get refreshments and had been seized by the Arabs. They landed all the goods from the ships on land and then armed them for war; seven or eight other vessels of their own joined them, thus forming a squadron."[214] In 1705, Lockyer reported that Muscat had 14 warships and 20 merchantmen, one of the former had 70 guns and none had less than 20, and that 14-16 vessels were not in port. He also mentioned that at Surat and the Indus River some Omani vessels were being built.[215] Hamilton estimated the naval strength of Muscat around 1720 at "one Ship of 74 Guns, two of 60, one of 50, and 18 small Ships from 32 to 12 Guns each, and some Trankies of rowing vessels from 4 to 8 Guns each."[216]

With this much naval power fired by an aggressive policy to establish Muscat's supremacy in the Persian Gulf, the Gulf of Oman and beyond, it came as little surprise that Omani attacks increased in number and vehemence. As long as the Omani actions were incursions only, the court in Isfahan did not worry too much. Even the sack of Bandar-e Kong in 1714 hardly bestirred the lethargic court. Aroused by the event for one week it then slipped back into business as usual. However, loss of territory and the probability of losing more was something it could no longer ignore. The first time Muscat's Imam Sultan Seyf b. Seyf II tried to annex Safavid territory was in May-September 1715 when he mounted a large-scale attack against Bahrain. The Qavasem Arabs of Sharjah and those of Qatar, who were traditional enemies of those of Bahrain, assisted the Omanis, who were defeated by the Safavid forces on this island.[217]

---

214. Martin, *Travels*, p. 416. Because Oman lacked timber the Omani ships were built in Surat and Bombay. Patricia Risso, *Oman & Muscat an early modern history* (New York, 1986), pp. 82-83.
215. Lockyer, *An account*, p. 207; Miles, *Tribes*, p. 224. On the quality of the ship builders see Martin, *India*, vol. 2/1, pp. 1003-04.
216. Hamilton, *A New Account*, vol. 1, p. 51.
217. NA, KA 1778, Isfahan to Gamron (18/11/1715), f. 328-31; Idem, Isfahan to Gamron (02/01/1716), f. 383 (Omanis lost 1,000 men on Bahrain); NA, VOC 1886, Oets to Batavia (24/03/1716), f. 18; Lockhart, *Fall*, p. 115; Mohammad Khalil Mar'ashi, *Majma' al-Tavarikh*. ed. Abbas Eqbal (Tehran, 1328/1949), p. 37.

In 1716 the Omanis again attacked Bahrain; initially with 15-16 vessels, which were later followed by 10-12 other vessels and many smaller craft.[218] As mentioned above, by that time the Omani fleet consisted "of one ship of 74 guns, of two of 60 and of one of 50, besides 18 smaller vessels carrying 32 to 12 guns, and some Trankis or rowing vessels of 8 to 4 guns," with which the Omanis terrorized the Indian ocean area.[219] The governor of Bahrain, Mehrab Sultan realized that he could do nothing against the large Omani force and therefore, he sent the fastest vessels to Rishahr to ask for help from the governor of Dashtestan. The latter came with troops to his support. Mehrab Sultan attacked the Omanis helped by the Safavid troops and the local population and the Omanis were again defeated. Many Omanis were killed and the rest fled.[220]

Although Muscat's fleet remained active in the Persian Gulf in 1716, it was only in 1717 that it attacked Bahrain again, this time with more success. According to a Safavid chronicle, the third Omani attack was carried out by 14 ships and maybe three to four times more troops than before. At that time Mehrab Khan had been dismissed from his post due to ill-wishers at court. The new governor was still en route. The Bani Otbah (most likely the Otub), Sunni Arabs from Qatar, who were the traditional enemies of the Bahrainis had made common cause with the Omanis for whom they acted as guides into the town and island. The population of the island was without a leader and thus was unable to effectively oppose them. Nevertheless, it was only after much fighting that lasted 45 days that the Omanis were able to capture the island.[221]

The conquest of Bahrain caused consternation in Isfahan. A Bahraini delegation led by Sheikh Mohammad b. Majed came to court to ask for action referring to the last Omani action, the Omani attacks on those

---

218. Coolhaas, *Generale Missieven*, vol. 7, p. 249 (30/11/1716).
219. Lorimer, *Gazetteer*, p. 403; Kroell, *Louis XIV*, p. 65, n. 210 (ships with 30 40 cannon); Ross, *Annals of Oman*, p. 55.
220. Mar'ashi, *Majma' al-Tavarikh*, p. 37 (The date for this event is: *qatalat ahl Oman* or 1128/1716); Matos, *Das relações*, p. 350 (26/02/1716).
221. Mar'ashi, *Majma' al-Tavarikh*, pp. 37-39.

going on pilgrimage to Mecca and their attacks on ships going to India. The Shah in response ordered Lotf Ali Khan, whom he made *sepahsalar* (commander-in-chief) and commander of the armies to Oman, take care of all issues raised by Sheikh Mohammad b. Majed.[222] Shah Sultan Hoseyn asked the Dutch ambassador, Joan Josua Ketelaar, who happened to be at his court to discuss a new commercial treaty, for Dutch naval support in retaking Bahrain. Ketelaar refused the loan of Dutch ships because he had no authority to grant such assistance.[223] Ketelaar gave the same reply to a similar request by Fath Ali Khan, the grand vizier, to support his nephew Lotf Ali Khan, who meanwhile had been appointed governor-general (*beglerbegi*) of Fars and Azerbaijan. Although the shah and his grand-vizier acquiesced in Ketelaar's refusal, Lotf Ali Khan did not. On his return to Bandar Abbas, Ketelaar was confronted by Ya`qub Sultan, one of Lotf Ali Khan's commanders, with the same demand. For not only had the Omanis taken Bahrain, once again, they had attacked and pillaged Bandar-e Kong, taken the islands of Larek and Qeshm, and were laying siege to the fortress of Hormuz. Both the Dutch and English Companies rebuffed Ya`qub Sultan. In desperation he laid siege to their factories to force the loan of their ships. Ya`qub Sultan eventually had to give in, and Lotf Ali Khan punished him for his allegedly unauthorized action. However, Lotf Ali Khan made it clear that he still insisted on naval assistance. The Dutch replied that both the Shah and the grand vizier accepted their reasons for not providing support and asked why lesser officials were not content with that reply. The Dutch also pointed out that in February 1718 they had given passage to Goa to a Safavid envoy Tahmurath Beg, whose mission was to ask the Portuguese for naval assistance.[224] The siege of Hormuz would last seven months, but

---

222. Mar`ashi, *Majma` al-Tavarikh*, pp. 38-39. In Dutch sources he is called the nephew of the grand vizier.
223. NA, VOC 1913, Ketelaar to Batavia (31/12/1717), f. 29, 49.
224. NA, VOC 1904, Oets to Batavia (07/11/1718), f. 2363-64; Ibid, f. 2403-05. Coolhaas, *Generale Missieven*, vol. 7, p. 440 (30/11/1719); on these event see Willem Floor, *Commercial Conflict between Persia and the Netherlands 1712-1718*, University of Durham Occasional Paper Series no. 37 (1988). On 09/02/1717 the Dutch in Bandar Abbas received news that five Omani vessels each with 100

the defenders held out and with the help of Ya`qub Sultan, governor of Bandar Abbas, they received sufficient water and food supplies.²²⁵

Lotf Ali Khan had to content himself with that reply, and swallowing it was made easier by his retaking of Bahrain. On 5 July 1718 he had put 6,000 troops ashore using small vessels supplied by coastal Arabs who recognized Safavid suzerainty. The Oman forces responded by raising the siege of Hormuz and regrouping on Larek and Qeshm.²²⁶ The Safavid victory was of short duration, however. In November 1718, the Omanis retook Bahrain and almost completely annihilated the Safavid relief force. Not only did Lotf Ali Khan lose many troops, he also lost many vessels. Because the promised Portuguese naval support had not yet arrived, Lotf Ali Khan needed ships badly. Therefore, he wrote the shah asking him to send money to buy 10 well-armed *grab*s, "for without ships there is nothing much that we can do to oppose the Muscat Arabs." Writing to Jan Oets, the VOC director at Bandar Abbas, Lotf Ali Khan regretted the fact that the Dutch had not shown friendship by helping him previously, but he hoped that they would prove their professed friendship by supplying him with at least five ships, for which he would pay in cash. Moreover, if they were to produce 30 ships, these too would be welcome and paid for within four months' time.²²⁷ Jan

---

men had landed on Hormuz; the vessels remained at anchor at Larek. NA, KA 1789, Ketelaar to Batavia (08/03/1717), f. 135.
225. Mar`ashi, *Majma` al-Tavarikh*, p. 38.
226. NA, VOC 1904, Oets to Batavia (07/11/1718), f. 2263vs-64r. The Imam of Muscat reportedly had already withdrawn troops at Larek and had sent them to Bahrain at the end of 1717. NA, KA 1805, Gamron to Batavia (31/12/1717), f.29. The siege of Hormuz continued and was executed by 4,000 men who bombarded the fort daily. There were some 30-40 small vessels and one Omani ship at anchor at Hormuz, which could be seen from Bandar Abbas and greatly hampered trade. Most merchants fled into the mountains. NA, KA 1805, Gamron to Batavia (17/02/1718), f. 72. For further information regarding the siege of Hormuz see also NA, KA 1805, Dagregister Gamron (01/02/1718 – 30/04/1718), f. 308, 310-13, 340-42, 346, 349-50.
227. NA, VOC 1928, Lotf Alie Chan to van Biesum (17/07/1718 received), f. 116; Ibid., Oets to van Biesum (15/09/1718), f. 179; Ibid., (01/10/1718), f. 181; Ibid., Lotf Alie Chan to van Biesum (received 18/09/1718), f. 118-22; Ibid., Schorer to

Oets, the new VOC director who had just arrived from Batavia, replied to the Shah and grand vizier that the Dutch ships had already left. In his letter to the grand vizier he added that since Lotf Ali Khan had written that Bahrain and the other island had been retaken, which at the time of Oets' receipt of the letter was no longer true, the support of Dutch ships was not needed. Lotf Ali Khan received a similar reply.[228] When Lotf Ali Khan made a new request for naval assistance, Oets replied that Ketelaar had discussed the issue with the shah and the grand vizier. He further drew Lotf ʿAli Khan's attention to the fact that he had brought with him the governor-general's reply to the shah's request, which Oets had given to the *shahbandar* to forward to the shah. Oets therefore had to act in accordance with that reply. Moreover, at that time there were no Dutch ships available to assist Lotf Ali Khan.[229]

In October 1718, not yet having received the governor-general's letter, Shah Sultan Hoseyn ordered the Dutch to send the three ships that had just arrived from Batavia to support Lotf Ali Khan and the Portuguese, who had promised to send five ships. If the Dutch refused to do so, they would be punished for disobedience. The grand vizier wrote Oets to the same effect and added that Lotf Ali Khan had money to pay the Dutch for any expenses they would incur. Lotf Ali Khan separately wrote to the Dutch and asked them to execute the shah's orders so that he could retake Bahrain and punish the rebellious Arabs. He added that after the Portuguese ships arrived and Bahrain retaken, it was his intention to execute another plan with the combined Dutch-Portuguese fleet. Although Lotf Ali Khan did not mention what this plan was, he probably intended to invade Muscat itself.[230] Because the Dutch ships had already left, the entire issue was a moot one.

---

van Biesum (13/08/1718), f. 71 (people are elated in Isfahan. The Shah is said to have appointed Lotf Ali Khan as *tofangchi bashi* (chief of the musketeers); Ibid., (12/10/1718), f. 80 (there were three days of bonfires at Isfahan to celebrate the conquest of Bahrain).

228. NA, VOC 1920, Oets to Shah, f. 221-24; Oets to grand-vizier, f. 224-28; Oets to Lotf Ali Khan, f. 232-35 (03/01/1718).

229. NA, VOC 1928, Oets to Lotf Ali Khan (24/08/1718), f. 126-27.

230. NA, VOC 1928, Shah to Oets (Dhu'l-Qaʿdeh 1130/October 1718), f. 219-21.

Even when the Safavids were repairing the fort of Hormuz, after having retaken it with a force of 8,000 men, the Omanis still occupied Larek and Qeshm. From there the Omanis asked why the Dutch did not come and trade in Muscat, to which they replied that the market was too small to be interesting.[231] In 1719, Imam Sultan b. Seyf died, and with his death the suppressed sentiments of those who had opposed him came to the fore. His contested successor Imam Mohanna` b. Sultan (1719-20) only lasted one year, before he was killed. He was remembered for his good administration and the promotion of trade to which end he even had abolished customs duties at Muscat.[232] The result of this succession conflict was an intense struggle between two major factions that resulted in a civil war that would last till 1728 and ultimately led to the demise of the Ya`ariba dynasty. The Omanis were now ready to conclude a peace treaty with the Safavids, and in 1720, they returned Qeshm and Larek to the Safavids, although the peace treaty had not yet been agreed. This was due to the murder of the Imam's regent, and the new regent did not want to sign the agreement.[233] As a result of these developments, along with internal troubles in Oman, the two warring parties started negotiations, which in 1721 led to a peace agreement. Muscat promised to return all conquered territories in exchange for commercial privileges at Bandar-e Kong and Safavid support in case of Portuguese attacks on Muscat. But when Lotf Ali Khan sent some troops to Bahrain to reinstate Safavid rule, they were sent back. A dispute had arisen among the Omani leaders, some of whom refused to accept the terms of the peace treaty.[234] In April 1721, Omani forces still occupied Bahrain, and it was unclear whether the peace treaty would be implemented.[235] Also, due to dynastic problems at the end of 1722, Oman was unable to maintain its power in the Persian Gulf. A nominally Safavid subject, Sheikh Jabbara of Taheri, one of the chiefs of the important Hula

---

231. Coolhaas, *Generale Missieven*, vol. 7, p. 407 (28/03/1719).
232. Ross, *Annals*, p. 57.
233. Coolhaas, *Generale Missieven*, vol. 7, p. 573 (30/11/1721). For an account of the civil war see Ross, *Annals*, pp. 56-74.
234. NA, VOC 1964, Oets to Batavia (15/02/1721), f. 76.
235. NA, VOC 1964, Oets to Batavia (05/04/1721), f. 767.

(or Huwala) tribe, then took possession of Bahrain on behalf of Shah Sultan Hoseyn.[236] By that time, Safavid rule had crumbled before the onslaught of the Afghan invaders who took Isfahan in October 1722 and forced Shah Sultan Hoseyn to abdicate.[237] Muscat had its own problems, for apart from political-dynastic problems, it also suffered from the havoc wrought by a hurricane that hit its harbor in August 1723; twenty-one ships and many smaller vessels were shipwrecked and many houses were destroyed as well.[238] For the rest of the decade Muscat was a spent power, both military and commercially, and given the gloomy state of affairs in the Persian Gulf in general it did not recover from its self-inflicted wounds. In 1725, the Dutch instructed one of its ships (*Nederhoven*) to call on Muscat and try to sell goods there. Although Bartholomeus Lispensier was welcomed and was able to sell some goods, the results were not encouraging and therefore, the Dutch dropped Muscat as a market to visit with a view to increase sales.[239] It was an indication of Oman's reduced might, and its power to intimidate, that the pasha of Basra extorted money from Omani merchants trading in Basra in the early 1720s. The Imam, therefore, decided to demand satisfaction. He seized the Surat vessel *Fattaa Remam*, which carried goods for the pasha, and threatened to take 260 *tuman*s from the ship, which was the exact amount taken from the Omani merchants. On September 1726 the Imam released the vessel. The new pasha on learning about the Imam's action retaliated by again taking money from Omani merchants and he

---

236. NA, VOC 2009, Oets to Batavia (15/11/1722), f. 47.
237. Lockhart, *The Fall*, p. 171; Willem Floor, *Afghan Occupation of Persia, 1722-1730* (Paris/Louvain: Cahiers Studia Iranica, 1998).
238. Kroell, *Louis XIV*, p. 175, n. 234. Muscat still had sent four ships plus 15 small vessels to Basidu (Qeshm) on March 15, 1723. The population surrendered and negotiations were ongoing to settle their conflict. It was also reported that the Imam of Muscat intended to launch an attack against Basra. NA, KA1891, Gamron to Batavia (30/04/1723), f. 424-25.
239. NA, VOC 2034, Instructie scheepsoverheden van 'tschip Nederhoven (15/06/1725), f. 324-26; Ibid., Instructie Lispensier (15/06/1725), f. 340-50; Ibid., Report Lispensier (11/08/1725), f. 35-65. The governor of Muscat, Sheikh Abdallah valad-e Mas`ud (sjeeg Abdulla waledde Mashoed), wrote in November 1729 to the Dutch requesting some goods. NA, VOC 2168, f. 6543.

even imprisoned some of them.²⁴⁰ In the past, the pasha of Basra would not have dared to take such a stand, fearing harassment of shipping in the sea lanes to Basra, if not a direct attack of his port. It would take many years before Oman would again play an important commercial and military role in the Persian Gulf.²⁴¹

---

240. NA, VOC 2079, de Cleen to 'tLam (07/11/1726), f. 71–80; NA, VOC 2105, Extract Dagregister Bassora, f. 854.
241. Risso, *Oman & Muscat*.

CHAPTER THREE
================

Ya`ariba Muscat (1650-1725)
===========================

Muscat Town

Population

Most of Muscat's population was Arab. According to Padbrugge, "the country and its people are rough from the outside, but polished inside. Their size favors short rather than tall size, but their dress makes them look like being of middle size."[1] Also, their behavior to people, including that to strangers was polite, friendly, generous and obliging. They also were very frank and wanted to be informed about everything and made this known in public loud and clear. However, these traits were not universally found among the urban population. For "This frankness is mostly found among the common man, who is not that very polite, while peasants are entirely boorish, who one may know from amongst all others, because they allow their hair to grow and don't cut it as is the

---

1. Floor, "A Description," p. 26. Both the Dutch and English did not use the term Omanis to refer to the inhabitants of Muscat and Oman, but rather that of Muscat Arabs or Muscateers or some variant thereof, see, e.g., Lorimer, *Gazetteer*, pp. 62-67, 1186.

custom of the Moslems."Virtue and bravery were admired and rewarded. The Imam made a public display to reward those of his men who had displayed such admirable behavior, most certainly when it helped him politically.[2] Wilmson, who lived for more than one year among the Omanis had a different opinion. According to him,

> In general, they are very miserly and stingy, and try to give all their doings the pretense of honesty. In their conversations they affect a great show of respectability and speak very slowly and softly. They have a reprobate mind, such that they feel themselves superior at the least sign of prosperity or humble in case of adversity. If they expect or hope for some advantage from someone, they abase themselves immensely before that person. Contrariwise they act very elevated from those whom they don't expect any advantage or whom they don't fear.[3]

In addition to Arabs, Indians (Sindis, Banyans), probably the largest minority group living in Muscat, there were Baluchis and Jews. There is some evidence that in the mid-1660s a community of Portuguese renegades still existed in Muscat, some of them former slaves who were not liable for ransom.[4] There are no data available on the total number of people living in Muscat or the breakdown by religious group. Despite the fact that the Omanis showed tolerance to other ethnic groups and religions, nevertheless, they did not entirely trust them or like them. For example, the large number of Indians mainly lived in a kind of suburb on the south side in the western part of the city, because "they are not trusted to be allowed to live inside the town."[5] This despite the fact that one Banyan merchant was rumored to have provided essential

---

2. Floor, "A description," pp. 28-29.
3. Floor, "A description," pp. 35-36
4. *ACE*, vol. 4-54, p. 154 (26/03/1666).
5. Floor, "A description," p. 24. According to Padbrugge, the Omanis wanted to get rid of the Banyans. NA, VOC 1288, Report Padbrugge, f. 436.

information to Imam Sultan b. Seyf, which enabled him to take Muscat.[6] This Banyan merchant Narutem had revealed Portuguese weaknesses to the Imam in 1649. As a reward, his family, but not the Banyan community, received tax exemption for his services.[7]

Although in 1650 many Indians left with the Portuguese, but despite Omani distrust, the Banyan community was large and was increasing after 1650.[8] In 1651, Banyan merchants were the main source of information to Elias Boudaens who visited Muscat at that time.[9] Those who had remained were mostly Kaphol Banyans from Diu (who were the wealthiest), while the newcomers were mostly Mappilas from Kerala. The former were permitted various exemptions from taxation.[10] In the 1670s the Banyan merchants owned houses and shops in and outside Muscat and were involved in trade with the interior.[11] Indians were not only traders, but also craftsmen such as builders, carpenters, and some may be shipbuilders. In 1668, some 3,000 captives were taken in a raid of Diu who in 1672 still squatted on the overcrowded beach of Makallah.[12]

---

6. C.H. Allen, "The Indian Merchant Community of Muscat," *BSOAS* XLIV/1 (1981), pp. 39-53," p. 40, n. 19; Floor, "A description," p. 33. According to Carsten Niebuhr, *Beschreibung von Arabien, aus eigenen beobachtungen und in lande selbst gesammleten nachrichten abgefasset nachrichten* (Kopenhagen: N. Möller, 1772), p. 207 the Portuguese captain had taken the daughter of a Banyan by force, who then betrayed the castle to the Omanis. According to *ACE* vol. 3-29, p. 517 (18/12/1650), the captain of Muscat had stored all the gunpowder, ammunition and arms in the factory rather than in the fort as he should have as per his instructions. Allegedly Narutem was able to convince him to disregard his orders in this respect. Narutem's story is borne out by Badger, *History*, vol. 1, pp. 81-84.
7. Badger, *History*, vol. 1, pp. 82-84.
8. NA, VOC 1259, f. 3375; Allen, "The Indian Merchant," for their origins.
9. NA, VOC 1188, Boudaens, "Schriftelijck relaes," (Surat 29/11/1651), f. 546.
10. Allen, "The Indian Merchant," p. 41; Barendse, *Arabian Seas*, p. 344.
11. Floor, "A Description," pp. 22, 37 (for the payment of poll-tax and other imposts see Ibid., p. 37); Lorimer, *Gazetteer*, p. 1182.
12. NA, VOC 1273, Goske to XVII (28/02/1669), f. 1940; Floor, "A Description," pp. 2, 25.

In the eighteenth century they constituted one of the largest Indian communities in the Persian Gulf.[13]

According to Wilmson, the Omanis "are very dirty of nature, both where their clothes are concerned as well as their way of living." Moreover,

> Their clothing is bad, to such an extent that is hardly possible to distinguish the best from the worst. Their belt is a leathern one with an orin or copper buckle. The Imam himself is not distinguishable [by his dress], whether he walks the street with shoes or with bare feet. The males hate to dress up in outward apparel, but they know how to dress the womenfolk with all kinds of silk clothes and gold jewelry. They have very little household effects or not at all. The rich sit on a simple mat woven from date fronds, or sometimes on small pebbles which serves them as a real carpet. Their night-goods consist of a rough woolen horse-blanket [filled] with flock-wool during winter. They mostly cover themselves with their mantles.[14]

Padbrugge noted that people squinted, which he ascribed to the fact that everybody rubbed herbal juice with a spatula under their eyes against the heat.[15] This had the effect that people (men, women, and children) had a blue ring around their eyes. The Omanis believed it made them look handsome. As protection against the heat they wore

---

13. Floor, "A Description," pp. 29-30. Niebuhr, *Beschreibung von Arabien*, p. 305 estimated the Banyan community of Muscat at some 1,200 persons in 1765.
14. Floor, "A Description," p. 35, see also Idem, pp. 26-27 which makes the same point as to the uniformity of clothes and provides a detailed description of how the Imam was dressed during an audience.
15. This refers to the use of kohl, see the article "Kuhl" *Encyclopedia of Islam*².

thick clothes.[16] They also rubbed themselves with sandalwood oil or some other oils.[17]

THE HARBOR

In 1672, the Dutch chief merchant Robert Padbrugge made a detailed description of Muscat port, which is reproduced here and speaks for itself.

> The town crawls into an oblong bay and is walled in by sky-high steep rocky mountains, many of which have been equipped with cannon, whilst others are only fit to serve as look-out.
>
> At the mouth of the bay's entrance there is a large village called Matairah (Matere), which has a passageway (*waterpas*) and a permanent guard of about thirty men. Offshore, at about one [German] mile[18] from its fixed western bulwark, there is a very conspicuous grey craggy outcrop protruding into sea, which can be observed from afar. North of it one enters straight into the bay. It is also possible to enter quite easily on the southern side, between the shore and the crag. The further one goes into the bay the better is the ground. Very close to the town and before a specific harbor just outside it, one finds very good holding ground. Contrariwise on the northern side of the entrance of the bay [the ground] is rather rocky. On our first arrival, we went here when we sailed into the bay past Matairah. This

---

16. About this subject, see the interesting articles on Bedouin clothes by A. Shkolnik, C.R. Taylor, V. Finch and A. Boruk, "Why do Bedouins were black robes in hot deserts?" in *Nature* 283 (24 January 1980), pp. 374 75 and R. Dmiel, A. Prevolutzky and A. Shkolnik, "Is a black coat in the desert a means of saving metabolic energy?" in *Nature* 283 (21 February 1980), pp. 761-62.
17. Floor, "A Description," pp. 27-28.
18. The German mile (7.4 km) is meant here and throughout this book.

was against the good advice of the government and we did the wrong thing.

At the entrance and the mouth of this bay, there are two passageways (*waterpassen*), which are situated at the foot of the rocky mountains. Recently, Mr. Godske has instructed us to use the northern one. It is well situated, for the Arabs, if they wish, can prevent anyone from entering it. Here they close the entrance at night, from sunset until sunrise, by stringing watch-barques over the entire entrance. There are another two [defenses] on the south side more into the direction of the shore. These protect and cover a long crescent shaped port, where one finds a shipyard. In it there are about 100 ships lying side by side, when the stern almost touches the bow. Here no more than three of the Imam's ships lay. Further along, [there were] all the foreign ones from Malabar, Suratte, Sindy, Persia, Bassora, Berem, Mocha, Mayottes, etc. The town itself is also situated in a crescent shaped area, except that almost one-third of [this area] has been cut off by the protruding mountains. At the moment the Benjaan prisoners of Diu have been put there. They are quite numerous and it is difficult to understand how the [Arabs] have been able to transport them all by sea.

The string of this bow [shape] or the straight line of the crescent is in an east-west of direction. On the east side it goes beyond a Portuguese church (which we think they may give us as a residency (*logie*), when we seriously start trading here or when we have a closer friendship with them). It has been well endowed with a wall and a shore lined with campshot. The Portuguese started to close the gap with the connecting curtain wall. However, the Arabs have so far neglected to complete this good and necessary work. The young Imam is not very pleased and very angry at the present governor because of this. The previous one had been urged [to finish] this work and was at the point of doing so, but since he has been dismissed from his governorship the work has not started. The wall closes about one quarter of the line, then there follows an open space (*vacht?*) of two, three hundred or more steps, which is not closed. The best thing that one may say (*'tbeste datter van sy*) about the crescent is that the houses are closely [knitted] together and most of them come right down to the shoreline. They are followed by round bastions, which are an obstacle and prevent rather than enhance a good enfilade.[19] The rest is closed by a thin wall as far as the new dock. It offers the advantage that the water borders on it (*daeraen vloeyt*). The dock has been dug, with difficulty, alongside the bottom of the rocky mountains. Even now its stones break away every day, yes even by night, at low tide. On both sides it has been drawn up with sloping and well built banks (*barmen*). Its width is estimated to be fifteen perches (*roedde*) and its length forty to fifty perches. The opening is closed with a palisade and only a narrow passage (*glop*) remains temporarily (*voor de loos*) closed through which the ships are allowed to enter and leave. Here lay twenty-six to twenty-seven native ships, amongst which was a rather large one taken from the Portuguese, which had a St. Maria on its stern. There were also a few of the Imam's own ships lying within that enclosed part cut off from the crescent by the protruding mountains. Situated to the South and extending as far as the mountains running parallel is a bow-shaped wall enclosing the town entirely, which even excludes the highest steep mountains.

Buildings and Walls

Muscat was a stronghold in more than one sense, for not only was it a well-protected and guarded gateway to Oman, but it also had very strong defenses. In 1672, Robert Padbrugge described these as follows:

---

19. A formation or position is "in enfilade" if weapons fire can be directed along its longest axis.

There are two gates on the landside and a dry moat all around. During the Portuguese period this wall was necessary, because the Arabs are experienced mountaineers. For, although, as has been said, the peaks of the mountains have been abundantly covered with block houses, the Arabs know how to climb even this steepness with great ability. [The town] is entirely circumwalled and enclosed enclosed by sky-high mountains; there are no more than two easy passes between the gaps (*cloven*) of the mountains, which have been closed by a wall in which a gate was made [reinforced by] two redoubts. Just above this gate is the other one, just on the summit of the same mountain. Apart from these two passes there are two gaps, but these are not very accessible due to the steepness and therefore, also totally closed by walls. The easy [gaps] are entrances to enter on the west and the east side on the landside. However, it is impossible to do so with horses, because they are followed by very difficult mountains. Therefore, if one wants to enter Muscat from the landside, one first has to go via the sea. These accessible gaps are impossible to capture or to take by surprise. The empty space (*vacht*) between the city walls and the gaps of the mountains is very wide. Moreover, it is intersected with many indentations in between the mountains. Some of which represent the best farming lands. However, most of it lay unused (*ledich*) and is covered with stones. Their cemetery is to be found there, likewise that of the Benjanen [Banyans], other Indians and that of Europeans, which is the closest to the town. On the south side, in the western section, the Indians live in great numbers and constitute a kind of suburb for they are not trusted [to live] inside the town. [The area] between that quarter and our [i.e. European] cemetery is mostly filled with horse stables, both of the Imam and the governor as well as of others, in addition to two rope-walks. After this detour we may as well enter [the town] again and will observe the fortifications on the seaside of the town. Here we also have only followed the straight line from the west to the east side and the dock and have left the rest of Muscat as yet unbuilt. Both ends or the corners of this half moon have been equipped with a good water passage (*waterpas*) and a strong castle on top of the steep cliffs. There is a brick-laid staircase against the cliffs that is used to climb from the water passage upwards. On the other side, where one looks from the east towards the sea, one sees another brick-laid staircase that had been built towards the foot [of the mountain] and another strong water passageway. There is yet another small narrow passage (*glop*) and entrance to the north side of this cliff through which many boats come daily, mostly laden with horse fodder. Next follows a sky-high rocky mountain, which encloses the entire east side of the bay. The two water passageways and their fortifications situated above them, which are mentioned, are in fact the entire defense (*gewelt*) of Muscat. Because of the water passageways they can prevent landing near the town, while the upper castles can only be taken through starvation, for on all sides there are steep and inaccessible cliffs.

The city did not change much between 1625 and 1725. Only the buildings having a Catholic religious function were given a secular function after the fall of Muscat in 1650. In 1651 Muscat was becoming dilapidated, "as is the custom of the Arabs," a visiting Dutch merchant observed. There was not one undamaged house and most of them were in ruins. The only construction activity that was ongoing was the repairs of the two forts. Many survivors of the Omani capture of Muscat had left and therefore, the town's population was much smaller than before.[20] In 1672, Robert Padbrugge described Muscat as follows:

> All Portuguese buildings have been destroyed. The Arabs, because of their great hate for the Portuguese, appear even

---

20. NA, VOC 1188, Boudaens, f. 545vs.

to have taken revenge on the buildings and did not want to leave one stone on the other. However, there still remain a church, a chapel, and a monastery, which is the Imam's court at present. Further there are some other almost dilapidated buildings. Among them, are a few partly destroyed buildings in which live Sheykh Abdallah (Chegh Abdul) and the chief of the soldiers. There are a few other [buildings] which are even more dilapidated. For the rest their dwellings are huts and holes (*moortkuylen*), which nevertheless are so full of people, that one is very much amazed and wondering where all these people, who gush forth from such a small dwelling, are coming from. The more so, since the greater part of the town is filled with merchandise. The streets are so narrow and winding that the town almost looks like a maze. Only in the widest street can a wool bale pass. A very lively wool trade is carried on here.[21]

In 1685, Kaempfer noted that many of the houses of the city were huts made of date fronds, but they were much neater, cleaner and larger, for they even had a courtyard, more than those on the Safavid Persian littoral. There were many ruined houses and buildings in the city; most of the houses were made of stone and were pleasing and spacious.[22] Georg Wilmson, a Dutch merchant who resided in Muscat in 1672-73, reported that the Omanis also built large houses, but this was exceptional. A certain Esma`il, a fugitive Arab from Basra, had built a very large house, which served as a kind of hotel for his compatriots indicating regular trade relations with Basra. Another Esma`il, nicknamed "Benderie" (i.e. Bandari), owned five 'hotels', but these were made of date fronds and mats, which he rented out per night at rates of two to three Abbasis, depending on their size.[23] According to Kaempfer, the Jesuit College, a nice Italianate building, was being used as storage and arsenal, and when the Imam was in town as his residence. There

---

21. Floor, "A description," pp. 24-25.
22. Kaempfer, *Die Reisetagebücher*, p. 148.
23. Floor, "A description," p. 60, n. 94; NA, VOC 1304, Report Wilmson, f. 483vs.

was still a Catholic white church with high roofs that was also used as storage area. The bazaar covered a large space and consisted of covered and partly vaulted alleys that ran parallel to each other and crossed each other regularly in a quadrate pattern. The shops were well-stocked with all kinds of goods.[24]

In 1721, according to Hamilton, the town was still very strong, although the buildings remained very mean. "Their Bazaars or Markets are all covered with Date Tree Leaves, spread on Beams of the Same Tree, that reach from House to House-top' and the Houses being all flat on their Tops, terassed with Clay and Straw mixt, in the aforesaid Months every Body lodges on them in the Nights; and the Nights afford plentiful Dews, that sometimes weet them thro' their thick Cotton Quilts."[25] The former Catholic cathedral had been transformed into the Imam's palace, when he resided in Muscat, which was one to two months per year. "The Wall of the Town that faces the Harbour, has a Battery of large Cannon, about 60 in Number, and there are 8 to 10 small Forts built on the adjacent Rocks or Mountains, which guard all the Avenues to the Town, both by Sea and Land; and there are none permitted to come in or go out of the Harbour between Sun-set and Rising."[26] Muscat had a Persian Gulf climate, which meant that from May to September it was excessively hot and humid.[27]

Religion

Although Jews and Banyans were permanent inhabitants of Muscat, in addition to the occasional Christians, they could not exercise their religion in temples and synagogues. In 1672-63, Georg Wilmson, a

---

24. Kaempfer, *Die Reisetagebücher*, p. 148-49 (he lists many of the products for sale). The Imam spent one third of the year in Muscat, according to Kaempfer. Curzon, *Persia and the Persian Question*, vol. 2, 1892: 440, says that the Portuguese cathedral was used as the Sultan's stables in the 1890's.
25. Hamilton, *A New Account*, vol. 1, p. 45.
26. Hamilton, *A New Account*, vol. 1, pp. 44-45. Bafqi, *Jame`-ye Mofidi*, vol. 3/2, p. 810 (At night nobody was allowed to pass the barrier.)
27. Della Valle, *Voyages*, vol. 4, p. 409; Hamilton, *A New Account*, vol. 1, p. 45.

Dutch merchant and resident of Muscat observed that "We have neither seen big temples nor churches or mosques. They all perform their religious duties by themselves everywhere. The Jewish church was in that quarter of the Sindi and Banyan prisoners at the foot of the mountains and [its construction] had nicely begun. However, the great hate these Arabs bear the Jews has prevented its continuation and completion, so that its construction has been stopped halfway and can still be seen in that stage."[28] Thus, it seems that the Omanis did not like to have special religious buildings, but it is more likely that this applied to Moslems, as is clear in the case of the synagogue. The absence of mosques in Muscat may have been due to the limited time that the Ya`ariba Imam had held the town as well as that most Omanis belonged to the Ibadi sect.[29] There was no *madraseh* or theological school either, for Wilmson noted that theological discussions were held in a covered space near the Dutch factory.

> Aside to it [the weigh-house] is a secluded place with banks and covered with mats, which is a kind of exchange or gathering place for the important merchants. Here one usually sees some jurists, important moolhaas (mollahs) or master exegetes of the Alcoran. Although they hold different opinions, they do not hate one another or argue among themselves as we have observed when Galiel (Khalil) took us there once and with great respect pointed out two exegetes. The one was of the old and Omers (Omar's) religion [i.e. Sunni Islam] and the other of Halys (Ali's) religion and persuasion [i.e. Shi`a Islam], but we were unable all to see something of that expressed in their faces. There were also a few books lying pell-mell and open, out of which, so it

---

28. Floor, "A description," pp. 24-25.
29. On the Ibadis see the relevant article in the *Encyclopedia of Islam*². On some of their religious practices see Floor, "A description," p. 36 ("The common man prays five times, while those who want to be considered a *mutawaas* (*muttawwa`*) or holy man pray seven times.") On the *muttawi`ah* among the Ibadis of Oman, see Lorimer, *Gazetteer*, vol. 2, p. 2374.

seemed, each in his turn read something more to edify than to cause dispute.[30]

Although the Omanis did not permit temples and the like they allowed non-Moslems to practice their religion and even have sexual relations with Moslem women. They also allowed cemeteries for non-Moslems.

Food Supplies

There was no agricultural activity in or around the town of Muscat itself, while after 1650 its population was growing. As in pre-Ya`ariba times, food supplies had to be brought in by sea. The main towns that supplied Muscat with food were Sib and Barkah.[31] Under the Ya`ariba dynasty, the country continued to be "unable to feed itself. Each year, most of its wheat and other grains are imported from Persia and other parts of the Indies, just as the rice from the Kanara coast."[32] Muscat had no real road to the interior, because the narrow passes were difficult to traverse by pack animals. Nevertheless, Muscat was "very well supplied with food of all varieties" by sea. Muscat had only one important economic resource, viz. fish, of which it had plenty. Hamilton noted the rich fishing grounds of Muscat, and that on the bare rocks slaves roasted fish, which was also eaten by cattle and horses.[33] Kaempfer made purchases for his sea voyage in 1685, and commented that only butter, milk and chickens were in short supply. He found that surprising, because the country neither lacked in

---

30. Floor, "A description," p. 25. See, also Hamilton, *A New Account*, vol. 1, p. 46 who states "their Molahs or Priests often preach themselves into violent passions, especially if the Subject of their Sermon be about the Verity of their Religion; and they challenge the Priests of any other Religion whatever, to confirm theirs with as good Evidences as they can."
31. Anonymous. *Relãçao das plantas*, pp. 12-13.
32. Floor, "A description," p. 30.
33. Hamilton, *A New Account*, vol. 1, pp. 45-46 (on the abundance of fish and how fishing was done). The fishing industry was so important that its revenues (*remda do arequim*) were the most important source of non-customs related income during the Portuguese period.

these products nor in sheep, goats and cattle, which peasants brought to the city by boat.³⁴

The Dutch mentioned the marketing of Muscat loaf sugar in Bandar Abbas in 1651.³⁵ In 1676 Batavia had become much worried about "the continued cultivation and culture of sugar on the coast of Arabia caused more and more oversupply in Persia and will be damaging for our trade."³⁶

> Sugar, which apart from dates is the country's only produce, is cultivated to some considerable extent around the surrounding places or towns, viz. Semmed (Samad), Menneh (Manah), Behlah (Bahlah), Sahrel, Gabbie (Ghabbi) and in particular near Nizwa where sugar, also from the other places, is pressed and manufactured. The Imam or some merchants also purchase sugar cane in the areas where it is cultivated and has it brought to Nizwa, for it is only here that loaf-sugar is manufactured. There the Imam jointly owns the two biggest mills with a merchant who has a quarter share. The sugar manufactured by others is of little importance. The drier the air, the better and whiter is the sugar. The sugar-cane is sown in the soil between March and April and cut in December. The sugar having been milled, it is put into bags of 25 *man*-e Muscat [one *man* = 8 lbs.] and consists of three qualities: cabessa (*cabeça* or head), bariga (*barriga* or belly), and pe (*pé* or foot), or in Arabic, 'saugatje' (*sawghat* or easy to swallow), 'amboneh' (*anbuh*?), and 'challal'

---

34. Kaempfer, *Die Reisetagebücher*, p. 149. For Omani products see also Anonymous, *Relãçao das plantas*, p. 12, which included vegetables, grapes, onions and some wheat.
35. NA, KA 1077, Sarcerius to Batavia (25/03/1651), f. 580; Bocarro, *Livro das plantas*, p. 52 and Anonymous, *Relãçao das plantas*, p. 12 already mentioned this product in 1633 or thereabouts.
36. Coolhaas, *Generale Missieven*, vol. 4, p. 92 (07/02/1676). "Their horses they mostly get from Garick (Khark) and Persia. They buy them young, feed and train them here and then sell them as Arab horses." Floor, "A description," p. 31.

(*halal* or permissible). The price of sugar fluctuates in proportion to the level of imports of that sweet produced by the Hon. Company in Persia. The ordinary price of the first quality is in Muscat 100 to 105, of the second quality 90 to 95, and of the third quality 80 to 85 *laris*. It is hard to learn how much is manufactured and exported it each year, because it is taken from Nizwa to the various sea-ports by camels and from there it is dispatched by ship to numerous countries. Moreover, the cultivation of sugar-cane crop depends whether previously good profits have been made on its yield. We were told that this country produces more than 5,000 to 6,000 chests of 22 Muscat *man*, of which Persia takes more than two-thirds; the remainder is taken to Bahrijn (Bahrain), al-Hasa, Bassura (Basra) and Mokha.[37]

Padbrugge noted that the Omanis outside Muscat:

> excel in agriculture and in the animal rearing, mainly rams, goats, and camels, which are of two kinds and quality. With regard to kind the difference is whether they have one or two humps on their back, like the dromedary. With regard to their quality the biggest difference amounts to the following: whether they can travel in one day from the court of Nizwa to Muscat, which normally may take four days. Such animals are mostly kept as riding camels. They assert that they are as easy to handle as horses, but we have experienced the opposite, for our ribs were creaking. That they are fast is true, this we saw when the Imam with his camel men passed us. ... They also breed mules, but these are smaller than the Persian ones and hard to distinguish from them.[38]

---

37. Floor, "A description," p. 31.
38. Floor, "A description," p. 27; see also Ovington, J. *A voyage to Surat in the year 1689* ed. H. G. Rawlinson (London, 1929), p. 246; Bocarro, *Livro das plantas*, p. 52.

In general both rich and poor lived very frugally. Their food mostly consisted of sun-dried whey, which was then softened between two stones. They ate it with some dates or rice and salt or fresh fish; sometimes with a little meat.[39]

Trades and Crafts

There were many people engaged in trades and crafts to serve Muscat's population as well as its maritime and commercial activities. However, in particular, it would seem that the Omani artisanal sector was not well developed.

> Trade and handicrafts are mostly carried out by the Sindis and Banyans in which pattern the prisoners from Diu can easily fit. Nevertheless, one finds many Arab gunsmiths and sword cutlers, anchor and bullet smiths, but they do not have the knowledge to smelt and cast iron. The coppersmiths make everyday consumer products quite well and properly. The hammers (*hamelslagen*) have not been well designed like ours, about which Dutch coppersmiths are very surprised. These consist of a very tiny grip which they bend a little; the hammering is done with red oxide which sticks very well to the copper. It also makes it more pliant and only fills the *duppen* or hammer dents and leaves the bosses elevated, which therefore are only hit by the hammer and evened out. We have made a large order for this red oxide in Persia so that our own coppersmiths may investigate it. How tar and paint are rubbed in to interchange between dark and red and new light red; how suitable it is for painting, the better it dries is perfectly known to Your Honour. There are several beautiful pieces of cannon (*clockspijs*) idle and totally unused due to the lack of good master craftsmen who might repair the widely burnt open fuse holes. The tinning with

---

39. Floor, "A description," p. 35. Ovington, *A voyage*, p. 248 gave a more positive picture of the food situation in Muscat.

Sal ammoniac is also very common here as in Persia, because all their pots, vessels, and plates are made of copper. They also know how to turn materials rather nicely and small, because the beads of their rosaries, which the Catholics call *pater noster*, all have to be turned, in which they have some dexterity. The potters are very good in glazing, but they are unfortunate in either having no good clay or not knowing well how to prepare it. They do not prepare the lead-ash for the glazing [process] as we do it by constantly stirring the melted lead with an iron claw. They just drop the molten lead in water, then take it out of the water again; they smelt it once more and pour it again in the water, and so on. This has to be a very slow process. But to return to the sifting, the ashes become cleaner, because only the thinnest and lightest particles mix with the water. To this one adds crushed and sifted charcoal and in this way the glue for the glazing is ready. This produces a red color or black when it is a little more heated or when some black [color] has been added. One gets a yellow or yellow-green color if one adds copper ashes in greater or lesser quantities to it.[40]

Therefore, it comes as no surprise that for example, Padbrugge reported that carpenters, in particular ship's carpenters, were in short supply and generally less competent than their European counterparts. Padbrugge stated that "With regard to other crafts [such as carpentry, brick-laying, silver and gold-smithing, etc.] they are not very good (*geen overvliegers*), therefore, these crafts are mostly taken up by the Sindis and Banyans."[41] In 1672, during the discussion with Padbrugge, his Omani interlocutors only once asked whether the VOC could supply them with carpenters. "However, when they heard how much these people earned they did not raise this matter again." This probably led to a better welcome of the two Englishmen who were staying in Muscat and who

---

40. Floor, "A description," pp. 29-30. The word *clokspijse* actually means the metal of which cannons are cast, but that does not make sense here.
41. Floor, "A description," p. 30.

had been well received by Sheikh Abdallah. On his departure, Padbrugge found that one of them, a carpenter, was instructing Omani carpenters how to repair damaged ships.[42]

System of Government

The Imam appointed a governor or *vali* to each town or district, who governed that jurisdiction on his behalf. This was also the case in Muscat. It was the governor's task "to administer justice on behalf of the Imam, to collect the country's revenues, to pay the militia remit. The remainder (for they keep tight strings on their purse) was put in the *beyt al-mal* or the State treasury, of which only the Imam is in charge. He administers it very honestly in such a way, that apart from a certain amount which he may use himself, it is solely used for the country's welfare and he (if one may believe it) does not even take one penny for his own upkeep. This amount is so small that we do not dare mention it in order to avoid appearing untruthful."[43]

Sometimes a qadi or judge was also appointed below the governor, whose task was "to see to that all court cases are scrupulously dealt with in accordance with their laws irrespective of persons and without connivance." There were no court houses, for justice was performed in public, in the open air, usually "in front of the governor's house or that of the Imam's courtyard, when he is in Muscat." The majority of cases were those between disputing merchants. "These cases, whatever their nature, are immediately judged by the governor who also gives his verdict at once."[44] As to these various laws Wilmson makes the following observations:

> In general, nobody may be beaten, let alone killed, because of some crime he has committed. However, they are not

---

42. Floor, "A description," pp. 11-12.
43. Floor, "A description," pp. 31, 34. On the term *beyt al-mal* see the relevant article in the *Encyclopedia of Islam*².
44. Floor, "A description," p. 34. For some of the their legal rules see Ibid., pp. 34-35.

very particular [about this law] when beating Banyans and other nonbelievers, whom they often treat rather harshly when they have to pay taxes.

All crimes, including murder, are punished by imprisonment, which is heavier or lighter in accordance with the crime committed. Although their law forbids execution, a human cannot live long in the prisons, which are subterranean and in the water, where one almost will die, because of the dirt and smell.

It is strictly forbidden to drink intoxicants. Both the seller thereof as well as those found drunk are punished with very long imprisonment. Nevertheless one finds more than ten to twelve araq shops, where intoxicants may be had for the heavy punishment is little feared, because of the high profits.

A slave who is tired of his master and takes an oath that he is a free man is considered to be free without recourse.

A witness is not allowed when the defendant states that he is an enemy.

Private contracts are invalid however, those registered with the *wali* [governor] are valid in law.

In a transaction, if one thinks to have been deceived, one does not have to fulfill the obligation.

After the beating of the drum nobody in Muscat is allowed to have a light or lamp burning. Those who are found out with it [i.e. lit lamps] are punished with the legal penalty.[45]

There was further a *shahbandar* in charge of the customs administration as well as the weigh-house, which was next to the Dutch factory

---

45. The drinking of coffee, the consumption of *bhang*, and the smoking of tobacco were all forbidden. Those who imported these latter two goods were severely punished and the goods burnt. All games were also forbidden. Public fornication is forbidden on pain of imprisonment and banishment, and the same holds for sodomy, "nevertheless the leading citizens are mostly afflicted with it. It is why we have seen that poor people who don't even have a piece of cloth to cover their knees and were found with naked knees were taken to the prison." Floor, "A description," pp. 34-35.

"and we believe that previously it was a water-gate, for during the Portuguese period it has been fit for that purpose, but no longer. The year of construction is stated in Roman letters on top of the gate and to the best of our memory [it was] 1624."[46] It was the *shahbandar* who in 1674 came to the Dutch factory to count and weigh the VOC merchandise and who calculated the amount of customs due. As previously mentioned, through these officials, the Imam controlled the finances, weigh-bridge and the defense of Muscat and he used only people of his own lineage and that of Sheikh Abdallah to run the administration. Sheikh Abdallah was the governor as of late 1671, one of his brothers was master of the weigh-bridge and the customs, and another brother was tax collector and in charge of the treasury in Nizva. All other functionaries in Muscat such as comptrollers of the weighbridge and tax officials were of the same lineage.[47]

To defend his country against invasion, "According to Galiel (Khalil), the Imam had 15,000 men in arms from Jolphaar (Julfar) until the main hook of Rasal Gatte (Ra's al-Hadd), both along the beach doing guard duty as well as in the fortresses."[48] However, according to Wilmson's observations, "The sea-towns which have fortresses and in which the Imam keeps soldiers are: Coriaat (Quryat), Muscat, Sohar, and Julfar or Cier,[49] which is situated on the inner side of Cape Musandam. Other small places with only redoubts were also to be found. Quite a few were situated on the coast with a force of five, six, eight to ten men of which places Muscat was the most important and "the key of Arabia."[50]

> The city [of Muscat] itself, situated in a plain between the two fortresses, has been enclosed in front and rear by a wall,

---

46. Floor, "A description," p. 25.
47. Floor, "A description," pp. 18, 56; NA, VOC 1288, Report Padbrugge, f. 444vs.
48. Floor, "A description," p. 27.
49. Sir, often identified as Abu Dhabi (e.g. by Badger) and discussed by Slot, *Arab al-Khalij*, pp. 40-41 as a place located somewhere between Sharjah and Musandam. Niebuhr said it took its name from the residence of the Qawasem Sheikh so it should certainly be between Sharjah and Jolfar (Ras al-Khaimah).
50. Floor, "A description," p. 32.

while on the east side there are inaccessible mountains. Thus, nature has made this place so strong that it only needs a small garrison [to ward off] enemies who come from outside. Ordinarily, the Imam only keeps little more than 100 to 150 soldiers in his service, If he expects an enemy the Wali sends for 300 to 400 peasants from the surrounding villages, who then on this order come to serve the Imam with their guns, pikes, swords and shields, and that only for simple and frugal fare. The castles in the town are equipped with only a few cannons, similarly with ammunition; in all their fortresses there are water-passageways; along the bay there are more than fifty pieces, amongst which are even eighteen and twenty-four pounders of metal; the remainder are iron cannons, which they take from and return to the ships according to their need.[51]

According to the Dutch merchant Padbrugge, "Most of the Imam's soldiers were from the Sindi coast, but recently he dismissed most of them, because he had to pay them. Now he uses his own people, who as soon as they are discharged return to their homes and work. Even important merchants volunteer for military operations out of love they assert for their country, but they also draw their pay and rations. The Imam at present has not more than 250 soldiers."[52] This maybe explains what Kaempfer wrote: "The soldiers looked as if they were pious, long-bearded respected village priests and clerics rather than martial warriors."[53] Their arms consisted of a sword and a dagger, but often also:

a good matchlock, [of the kind where] the cock hammers down, being forced by the lever (*beer*) and reaches the pan with a burning fuse, whose fuse is thin, firm, nicely and well designed, well carbonized and made of cotton. Usually the

---

51. Floor, "A description," p. 32. For a description of the arms and equipment of the soldiers, which they had to buy themselves, see Idem, p. 27.
52. NA, VOC 1288, f. 445; Floor, "A description," p. 63, n. 130.
53. Kaempfer, *Die Reisetagebücher*, p. 150.

fuse is fixed with one end attached to the lock. The butt-end is very short and small. The rammer is made of iron, thin, and touches the cheek, the thumb is under the nose, and they put their elbow level and stand in proper position. They shoot very straight. The powderhorn is hanging in different ways, and the same holds for the small horn with loading powder, some have it on the right, while others have it on their back. Poor soldiers who have no mantle are often found [wearing] only a robe over which they have a bad dress (*rockie*). But there are few of them. Everyone is free to choose the kind of gun of his own liking. They have to pay for it themselves, about which they are proud. That is why one mostly sees nice-looking (*sinnelijk*) matchlocks, which, however, are all top-heavy. Very few have half-pikes amongst which one observes those which are of iron. This must be very awkward, because the shaft is not thicker than that of a normal curtain-pole. According to Gail (Khalil) the Imam had 15,000 men at arms from Jolphaar (Jolfar) until the main hook of Rasal Gatte (Ra's al-Hadd), both along the beach doing guard duty as well as in the fortresses.

Wilmson reported that neither the Imam nor the Portuguese used the Baluchis (or Sindis) as soldiers, but only as sailors. When the Omani fleet sailed on 23 January 1673 Wilmson explicitly watched out for Baluchis and observed that among the crews many Baluchis were to be found. In 1672, the Baluchis had come in great number with their families in barques from Kij-Makran during the Persian invasion of their territory.[54] Wilmson also states that the Baluchis were well known as good soldiers and good shots. Merchants used them as soldiers on voyages to Mokha, Sind and India and paid them well, namely 18 to 20 *laris* per month exclusive of the right to ship some goods free of charge. Wilmson did not investigate whether Baluchis would be willing to sign on with the VOC for voyages of two to three years' length, because he

---

54. Floor, *Five Port Cities*, p. 363.

had been ordered not to do so. He also wanted to prevent the Omanis thinking that the VOC needed soldiers.[55] As stated previously, Wilmson further noted:

> that every time the Portuguese fleet sailed into the Gulf, the Omanis had to take cannons and crews and navigators from the mercantile fleet to man and arm their war fleet. This was an important handicap in mounting operations against the Portuguese, which had been put off many times. On several occasions the war drum had been beaten and not enough men had presented themselves. ... Their crews were inexperienced men such as porters, fishermen, boatmen etc. amongst whom were many Baluchis. If prospects for booty looked bright there were sufficient recruits, but when the enemy fleet was expected to be at sea it was hardly possible to find anyone. Soldiers were recruited from the outlying villages at 9 to 12 *laris* per month. Their tactics were of a hit and run kind rather than of protracted resistance, for the Omani ships soon disengaged when the opposition was fierce. There was no discipline among the fleet, and if a crew did not want to fight it just did not partake in the battle. They also lacked a proper commander of the fleet or *saran* as they called him, while they do not know how to handle cannons either.[56]

To finance the government, the Imam not only taxed international trade, but also all his subjects and their property, local trade and agricultural output, in accordance with the relevant Islamic religious injunctions. In 1672, according to Georg Wilmson, the rates for these various activities were as follows:

---

55. Floor, "A description," p. 58, n. 55; NA, VOC 1304, Report Wilmson, f. 482 vs.
56. Floor, "A description," p. 17. *Saran* probably is *sarhang*, a Persian word meaning 'general, commander, captain, chief.'

Taxes. We were told that the taxes which the Arab inhabitants as well as the other Moors are obliged to pay yearly are the following,

Everyone is obliged to pay 2.5 percent of all his cash, silver and gold, including the jewelry of children and women, also on their copperware, [such as] pots and pans, etc. each year.[57]

Of all grain that is sown, when it is harvested, of each 100 *parra*s, three *parra*s[58] [have to be paid].

From sugar nothing is levied before it has been marketed, then 2.5 percent is taken from the proceeds.

Dates, be it dry or [wet] in packages, pay for each 100 *man* ten *man*.

Animals. Of 100 camels one every year; of 50 a small one. Of 100 sheep, rams or goats also one.

Poll-tax. Everyone, be it man, woman, child or slave has to pay 0.5 ma. [*mahmudi*] each year. This is money for the poor and is collected after the end of their month of fasting.

All those Banyans who trade have to pay for 0.5 *lari* per person, per month. This is a fixed rule. However, they are sometimes 'shorn in proportion to their quantity of wool,' and some pay double or treble this amount. In exchange, they are exempt from paying the annual *zeekat* [*zakat*],[59] which is levied on the Moors. This [tax] yields annually 120 to 130 *tumans*. In addition, some Indian Banyans have thirty to forty houses (*land huiz*) for which they pay annually 12,000 *laris*.

---

57. For further information on Islamic taxation regulation, see the article "Kharadj" in the *Encyclopedia of Islam*².
58. A *parra* is an Indian weight used for transactions in grain measures of capacity. Twenty *parra*s are equal to one *candi* or *kandi*, or about 500 lbs. In the nineteenth century the *parra* or *farah* as it was also called, consisted "of 40 *sidi*s, and 2 1/2 *farah*s of ordinary wheat are equal to 2 Karachi maunds." Lorimer, *Gazetteer*, vol. 2, p. 1188.
59. *Zakat* or alms tax, one of the principal religious obligations of Islam, see 'Zakat, "*Encyclopedia of Islam*².

The shops of the bazaar yield more than 18,000 *laris* annually. In addition to that, they also have to pay a considerable sum for the ground rent of their houses, the precise figure we have been unable to learn.

Ships (*barquen*). When the owner of a barque sails to some place with freight he has to pay 2.5 percent for half, which is his loss, the other half of the freight is for the crew and he pays nothing.[60]

International Trade in Muscat.

Muscat carried on a sometimes lively trade with Sind, West India, East Africa, Yemen and with ports in the Persian Gulf itself. Both the volume and direction of trade was, of course, subject to ups-and-downs, both a function of international/regional developments as well as internal ones. Muscat was not the only port that traders visited on the Omani coast. Jolfar also was a good harbor, "where many Indian barques carrying money, come to buy Dates, and pearls which are Fished all along that Coast from mascat to bahrem; there is a good Castle at Julfar."[61] Muscat trade was mostly with Sind, Kutch, Patan, Konkan, i.e. Rajapur and other ports held by the Shivaji, Surat, Karwar, the Canarese and Malabar Coast, Mokha, Aden, Malindi (East Africa) and the Maldives. The imports were mostly textiles, rice and coffee, in addition to some minor products as well as 150-200 slaves. Muscat's own exports were limited to dates, loaf-sugar, horses, and cash. Muscat also exported some Persian and Indian goods to its trading partners, but the range of products and its volume was limited. Muscat was not the final market for most of the imports (with the exception of rice), but a point of transshipment. The majority of products were forwarded to the smaller Safavid Persian ports, Basra, Bahrain, Qatar and Hasa.[62]

---

60. Floor, "A description," p. 37.
61. Thevenot, *Travels*, vol. 2, p. 182. Bahrem is Bahrain.
62. For detailed description of what was imported and exported from Muscat and to/from which port in 1673, see Annex 2.

On arrival in the bay of Muscat, which was closed by an iron chain each arriving vessel was met by a guard-vessel, which ascertained whether the new arrival was friend or foe and the nature of its business. If a friend and mercantile, the ship was allowed into the inner bay, but it had to stow its sails. When the ship came to anchor, a guard was put on board, who stayed there until the ship departed. Nobody was allowed to leave the ship or come aboard after sunset. Likewise, no ship was allowed to depart before having shown a pass to the guards at the western water passage-way. Some ships only came to get water and firewood, but many came to trade. Those unloaded their cargo with lighters, which was then taken to the weigh-house where the goods were weighed, counted and sealed (in case of textiles). All goods had to be unloaded, unless an arrangement had been agreed prior to entering the inner-harbor.[63]

> Weighable goods are mainly packed according to a standard weight and are taken to the merchants' houses after having been counted and registered. If part of it is sold, the goods have to be taken to the weigh-house to be weighed; here the buyer's and seller's names, the date and the price of the transaction are also recorded in order to calculate the amount of tolls to be paid after the end of the monsoon or on departure of each ship. If the year has expired and some goods are still unsold, no toll is demanded however until they are sold or transported elsewhere.
>
> **Textiles** (*cleeden*) are taken to the weigh-house, are registered and on each pack a seal is affixed, so that they cannot be changed. Nobody is allowed to open any pack in his house without the presence of an official. The settling of the toll account to be paid is done in the same as with the weighable goods.[64]

---

63. Floor, "A description," p. 49.
64. Floor, "A description," p. 41. For the rates paid in the weigh-house, which varied per product, see Idem, p. 47.

The weights used at Muscat in the 1670s were as follows:

Table 3.1: Weights used in Muscat (1673)

Name	Subdivision (in *man* of 8 lbs.)	Weight equivalent (in lbs.)
Great *bahar*	200	1,600
Small *bahar*	80	640
Candi	60	480
Feraseleh (*farsaleh*)	10	80
Mandilij (*man* of Delhi)	3	24
Man of Muscat	1	8
20 *parren*	Equals one *candi* of rice, wheat, etc. *	

* For an explanation of the various weight terms see Hinz, Walther. *Islamische Masse und Gewichte* (Leiden, 1970), Willem Floor, "Weights and Measures in Qajar Iran," *Studia Iranica* 37/1 (2008), pp. 57-115, and Yule, *Hobson-Jobson*.

Source: Floor, A description," pp. 49-50.

After having being taken to the customs-house (*bangsar*) and the weigh-house, the goods were permitted to be taken to the merchant's house or lodgings. As of around 1670 the brokerage for all trade and Muscat's weigh-house had been farmed by a Banyan, called Thewil for an amount of 30,000 *laris*. In addition he also farmed 30-40 houses.[65]

> He appoints for each ship a broker to whom they are obliged to pay 1½ per cent of all items sold. One per cent is for the main-broker (i.e. Thewil) and ½ per cent for his deputy broker; yes, even for the freight-goods which a ship takes from here on its return voyage.

---

65. Floor, "A description," p. 47. In 1682, a Moslem merchant, Hajji Mohammad, farmed the administration of the customs-house in Muscat. NA, VOC 1379, Casembroot report (25/11/1682), f. 2721.

> Similarly, this broker allots to each ship or its crew one of
> the said houses for which he gets 5, 6 to 8 *abbasi*s depending
> on their size or location, until the day they leave. Someone
> who stays here until the end of the monsoon makes a
> contract with him for the second journey from the end of
> May or till the end of September or October for that whole
> period.

This did not include the brokerage for the horse trade, which was farmed separately and was held in 1673 by a man called Khalil, who had paid 1,600 *mahmudi*s. He recuperated his invested by charging 29 *lari*s per horse, of which buyer and seller paid half each. The farmer also charged rent for the area where the horses were corralled; a fee of two *mahmudi*s per head per month. He also received 10 *mahmudi*s for the transportation of each horse, of which the merchant and the ship's captain (*nakhoda*) each paid half.[66]

Initially the right of entrepot for all traders existed in Muscat, irrespective of the religion or origin. This meant that merchants did not have to pay customs duties, even when their merchandise had been taken ashore, or when the goods were forwarded to other ports or markets. This was changed in 1672, probably due the monopolistic position taken by the new governor Sheikh Abdallah, about which later. Under the new rules, "both Moors and Banyans have to pay the legal toll on all goods, which are taken ashore. However, if a ship continues its journey, only a toll is levied on goods taken ashore or transshipped; in case of Moors sometimes allowances are made." There was no export duty, because an import duty had already been paid, while all local produce (loaf-sugar, dates, etc.) did not have to pay any export duties.[67]

After the conquest of Muscat, the Ya'arabi Imam initially levied no customs duties, neither from Moslems or non-Moslems. In fact, according to Wilmson when he arrived in Muscat it was the very first time that Banyans had to pay customs duties. "Those who possessed a house

---

66. Floor, "A description," pp. 47-48.
67. Floor, "A description," p. 47.

(*landshuis*) in the country had to pay 5 and others 10 per cent. Therefore everybody was forced to take a house in the country, even though it was only a shop." Moslems had to pay 2.5 per cent (the *zakat* rate). On return from a voyage no duties were levied from them if they had a document showing that they had paid their taxes. "However, they have to make so many voyages with their merchandise that they have to pay tolls every time and to show documentary proof thereof at the place of their residence."[68] The rates were raised to 5% in 1671/72 and even to 7.5%.[69] The introduction of higher rates coincided with the temporary closure of the port to foreign vessels, internal political troubles in Oman and the overture to peace with the Portuguese as discussed below.[70] Klein suggested that rather than a quadrupling of rates, new rates were introduced reflecting Ibadi law, i.e. low rates for Moslems (*zakat* rate), a higher one for *dhimmi*s (adherent to an officially tolerated non-Moslem religion) and the highest for those living in the *dar al-harb*, i.e. lands outside of Moslem rule as well as unbelievers. However, in actual practice this rule was not strictly adhered to.[71] In 1673, Moslem merchants paid 2.5%; Banyans who had been exempt, then had to pay 5%, if they could prove that they were homeowners, in which case they were charged with a heavy real estate tax, otherwise the rate was 10%. A high rate of 8% was charged to Moslems and Banyans coming from pagan-held lands, such as Kutch as well as from Shivaji-held lands.[72]

---

68. Floor, "A description," pp. 46-47.
69. NA, VOC 1279, de Haze to Batavia (16/05/1672), f. 955 suggests that there was a flat rate for all merchants, however.
70. NA, VOC 1259, van Wijck to Batavia (12/03/1666), f. 3311 (customs duties raised to 10%); Coolhaas, *Generale Missieven*, vol. 3, p. 598 (05/10/1667).
71. NA, VOC 1259, Gamron to Batavia (12/03/1666), f. 3311. On Ibadi law see Wilkinson, *The Imamate Tradition*, p. 181.
72. Floor, "A description," p. 46.

Table 3.2: Customs duties charged at Muscat in 1673

Country	Moslems or Moslem-owned goods in %	Banyans in %	Remarks
Sind	2.5	5	
Kutch	8	8	Higher rate because it was ruled by an infidel
Patan	2.5	8	
Surat	2.5	5	
Rajapur	8	8	Because it is in the realm of the Shivaji
Vengurla	8	8	
Karwar	2.5	-	
Basrur, Mangalore, Bhatkal	17.5	17.5	Because that is the rate that the Omanis had to pay
Basra	2.5	5	
Persia	2.5	5	
Mokha	2.5	5	

Source: Floor, "A description," p. 46.

One of the main problems in the 1670s was that trade arrangements as well the customs rates that were lowered or increased based on political expediency and economic self-interest. The Imam's *vakil* or agent controlled the customs-house and trade itself, because he insisted on his right of first purchase. Nobody was allowed to sell or buy anything without Sheikh Abdallah's permission. The Malabar trade (coconuts, pepper, spices, coir, construction wood) was almost exclusively reserved for him. Sheikh Abdallah in general was only interested in so-called weighable products (rice, pepper, spices), but also in textiles. He kept most of these goods until the end of the trading season to drive up prices, for he only sold when profits were high. These goods were then distributed over the Persian Gulf ports. Only the Imam was allowed to buy military goods such as coir ropes, planks, masts, cannon, and iron, i.e. all goods needed to outfit the navy. What he did not need was resold in the market.⁷³ To tilt the market to his advantage Sheikh Abdallah changed the rules when it suited him. Sometimes he bought an entire ship's cargo sometimes a part thereof. The ship's *nakhoda* had to present himself to Sheikh Abdallah's house with the bill of lading and a sample of his merchandise. Although many Banyan merchants were also present only Sheikh Abdallah was allowed to make a bid for the goods. He invariably bid lower than the going market rate, but the *nakhoda* had to accept it else he was thrown into prison. The goods bought by Sheikh Abdallah were then taken ashore to the weigh-house and from there to the Imam's warehouse. The *nakhoda*'s remaining goods he took to his own lodgings, but he was allowed to sell them only after permission from Sheikh Abdallah. To be exempt from these impositions, some merchants made a separate settlement with Sheikh Abdallah, i.e. they paid him a lump sum. In exchange for this payment, merchants were allowed to sell their goods to the highest bidder. Even then he might interfere, for it could happen that after a transaction and the goods were being weighed, Sheikh Abdallah liked the price (or rather the expected profit) and he then forced the buyer to accept him as a partner for half of the purchased goods. It even happened that when rice in bulk yielded a higher price than bagged rice he forced the sellers of bagged rice (who already had paid customs duties to be allowed to sell their goods freely) to sell their rice in bulk.⁷⁴

As to export products, the Imam also was a major player in the market. He was a major producer of loaf-sugar, as discussed above, and thus also dominated this market segment. The other important export product, horses was also under the Imam's (or rather his agent's) control. Not all horses sold in Muscat came from Oman, for each year the Imam sent an agent to Safavid Persia to buy 20 to 30 horses. In addition, 200 to 300 other horses were sold to Indian merchants, who mostly exported them to Konkan (Kerala). Many, if not all of them, also came from Safavid Persia for Persian horse traders kept many horses in stables in Muscat. However, the purchase of horses was conditional upon having

---

73. Floor, "A description," p. 45.
74. Floor, "A description," pp. 43-46.

bought one or more horses from the Imam's agent. Sometimes, the merchants had to buy all the Imam's horses, before he allowed others to be sold. To make high prices the Imam's agent usually waited with the sale till the end of the monsoon.[75]

Despite the dominant and oligopolistic role of the Imam's agent, Sheikh Abdallah trade flourished. This was partly due to the fact that both Seyf b. Sultan (1680-1692) and Sultan b. Seyf I (1692 - 15 Oct 1711) promoted trade and expanded the wealth that they inherited.[76] The Imam owned ships which were mainly involved in trade with the Red Sea and East Africa.[77] Further, it was partly due to the fact that the trade of Muscat was entirely controlled by a group of Indian merchants associated with the Imam's agent, the admirals of the Muscat war fleet and tribal notables. This made it easier for West Indian merchants to call on Muscat, for they were bound by ethnic, religious and in many cases also by family relations. The mercantile community of Muscat was small; most came from Sind, Gujarat and Kerala.[78] There were two important Arab wholesale merchants, Esma'il al-Basri and Esma'il Bandari, who as their names suggest had links with Muscat's two main markets, i.e. Basra and Bandar Abbas.[79] Also, there were some Armenian traders who called on Muscat.[80] The Sindis played a special role with regard to textiles.

> From the textiles which are brought here from there [i.e. Sind], of the 800 packs, Muscat consumes little more than one quarter; the remainder is taken to Bahrain, Katijf (al-Qatif), Qatar, Basra and Persia in the following manner. Those from Sind have their representatives here to whom

---

75. Floor, "A description," pp. 30, 48.
76. Ross, *Annals*, p. 56.
77. Floor, "A description," p. 40.
78. *ANTT*, DRI LIX, f. 86r-vs; Floor, "A description," p. 45; Allen, "The Indian Merchant," pp. 39-53; Foster, *English Factories*, vol. 5, pp. 126-27; Barendse, *Arabian Seas*, p. 344.
79. Floor, "A Description," p. 61, n. 94.
80. Meier-Lemgo, K. *Die Briefe E. Kaempfers* (Mainz, 1965), pp. 267-314, no. 25; Baladouni and Makepeace, *Armenian Merchants*, pp. 39, 246.

they send their goods each year. These keep all that is consumed in Muscat and send the rest to the said places to other representatives who mostly reside there on their behalf to sell these goods. They send the proceeds mostly via Congo (Bandar-e Kong) back to Sind.[81]

Muscat also gained wealth from Mecca pilgrims who came from India, and "it was much frequented by Merchants over the Deserts, and no less by those of Mocha in the Red Sea, and by the way of Grand Cairo; it vends all Drugs and Arab steeds, and pays Gold for Indian Commodities: Here they keep safe those Ships they steal or purchase, for Wood, nor Timber growing here."[82]

Because like other markets in the Persian Gulf, Muscat also had a negative trade balance with India the lack of exportable goods was compensated for by the export of specie. It would appear that Muscat itself did not coin its own money. In 1673 the following coins were in use:

> The money which is current is abbasis, five shahis, and *mahmudis*. The small coins are [made of] spiaulter (zinc), and were introduced by the Portuguese and are still used. Their rate is 31 to 32 to one *mahmudi* depending whether many of them are brought from the other side of the Gulf, where they used to be coined in former times. Silver coins are full, half, quart and eight *laris*, which are exported by the Indians, who import others consisting of half copper, a reason why this trade had finally been forbidden altogether.[83]

---

81. Floor, "A Description," p. 41. For a breakdown of the kind and quantity of fabrics consumed in Muscat in 1672, see Annex 2.
82. Fryer, *A New Account*, vol. 2, p. 156.
83. Floor, "A Description," pp. 31-32. The zinc coins most likely were struck in Goa, Diu, Daman and Chaul and the alloy used was composed of copper (40.4%), zinc (25.4%), nickel (31.6%), and iron (2.6%). Teixeira de Aragão, *Descrição geral e histórica das moedas cunhadas em nome dos reis, regentes e governadores de Portugal*, 3 vols (Lisbon, 1874-80), vol. 3; Vaz, J. Ferraro and Sousa, M. Correia de. *Dinheiro luso-indiano (Indo-Portuguese Money)* (Braga, 1980).

Conclusion

The fall of Hormuz in 1622 did not lead to the rise of Muscat, although the Portuguese had certainly hoped that it would. This was not only due to the fact that the Dutch and English had started trading in Bandar Abbas, but more importantly, the Portuguese instead of being friendly with the Safavids now considered them enemies as well. Therefore, they strengthened and formalized their relationship with Basra, whose governor also received Portuguese military assistance when attacked by the Safavids. To further 'defeat' the Safavids the Portuguese began a decade-long reign of terror in the Persian Gulf, led and orchestrated by Rui Freire de Andrade. Although the Portuguese fought a sometimes fierce rear-guard battle they finally had to give in to the superior naval power of the Dutch and English and not only lost their control over the Persian Gulf, but over the Indian Ocean as well. By 1614, its possessions on the Persian littoral had already been incorporated in the Safavid kingdom, while most of its Omani possessions lasted another 20 years before they all gradually started to fall into the hands of the Ya`ariba Imam, a process that was completed by January 1650.

Continued Portuguese control over Muscat was problematic. This entailed a heavy military expenditure due to the need to maintain a standing fleet, a large number of troops (240% more soldiers in 1630 than in 1603) and the construction of a significant number of forts between 1620 and 1624. The result was that the Portuguese lost money in the Persian Gulf, because Muscat was a budget drain. Moreover, they had no access to the Safavid Persian market. This was finally corrected by the agreement of 1630 giving them access to that market via the port of Bandar-e Kong and formally, although not in actual practice, to half of its customs revenues. Muscat's main role remained that of a forwarding station for the Sind-Basra trade. Neither the Dutch nor English were active there before 1636, which allowed the Portuguese unhindered access to the upper Persian Gulf. However, by that time, the Portuguese had lost the war for supremacy in the Persian Gulf to the Dutch and English. Also, at that time, the Ya`ariba Imam had begun his inexorable progress to oust the Portuguese from all their positions along the Omani coast, a process completed by January 1650. By then, the Portuguese were a spent force and after 1652 they were no longer involved in any direct commercial activities in the Persian Gulf.

Instead of trying to come to some kind of peace agreement with Oman, the Portuguese could not accept the fact that they had lost.[84] Therefore, they tried to regain Muscat by seeking allies among those sheikhs that did not like Ya`ariba rule. This policy forced the Imam of Oman to attack the Portuguese wherever his ships would encounter them. At the same time, the Imam was trying to build a commercial fleet. To do so, starting with very little, the Omanis also engaged in piracy to boost their commercial start-up. Since the Portuguese responded in the same vein, it was no surprise, even if the Imam had not declared the *jihad* against them, that the Omanis took the war to the Portuguese possessions in India and Africa, where they also had commercial interests. In the ensuing war between Omanis and Portuguese, few warships were taken or sunk, but many merchantmen of both sides were taken.[85] Hatred for the Portuguese did not change the multi-ethnic character of the town of Muscat. Although the Omanis did not necessarily like or appreciate other beliefs, they tolerated the presence of their adherents in Muscat to assist and maintain the commercial and infrastructural development of the port. The town did not grow much in size and depended for crafts and many of the trades on Indians (Baluchis, Sindis, Banyans), Jews and others.

Meanwhile, the Ya`ariba Imamate developed its own agricultural resources and foreign trade. Muscat, which was able to attract much trade from India, Yemen and Africa, served as one of the points of transshipment in the Persian Gulf. This development came under serious threat when the Portuguese began a major naval offensive against Muscat between 1667 and 1675. Politically the Ya`ariba dynasty had been less

---

84. Martin makes several remarks about Portuguese conviction of their superiority so that they were disdainful of the abilities of their enemies. Although they paid dearly for this attitude they refused to change their attitude. Martin, *India*, vol. 1/2, p. 666, 690.
85. Hamilton, *A New Account*, vol. 1, p. 51.

successful. It felt threatened both externally and internally. The Imam even considered accepting an English presence in or near Muscat, when in 1659 the English were considering moving to Muscat, because of problems with the Safavid government. The internal opposition against Ya`ariba rule was still strong in Oman and the Portuguese tried to use it to their own advantage and find allies against the Imam. This rebelliousness at home, of course, handicapped Oman's ability to act more strongly externally. The new Portuguese offensive as of 1667 coincided with a serious political crisis within Oman. In 1672 the country was on the verge of revolt and only repression and the absence of a capable leader to head the discontent saved the Ya`ariba Imamate. The Imam's regime became so weak that it even sought to attract the Dutch to move operations to Muscat as well as to provide it with military assistance against the Portuguese. The Dutch declined to give military support (they were at peace with Portugal), but they came to Muscat and stayed for three years (1672-1675). They used it as a lookout to warn Dutch ships if there were English or French ships in the Persian Gulf, with whom they were at war at that time. When this threat disappeared the Dutch withdrew from Muscat in 1675. Under two very energetic Imams, Oman was able to overcome this period of weakness and internal dissent and emerged from it stronger than before. Trade continued to grow, and for a time (mainly during 1693-99 and 1714-19) a number of naval engagements took place between the Omanis and Portuguese in which the latter prevailed. The Omanis retaliated by destroying Bandar-e Kong, Diu, Mangalore and Mombasa, and even occupying the latter.[86] However, rather than aiming to replace the Portuguese in India the Omanis wanted to do that on the coast of East Africa. In this connection, it is of interest that the Omanis never attacked Dutch or English shipping and settlements. The Portuguese could have learnt something from this, but they were too obsessed with their right, pride, reputation and resentment that they never were able to seek a peace agreement with the Omanis to their own considerable cost.

---

86. See Subrahmanyam, *Portuguese Empire*, p. 191 for the argument that the Omani raids were one of the contributing factors for the decline of Diu.

Not only Portugal but also Safavid Persia felt threatened by the increasing Omani depredations, which led to two attacks on Bandar-e Kong (1695, 1714) and finally to attacks on Bahrain, Larek, Qeshm and Hormuz (1716-1719) and their occupation. The Safavid court began its drive for an anti-Omani league in the early 1690s and was able to get the Portuguese (1695-96) and the Dutch (1697) interested, but each time the Safavids were unable to hold up their end of the agreement. Thereafter, no other country was willing to respond positively to Safavid invitations for an invasion of Muscat and this was not for lack of Safavid trying. It is amazing that the Safavid court regularly raised this figment of its imagination, despite its lack of funds, troops, supplies, and the political and organizational ability to carry out a sustained military campaign to conquer Muscat. There was no doubt that many at the Safavid court, and the Shah foremost, believed that it was a good idea to attack Muscat, but so was hunting and carousing, and that was something that the effeminate and dissolute court could handle and finance, and that is what it continued to do until it was swept away in 1722. It reminds one of the incessant annually repeated refrain, or should one say credo, of the Portuguese that they should retake Hormuz, but without breaking the good relations with the Shah, which was another figment of the imagination.[87] Finally, in 1719 the Portuguese were once again willing to lend the Safavids a hand, which resulted in naval success, but not in Omani withdrawal. It was the civil war in Oman itself rather than Portuguese or Safavid actions that led to Omani abandonment of Larek and Qeshm as well as the handover of Bahrain in 1722. Muscat's military strength was sapped by the civil war, while commercially it was also weakened, a situation that was reinforced by the economic crisis that befell the entire Persian Gulf and its hinterlands due to the Afghan occupation of Safavid Persia. It would take a few decades before Muscat became a regional power again.

---

87. The Portuguese even raised the matter of the return of Hormuz in 1729. Matos, *Das relações*, pp. 357-58.

CHAPTER FOUR

THE SECOND PERIOD OF DUTCH-OMANI CONTACTS 1755-1806

Trade with Muscat was not something new for the VOC and it contemplated to start trading with Muscat again in 1756 and 1757. However, because these sales negatively impacted sales of its Khark factory, the VOC abandoned Muscat as a possible outlet for its merchandise. In 1766, the VOC abandoned the Persian Gulf trade altogether after it had been ousted from Khark Island, off the Persian coast. Nevertheless, the Dutch resumed trade with the area one decade later with direct voyages from Batavia to Muscat to sell sugar and some spices. However, these voyages were made by private Dutch merchants who bought their merchandise from the VOC. This chapter relates to the development and demise of the commercial contacts between the Dutch and Muscat in the second half of the eighteenth century.

INTRODUCTION

In 1756, when the VOC extended its trade to Muscat, the event greatly disturbed the EIC Council in Bombay and their superiors in London.

The English Company servants believed that the Dutch sought no less than complete control of the Persian Gulf. The English and some of the local chiefs such as Sheikh Naser of Bushehr took this view because the Dutch had first taken military action against the governor of Basra to force him to refund the money he extorted from VOC servants. This successful action was followed by the establishment of a factory, or rather a fortress on the island of Khark, while at the same time the Dutch factories in Basra and Bushehr were abandoned. The English, chagrined at the Dutch success, and believed that the latter would continue with their forceful policy and seize Bahrain. Such an operation was indeed proposed by von Kniphausen, the VOC Resident of the Khark factory. However, both the High Government at Batavia and the Company directors in the Netherlands had rejected the proposal.[1] In response to these Dutch activities, the English established a factory in Rig, but it was destroyed less than one year later by the chief of Rig, Mir Mohanna. The English were convinced that the Dutch at Khark were involved in this as well and probably were even the instigators.[2] A punitive expedition against Rig also failed and in that same year, the Dutch arrived with two large ships at Muscat.

The English were understandably apprehensive about Dutch encroachment on their position in the Persian Gulf, particularly as they had been ordered by the Court of Directors in London to advise it on "what new avenues may be opened" to expand their trade.[3] The fact that the Dutch had been able to settle in "one of the most important trade centres in the Gulf whose rulers had hitherto refused to allow any European to open a factory on their territories" must undoubtedly have alarmed the EIC directors.[4]

---

1. See Willem Floor, "The Bahrein Project of 1754," *Persica*, vol. 11 (1984), pp. 129-148.
2. See Willem Floor, *The Persian Gulf. The Rise of the Gulf Arabs. The Politics of trade on the northern Persian littoral 1730-1792* (Washington DC: MAGE, 2007).
3. A.A. Amin, *British Interests in the Persian Gulf 1747-1780* (Leiden, 1976), p. 146.
4. Amin, *British Interests*, p. 145.

However, the English did not know that there was no grand design for Dutch control of the Persian Gulf. Some VOC servants like von Kniphausen may have harbored such thoughts, but these were not shared by their superiors either in Batavia or Amsterdam. What appeared to have been a consistent Dutch commercial expansion policy was in fact merely a succession of uncoordinated and chance incidents that were in search of a policy. While it is true that Dutch activities at Basra, Khark, Bahrain, Bushehr and Rig were all engineered by von Kniphausen, not all of his actions had the approval of his superiors. Moreover, his activities had nothing to do with the events in Muscat, which he actually opposed.

Proposal for Annual Muscat Voyages

The idea of extending Dutch trade to Muscat originated with the VOC Resident in Bandar Abbas Jacob Schoonderwoerd. On 31 March 1755 he suggested to the High Government in Batavia that the VOC accept the invitation of the pasha of Baghdad to resume trade in Basra. He proposed that the Dutch remain on Khark and sent two assistants to Basra, who would order more goods from Khark once they had sold their existing stock. To enable them to do so Schoonderwoerd further suggested that one small barque be put at the disposal of the VOC staff in the Persian Gulf. This vessel might also be used to send goods from Bandar Abbas to Muscat at times when certain merchandise fetched higher prices there.[5]

Schoonderwoerd's suggestion was approved by Batavia and von Kniphausen was ordered to appraise its feasibility; the proposal to extend trade to Muscat was made conditional on his approval. This condition was of a formal nature rather than one of policy, for Schoonderwoerd, who until then had been the highest ranking VOC servant in the Persian Gulf, was to return to Batavia. Since he was succeeded by a lower ranking colleague, the High Government had decided to make the Khark factory the Residency of Dutch activities in the Persian Gulf. If von Kniphausen

---

5. NA, VOC 2803, Gamron to Batavia (31/03/1755), f. 18-19; see also Floor, *The Rise*, chapter four regarding the resumption of trade at Basra.

agreed to send surplus goods from Bandar Abbas to be sold in Muscat instead of Khark, Schoonderwoerd would be authorized to make the voyage to Muscat.[6] Seeing that the reply from von Kniphausen was not forthcoming, Schoonderwoerd decided to leave Bandar Abbas for Muscat on 29 December 1755.[7]

He arrived in Muscat on 7 January 1756 on board the *Vlietlust*. On arrival he was informed that the Imam of Muscat, Ahmad b. Sa'id (1744-1783) had come to the city a few days earlier from the royal residence at Rustaq. Schoonderwoerd went to pay his respects to the Imam, who received him warmly. Also, he told Schoonderwoerd that it would please him if the VOC established a factory in Muscat. He also inquired whether the Dutch might be able to supply him with a ship identical to the *Vlietlust* at cost price. Schoonderwoerd made it clear that he had no authority to commit the VOC on these matters. Moreover, he had to react cautiously, as the Imam might not agree to the price that the High Government would ask. Therefore, Schoonderwoerd offered his opinion that payment would have to be in advance of delivery for Batavia to agree to such a transaction. The Imam assured Schoonderwoerd that the Dutch need not worry about payment or price, on which they would surely reach agreement. To that end he suggested that the Dutch send an official with power of attorney to deal with these matters. The Imam indicated his sincerity by giving Schoonderwoerd a letter to Jacob Mossel, governor-general of the VOC in Batavia, in which the Imam formally proposed the establishment of a Dutch factory and ordered the delivery of one ship of the *Vlietlust* class.[8] As evidence of his friendly intentions and his wish to promote amicable relations with the Dutch, the Imam presented Schoonderwoerd two stallions and fodder for Mossel. In return Schoonderwoerd presented the Imam a gift worth Dfl. 605.[9]

---

6. NA, VOC 1009, Batavia to Gamron (18/07/1755), f. 249.
7. NA, VOC 2885, Gamron to Batavia (28/12/1755), f. 21.
8. NA, VOC 2885, Achmed Bein Sijjd to Mossel (Muscat, 24/01/1756), f. 57-59 (Dutch translation only).
9. A Dutch florin or Dfl. is a *gulden* or guilder of 20 *stuivers*.

Although Schoonderwoerd's voyage to Muscat was a diplomatic success, his commercial activities were not. Immediately on arrival Schoonderwoerd inquired about the state of the market. It became clear that trade prospects were not bright; a few days before an English sloop, the *Kedrie*, had arrived from Bengal with a cargo including zinc and iron. Schoonderwoerd could only get an offer for zinc at cost price and for iron at the VOC's fixed price. He therefore sold part (24,200 lbs.) of his iron at Dfl. 17 per 100 lbs. and 300 *canisters*[10] (100,121 lbs.) of powdered sugar at Dfl. 16 per 100 lbs. Schoonderwoerd was unable to sell more for ready cash, but he believed that if he could have stayed for another three months the entire cargo might have been sold.[11]

Although he sold little, Schoonderwoerd believed that a profitable business might be done in Muscat. For this it would be necessary to send a medium-sized ship for three or four months. The merchants would have to be granted a short period of credit, which at the same time would have an inflationary effect on prices. The best time for trading in Muscat, Schoonderwoerd believed, would be at the beginning of October when the so-called Mokha monsoon began.[12] At that time coffee could be purchased at six *stuivers* or slightly more per lb.; high quality aloe from Socotra and other kinds of gums were also procurable. Finally, the cash situation in Muscat was then most favorable and as the Dutch had orders to sell for cash this was an important factor. Schoonderwoerd also reported that he had again been asked by a

---

10. A canister or canaster was a bale of twined bamboo to transport, for example, sugar, tobacco and mace.
11. The cost price of iron was Dfl. 2,902:15 (including 2 per cent costs in Batavia). The proceeds were Dfl. 4,117:8 at a net profit of Dfl. 1,214;13 or 41 per cent. The cost price of sugar was Dfl. 8,638:13 (including 2 per cent cost in Batavia). The proceeds were Dfl. 16,019:7 at a net profit of Dfl. 7,380:14 or 85 per cent. Total costs were Dfl. 11,541:8, while the total proceeds were Dfl. 20,136:15 or a net profit of Dfl. 8,595:7 or 75 per cent. NA, VOC 2885, Schoonderwoerd (Muscat) to Batavia (24/01/1756), f. 53.
12. The Mokha monsoon refers to the coffee traders who traveled from Mokha (Yemen) to Basra in July to sell their coffee and buy dates and other goods. On their return to the Red Sea many stopped at Muscat in the hope of benefiting from lower prices.

representative of the king of Sind to come and trade. Although he had little knowledge of that country or its trade, he believed that the proposal was worth further investigation.[13]

THE FIST MUSCAT VOYAGE

Meanwhile the High Government had decided to send the *Marienbosch* to Muscat instead of Khark with a variety of goods, but mainly sugar, to be followed later by a second ship. When Schoonderwoerd finally arrived in Batavia towards the end of May 1756, the High Government accepted his proposal with minor changes. Thus, on 8 June 1756 the council decided that the second ship, *'tPasgeld*, would travel to Diewil-Sind if trade prospects in Muscat were unfavorable.[14]

On 9 July 1756, Captain de Nijsz of the *Marienbosch* and Captain Brahé of *'tPasgeld* received their orders for the voyage to Muscat.[15] The ships were to sail together to Muscat and try to sell their goods there. Only if it proved impossible to sell the cargoes of both ships was Brahé to set course for Sind. Because the greater part of the cargoes consisted of sugar, de Nijsz and his colleague were allowed to follow the market trend. Nevertheless, they were to seek the highest possible prices. The High Government had fixed the prices for the other goods that they carried.[16] If possible, both captains were instructed to deliver the goods only after payment had been made aboard their ships. If cash was scarce, they were permitted to make a deal with the Imam of Muscat for the sale of goods on four months' credit. This was a practical measure, since the *Marienbosch* had to stay in Muscat for that period anyway.

---

13. NA, VOC 2885, Schoonderwoerd (Muscat) to Batavia (24/01/1756), f. 52-56.
14. NA, VOC 786, year 1756. See the resolutions of March 30, April 20 and 30, June 8 and July 5, 1756.
15. NA, VOC 1010, Instructions from the High Government for Captains de Nijsz and Brahé (Batavia, 05/07/1756), f. 213-15.
16. Prices per 100 lbs. after deduction of expenses were as follows (in Dfl.): iron 18; tin 40; zinc 22:10; pepper 35; mace 640; nutmegs 280; cloves 500; and cinnamon 600.

Because of the fluctuating exchange rates owing to the scarcity of cash and the changing intrinsic value of coins, the High Government charged the captain to employ only trustworthy money changers. They were authorized to accept the various currencies only at the following fixed rates:

Keyzerdaalders	60 *stuivers*
Rupees	26 *stuivers*
Golden rupees	Dfl. 18:18
Venetian ducats	Dfl. 6:12
Copperware	Dfl. 80:00 per 100 lbs.

On arrival in Muscat the captains were to contact the VOC factories in Bandar Abbas and Khark. They would provide them and Batavia with information about trade and other matter and perhaps with letters for Batavia. The captains were also instructed to proceed to these factories if sales in Muscat proved to be unsuccessful.

The vessels left Batavia on 19 July 1756, but en route the *Marienbosch* proved to be faster so that it arrived in Muscat on 27 August 1756.[17] De Nijsz and his deputy Gotsche went ashore the next day and were well received by the governor (*vakil*) of Muscat, Khalfan b. Mohammad. They told him that they had a letter and presents from the governor-general for the Imam.[18] The governor immediately sent runners to the Imam, who at that time was staying at Rustaq. Pleased with the arrival of the Dutch ship, the Imam invited de Nijsz to visit him. The captain and Gotsche left Muscat on 3 September 1756 by native craft for Bocca,[19] which they reached the following day. They learnt that the Imam had arrived there the night before. Therefore, de Nijsz had his presence

---

17. The following is based NA, VOC 2909, De Nijsz to Batavia (06/05/1757), f. 6-15, unless otherwise indicated.
18. For the Dutch text of this letter see NA, VOC 1001 (06/07/1756), f. 216-19.
19. I have been unable to identify Bocca. Dikkah is probably meant here, which is almost a suburb of Matrah.

announced by a Banyan.[20] The Imam sent military group to welcome de Nijsz and escort him to the palace. An hour later the Dutch party arrived to be greeted by a guard of honor; they were then taken to the Imam, who received them warmly. After the usual compliments he requested that de Nijsz read the governor-general's letter aloud in Dutch and have the Banyan translate it into Arabic.

In this letter the governor-general gladly accepted the Imam's offer of friendship with the Netherlands. To indicate Dutch goodwill, he announced the arrival of the *Marienbosch* to initiate Dutch trade in Muscat and requested the Imam's assistance in promoting it. As to the sale of a Dutch ship to the Imam, the governor-general regretted that no such vessel was available at that moment. If the Imam was prepared to wait, however, he would see to it that a ship would be sent as soon as the opportunity arose. The governor-general also mentioned that a ship would cost some Dfl. 150,000. Finally, he thanked the Imam for the gifts that he graciously sent to Batavia, a gesture that the governor-general reciprocated.[21]

After the official audience was over, de Nijsz requested the Imam's protection and assistance in furthering Dutch trade in Muscat, which the latter promised. He added that he would grant the Dutch more privileges than any other nation and he invited the Dutch delegation to stay at Rustaq with him during the holidays.[22] De Nijsz politely declined the invitation, pointing out that his absence would delay trading activities too much. De Nijsz then took his leave accompanied by two of the Imam's secretaries.

On 6 September 1756 the Dutch returned to Muscat where the governor, accompanied by some merchants, visited them at their residence on 9 September. The governor told de Nijsz that he had received

---

20. The Dutch used the term Banyan to refer to Hindu merchants from India, especially those from Gujarat.
21. For a list of the gifts, see NA, VOC 1001 (06/07/1756), f. 216-19.
22. The holidays referred to are *'id al-adha*, on 10 Dhu'l-Hijja and *'id al-kabir* on 18 Dhu'l-Hijja. In 1756 the corresponding CE dates were 6 and 14 September respectively.

a letter from the Imam granting the Dutch the right to build a house in Muscat wherever they desired.[23] De Nijsz thanked the governor for this privilege, but told him that for the time being the rented house sufficed. Nevertheless, he would convey notice of this favor to the High Government and let them decide on the matter.

Then they discussed trade. De Nijsz asked the governor what duties the Dutch would have to pay. The latter stated that the English and French had to pay seven per cent,[24] to which de Nijsz replied that the Dutch were not in the habit of imitating their competitors, false though this claim was. He therefore asked for total exemption from customs duties for Dutch goods. Replying that the Dutch were to pay less than other nations, as ordered by the Imam, the governor therefore proposed a duty of three per cent. De Nijsz, however, continued to insist on complete exemption. The governor finally promised to inform the Imam about this demand. Since the matter was not raised again either by the Imam or the governor during the Nijsz's stay in Muscat, the Dutch paid no customs duties on the goods that they sold.

On 19 September 1756 *'tPasgeld* arrived in Muscat. In view of the dim prospects of selling a second cargo of merchandise, it was decided that the ship would set course for Sind in accordance with

---

23. Amin mistakenly states that the Dutch requested permission to build a factory and hoist the Dutch colors. This also holds for the Imam's alleged reply to this request, viz., "The Imam agreed that the Dutch land their cargo, hire a suitable house, and leave proper persons to carry out the business, but he refused to permit them to build a factory or hoist their colors." Amin, *British Interests*, p. 145, n. 5.

24. According to Dutch sources, the English and French paid a customs rate of 7 per cent; see NA, VOC 1011, instruction for Rood, Karsseboom, Verschuur (Batavia, 25/07/1757), f. 204. According to English sources, however, the customs rate in 1756 was as follows: "Import duty in those days was determined by national or religious status of the merchants; it was 5 per cent. ad valorem for Europeans, 6½ per cent. for Muhammadans, and 9 per cent. for Hindus and Jews." Lorimer, *Gazetteer*, vol. 1, p. 416.

their orders. Therefore, *'tPasgeld* left Muscat on 26 October 1756.[25] Trade in Muscat was slack so that only by 15 February 1757 had all goods been sold, with the exception of one bale of Ceylonese cinnamon and five cases of manufactured goods. Deputy Gotsche did not live to see this outcome, for he died on 29 January 1757.[26]

The Second Muscat Voyage

The profit realized by de Nijsz was not encouraging, for only Dfl. 85,134.18 net was made, while both prices and the rate of exchange in specie had been disappointing. Nevertheless, Mossel and his High Government decided to send another ship, the *Barbara Theodora*, to Muscat in the hope of better results. Not only did the council wish to get rid of surplus stocks of sugar, but the mere eight-month voyage to and from Muscat was considered promising. The captain of the *Barbara Theodora*, Simon Rood or Root, was therefore ordered to sail directly from Batavia to Muscat and to sell sugar at the highest possible price, since the High Government believed prices had risen in Muscat. To give Rood an indication of what was expected the council informed him that the 1756 prices for powdered sugar and candy sugar had been rupees 15 and 13.5 respectively (both yielding a 50 per cent profit), but these had been insufficient.

Although given a free hand where sugar was concerned, Rood was required to stick the prices fixed by the council for the other commodities, which were the same as in 1756. The same held for the rates of exchange where specie was concerned as well as the period of credit Rood was allowed to extend to trustworthy merchants.

---

25. See Willem Floor, "Dutch East India Company's Trade with Sind in the 17th and 18th centuries," *Moyen-Orient & Ocean Indien*, vol. 3 (1986), pp. 111-144. This study was re-published by the Institute of Central & West Asian Studies (University of Karachi, 1993-94) enriched with comments from Pakistani scholars.
26. This ends the information based on NA, VOC 2909, De Nijsz to Batavia (06/05/1757), f. 6-15.

Furthermore, Rood was instructed to inform the Imam that the VOC did not wish to construct a factory in Muscat as already it had sufficient factories in the Persian Gulf. The VOC did, however, wish to extend its commercial operations to friends and neighbors, which was why the Dutch had come to Muscat. Captain Rood was to communicate this only if asked why Batavia had not responded to the Imam's offer.[27]

The *Barbara Theodora* left Batavia on 27 July 1757 and arrived in Muscat on 21 September 1757.[28] Rood had his presence announced to the governor of Muscat, Sheikh Khalfan b. Mohammad, through the VOC broker, the Banyan Narrotam.[29] Rood inquired whether the Dutch would again be allowed free trade in Muscat and whether they would enjoy the same privileges they had received in 1756. He pointed out that this was the reason why the High Government had again decided to send a ship to Muscat. Rood then presented the governor with the governor-general's letter[30] for the Imam and mentioned that he had brought gifts for the Imam as well. The governor received the governor-general's letter with bows and kisses and gave Rood and his men a friendly welcome. He told Rood that he had been looking forward to the return of the Dutch and that he was certain that the Imam would grant them free trade this year as well. At Rood's request, the governor advised him to wait few days in Muscat before presenting the Imam, who was due to arrive in Muscat shortly, with the gifts from the governor-general.

---

27. NA, VOC 1011, Instructions for Rood, Karsseboom, Verschuur (Batavia, 25/07/1757), f. 198-205.
28. Unless otherwise indicated the following is based on NA, VOC 2937, Rood to Batavia (08/03/1758), f. 77-104.
29. The broker was Narrotam (or Noerotoem) Anak Rama Djiendil Djoezie, see NA, VOC 2937, f. 107-09, which includes a letter from him to Mossel. The broker received separate appointments for each voyage. He sent presents to Mossel, who reappointed him for the second voyage, exhorting him to sell the VOC goods at higher prices. NA, VOC 1011, Mossel to VOC broker (Batavia, 25/07/1757), f. 209-11.
30. For the Dutch text see NA, VOC 1011 (Batavia, 25/07/1757), f. 205-08.

On 23 September 1757 the governor suggested to Rood that trade negotiations could begin, for a number of merchants were on the point of leaving for the upper part of the Persian Gulf. However, the prices these merchants were willing to pay were too low. They bid only 13-14 rupees per *picol* for powdered sugar and 19 Rupees of candy sugar and asked for five months' credit. The only attractive part of the offer was that they were willing to buy the entire stock of sugar. However, Rood did not accept their offer.

No trade was done until 25 September, when the merchants returned. After much haggling they offered 15 Rupees per *picol* for 800-1,000 canisters of sugar at five months' credit and payment in monies current in Muscat. Rood finally accepted this offer, fearing that with the departure of these merchants he would have less chance of selling his cargo. He reduced the period of credit, however, to three months and required that both the governor of Muscat and the VOC broker guarantee the time of payment and the currencies used. These conditions were accepted by both the governor and the broker.

Table 4.1 List of all goods offered for sale in Muscat in 1757 and the usual prices obtained

Name	Price (Rupees)	Price (Rupees)
Old copperware per *man* of 8 lbs. at 5 ½ -5 ¼ Rs per 100 lbs.	68 ¾	68 5/8
Asafetida per *picol* of 125 lbs.	110	105
Hing Herati (asafetida from Herat, fine, per *picol* of 125 lbs.	225	250
Hing Troesie or Toercesa [?] per *picol* of 125 lbs.	126	125
Gum Arabica per *picol* of 125 lbs.	13	12
Gum myrrh per *picol* of 125 lbs.	44	42 ½
Gum olibanum per *picol* of 125 lbs.	8 ½	8
Socotra aloe per *picol* of 125 lbs.	56	55
Persian *runas* [madder] per *picol* of 125 lbs.	40	35

Name	Price (Rupees)	Price (Rupees)
Dry dates per *bar* of 200 *man* of 1,600 lbs.	60	65
Wet Muscat dates per *bar* of 1,600 lbs.	50	52
Wet Basra dates per bale of 144-145 lbs.	5	6
Persian rosewater per case of 50 bottles	23	20
Moorish coffeebeans per *man* of 8 lbs. Rs 3-2 ½ or *per* picol of 125 lbs.	46 7/8	39 1/16
Sulfur soil per *picol* of 125 lbs.	11	10
Kapok per bale of 20 *man* of 460 lbs. at Rs 160-150 or per 125 lbs.	43 ½	41
Elephants tusks from Mombasa per *picol* of 125 lbs.	150	140

Source: VOC 2937, f. 11 (Mascate, 07/12/1757).

In November 1757, the Imam finally came to Muscat, accompanied by his youngest son Mohammad and three mullahs. On the advice of the governor, Rood and his officers welcomed them at Matrah, according to the country's custom. The Imam had come from Rustaq to send off two small ships, two *grabs*[31] and two to three *gallivats*[32] to Mombasa[33] with military supplies to punish rebels, who challenged his rule.

On 3 November 1757 Rood, accompanied by 26 European and Buginese[34] soldiers and the VOC broker, marched to the Imam's palace to offer him the governor-general's gifts. During the presentation the VOC soldiers offered three salutes with their matchlocks, while the *Marienbosch*, the Imam's admiral's ship and the Muscat forts fired their guns. The reception of Rood and his party was very friendly. The Imam expressed the hope that the Dutch would continue their annual visits, for they were, so to speak, like brothers to him and were as free in his

---

31. A common type of small sailing vessel at that time, popular with country traders.
32. A kind of war boat with oars and sails, of small draught.
33. Zanzibar, Mombasa and some other parts of the East African coast were part of the Imam's dominions.
34. Inhabitants of the Indonesian island of Bugi (Central Sulawesi).

country as in their own home. He then invited Rood and his officers to his residence in Rustaq, but the captain politely declined this honor, since time was pressing. Accepting this reason, the Imam nevertheless insisted that Rood and his party visit the largest fort of Muscat on the east side of the bay.[35]

On 7 November 1757, Rood and his officers were given a tour by the Imam and saluted by gunfire from all forts and ships in the bay. The Imam took the opportunity to show Rood how many of the guns and gun carriages had deteriorated with age. He asked that Rood report this to Batavia and he also ordered ten new pieces. He further mentioned to Rood that never before had any nation been honored by him with even one salute. Rood obliged by thanking the Imam for this unique honor as well as inviting him to visit his ship the *Barbara Theodora*. After the Imam accepted this invitation they returned to his palace. The Dutch continued to be saluted until their arrival there. Later that day the Imam sent fruit and sweetmeats to Rood.

On 10 November 1757 the Imam, his sons, the governor of Muscat and a party of officials were given a stately reception aboard the *Barbara Theodora*. The Imam visited all parts of the ship and compared it with his 130-feet admiral's ship, which had been built in Bombay and bought for 90,000 rupees from the English in 1757. According to Rood, the Dutch ship was considered a better vessel by the Imam, but then he could hardly have said anything else.

On 18 November 1757, the Imam returned to Rustaq and Rood took his leave. The Imam presented him with two Arab stallions for the governor-general and instructed Khalfan b. Mohammad to write a letter to the governor-general.[36] He then asked when Rood would return to Batavia. Rood replied that he would leave as soon as possible after he had collected his money. To that end he seized the opportunity to take up the main problem in this respect, viz. the high price of exchange for golden rupees and ducats. Rood requested that the Imam fix the rate

---

35. This probably is the Jalali fort, see Lorimer, *Gazetteer*, vol. 1, pp. 1180-81.
36. For the text of this letter (Dutch translation only) see NA, VOC 2937, f. 105-06.

of gold coins at their intrinsic value or at a minimum at five rupees. The Imam replied that he was unable to do so in view of the scarcity of specie in his country, which was the real cause of the high rates. He would, however, order the governor to see to it that the merchants honor payment of their debts speedily. Rood had to be satisfied with that reply and thanked the Imam for all the honors shown to the VOC. The Imam then wished Rood a safe voyage and left for Matrah, where the official farewell took place. There, mounted on camels, the Imam and his entourage continued their journey.

Having no other official duties to perform and wishing to return as soon as possible, Rood sold his remaining stock on 29 November to the VOC broker, which no merchant had expressed an interest in buying. Barring these few items, Rood was very pleased with the trade results. Not only had he sold his entire cargo, in spite of the fact that that three VOC ships had preceded him to Khark and Bandar Abbas, but most of his transactions had been in cash and he was able to make a profit of 101 per cent, or 30 per cent more than in 1756. This was mainly due to the sale of greater quantities of sugar and at a lower price than in 1756.

In early December 1757 Rood left Muscat. A few days prior to his departure the Imam had sent him a letter for the governor-general requesting that two of his servants be allowed to make the voyage to Cochin. The servants had been charged to settle an affair with the king of Calicut. Because the *Barbara Theodora* was scheduled to call on Cochin to take in water and firewood, Rood could not refuse. After an uneventful voyage he returned to Batavia on 8 March 1758.[37]

---

37. Here ends the information based on NA, VOC 1011, Instructions for Rood, Karsseboom, Verschuur (Batavia, 25/07/1757), f. 198-205.

Table 4.2: Profit and Loss Account of the *Marienbosch* (in Dutch guilders)

Imports according to the Batavian invoice			113,605: 2: 8
Ship's supplies in Batavia			15,292: 8: 0
Profit after deduction of brokerage and commission	107,338: 4: 0		
Less underweight of benzoin	274: 0: 0		
Gross profit		107,612: 4: 0	
Deduction of the cost of 2.5 month's stay in Muscat			
Supplies and domestic needs	656:19: 3		
Ship's expenses and cost of voyage	1,636: 4: 0		
Fodder for horses 160:13 Rupees			
Two grooms at 6 Rupees/month at two month's advance 32:8			
	193: 1: 0		
Cost dispatched documents to Khark and Gamron	16:17: 8		
Payment for letter received	6:15: 0		
Supplied to ship in Batavia	15,292: 8: 0		

Supplied in addition to the cargoes	141: 6: 8		
Various presents	1,993: 9: 8		
Commission for the ship's officers	2,319: 0: 0		
		22,255: 1: 0	
Net profit on cost price 1,059,42:11.8 = 80.6%			85,357: 3: 0
Total			214,254:13: 8

Source: VOC 2937, f. 89-91.

VOC Decides to Discontinue Muscat Voyages

Although the High Government was extremely pleased with the trade results of the *Barbara Theodora* and its quick journey, nevertheless it decided to discontinue all voyages to Muscat. The chief of the Khark factory, Tido von Kniphausen, had complained that Muscat's profit was Khark's loss. In view of inter-Gulf trade relations, goods sold in Muscat could not be sold at Khark, as the Persian Gulf merchants frequently called on all ports in that region. As far as the High Government was concerned Java sugar could just as well be sold in Khark, which already had a VOC factory and therefore, had to show a profit. The High Government stressed the need to sell all the sugar they sent, so that they finally could be rid of it. Von Kniphausen was instructed to inform the Imam of Muscat that no VOC ships would call in 1758 due to a delay, which made it impossible to undertake the voyage. Company ships would return to Muscat at a later date, if possible. This fabrication was intended to save face, for the council felt embarrassed about the turn of events. It also wished to maintain friendly relations with the Imam.[38]

---

38. NA, VOC 1012, Batavia to Khark (25/04/1758), f. 123-24, 131.

In view of the delicate commercial situation of Khark the High Government's decision was completely logical.[39] Rood's argument for continued voyages to Muscat was too weak and an uncertain basis to rely on. He pointed out that much rice had always been carried from Bengal and Malabar to Muscat. In 1757, five small private English *grabs* had come from Malabar with rice, pepper, sandalwood and cardamom. They had bartered these goods for dry and wet dates and other items. Because the trade carried on by the English country traders was not as important as before, Rood proposed that one ship from Batavia (carrying spices, sugar, and base metals) and two from Bengal (carrying rice and textiles) be sent to Muscat each year. However, in that case the second ship from Bengal would have to depart three months after the first one. This schedule would allow the return of such a ship as soon as possible. These goods were to be bartered for pearls, copperware, rosewater, dates, various gums, brimstone, rock salt and drugs in addition to gold ducats. In this way, Rood argued, the VOC could take away business from English country traders, see what prices the VOC might obtain for its goods from Batavia and make short swift voyages.

Table 4.3 Proposed cargos for continued voyages to Muscat

Commodity	Quantity	Price (in Rupees)
From Batavia		
Powdered Java sugar	2,000 canisters	-
Candy sugar	100 canisters	-
Iron bars	800 *picol*	-
Lead	200 *picol*	-
Tin	200 *picol*	-
Steel	100 *picol*	-
Sappanwood, thick, long, straight	400 *picol*	-
curcuma [turmeric] from Java	250 *picol*	-

39. See Floor, *The Rise*, chapters four and five.

Commodity	Quantity	Price (in Rupees)
curcuma from Malabar, new variety	250 *picol*	-
cloves, not mixed with nutmegs	40 chests	-
Cochineal	5 *picol*	-
camphor, Chinese or Japanese	100 *picol*	-
benzoin, zinc, macis	on account of abundance little trade	
From Bengal		
fine and coarse Bengal rice in gunny bags of 150 lbs. each	Two cargos	6½–7 Rs per bag fine kind 5½–6 Rs per bag for coarse kind
new dried ginger	250 gunny bags	12½–15 Rs per picol of 125 lbs.
curcuma from Bengal	250 gunny bags	9–10 Rs per bag
Bengal gum-lac on sticks in bags of 70-80 lbs.	250 gunny bags	30–32 Rs per 125 lbs.
unbleached *baftas*; 150 per bale; each piece 24 long, 2 cubits wide	25 bales	78–88 Rs per *corgie*† of 20
Soesjes‡ with red-yellow stripes in 3 varieties; each bales with 200; each piece long 40, wide 2 cubits; 2nd variety long 50, wide 1½ cubit, and 3rd variety long 40, wide 1½ cubit	25 bales	12–13 Rs/piece variety one 12–13 Rs/piece variety two 7–8 Rs/piece variety three
Sjeklassen§; 150 per bale; each piece long 40, wide 2 cubit	2 bales	11–12 Rs per piece
various textiles of all kinds	2 pieces of each kind	sample as a try-out

† *Corge* or *corgie*, a term of Indian origin meaning 'a unit of twenty, a score.'
‡ Light East-Indian cotton cloth made in colored and white stripes, used for head covering. § Unidentified Indian fabric.

Source: VOC 2937, Root-Karseboom to Batavia (08/03/1758), f. 101.

Clearly Rood had no idea of the desperate financial position that the VOC found itself in at that time. Even Khark had no means of direct navigation with Bengal, although von Kniphausen, the chief of the Khark factory, pointed out that this meant the VOC's loss of the textile market in the Persian Gulf. Moreover, the Muscat voyages were but a gamble by the High Government to rid itself of large stocks of Java sugar; there was no future in the continuation of these trade relations with Muscat, because this would negatively impact the financial performance of the Khark factory.[40] The total commercial failure of *'tPasgeld* voyage may have contributed to the High Government's decision to discontinue the Muscat voyages.[41]

The decision met the total approval of the VOC's managing directors, the *Heeren XVII*. In 1759, they expressed their surprise at the Muscat voyages. Whereas Schoonderwoerd had proposed that a medium-sized ship be employed, the High Government had sent one of its largest ships, one of 140 feet length, to Muscat in 1756. In view of the slack market, one had to expect low profits, for what else could Batavia expect of two fully laden ships? The XVII bitingly observed that the so-called profit made by de Nijsz in 1756 amounted to little. Moreover, *'tPasgeld* had not yet returned from its voyage to Sind. Notwithstanding these hard facts, the High Government had decided to send the *Barbara Theodora*. This decision had only been taken to dispose of sugar and not so much with a view to the profitability of the Muscat trade, the directors commented. Since the voyages to Muscat and Sind were considered disadvantageous for the VOC factories in Khark and Surat, the directors insisted that Batavia discontinue all voyages to Muscat as soon as it had disposed of its sugar stocks.[42]

Upon hearing of the outcome of trade on the *Barbara Theodora*, the XVII could not help but point out that its results only backed up their earlier position. The net profit was hardly enough to cover the ship's

---

40. NA, VOC 2937, Rood to Mossel (Batavia, 08/03/1758), f. 87 (should be f. 101).
41. See Floor, "Dutch East India Company."
42. NA, VOC 334, XVII to Batavia (12/10/1759), section Masquetta, not foliated.

expense, the loss on the rate of exchange and other costs, so that in fact little profit remained. Moreover, sales at Muscat had resulted in lower profitability of the Khark factory. Therefore, the directors were pleased with the High Government's decision to discontinue the Muscat voyages.[43]

However, the decision did not signal the end of relations between the VOC and Muscat. In reply to a request of the former VOC broker, in 1761, the High Government had written that the Company would not resume trade. The XVII commented that even were the Imam himself asked, the answer remained negative.[44] Nevertheless, friendly relations were maintained. The Khark factory communicated with Muscat in connection with trade matters, ship wrecking, and private trading by VOC servants. The Dutch were still very much in the favor of the Imam of Muscat. When survivors of the Khark debacle arrived in Muscat, they were warmly welcomed and in 1766 when a Dutch ship sent from Surat came to see what could be salvaged, the Imam even offered naval and military assistance to help the Dutch retake Khark.[45] This ship carried a VOC servant to Muscat, who was to remain behind and serve as the Company's eyes and ears in the Persian Gulf. However, he was soon withdrawn, when the Surat factory received notice that the VOC decided to cease all activities in the Persian Gulf.[46]

Resumption of Annual Muscat Voyages

The eclipse of the VOC in the Persian Gulf did not preclude the sailing of Dutch ships to the area, as has been asserted by Amin, for instance.[47] The VOC factory at Surat continued to maintain contact with Basra for the purpose of forwarding letters, but shipping from Batavia to Muscat and the Persian Gulf was resumed only in 1777. On 15 July 1777 the

---

43. NA, VOC 334, XVII to Batavia (30/09/1760), section Persien, not foliated.
44. NA, VOC 335, XVII to Batavia (25/10/1762), section Masquetta, not foliated.
45. See Floor, *The Rise*, chapter four; Lorimer, *Gazetteer*, vol. 1, p. 411.
46. NA, VOC 795, Resolution of the High Government (Batavia; 20/06/1765), f. 521ff.
47. Amin, *British Interests*, p. 132.

High Government allowed merchant Willem van Hogendorp to buy 1,500 canisters of sugar from the VOC stocks at 5 *rijksdaalders* per *picol* plus 30 *stuivers* per *picol* as tax, on the condition that he also purchase and export 150 *leggers*[48] of arak and transport them in his own private ship to Muscat.[49] Van Hogendorp's initiative set an example and soon it was followed by other private Dutch merchants, who likewise requested permission to send ships with sugar and arak to Muscat.[50] By 1780, two ships per year were sailing to Muscat (see Table 4.4), causing the High Government to reconsider the feasibility of direct VOC trade in the Persian Gulf. The private merchants van Hogendorp and Wiegerman were therefore instructed to examine the quantities of and prices for cloves, nutmegs and mace. In 1781, both merchants reported that nutmeg and mace were not much in demand in Muscat, but predicted a sale of 28 *picol*s of cloves as the price and demand were good. They were unaware of trading possibilities in the rest of the Persian Gulf area, as they had been unable to penetrate further into the Persian Gulf during their voyages.[51]

Table 4.4: Dutch ships sailing to Muscat, 1777-1793

Year	Name ship	Source
1777	Unknown	NA, VOC 807, f. 759
1778	De Snelheid	NA, VOC 809, f. 251
1779	De Snelheid; Concordia; Hercules	NA, VOC 809, f. 251, 380vs; NA, VOC 810, f. 1308
1780	Nepthunus; de Snelheid	NA, VOC 810, f. 662, 1308

---

48. A barrel with a capacity of 400 or 563 liters.
49. NA, VOC 807, Resolution High Government (Batavia; 15/07/1777), f. 759. One *rijksdaalder* equals 2.5 guilders and one *stuiver* equals five cents or *duiten*.
50. For example, Mr. Boesjes, owner of the grab *de Snelheid*. NA, VOC 809, f. 251 (23/11/1779) (left with 300 canisters of sugar, 100 barrels (*leggers* of 440, 563 liters) of arak and some mace [a spice made from the inner husk of the nutmeg]); NA, VOC 810, f. 622 (30/06/1780) (left with a cargo of 400 canisters of sugar). See also NA, VOC 809, f. 380vs (17/12/1779) (*Concordia*); NA, VOC 810, f. 1307 (12/09/1781) permission granted to Jan Hendrik Wiegerman, president of the council of aldermen of Batavia to make voyages to Muscat with details of the cargo; see also NA, VOC 811, f. 287-88 (07/12/1781).
51. NA, COC 811, Resolution of the High Government (Batavia; 07/12/1781), f. 287ff; NA, VOC 810, f. 1308-09 (12/09/1781).

THE SECOND PERIOD OF DUTCH-OMANI CONTACTS 1755-1806 · CHAPTER FOUR · 163

Year	Name ship	Source
1782	*Hoorn;**	NA, VOC 813, f. 232
1783	*Hoorn*	NA, VOC 813, f. 232
1784	*Battavier* [sic]	NA, VOC 814, not foliated
1785	*Nepthunus, Hercules;*†	NA, VOC 815, f. 284, 287
1786	*De Nagel,*‡ *Nepthunus, Hercules,*§ *Java's Welvaren*	NA, VOC 815, f. 284, 395, 555-56
1787	*Hercules, Nepthunus, Java's Welvaren*	NA, VOC 819, f. 469; VOC 818, f. 868, 1292; VOC 820, f. 1243
1788	*Nepthunus, Java's Welvaren*¶	NA, VOC 820, f. 102, 972, 1243
1789	*Hercules*	NA, VOC 821, f. 1046
1790	*Nepthunus, Java's Welvaren*#	NA, VOC 825, f. 268-69
1791	*Java's Welvaren, Hercules*	NA, Hooge Regering Batavia, not foliated; see index on resolutions (04/01/1791)
1792	*Java's Welvaren*	NA, VOC 827, f. 3559
1793	*Maria Catherina***	NA, Archief Oost-Indisch Comité, nr. 78, Dagregister Batavia 1793/94, f. 195

* NA, VOC 811, f. 287 (07/12/1781) also mentions a voyage by de Jonge Hugo with, among other things, 300 lbs. of spices. † The alderman Alexander Agerbeek financed the voyage of both the *Nepthunus* and *Herculus*; both carried sugar and spices as well as 30 picol of macis for the account of the VOC. NA, VOC 815, f. 284-87 (22/11/1785); see also NA, VOC 815, f. 228 (11/11/1785). ‡ De Nagel was a ship that had just been built in Batavia. It was commanded by captain Hermannus Folkers. NA, VOC 815, f. 396 (16/12/1785). It left with 38 picol of macis. § Alexander Agerbeek asked for permission to repair de Hercules in the VOC yard to make another voyage to Muscat. This was approved, but on condition that he would invest half of the cash with which he would return from Muscat in VOC letters of credit (credietbrieven), amounting to 50,000 rijksdaalders. In addition the VOC would earn 7,415 rijksdaalders, the proceeds of its 30 picol of mace that had been part of the ship's cargo. NA, VOC 817, f. 555-56 (28/11/1786). In 1787 the mace yielded 6,846 rijksdaalders. NA, VOC 819, f. 470 (18/12/1787). In 1788, it yielded 6,890 rijksdaalders. NA, VOC 820, f. 972 (15/07/1788). Java s Welvaren returned with half of its proceeds in gold and half in keijzerdaalders. The sale of VOC mace had yielded 6,650 rijksdaalders. NA, VOC 820, f. 1243 (1788). # William Francklin, Observations made on a tour from Bengal to Persia in the years 1786-7 (London, 1790), p. 38 noted that in January 1787 there "was a Dutch ship lying in the harbour [of Muscat], commanded by Captain Stewart."

** *De Maria Catherina* may have been a Portuguese ship, as stated in the index of the *Dagregister*, but the text itself refers only to "a private (*particulier*) ship." The cargo of these ships invariably consisted of powdered and candy sugar (generally 1,200 canisters of the former and 300 of the latter) and 38 *picols* of cloves.

The profits made by private merchants, together with the sales prospects for cloves, prompted the High Government to promote such voyages. It allowed the VOC to sell 30 *picol*s of cloves per year, enabling the Company to acquire much needed cash for its commercial operations. Therefore, the High Government decided that private merchants could continue their voyages to Muscat provided they sold 30 *picol*s of cloves on behalf of the VOC and invest half of the proceeds of the voyages in VOC letters of credit.[52]

To sustain the pattern of Muscat voyages, the High Government assisted the private merchants in various ways. When in October 1779 Wiegerman's ship, the *Nepthunus*, suffered heavy damage near Bantam (Indonesia) and had to return to Batavia, the High Government permitted Wiegerman to hire a VOC ship of 140 feet length. It realized that repairs would take some time, forcing Wiegerman to store his cargo of sugar and so lose a great deal of money. It further agreed to this request, because the export of sugar was in the interest of the economy of Batavia, and ships were lying idle due to lack of crews, and charged Dfl. 16,000 for the ship's lease.[53] The High Government also permitted Wiegerman to export tin, believing his voyage would set a good example for other private merchants.[54] In addition, it permitted repairs to be made in the VOC shipyards and encouraged the import of *aureum pigmentum* (yellow arsenic sulphide) and sulfur.[55] Even when stocks of sugar were

---

52. See, for example, NA, VOC 815, f. 284-87, 395; NA, VOC 817, f. 555, NA, VOC 818, f. 1321 (24/07/1787); NA, VOC 820, f. 1243 (1788).
53. NA, VOC 810, f. 210-13 (24/10/1780).the *Nepthunus* carried 2,000 canisters of powdered sugar, 60 canisters of candy sugar and 20 barrels (*leggers*) of arak. NA, VOC 810, f. 622 (30/06/1780). The High Government also agreed to the request by J.H. Wiegerman in 1784 to be allowed to repair the cutter *de Battavier* to make a voyage to Muscat with about 400 canisters of sugar. NA, VOC 814, not foliated (02/03/1784).
54. NA, VOC 810, f. 1308-09.
55. NA, VOC 814, not foliated; NA, VOC 717, f. 555. The reason was that the factory owner Cornelis de Keyser and the manager of the plumber's manufactory Godfried Welke liked the *aureum pigmentum* that had just arrived with *de Hoorn* coming from Muscat, which product was better than the so-called royal yellow. The High Government therefore ordered the captain of *de Hoorn*, Gerrit Bruijn,

low, the High Government allowed some export to Muscat, because of the advantages this afforded the VOC. It also held hopes of reestablishing trade relations with Persia via these voyages.[56] However, the so-called East Indies Committee that had replaced the High Government took a rather negative view of these voyages in light of the difficulties involved. It was for this reason that the Committee had decided to refuse the invitation of the Pasha of Baghdad to reestablish VOC trade in 1793.[57]

To the best of my knowledge, voyages to Muscat continued until 1796,[58] although the available Dutch documents do not yield further information on departing ships after 1793. The Batavia Diary (*Dagregister*) for 1793 mentions one ship returning from, and another en route to, Muscat, but the 1794 diary does not mention any ship bound for that

---

to buy 100 lbs. of *aureum pigmentum* on his next voyage, which he was about to start. NA, VOC 813, f. 232 (02/05/1783). Batavia's 4-year reserves of brimstone amounted to 350,000 lbs. The High Government needed 50,000 lbs. per year for the production of gun powder and in addition for other users (ships, etc.) it required 87,500 lbs/year of that ore. It therefore was ordered to buy 350,000 lbs. at Muscat. NA, VOC 818, f. 1615 (21/08/1787).

56. NA, VOC 825, f. 268; NA, VOC 815, f. 228, 285; but it did not allow the export of additional quantities of sugar in times of scarcity. NA, VOC 820, f. 102 (21/01/1788). The Omanis also sent their own ships to Batavia. Risso, *Oman & Muscat*, p. 101. Captain Johannes Florens of *de Hercules* was fined Dfl. 500 because he had called on Poeloe Pinang, an English port to buy 300 bags of saltpeter. He was, however, allowed to ship them to the Persian Gulf for sale to Persia. NA, VOC 821, f. 1046-47 (13/12/1788). The Netherlands was at war with England at that time, hence the fine.

57. NA, Archief Oost-Indisch Comité, nr. 71, f. 575 (08/11/1793). Contacts with the Persian Gulf continued to be maintained; in 1798 a letter was received in Batavia from the Dutch ambassador in Istanbul requesting Dutch ships to call on Basra. NA, Archief Oost-Indisch Comité, nr. 10, f. 78 (21/06/1798). Earlier requests from the governor of Basra had been made in 1771 and 1780. NA, VOC 791, Resolutions High Government (27/05/1771) and NA, Legatie Archief Turkije nr. 784.

58. The voyage of *Java's Welvaren* in 1791 had been disappointing due to low sugar price and the long voyage. The return cargo consisted of gold and silver specie plus gum Arabica. The VOC mace, 60 *picol*, had not been sold and it was returned to the Company at the fixed price of 90 *stuivers* per lb. NA, VOC 827, f. 3559 (19/12/1791).

destination.[59] The documents offer no clues either as to why these voyages seem to have been discontinued.[60] Perhaps profits had diminished; although this seems unlikely considering that a proposal was made in 1796 to send a VOC ship to Muscat financed by private merchants. Moreover, two private merchants asked permission to send ships there in the same year.[61] Therefore, it seems that these voyages were indeed made, be it that Dutch ships may have sailed under foreign flag, because of the war between France and England. The new Dutch or Batavian Republic became an ally of France, which automatically meant that the English considered Dutch ships enemy ships. The Batavian Republic further nationalized the VOC in 1796, which meant that its ships were considered to be legitimate targets for British ships. Therefore, the Bombay Council instructed its broker in Muscat to oppose "by every means in your power to prevent these Nations' ships [i.e. French and Dutch] sailing to and from Muscat under Arab and particularly the Imam's color."[62] Apparently two Dutch ships flying Arab colors had been to Muscat in 1796 that came from Batavia, the *Jupiter* (named as an 'Arab' ship), sailing Batavia-Muscat-Batavia and *Graaf Bensdorff* from Batavia to Muscat and then to Europe. There may also have been one in October 1797, a dinghy, called the *Latokinu* commanded by Captain Crouch, but it may not have been a Dutch vessel.[63]

---

59. NA, Archief Oost-Indisch Comité, nr. 78, Dagregister Batavia 1793/94, f. 57 (return of *Java's Welvaren* on March 30) and f. 195 (departure of *de Maria Catherina* on November 7). The likely reason for the discontinuation of these voyages is the closure of the Dutch factory in Cochin in 1793. Ashin Das Gupta, *Malabar in Asian Trade 1740-1800* (Cambridge, 1967), p. 122

60. Most of the information on ship movements was obtained from the resolutions of the High Government, which do not exist from 1793 and thereafter. The Batavia Diary continues only to 1794 and does not mention any ships leaving for Muscat. Other sources do not yield information either.

61. NA, Hooge Regering Batavia, nr. 873; see index on resolutions in 1796 under "Persien in 't algemeen" and "Musquette in Persien." The texts imply that the ships may have left, for the committee did not oppose the voyages.

62. J. A. Saldanha, *The Persian Gulf Précis* 10 vols. (Gerards Cross: Archive Editions, 1986), vol. 1, p. 336 (Bombay; 25/03/1797).

63. Risso, *Oman & Muscat*, pp. 145-46 (the broker Norotam Josey, who worked both for the Dutch and English, reported to Bombay that in 1796 two Dutch ships had come to Muscat with sugar and spices, which had hoisted Arab

In December 1799, the Batavian Republic did not renew the charter of the VOC, which then formally ceased to exist. This constituted a further obstacle for continued voyages to Muscat, and thus ended Dutch trade relations with Muscat in the eighteenth century.

The above described political developments explain why no longer Dutch ships were coming to Muscat after 1796. Imam Sultan b. Ahmad (1794-1806) wanted to know what the reason for this was. It may have been that he knew or guessed why, because in 1796 the Imam had concluded a treaty with the English East-India Company, in which he promised not to allow Dutch and French vessels in his territory nor allow them to establish trading stations there.[64] Therefore, he may have wanted to know what their reaction was to this treaty, because he was none too happy about this commercial restriction himself. Although sugar and spices were availabe in Western India, prices in Batavia were more competitive. Therefore, in August 1798, the Imam sent the ship *Sib Badam* under captain Abdol-Rahman, assisted by mate al-Mu`allim Wazir, to buy sugar and other goods in Batavia. The Imam clearly wanted to renew commercial relations with the Dutch, so that they might continue with their annual voyages, as had been done since 1777, or if that was not possible that Omani ships would make these voyages. The Omani ship also carried some unnamed cargo and two horses as a present. The Imam asked the governor-general of the VOC for special treatment given the old existing friendship between the Dutch and Oman. The *Sib Badam* had a successful journey and returned to Muscat with presents and a letter from the governor-general in Batavia. Although the contents of this letter are unknown, it must have been made clear or otherwise the Imam's captain would have done so, that the Dutch were unable to continue to sail to Muscat, because of the war with Great Britain. This seems to have been no obstacle for the Imam, for now that

---

colors; however, *vali* Khalfan wrote to Bombay that the two vessels had Danish and American colors); Saldanha, *The Persian Gulf Précis*, vol. 1, p. 337 (Bombay; 25/03/1797) and p. 338 (Muscat, 27/12/1797); National Archives (Kew Gardens), HCA 30/754.

64. For the text, see Risso, *Oman & Muscat*, pp. 218-19.

friendly commercial relations had been re-established, the Imam wanted to make them more regular. In August 1800, the Imam sent the vessel *Janjawar* under Hajj Mahmud b. Mohammad b. Mashkur to Batavia, again with the main objective of buying sugar in addition to some other unspecified goods. The *Janjawar* returned safely with the desired cargo and a letter from the governor-general, about which the Imam wrote: "Whatever you told us is now known to us" and he thanked him for the friendly treatment given to the ship and crew. Therefore, in August 1801, the Imam decided to send the *Fath Islam* to Batavia, which first had to go to Calcutta for repairs and then continue to Batavia. According to the English, in 1801, the Imam concluded a trade agreement with Batavia. Nothing of the kind is suggested by these letters, while Dutch sources make no mention of such a treaty.[65] Whether there was such a treaty the fact is that that the Omani trade with Batavia was as of that time the Imam's monopoly usually sending two or three ships per year to Batavia.[66]

The next letter that mentions the departure of an Omani ship to Batavia is from May 1806, in which Imam al-Sayyed Badr b. al-Sayyed Seyf, son of the previous Imam Sultan b. Ahmad wrote to Governor-General Albertus Henricus Wiese (1804-08). It refers to the death of the Imam Sultan b. Ahmad and his accession to the throne and, most importantly, "we request from God that the renewal of the friendship and love between us and you is stable, as it used to be from our fathers to you, since the love between the fathers creates a bond between the sons." The Imam's letter was sent with the vessel *Khalili*, which belonged to Hajji Anbar Dawud Khalil and was captained by Ibrahim b. Hasan, who, in 1800, had been a member of the crew of the *Sib Badam*.[67]

---

65. Redha Bhacker, *Trade and Empire in Muscat and Zanzibar: The Roots of British Domination*. London: Routledge, 1992, p. 29. The *Janjava* may be the same ship mentioned in British sources as *Gunjava*, which was a square-rigged vessel of 1,000 tons and 32 guns, see Risso, *Oman & Muscat*, p. 171.
66. Risso, *Oman & Muscat*, p. 198.
67. For the facsimile, text and translation of these letters, see Jan Just Witkam, "Wood, horses and friendship. The Arabic letters from Muscat to the Dutch in Kochi (1779) and Batavia (1798-1806)" in AbdulRahman al-Salimi and Heinz

Unfortunately, no other letters seem to have been preserved, but the letters suggest that starting from August 1798 each year at least one Omani vessel sailed to Batavia to buy sugar. Whether these voyages continued after 1806 is unknown, but seems likely. It was only in 1824 that the government of the Dutch East Indies sent the vessel *Baron van der Capellen* to the Persian Gulf with a typical eighteenth-century cargo: sugar, tin, copper, spices, steel, nails, iron, and sappanwood with a total value of Dfl. 125,000. The ship not only called on Muscat, but also Bandar Abbas and Bushehr. The captain was able to sell his goods and for his return voyage took on horses, rose water, gallnuts, opium, and especially specie, which accounted for two-thirds of the value of the first return cargo. The profits were attractive enough to encourage merchants to finance four other voyages of a single ship each, between 1828 and 1831. But the fact that the Dutch had no agent representing their interests on the spot was a disadvantage. Moreover, as security on the Persian Gulf coast was uncertain it was decided to discontinue the voyages.[68] However, Armenian merchants based in Batavia continued to sail between Batavia and the Gulf, mainly with a cargo of sugar.

Conclusion

The pattern of Dutch relations with Muscat reflects trade with the Persian Gulf area in general. We observe a decrease (and in the VOC case a complete abandonment) of trade by European Companies and an enormous increase in the so-called country trade.[69] The Dutch flirtation with Muscat had no real economic basis, and only served to rid Batavia of its surplus stocks of Java sugar. The speedy abandonment of Muscat by the VOC bears this out. That it took ten years before Dutch country traders returned to Muscat was probably the resulting impact of the sack of Khark. Undoubtedly, merchants in Batavia were informed

---

Gaube eds. *Studies on Ibadism and Oman*. Hildesheim: Olms, 2013, pp. 265 97; which is reprinted in Annex 5.
68. N. J. den Tex, "Onze Handel in de Perzische Golf en de Roode Zee," *De Economist* 1 (1871), pp. 23, 28.
69. Amin, *British Interests*, pp. 127ff.

as to the profitability of trade with Muscat through their contacts with the VOC factories in Surat and Malabar, which had regular contacts with Muscat. When these country traders finally reestablished contact an annual trade pattern came into being,[70] which was temporarily disrupted by the Napoleonic wars, the occupation of Java by the English and thereafter the build-up of Dutch rule in the East-Indies. That this trade pattern of annual voyages probably was continued in 1798, but this time from Muscat, as well as the fact that it also remerged from Batavia at the beginning of the nineteenth century is a sign of its tenacity and financial attraction.[71]

---

70. "The Sugar, Sugar Candy, Metals and Prices imported at Bushire, by Boats, from Muscat, is commonly brought to the latter on Dutch and French Vessels." Saldanha, *Précis*, vol. 1, p. 423 (Report on the Commerce of Arabia and Persia by Samuel Manesty and Harford Jones, 1790).

71. For the resumption of these voyages in the 19th century see Willem Floor, *Traditional Crafts in Qajar Iran* (Costa Mesa, 2003), pp. 332-33.

ANNEX I

A Report on the Discovery of the Coast of Oman in 1666

[**3366**] Description of a voyage along the coast of Arabia beginning at a place called Chassab,[1] which is situated at 9.5 [German] miles[2] West of Cape Mozando,[3] and further along all places, bays, ports, rivers, depths, shoals, sandbanks, shallows as well as the nature of the interior of the country adjacent to the said coast as far as the Bay of Mascatta by junior merchant Jacob Vogel, having been ordered [by the director Hendrick van Wijck[4]] to board the hooker the *Meerkadt* together with junior mate Adriaen vander Werff, the aforementioned Vogel for the said reasons and the abovementioned vander Werff to draw a map of the said coast together with the captain and mate of the said hooker as is clear in more detail from the instruction given by the said director.

---

1. Chassab or Chaszab is the town of Khasab.
2. The German mile (7.4 km) is meant here and throughout this report.
3. Cape or Ras Musandam to the Europeans and to the Arabs Ru'us al-Jibal or Cluster of Peaks.
4. Hendrick van Wijck, chief merchant, chief of the Bandar Abbas VOC trading station and chief of VOC trade in Persia (1661-66).

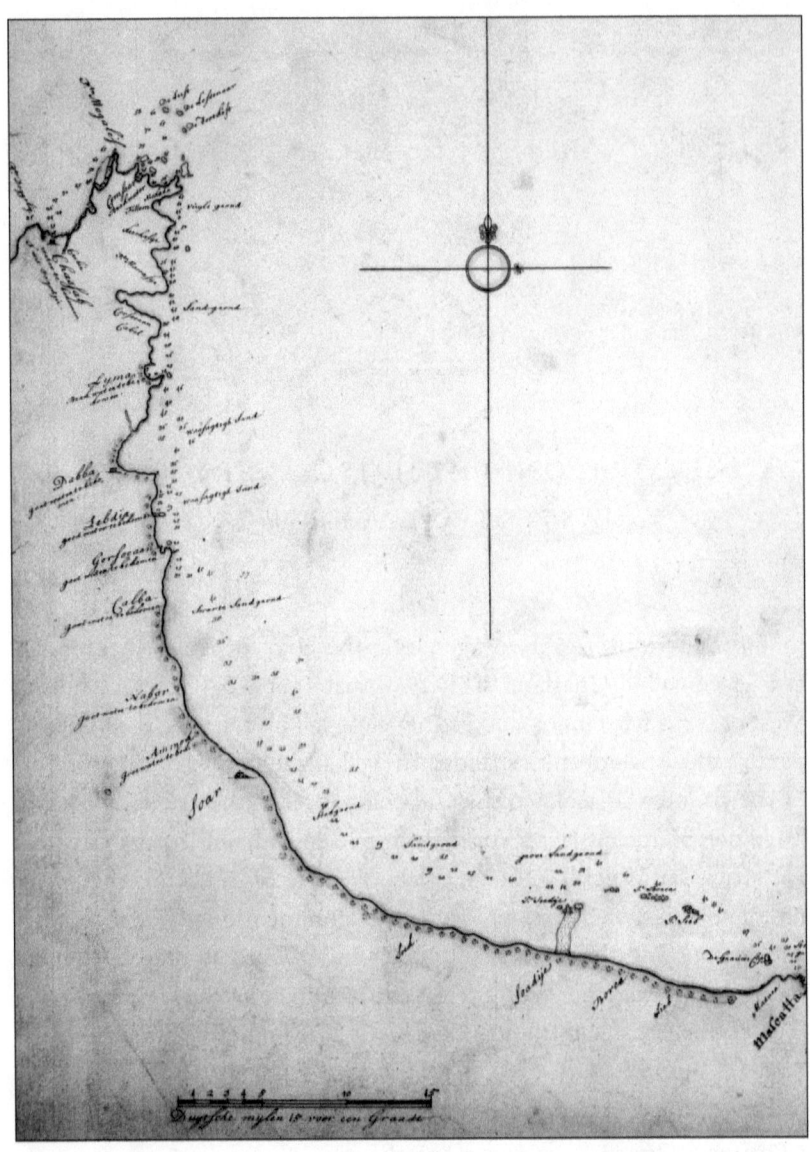

The Coast of Oman, showing the various places mentioned in the report with additional notes where (good) water could be obtained and what kind of holding ground was to be found along the coast. The scale of the map is 15 German miles equals one degree. All three maps from Nationaal Archief, The Hague, Nr. 4. VEL 222

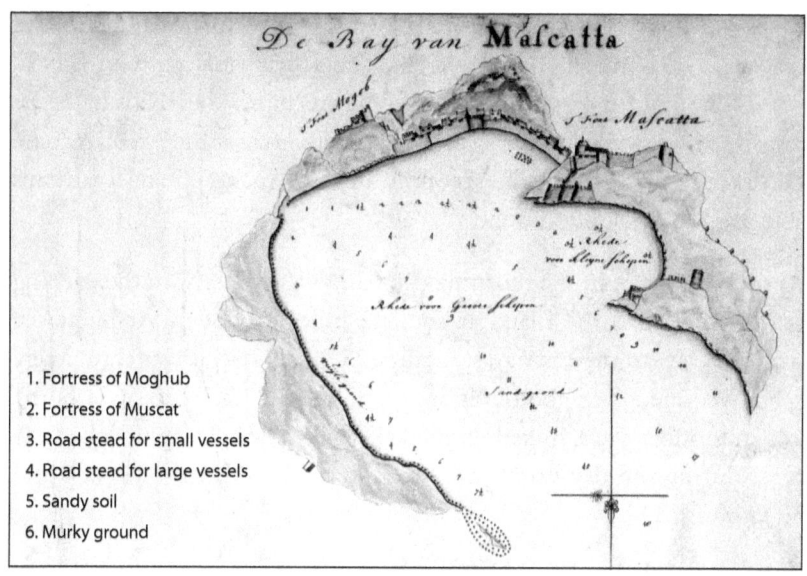

1. Fortress of Moghub
2. Fortress of Muscat
3. Road stead for small vessels
4. Road stead for large vessels
5. Sandy soil
6. Murky ground

Bay of Muscat

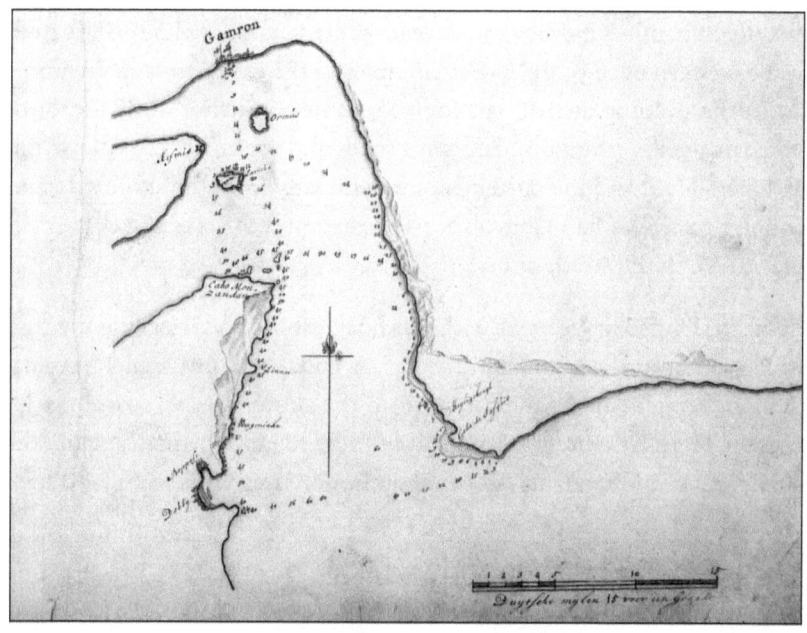

The Mouth of the Persian Gulf and the Strait of Hormuz, showing Bandar Abbas (Gamron), Qeshm and Larek Islands and Cape Musandam.

April 26, Monday morning. At sunrise we weighed anchor and [left] the roadstead of Gamron [Bandar Abbas] and sailed away with an E.N.E. wind. The course was to sail between Lareecque[5] and Kismis[6] to be returned in this way to Chassab, which is situated on the Arabian coast. During the first bells of the second watch we anchored at 13 fathoms above a good holding ground.

April 27, Tuesday. In the morning the wind was westerly; in the evening at sunset we had the island at about 2 miles east of us. At night the wind was S.S. to the east and sometimes S.S.E. [3367] it was completely calm. We sailed over good holding ground at 62, 63, 50 to 56 fathoms, which grounds were mixed with black sand. When we approached the coast during the day watch we encountered muddy grounds at 56 to 50 fathoms.

April 28, Wednesday. In the morning it was dead calm with hazy (?) (*disigh*) weather. With a Southern sun we saw Cape S. to the east half easterly at about 3.5 miles and a small white pagoda,[7] which is situated at the western edge of the bay at 2.5 miles to the east, 2 miles away from us. In the evening at half past four we came to anchor at 22 fathoms on coarse sandy ground mixed with shells and rocks, because the wind had died down and the current, coming directly from the shore side ran counter to us. We had Chassab S. to the east and the western corner of the bay W. to the south of us.

April 29, Thursday. We went with our boats ashore and in sailing the bay we passed grounds at 20, 15, 12, 8, 6.5, 5, and 4 fathoms, which [point] is about a pig of iron's shot away from the shore, it is all coarse sandy ground. Here we were received in a friendly manner by the captain (i.e. chief) and the inhabitants. The captain honored us with a goat and had

---

5. Larek Island, 32 km south by east of Bandar Abbas.
6. Qeshm Island at 24 km south by east of Bandar Abbas.
7. Maybe the tomb of Sheikh Zuhayr, a Moslem saint, is meant here. It is built of stone and Madripore corral and has the appearance of Persian work. It stands between al-Sha`am and Khasab, see Miles, *The countries*, p. 445 see also next note.

our two barrels, which were in the boat, filled with water. This [water] was good, but a bit far away from the beach to fetch it.

Chaszab is a small place with a small fortress in which a captain and about 30 to 40 soldiers are garrisoned. Its walls are made of stone and clay, constructed in a square of 5 fathoms high; it has no cannon, however. It is situated in a valley where there are plenty of date trees. Under them, people have built their dwellings or huts after the Indian fashion. Some are made of stone and clay, others of date fronds; they are about 8 to 9 feet high and are at a distance of 10 roods from each other. Their number is estimated to be 50 to 60.

It is situated at 26 degrees and 9 minutes Northern latitude between the Puncto de [?][8] and the river Ciebij,[9] which puncto and river are situated about 2.5 miles apart from each other [**3368**].

The countryside behind the said valley is rocky and mountainous, where one finds a few goats. Because of the population's poverty and the aridness of the country there is little selling and buying to do here.

There is some fresh [food] to be had such as goats and chickens although little. One may also obtain water, but it is a somewhat far to fetch.

When the dates are ripe, all people from the neighboring places come to harvest them. This takes place in the month of June and the people stay here until September, when each returns home with what he has plucked. These people mostly live from fishing and have nothing else to eat but these dates, which they eat with fish instead of bread.

It has a bay with a good holding ground at 12 to 8 fathoms. On the western side there is Puncto deggebay where in a valley there a small

---

8. The copyist has dropped a word here, viz. Doggebay. I have been unable to explain this name, but the authors of the journal clearly refer to Ras Sheikh Mas'ud. In a little bight at the northern end of the cape is the tomb of Sheikh from which it takes its name.
9. The Sib River or Khur al-Sham.

temple.[10] On the eastern side one finds the river Clobije,[11] where in former times the Portuguese used to put their frigates.

From the river Ciebie to the creek of Cabalje[12] the course is N.E. and then in northern direction for 2 miles and the depth is 25, 26, 27 to 30 fathoms over murky ground.

Cobalje is a place situated in a valley in the mountains. There are 5 to 6 huts in which fishermen live.

From the refuge of Cabalje until one is east off Puncto Mogoleff[13] (on its corner a crag is situated) the course is N.N.E. for 3.25 miles and from there until the aforementioned puncto the course is east for one mile.

Almost right between Cobalje and Puncto Mogaleff, the Ilje de Gaselle[14] island is situated at 0.25 mile off the coast. The depths between this [island] and the coast are 19, 15, 11.5, 9.5, 10.5, 12, 15, 14, and 19 fathoms mostly [over] murky ground, although it is now and then too rocky.[15] At a distance of a cannon's shot out off the island the sea has a depth of 48, 60, 50 and 65 fathoms [over] murky ground. [**3369**]

From Puncto Mogaleff until the western corner of the bay of Comzaar[16] the course is E.S.E. for 1.75 miles and the depth 53, 70, 75 to 65 fathoms [over] murky ground.

Camsaar is a place situated in a valley close to the mountains, where about 50 to 60 houses have been built of rocks to which clay is added. These are all inhabited by fishermen.[17]

---

10. See note 7.
11. Copyist's error; the Sibi River is meant here.
12. Cabalje or Cobalje is the Colville Cove, or the Khor Groob Ali or in Arabic Ghubb Ali.
13. Ras Mukhalif.
14. Jazirat al-Ghanam or Sheep Island.
15. This passageway is called Discovery Strait or Khur Qoway.
16. Kumzar is unique as being the only purely Persian town on the Arab coast. Miles, *Tribes*, p. 448.
17. There are three different traditional houses in Oman. First of all, there are *barasti* huts. These were built with palm fronds. The other one is called round

There is also a water well here, but it is not large and it is far to fetch. The bay is fit for small craft, but not for others vessels, for there are strong currents here, so that it is very difficult to get in or get out [of the bay]. At the N.W. side there is a small island and to the N.E. side there are two small islands. The depth here is 64 to 50 fathoms [over] murky ground. From here one sees in N.N.E. direction the small islands de Leest',[18] Lessenaren,[19] [and] Doodkist,[20] which are situated at about 3.5 miles offshore.[21] The depth of the S.W. side of [the island of] de Leest is 53 to 65 fathoms [over] coarse sand ground. Three miles east off the western corner of Comzaar there is an island[22] on the corner[23] of Cape Mosandon. The northern corner of this island lies at 26 degrees, 24 minutes northern latitude. The depth is 70 fathoms sandy ground. To the south at 1 mile off Cabo Mosandon one sees a mountain where some huts have been built, but which are no longer inhabited. In former times this has been a place that is called Cheijsa[24] by the Arabs.

On the other side of the aforementioned mountain on which Cheijsa is situated one finds the bay of Fillm.[25] On its northern side is Mocha[26] to which the same applies as to what has been observed with regard to Cheijsa.

---

house. These were made of stones and the roof was made of wood and grass. The last one is called *bait al-qufl*. These were strong houses built of large stones and their walls were thick.
18. The Last.
19. The Lectern.
20. The Coffin.
21. The Quoins, three wedge-shaped islands, the highest of which is 180 m high, called by the Arabs "Salama-wa-bent or 'Salama and her daughters." Miles, *Tribes*, p. 540 (Salamah wa-Banatha).
22. The island of Musandam.
23. Ras al Bab.
24. The village of Shaishah on Ras Qabr Hindi or the "Indians Grave."
25. The bay of Film, which forms part of the very large inlet known as Khor Ghazirah or Ghubbat Ghazirah. It is also known as Malcolm's Inlet.
26. Moqaqah.

From the northern corner untill the southern corner of Fillm bay the course is S. to the west for 1.5 mile and the depth [**3370**] is 48, 46, 45, 40 to 38 fathoms [over] good sandy ground. At a distance of about the range of a pig of iron shot from shore, a small island is situated at 1 mile E., to the south off the corner of Kierkasie.[27] The depth between this island and the shore is 40 fathoms [over] sandy ground.

From the Hook of Kierkasie until Puncto Marrazie[28] the course is S. and half to the west for more than 2.5 miles. One sails over sandy ground with depths of 46, 45, 40 to 38 fathoms.

Between these two hooks there is an inlet of about 1.25 miles which has good holding ground to the South side of the bay at about 0.25 mile offshore at a depth of 36 to 37 fathoms [over] grey sandy [ground].

From Puncto Marrazie until the Hook of Corsecaan[29] the course is S. to the west for 2 miles. One has depths of 40, 42, and 45 to 48 fathoms [over] sandy ground.

Here one has a bay[30] between the two streams aforementioned, the circumference of which is about 3 miles. At the inlet the depth is 42 fathoms [over] sandy ground.

From the Hook of Coersocaan to the southern hook of the bay of Lijma the course is S. for 3 miles and the depths are 38, 35, 33, 28, and 26 to 25 fathoms [over] sandy ground.

Between these aforementioned hooks there is also a cove where 3 to 4 huts stand. These are uninhabited and [this place] is name Cabil.[31]

Lijma is a place situated on a sand mountain. It has 50 to 60 small houses or huts that are constructed with rocks and clay and with date palm fronds of 8 to 10 feet [length]. It is situated at 25 degrees, 34 minutes northern latitude.

---

27. Probably (Qaryah) Karshah is meant here. The island probably is Umm al-Faiyarin.
28. Here probably Duhat Shaishah is meant.
29. Here probably Ghubbat Shabus is meant or Ras Sarkim.
30. This is the bay of Lima.
31. The cove referred to, is the Duhat Qabal named after the village of Qabal.

Behind this sand mountain there is a valley where some date palms are to be found and where some mustard-seed grows. The population lives off these. In the aforementioned valley there is a well, but the water is not so good, for it is brackish and almost undrinkable. It is situated at about 0.25 mile from the beach.

At a distance of a cannon shot off the aforementioned sand mountain on the southern side of the bay, there are at least some 50 to 60 small houses such as those mentioned above on the mountain slope, where the fishermen live. [**3371**]

The countryside around and behind the aforementioned valley is stony and mountainous, where one finds some goats, albeit very few. Therefore, there is nothing much to do here, because of poverty of the population and the aridness of the country. It has a beautiful bay, however, which is 1 mile wide and 0.75 mile deep. It has everywhere fine grey sandy ground. At the inlet the depths are 22, 20, 18, 15, 12, 4, 8 and 7 fathoms, while one is still at a distance of a pig iron's shot offshore.

At the southern corner of the bay, there is a small island at a distance of about a cannon's shot. The depth between them is 20 fathoms [over] murky ground.

To the south of the bay of Lijma at one mile's distance, there is a small bay in which Lijma Cadijma[32] is situated, which consists of 7 to 8 huts, but which are uninhabited.

From the southern corner of the bay of Lijma until the southern corner of Dabba[33] the course is S. half to the west for 5.75 miles. The depths are 40, 45, 48, 35, 36, and 30 to 25 fathoms mostly [over] waxy sandy ground.

Dabba (which we were unable to visit because of calm and counter currents) is a place (according to the interpreter assigned to us) with about 300 small houses constructed date palm fronds in the aforementioned manner. It is situated at 25 degrees, 12 minutes northern latitude.

---

32. Lima Qadimah or Old Lima.
33. Diba.

During the days of the Portuguese, there were 4 forts of which the largest is still standing.

This place also has a valley with a lot of date palms under which there are water wells, where one may get fresh water.

At the northern side of Dabba there is a small fresh water river where the fishermen live.[34]

From the southern corner of Dabba until the small island, which is situated in from of Lebdia,[35] the course is south for 2.25 miles, while one passes over depths of 21, 20, 19, and 22 fathoms of waxy sandy ground.

Lebdia is a place of about 200 small houses [**3372**] which are all built with date palm fronds and is situated close to the beach. It lies at 25 degrees, 5 minutes northern latitude. Behind these houses there is a beautiful valley where one finds a great many date palms and some fig trees. Under these [trees] there are several wells, one of which is situated a pistol's shot distance from the beach, from which well one may get very good and fresh water.

In the said valley there are growing some melons, water melons, and onions, but very few.

Behind this valley there is nothing but stony mountains so that not much trade can be carried on here.

Here one may obtain some fresh food such as cows, goats, chickens, melons, water melons, limes and onions, but not very much.

This place has no bay, but [only] a public roadstead, where at a 0.25 mile offshore one has a depth of 10 to 12 fathoms [over] waxy sandy ground.

From the small island on the southern side of Lebdie until the small island[36] situated at the southern corner of the bay of Gorfodeo[37] the

---

34. This refers to Bai`ah, "from the sea the two places appear to form one town, but in reality there are separated by a water course." Lorimer, vol. 2, p. 264.
35. Probably (al-)Bidyah is meant here. The island is called Jazirah Bidyah.
36. The islet is called Sirat (Sereet).
37. Copyist's error for Gorfocan or properly Khur Fakkan.

course is S. to the east for 1.75 mile. The depths are 16, 19, 22, 25, and 30 to 35 fathoms [over] waxy sandy ground.

Gorfocan is a place situated on a cove where about not less than 200 small houses have been built. All of them are made with date palm fronds and are close to the beach.

On the northern side it had a triangular fort from the days of the Portuguese, and one can still see the ruins of its walls. On the southern side in a cove [inboschies], which connected to a bay there is another fort on a mountain, but it has neither garrison nor guns, so that the place is totally dilapidated.[38]

This place has a beautiful valley with a great many date palms and some fig trees. Melons water [melon], limes and onions also grow here. **[3373]**

Under the trees there are several water wells with which they irrigate the land. It is good fresh water and somewhat farther to fetch than in Lebdie.

In the mountains, to the south of this valley there are some orange and lime trees.

For the rest the countryside surrounding this valley consists of rocky mountains, so that these people live from what grows in the valleys here. Because of poverty of the population and the aridness of the country it is no use carrying on trade here.

Fresh food to be had here consists of the fruits mentioned above and for the rest of some cows, goats and chickens, but of these, there not a great many.

The cove here has a width of one and a depth of 0.25 mile. On its southern side is a small island[39] at about a matchlock shot distance off shore.

---

38. Miles, *Tribes*, p. 452 believed these ruins to be a fort built by the Persian general Mohammad Taqi Khan Shirazi in 1742.
39. The islet is called Sirat (Sereet).

Here the sandy beach ends, which begins at the southern corner of Dabba. South of Gorfocan one again only meets with rocky mountains as far as Colba. Between these [places] one finds some sandy bays.

From the small island situated on the southern side of the bay of Gorfocan as far as a point off a place called Colba,[40] which is about 3.5 miles distance, one sails over depths of 20, 18, 22, 25, 30, 40, and 45 to 57 fathoms of black sandy ground, one being 9 miles off shore.

The land between the two aforementioned places runs from south to north and has no crags or shoals off shore.

South of Colba at about 5.5 miles is Nabor[41] and at both places fresh water can be obtained.

Going to the south from Nabor for about 3 miles, one finds a place called Ammock,[42] where one also may get fresh water.

The distance from Ammock until Soar[43] is about 3.5 miles, where also fresh water can be had. [**3374**]

The coastline between the aforementioned places mostly runs S.S.E. and N.N.W. and is low land with here and there tamber[44] and other wild trees. However, 7 to 8 miles upcountry one observes again high mountains.

Along the coast here one finds neither bays nor crags or shoals so that one only has to stay clear of the shore.

Sailing from Calbo to Zoar and staying 3 to 4 miles off shore, one passes over depths of 40, 38, 38, 3, 35, 30, 35, 50, 40, 35, 31, 22, 19, 10 to 15 fathoms of black sandy ground, which is south of Soar where we have dropped anchor.

---

40. Kalba.
41. Nabar.
42. Amq.
43. Sohar.
44. *Tamr* or *thamr* or date palms.

It is about 21 miles from Soar to the small islands named Ilje de Soadije.[45] The coastline runs from Soar S.E. to the south for 6.5 miles and then to the abovementioned small islands E. to the south.

To the west of Soadije at about 8 miles there is a place called Soceck,[46] where only 5 to 6 huts are standing.

The depths between Soar until the abovementioned islands while sailing 4 to 5 miles offshore are 30, 38, 25, 18, 20, 35, 23, 25, 21, 19, 18, 22, 21, 30 fathoms of sandy ground.

It is again lowland with mountains [inland] as before. The coast is most of the time beautiful, but it has no bays.

The islands of Soadije number six and are situated at about 3 miles offshore. They are named after a place that is situated opposite them onshore called Soadije.

Here there is a reef from the said islands to the shore, so that vessels cannot pass between them.

Having the islands at S. to the north for 2 miles the depth is 31 fathoms of coarse sandy ground.

From the islands of Soadije until the islands of Borca[47] the course is E.N.E. for two miles. [**3375**]

The two islands of Borca have 5 to 6 crags. They are situated at 4 miles offshore and are also named after a place called Borca just as above.

Having the said island S.W. of you for 1.5 mile, one passes over a depth of 60 fathoms of the same ground as above.

From the islands of Borca until the islands of Sib[48] the course is W. and half to the south for 1.75 mile.

---

45. The Suwadi islands.
46. Suwaiq.
47. Barkeh.
48. Sib.

There are 5 islands of Sieb[49] and near them 4 to 5 crags are found. They are situated 4.5 miles off shore. They are also named after a place that is situated right opposite them onshore and which is called Sieb.

Having the said islands S. of you at 0.75 mile one the depth is 40 fathoms above sandy ground.

One and a half mile to the east of the islands of Sieb, there are 3 islands with 3 crags. When you have these at 1 mile W.S.W. from you the depths are 42, 41 to 40 fathoms of good holding ground mixed with sand. They are situated at 4.25 miles off shore.

Here ends the lowland that began at Colba. Here the rocky mountains start showing along the coast. From the said island until the Grey Rock[50] the course is S.E. to the east for about 5 miles, which Rock is one mile off shore.

From the Grey Rock until the eastern corner of the bay of Mascatta, the course is E.S.E. for 2 miles and [the depths are] 18, 16, 15, 12, 11 and 10 fathoms of sandy ground.

Mascatta is a city having stone walls all around. To the side of the bay there are some cannons [on the walls]. Its size is about that of Gamron and the houses are built in almost the same way. It is well populated by all kinds of Indians, who come to carry on their trade here. It lies at 23 degrees, 18 minutes northern latitude.

This city is situated against the mountains and has three forts which are on the seaside, to wit: [**3376**]

At the eastern side of the city the fort of Mogob[51] is situated on a mountain. The only entrance is via a staircase that has been hewn into the rock.

---

49. The islands of Barkeh and Sib are called "the Deymanieh [Dimaniyat]; they are sterile, waterless and uninhabited, and two have separate names-Joon and Khararba. (The Deymanieh group is often called by fishermen the 'Saba Jezair' or the Seven Islands, and derives this appellation 'Deymanieh' from a tribe of that name, of which a small remnant still exists in Oman; the name has remained unaltered since the time of Pliny)," Miles, *Tribes*, p. 459.
50. The island of Fahal (the stallion) is meant here.
51. Mughab, at the turn of the 20th century there was a city quarter of Muscat of that name.

At the western side of the said city the fort of Mascatta is also situated on a mountain, having at the mountain foot a bulwark from which one may enter the said fort via a constructedstaircase.

To the north and at a matchlock's shot distance from the bulwark (which is situated below the fort of Mascatta) there are two bulwarks named St. Anthony[52] on and below the mountain. Behind these bulwarks in the mountains there at least 8 to 9 guard-houses. Behind the city there is nothing but rocky mountains. However, trade is important here and is carried on by Moors,[53] Banyans,[54] and Mallabars,[55] who with their ships make a major voyage and come here. They bring all kinds of textiles, and clothes in addition to pepper, cinnamon, ginger, *borre borry*,[56] rice, sandalwood, iron, and un-tanned hides.

The bay has a width of about 0.13 mile and a depth of 0.14 mile. On the western side between the bulwark below the fort of Mascatta and St. Anthony there is an inlet, which is the roadstead for small vessels. The bay is the roadstead for big vessels that are usually anchored at depths of 9, 8 to 7 fathoms of ground abovementioned.

Concerning fresh food one can get everything here for the ships, but all things are expensive with the exception of fish which is caught here in abundance and is to be had at a reasonable price.

Verified and agreed with the principal [text].[57]

---

52. Probably Fort San Joao or St. John is meant here. The forts were known under different names to those mentioned in this journal, see Miles, *Tribes*, p. 463, see als Lorimer, *Gazetteer*, vol. 2, p. 1180.
53. Moslems.
54. Europeans referred to Hindu merchants from Western India, especially Gujarat, as Banyans.
55. People from the Malabar coast are meant here.
56. *Borre borry* is a yellow ungeant prepared from coco-nut oil, curcuma, and sandalwood.
57. The text of this journal (a copy of the original which has not been preserved) is to be found in NA, VOC, folios 3366-76. The translation is a reproduction of Willem Floor, "First Contacts between the Netherlands and Muscat," *Zeitschrift der Deutschen Morgenländischen Gesellschaft* 132 (1982), pp. 289-307.

Annex 2

The Trade of Muscat in 1673

Muscat.[1] To analyze the trade of Muscat to the best of our meagre ability, we first will mention all things brought from other countries in the year 1673, and after that what we have further observed.

We therefore, begin with **Sind** (Sindy).

Fourteen barques came here, to wit: four on 16 February, seven on 17 February, one on 20 February, one on the 1 March, one on 4 March, or in total fourteen small and large barques. They have brought the following items:

770 . . . . packages with various kinds of textiles (*cleeden*).
250 . . . . *candis* (*candijs*)[2] *borborry*[3]

---

1. This annex is taken from merchant Georg Wilmson's report (VOC 1305, f. 473-91vs) as published in Floor, "The Description," pp. 37-50.
2. *Candi* is weight used in South-India, which is roughly about 500 lbs, but varying much in different parts. It was generally equivalent to 20 *man*. In Tamil the word is *kandi*; the Portuguese write the word as *candil*.
3. *Borborrij* a word derived from Javanese *boreh*, is a yellow ointment prepared from coconut oil, sandalwood and curcuma.

6	. *candis* putchok (*petsjock*)⁴
108	. *candis* lamp-oil
50	. *candis* salammoniac
50	. *candis* saltpeter
40	. *candis* lack called *tockte*⁵
4,000 . . .	. pieces of hides
30	. *candis* cumin

Kutch (Ketsi).⁶ Four small ships came here to wit: one on 8 May, one on 13 May, one of 14 May, one of 15 May; they brought the following to the market:

350	. *candis* lamp-oil
1/2	. *candi* silk *t'sjadder*⁷
115	. packages of cotton
60	. *candis* of *cajang*⁸
60	. *candis* of cotton yarn
57	. *candis* of peas

---

4. *Poetsjoek* or putchock is the trade name for a fragrant root, a product of the Himalayas. It is used as a chief ingredient of Chinese pastille rods commonly called jostick.
5. *Lack* or lacca from the Hindi word *lakhi*, the resinous incrustation produced on certain trees by the puncture of the lac insect (*Coccus lacca*). The term tochte maybe the Persian word takhteh, meaning among other things 'a board, plank, or a sheet of paper.'
6. Ketsi may be identified with Kutch (Gujarat), the home base of the Sanganian pirates.
7. *Tsjadder* from *chador* (Persian) meaning 'veil, tent.' Here undoubtedly fabrics are meant that were used as veils.
8. This was a Malay term for groundnut, but was also used in VOC records as the generic name for pulses.

240	. . . . . *corges*[9] of red and white *sjoerij*[10]
15	. . . . . *candis* of *milij*[11]
5	. . . . . *corges* of *kad aewasije*[12]
1	. . . . . *corge* of silk *longis*[13]

Patan.[14] Two small ships came here, to wit: one of 23 April, one on 6 June, which brought the following to the market:

40	. . . . . packages of *bhaer*[15] of cotton
90	. . . . . *candis* of lamp-oil
23	. . . . . *candis* of ground-nuts
17	. . . . . *candis* of *milij*
42	. . . . . *candis* of peas
16	. . . . . *candis* of sesamium
50	. . . . . *corges* of *zjoerijsen*[16]
12	. . . . . *candis* of cotton yarn

---

9. A term of Indian origin meaning 'a score,' or a unit of 20.
10. I have been unable to identify this term; it may be the same fabric referred to as *jurries* by Hamilton, vol. 1, p. 77.
11. *Milij* from the Portuguese *milha*, meaning millet, but in Dutch mostly used to refer to maize or so-called Turkish wheat.
12. *Kad* from *qadak*, meaning "of a person's size" (*be andazeh-ye qad*), was a tightly woven Persian cotton fabric which is also referred to as *nankeen* in European sources.
13. *Longijs* from the Persian *longi*, a cloth worn around the loins and passed between the legs. Here is refers to the kind of textile used for that purpose.
14. Patan (Maharashtra State) in India.
15. A *bahar* is a unit of weight used in India and Persia, whose weight varies per location and per product, see Willem Floor, "Weights and Measures in Qajar Iran," *Studia Iranica*, 37/1 (2008), pp. 57-115.
16. *Zjoerijsen* or *sjoerij*, I have been unable to identify this term; it may be the same fabric referred to as *jurries* by Hamilton, vol. 1, p. 77.

From the sea ports in the **domain of the Shivaji** (Sewagie)[17] fourteen ships came here, both large, such as grabs (*goerab*)[18] and small ones, to wit:

Two from Sangameshwar (Songmeijser)[19] on 6 February.

One from Killiesie[20] on 6 February.

Two from Hardtsjerie,[21] one of 7 March, one of 9 April.

Five from Rajapur (Ragiapour),[22] one of 20 April, one on 9 May, one on 12 May, one of 18 May, one on 19 May.

One from Harapatnam[23] on 12 May.

One from Aatsjerek[24] on 10 May.

Two from Vengurla (Wingurla),[25] one of 20 January, one of 6 April.

Altogether fourteen ships and *grab*s came, which brought a variety of goods that we therefore, have tabulated and which consisted of the following:

1358	. packages of various kinds of textiles
73.5	. *candi*s of cardamom
243.5	. *candi*s of *borborrij*
117.5	. *candi*s of sandalwood

---

17. Shivaji Bhosale (r. 1674-1680), the founder of the Maratha Empire.
18. *Goerab* or *grab* (English) from Arabic *ghurab*, meaning 'raven,' was a galley, a two or three-masted square-rigged vessel, sometimes with and sometimes without a bowsprit.
19. Sangameshwar (Maharashtra State) in India.
20. Killesie, probably Kelashi or Kelshi, now a village on the west coast of India (Maharashtra State).
21. Hardtsjerie, unidentified place on the west coast of India (Maharashtra State).
22. Rajapur (Maharashtra State) in India.
23. Harapatnam, unidentified place on the west coast of India (Maharashtra State).
24. Aatsjerek, unidentified place on the west coast of India (Maharashtra State).
25. Vengurla is a town in Sindhudurg district of Maharashtra, India just north of Goa.

83.5 . . . . . *candi*s of ginger
70 . . . . . *candi*s of black sugar[26]
271. . . . . *candi*s of hemp
123.5 . . . . *candi*s of white and cooked areca[27]
140. . . . . *candi*s of tamarind
110. . . . . *candi*s of *helileh*[28]
8 . . . . . *candi*s of *Cassia fistula*[29]
26 . . . . . *candi*s of *goony*[30]
66 . . . . . *candi*s of *coetlij*[31]
293. . . . . *corge*s of white rice *dengie*[32]
500. . . . . packages of ordinary rice
83 . . . . . *candi*s of coir (*caijer*)
23 . . . . . *candi*s of lamp-oil
50 . . . . . packages of glass beads
100,000 . . . coconuts

From **Surat** and **Broach** (Brootchia)[33] two small ships called here, which brought the following to the market:

200. . . . . packages of textiles
122. . . . . *candi*s of lamp-oil

---

26. *Jaggery* or *gurh*, traditionally produced sugar from date, cane juice or palm sap, mixed with a variety of other ingredients; it is brown in color.
27. This refers to the areca nuts from the areca nut palm of the Malabar coast, which, fresh or dried, were used for chewing.
28. *Terminalia chebula* or *myrobalan migrae*, a dye known in Persian as *halileh-ye siyah*, or *myrobalan nigrae*.
29. Its root was used as a purgative,
30. *Goony* from Hindi *goni*, a sack, sacking. It was the popular and trading name of the coarse sacking and sacks made from the fiber of jute.
31. *Coetlij* or properly *sutli* means 'yarn, string.'
32. *Dengie* rice, perhaps refers to the Gujarati word for 'unmilled rice,' *dangar*.
33. Broach a port at the mouth of the Narabada, north of Surat.

104 . . . . . *bahars* of 640 lbs. each of cotton
20 . . . . . *candis* of *borborrij*
45 . . . . . *candis* of white rice *dengie*
3 . . . . . *candis* of zinc
1/2 . . . . *candi* of aguilwood.[34]

From **Karwar** (Karwaar)[35] a small ship called on 14 April that brought the following:

300 . . . . . packages of textiles
83 . . . . . *candis* of white rice
22 . . . . . *candis* of hemp
14 . . . . . *candis* of ginger
18 . . . . . *candis* of areca
45 . . . . . *corges* of *goony*
19 . . . . . *candis* of *soetlij*

From the **Canarese coast**, from ports such as Bhatkal (Batticale),[36] Basrur (Bassalore),[37] and Mangalore (Mangaloor)[38] twenty-seven ships and *grabs* came here with cargos of rice from 1 December of last year until the end of May, some of which made two voyages. These, according to a rough estimate, have brought here, both in packages and in bulk, more than 7,000 *lasts*.[39]

---

34. Aguilwood or eagle-wood is the name of an aromatic wood from Cambodia and some Indian regions. It is also another name for aloes-wood, It is derived from Tamil, *agil*.
35. Karwar in Mysore, India.
36. Bhatkal on the isthmus connecting Karwar Head in Kanara with the land is situated close to Karwar.
37. Basrur is a port on the Malabar Coast (Kerala State).
38. Mangalore a port in Mysore.
39. One *last* is 2 tons.

From the **Malabar coast,** seven small ships came here fully laden, to wit:

One from Calicut[40] on 10 March.

One from the same on 22 March.

One from Ponnani (Pannanij)[41] on 23 March.

Two from Dharmapatam (Dermenepatan)[42] on 22 March.

One from Cannanore (Cannanoor)[43] on the same date.

One from the same place on 14 April, or in total seven small ships from the Malabar coast, which brought the following to the market here:

1,300	*candis* of copra or *kokospit*
555	*candis* of pepper
97	*candis* of red areca
276	*candis* of *borborry*
135	*candis* of fried ginger
120	*candis* of cardamom
154	*candis* of iron
113	*candis* of sappanwood
146	*candis* of *trehiel*[44]
170	*candis* of coir
50	*candis* of *soetlij*
210	planks
123,000	coconuts

195 bundles of reeds plus bamboo, conifers and other timber.

---

40. Kozhikode, also known as Calicut, is a city in the state of Kerala in southern India on the Malabar Coast.
41. Ponnani is situated south of entrance to Bharathpuzha River on the Malabar coast (Kerala).
42. Dharmapatam town is situated on an island formed by the mouths of the river of the same name on the Malabar Coast, 5 km north of Tellicherri.
43. Kannur, also known as Cannanore (Kerala).
44. I have not been able to identify this term.

From **Mokha** and **Aden** (Adon), three small ships arrived here between 28 May and 4 October, two belonging to the Imam and the third one to Alaur Aga.[45] These ships take most of their cargo to Persia and other parts of the Gulf. In addition fifteen to sixteen barques arrived; all of them carried the following from there to Persia and beyond:

3,000	*candis* of coffee
345	packs of pepper
53	large packs of *ruinas*[46]
22	packs of cardamom
22	packs of dried ginger
22.5	*candis* of wax
4	*candis* of camphor
2.5	*candis* of benzoïn.

From **Patta** (Pate),[47] situated on the Melinde coast,[48] two small ships arrived here, one belonging to the Imam, which left thither mid-February and returned on 4 October, one vessel from Pata also arriving on 4 October. These two small ships brought the following:

---

45. I have not been able to identify this person.
46. *Ruinas* is a corruption of the Persian word *runas*, meaning madder, a red dye.
47. Patta Island is situated on the coast of Kenya, north of Witu. Hamilton, *A New Account*, vol. 1, p. 18 states that "Patta is now in the hands of the Musqat Arabs, and affords good Store of Teeth [tusks] and slaves for Musqat."
48. The Malindi coast is situated in Kenya.

570. . . . . slaves, 450 for the Imam's account and 120 for that of those of Pate

250. . . . . planks for the Imam's account

8 . . . . . masts

Further, some amber and civet [skins?].

From the **Maldives** two vessels called here, which only brought coir, coconuts and chanks.

All goods that are brought here from foreign parts have to be unloaded at the bankshall (*bankschael*)[49] and have to be recorded there.

Weighed goods are mainly packed according to a standard weight and are taken to the merchants' houses after having been counted and recorded. If part of them is sold, the goods have to be taken to the weigh-house to be weighed; here the buyer's and seller's names, the date and the price of the transaction are also recorded to calculate the amount of tolls to be paid at the end of the monsoon or on departure of each ship. If the year has expired and some goods are still unsold, no toll is demanded until they are sold or transported elsewhere.

Textiles (*cleeden*) that are taken to the weigh-house are recorded and on each pack a seal is affixed, so that they cannot be changed. Nobody is allowed to open any pack in his house without the presence of an official. The settling of the account of toll to be paid is done in the same manner as with the weight goods.

Having discussed the trade of various foreign parts carried on here, Your Honor may observe next the following, to wit:

Sind. From the textiles that are brought here, Muscat consumes 800 packs or a little more than one quarter; the remainder is taken

---

49. Bankshall (Bengali *banksala*) a term used to denote a warehouse or the office of the Harbor Master.

to Bahrain, al-Qatif (Katijf), Qatar, Basra, and Persia in the following manner. Those [traders] from Sind have their agents here to whom they send their goods each year. These keep all that is consumed in Muscat and send the rest to the above places to other agents, who mostly reside there on their behalf to sell these goods. Mostly, they send the proceeds via Bandar-e Kong (Congo) back to Sind.

The fabrics (*lijwaten*) and materials that Muscat consumes have been reported to us to consist of the following varieties and quantities:

	length	width
500 *corges* of *goeries*[50]	24	1.25 *cobido*[51]
200 *corges* of *goeries*, coarse	24	1.25
50 *corges* of black *baftas*[52]	28	1.50
20 *corges* silk *alegia lackij*[53]	25	1.50
40 *corges* long *loebieij*[54] 6 make one piece	24	2
50 *corges mawijs*[55]	4	2
15 *corges mawijs* 2 make one piece	12	1.50
25 *corges tsiadder 'tsjonnie*[56]	12	1.50
80 *corges kad kenaiedaar*[57]	24	1.25
15 *corges longijs sabonie*[58]	12	2

---

50. I have not been able to identify this fabric.
51. Cubit or ell.
52. *Baftas* from Persian *bafteh* or woven; these are fine cotton fabrics.
53. *Alegia* are fine fabrics made of so-called *legi* silk; they were five yards long with a wavy pattern running in the length of either side. I have been unable to identify the word *lackij*.
54. *Long* probably is *longi* (see above) and *loebieij* perhaps the place of origin.
55. I have not been able to identify this fabric.
56. Probably a corruption of the word *chador-e chaneh*, or face veil from the Persian words *chador* (veil) and *chaneh* (chin, jaw).
57. For the term *qad* see above. The word *kenaredaer* is from Persian *kenarehdar*, meaning 'having a hem, bordered.'
58. *Longi*, bath cloth; *sabonie* perhaps from Persian *sabuni*, meaning 'soap.'

200 *corges paleng peosj moltony*[59] per pair   11   4

Further, many small goods of various kinds of silk as well as cotton materials, but only a little of each.

The fabrics (*lijwaten*) of which a large quantity is transported to other parts are the following:

	length	width	
White *goeries*	24	1.25	Bahrain, Basra, Persia
Idem	32	1.50	idem
Idem	32	2	idem
Idem, coarse	24	1.50	idem
Kadmiersay[60]	20	1.25	idem
Black *baftas*	28	1.50	Mokha, Hasa, Basra, Persia
Alledzja molla abrahunnij[61]	24	1.50	Persia
Alledzja mioneh[62]	24	1.25	idem
Alledzja kalberga[63]	24	1.25	idem
Alledzja zjome waar[64]	11.50	1.25	idem

---

59. Properly *palang-push-e Moltani*, or a cloth cover (Persian *push*) for a palanquin made in or of the design of Moltan (a region in Sind).
60. I have not been able to identify this fabric.
61. *Alledzja*, see above. Mullah Ibrahimi refers to the original designer or manufacturer of this special variety of this silken fabric.
62. *Miyaneh*, a Persian word meaning 'middle,' here referring to a special quality of this silken fabric.
63. Kalberga refers to the place of production, i.e. Gulbarga a city in the Indian state of Karnataka, which formerly part of Nizam's Hyderabad state. Gulbarga is 200 km from Hyderabad.
64. *Jamehvar*, a Persian word referring to a kind chintz or flowered sheet or shawl; here it indicates a quality of fabric.

Alledzja zjome shah[65]	11.50	1	idem
Chitsware	18	1.50	idem

Sole-leather

Indigo [to] Basra, al-Hasa and Persia

Salammoniac, mostly to Persia

Irias,[66] *putchok* in the Hindi fashion on lead (*op loot*)[67] is made in Sind and has been brought here by the English for two consecutive years.

Kutch. All goods coming from there are sold in Muscat. Afterwards, part of it is taken by buyers from al-Hasa, Bahrain, etc. Trade from those parts does not amount to much value. If the Sanganians (Sanganers)[68] have taken vessels coming from Sind they take the goods in those vessels to their [own] vessel here to which are added other goods from Kutch.

Patan. Trade from those parts is of no importance, it mostly consists of all kinds of grains, lamp-oil, *Cassia fistula*, and cotton. It is all sold in Muscat and it is shipped from there to other parts.

Konkan (Conken).[69] This is the popular name for all sea-ports in the possession of the Shivaji. It also includes Karwar. From there, a considerable quantity of textiles and other merchandise is brought here. The weighed goods are mostly sold here and then taken elsewhere by the buyers, who then sell these goods to Arab and Persian merchants.

---

65. Royal *jamehvar*, refers to a special quality or pattern of this silken fabric.
66. From the root of the iris (orris root) an oil was made, known as irias, used as a medicine.
67. I have been unable to understand the meaning of this part of the text. "*Poetjoek op sijn Hindies op loot valt in Sindij,*" where the words *op loot* don't make sense to me, unless the meaning is that the jostics rods were made of lead (*loot*).
68. The Sanganians inhabited the coast of Kathiawar and Kutch, Beyt being their principal center, see Ovington, *Voyage*, pp. 99, note 2 and 254f.
69. Konkan, the low country of Western India between the Ghauts and the sea, extending roughly from Goa northward to Gujarat.

Of the 1,500 to 1,600 packs, Muscat consumes little more than 300 to 400 consisting mostly in dongrys with black and red heads, *chadors* of all kinds, coarse *chillas* named *cahonie* of an inferior quality,[70] common *parcallen*,[71] long 24, wide 1.5 [cubits], cotton yarns, etc.

All weighed goods are sent from here to Persia and the Arabian coast.

The remainder of the textiles (*cleeden*) consisting of various kinds bought by Persian merchants at Golconda are taken here and then shipped to the small sea-ports of Persia, because they pay lower imposts, so that Muscat only serves as a transit station.

Surat. From there little trade is carried on here. The only ships that come here in the bay do so out of necessity or out of fear of the Portuguese. The goods taken here by two small ships have already been sold. The textiles consisting of two kinds, namely *kahonie* and *patha*,[72] which for the greater part is taken by Muscat, only a small quantity was taken to Basra.

Kanara. This is the store-room of Persia and Arabia. Its rice is sold here and then transported in small lots, mostly by barques, except that consumed in Muscat itself.

Malabar. All that is brought from to Muscat is for the greater part reserved by the Imam's agent, for he considers this to be the most profitable trade. He keeps the goods until the end of the year and will not sell them if he cannot make a considerable profit. These goods are transported to the surrounding Arabian and Persian sea-ports, which

---

70. *Chilla* (from Sanskrit *chela*) refers to a fine cotton fabric. *Cahonie*, probably a copyist's error for *catoni*, derived from the Arabic *qutni* (also atlas) referring to a mixed silken-cotton fabric. For the various textile terms, see Willem Floor, *The Persian Textile Industry in historical perspective 1500-1925* (Paris, 1999), chapter 2.
71. This word already occurs in Middle Dutch as *perkaal*. It is probably derived from Persian *pargaleh* and referred to a plain, un-patterned cotton fabric. For other possible meanings, see Hobson Johnson q.v. *percaulas*.
72. I have not been able to identify the term *patha*. Possibly, *patha* just refers to the Sanskrit word *patta*, meaning 'fabric, strip of cloth,' or to the famous *patola* fabrics from Gujarat, which are colorful silken *ikats*. For the term *cahonie*, see note 70.

trade he increases or decreases, depending on the state of the market in Persia or elsewhere.

Mokha. Coffee is the main item from Mokha, all of which is taken to Basra and Persia. Only a little is stored and brought here by Arab merchants; the greater part is transshipped or forwarded by the same barques. The fact that this year pepper, cardamom, and ginger were brought here was caused by the abundant import and low prices of these goods in Mokha. Formerly, they used to sell better there.

Patta, situated on the Melinde coast. This trade is carried on by the Imam. He only takes cash, rice and dates when he sails thither. From Patta 400 to 500 slaves, masts, planks and other construction timber are taken. The annual trade carried on by the citizens [of Patta] with a small vessel is of little importance. They bring more or less 150 to 200 slaves, some ambergris, some tortoise shell, further conifers and other construction timber.[73]

Maldives. We have already mentioned what is brought from there, which only consists of trifling goods.

The prices of weighed goods fluctuated during the trading season. We have noted it every month and recorded it at the end of the *Dagregister* (Journal) to which we humbly refer. The same holds for the list of fabrics (*lijwaten*), which we have already sent.

The abovementioned places take various goods from Muscat and are reported to consist of the following:

Sind annually imports around 1,400 to 1,500 great *bahars* of 1,600 lbs of dry as well as wet (*pakdadel*) dates; 400 to 500 candis of copra; 300 to 400 candis of white areca depending on the size of the imports [into

---

73. Robert Padbrugge suggested in his report (VOC 1288, f. 437r-vs) that it would be worthwhile to investigate the slave trade of the island situated on the coast of Sofala (Caffala/Mozambique) where many castrated negroes (*caffers*) were offered for sale. Here they were bought with prices ranging from 10 to 14 Spanish reals (*Spaanse matten*) and sold at 25 to 36 *rijksdaalders* (the Dutch base unit of account) equal to 2.5 Dutch guilders) per slave. The slave dealers refused to sell slaves to Padbrugge, because they feared that the negroes might become violent [?] (*voor den droos hebben*).

Muscat]. Furthermore, *ruinas*, pepper, cardamom, lead, tin, sandalwood, is taken depending on the market situation there [i.e. Sind].

Kutch annually imports 600 to 700 *bahars* of dried and wet dates; 100 to 150 candis of copra; 40 to 50 candis of white areca; 35 to 40 candies of *tebhiel*,[74] *hing*,[75] pepper, etc., depending on whether the Malabar spices are expensive or cheap in Patan.

Patan annually imports 200 to 300 *bahars* of dry and wet dates.

Konkan imports nearly 1,000 *bahars* of dry and wet dates; 100 candis of *ruinas*; 100 corges of *japancij*;[76] 400 candis of *hing*; 100 to 150 horses; some rosewater and fruits; and cash.

Surat imports. Depending on whether ships call here, 200 to 300 *bahars* of dry and wet dates per ship in exchange for cash.

Kanara only imports cash, but sometimes also 30 to 40 horses for the *Neijk*[77] or ruler of their land.

Malabar. Little else is taken back to their country other than cash, except for some saltpeter, rosewater, Persian earthenware, and fruits.

Mokha. If spices such as cloves and nutmegs had a willing market there, they take some of these goods from Kong, sometimes also from Muscat. Furthermore, native loaf-sugar, textiles from Sind and great quantities of wet dates.

Patta imports the following from Muscat: [blank] *bahars* of dates; Spanish reals called *foulerie*;[78] some Persian porcelain, some 10 to 20 chests of Muscat loaf-sugar; black coarse *longi* from Vengurla; *chador daboelij*[79] of

---

74. I have been unable to identify this product.
75. Asafetida, a fetid smelling spice, much used in Indian cooking. It is made from the dried latex exuded from the living underground tap root of several species of Ferula, which is a perennial herb.
76. *Yapanji*, a felt cloak or great coat used to protect the wearer against the cold and rain.
77. *Neijk*, from Hindi *nayak*, meaning 'leader, chief, general.'
78. I have not been able to identify this term, which is not known to numismatists.
79. Referring to a *chador* coming from Dabhol, a famous Konkan port.

poor quality; *paatsjehaer* called *chonne*[80] produded in Masulipatnam; Surat textiles (*cleeden*); blue *baftas*; some chintzes; *patha*; *chador cambatij*,[81] black *cannekijns*.[82]

Bahrain, **Qatar** and **al-Hasa** buy from the merchandise that comes here from all parts in such large quantities as will not be seen anywhere else.[83]

There are a few goods of which they only take a small share. They only enter the market for cash.

The trade of Abdallah. We can hardly say anything definite about trade in general, because the Imam's agent, without whose prior permission no foreigner may buy or sell anything, daily issues new trade regulations. During our stay here, we observed that he sometimes acquired a whole ship's cargo, sometimes half, and also a quarter [of a cargo]. He allowed himself to be guided by his expectation of the profit likely to be earned from the imported goods. All this is done under the guise of an honest sale, and they [the importers] are hardly allowed to show that they feel wronged in some way, or else prison is their future. The *nakhoda* (*nachoda*) or commissioner of any ship that arrives from abroad has to submit the bill of lading. He is then ordered to provide samples of each good ashore. Then he has to go to Abdallah's house, who is there with a company of Banyans and others, to contract a sale. But only he [i.e. Abdallah] is allowed to make a bid, which is rather unsettling, for it is so low that the seller is taken aback. However, whatever the market situation

---

80. *Paatsjehaer* or patchery, were so-called Coromandel textiles (*doeken*), which usually were two in one piece of double width. The term *chonne* I am unable to explain, unless the Persian word *khaneh* (house) is meant, which is unlikely.
81. The *Cambatij chador*s are those coming from Cambay, the famous port of Gujarat, which Arab authors usually rendered as Kanbayat.
82. Fine cotton fabrics; the word is derived from the Portuguese *canequim*.
83. According to Robert Padbrugge (NA, VOC 1288, f. 437), each year 1,000 *last* (a Dutch measure equivalent to two tons) of pepper were imported from Malabar. The greater part of this pepper was re-exported with caravans to/from Mecca. He also reported that the best-selling products were those of inferior quality.

is, he is obliged to part with his goods- the one more, the other less-, at a difference of 1.5, 2, 3, 4 to 5 *laris* per *man* of 24 lbs. or per *candi* of 480 lbs. with the current rate.

The goods, which Abdallah wants to buy and to have sole possession of, are taken ashore and via the weigh-house taken to the Imam's warehouses. The remainder is stored in the seller's house, where they may be sold to the highest bidder, provided Abdallah has given permission and that it is sold with a considerable profit. In case of a sale at higher prices than at first was fixed, the first transaction automatically becomes null and void, without any further ado [by Abdallah]. When these people are about to leave, and he still may have a liking for some goods, he then again concludes a transaction with them, but as has been stated above, [at a price] lower than the market rate. This mostly happens with weighed goods, for he seldom takes an interest in textiles (*cleeden*). Several goods such as anchors, coir, and coir ropes, planks and masts, cannons and iron are mostly bought on the account of the Imam. He, after having taken from these goods what he needs, then sells the remaining coir, iron, etc. to others.

If one of the arriving merchants wants to be exempt from these servitudes, he settles with him [Abdallah] for a certain amount, or he only profits from a share of their goods in order to be allowed to sell the rest of them to their own liking. All this having been done, nothing may be sold [nevertheless] before the broker has obtained his prior permission to do so after having informed him that there might be something to his liking. In that case, when the goods have already been put on the scales, and he pereives a profit for himself, the purchaser has to withdraw. Or if Abdallah allows him [the purchase], it has happened that he will take half of it. Thus, hardly anything is sold by foreigners that he does not have a share in it. Yes, it even happened that at a time that rice in bulk (*stort rijst*) yielded more profit than rice in straw packages, he ordered those traders [with the packaged rice], for which they had already paid 0.25 *mahmudi* per package or less, depending on whether they were big or small, to unpack it to be allowed to market it freely. When they sold it by measure again they had to pay a certain amount for each *candi*. This is the way trading practices of the Imam's agent were carried out during our stay. What else he will think of is as yet unknown. The majority of the Basrur voyagers [*vaarders*] have left almost bankrupt from here, because of the extraordinary imposts and the assignations with which they have been paid, from which they may expect little merchandise or money. [For example,] there was a Brahmin (Bramene) whom they forced to buy more than 40 horses at an unusual high price, in addition to another from whom they took his ship half by force. Those people thought that they could pay with an assignation after deduction of 17.5 per cent tolls on the price agreed upon. [The Basrur voyagers] were not prepared to accept this and lodged a complaint with the Imam, but found little consolation. For as soon as the latter had turned his back, they were put in prison for quite some time. However, they could not be persuaded to agree to the unreasonable transaction and were released. Because the monsoon had long since come to an end, they [the Arabs] suggested that the [Basrur voyagers] took the ship back. Nevertheless, they were held liable for a mere 1,000 *laris*, which the Arabs thought they could claim from their fellow-countrymen. The *nakhoda* again refused to give in and was again put in prison, where he finally died. In this way and the previously mentioned manner, foreigners are treated here.

The **tolls** that were levied on the merchandise coming from the various parts and which were traded here during the year 1673 are reported to be as follows:

Sind, Moorish goods brought here from there paid 2.5 [per] 100; Banyans: 5 per 100.

Kutch, both Moors[84] and Banyans, because they are ruled by a heathen[85] government: 8 per 100.

Patan, Moors: 2.5 per 100; Banyans 8 per 100.

Surat, Moorish goods: 2.5 per 100; Banyans: 5 per 100.

Rajapur, both Moorish and Banyan goods, because the ports are in the dominion of the *Shivaji*: 8 per 100.

---

84. Meaning Moslems.
85. Heathen meaning a non-Moslem government.

Vengurla, the ame: 8 per 100.

Karwar, Moors: 2.5 per 100; Banyans: 5 per 100.

Basrur, **Mangalore**, and **Bhatkal**, because they took so much from the Imam's men: 17.5 per 100.[86]

Basra, Moors: 2 1/2 per 100; Banyans: 5 per 100.

Persia, the same; idem.

Mokha, the same; idem.

The inhabitants [of Muscat/Oman] being Arabs used to stay there once a year, and pay 2.5 per cent of their property (*middelen*). If they go on a voyage and return with cargo, nothing is collected, when they showed a document stating that they had paid their taxes. However, they have to make so many voyages with their merchandise that they have to pay tolls every time, and to show documentary proof thereof at the place of their residence.

The Banyans living or residing in Muscat did not pay anything on their imported goods in former times. However, on our arrival, a toll was levied for the very first time. Those who possessed a house (*landshuis*) in the country had to pay 5 and others 10 percent. Therefore, everybody was forced to take a house in the country, even though it was only a shop. Similarly, nothing was taken, be he Moor or Banyan (even when the goods were taken ashore), when the goods were sent to other parts. However, this also changed during our stay, for now both Moors and Banyans have to pay the legal toll on all goods that are taken ashore. However, if a ship continues is journey, only toll is levied on that which

---

86. Those of the Indian coast retaliated by coming with a few ships only, which created a scarcity of rice and other products in Oman. In 1674, the Imam, therefore, tried to attract merchants from the Kanara and Malabar coast by lowering the customs duties for them to 2.5 percent only, see NA, VOC 1297, Bent to XVII, Gamron 1 April 1675, f. 1015. In 1674 rice was hardly obtainable in Muscat and it was one of the best-selling goods, because during the last monsoon only four vessels from Cannanore had come with pepper, ginger, cardamom, coir, etc., see NA, VOC 1304, Ritsert to Maetsuycker, Mascate, 19 September 1674, f. 523.

was taken ashore or that which was transshipped; in case of Moors sometimes allowances are made.

From exports nothing was levied during our stay, when the importer had already paid tolls on them.

Similarly, nothing is paid on exports of dates and loaf-sugar and everything that may be produced in the country itself.

The brokerage (*makalardij*). The brokerage of all coming and going ships in addition to the city's weigh-house and thirty to forty houses have been farmed out to a Banyan, called Thewil, for an amount of 30,000 *laris*.[87] He appoints a broker for each ship to whom they are obliged to pay 1.5 percent of all goods sold. One percent is for the main broker and 0.5 percent for his deputy brokers, yes even for the freight goods, which a ship takes from here on its return journey.

Similarly, this broker allots to each ship or its crew one of the said houses, for which he gets 5, 6 to 8 *abbasi*s,[88] depending on their size or location, until the day they leave. Someone who stays here until the end of the monsoon makes a contract with him for the second journey from the end of May or till the last of September or October for that whole period.

The weigh-house. The sum that is paid for each pack, be it two or up to 50 *man* of 8 lbs. amounts to:

	1/16 *mahmudi*[89]
apart from cloves, each pack	0.25
rompen,[90] each pack	idem

---

87. A *lari*, meaning [coined in] Lar, a town in southern Persia, is a coin shaped like a bent hairpin. They were struck with circular or rectangular dies in Persia, Ottoman Empire, Arabia, India, Sri Lanka and the Maldives and a popular coin for international trade.
88. A Persian silver coin first issued in the late 16th century.
89. A Persian silver coin first struck in the 1580s.
90. A kind of inferior nutmeg.

cinnamon, each pack	idem
one *bahar* of cotton of 640 lbs.	5/8
tin or lead per *schuit*[91]	1/16
silk per pack	2
elephants tusks per candi	idem
for the measurable products (*meetwaren*), the buyer pays for each candi	0.5
in case of *parren*,[92] insufficient to make up one candi each	1/32

The weights that are used are as follows:

the great *bahar* is	200 *man* of 8 lbs or	1,600 lbs.
the small *bahar* is	80 *man* of 8 lbs. or	640 lbs.
the candi is	60 *man* of 8 lbs. or	480 lbs.
ferasileh (*farsaleh*)[93]	10 *man* of 8 lbs. or	80 lbs.
mandilij	3 *man* of 8 lbs. or	24 lbs.
man Muscat	1 *man* of 8 lb.	8 lbs.

20 *parren* equals one candi of rice, wheat, etc.

The horse trade is also of great interest to the Imam's agent. Every year he sends a factor to Persia who buys twenty to thirty ordinary horses on the account of the Imam. In addition 200 to 300 horses, one year more, the other less–, are marketed here and sold to Indian merchants. Those that remain unsold, the [horse] traders take them to Vengurla, Rajapur and other Indian seaports. No Indian merchant is permitted to buy any horse, before he has bought one, two or three from the Imam's

---

91. Metal was cast in the mould of a *schuit* or boat. In Japan, for example, *schuitzilver* (boat silver) was the base unit of account. In British records tin is usually recorded in a number of 'pigs.'
92. I have been unable to identify this product.
93. *Feraseleh* a weight of 10.5 kg.

agent, so cheap that he has to scratch his head. Sometimes, they have to buy all his horses without being permitted to buy [horses] from anybody else. He himself has no stables, but on learning that there are some prospective buyers, he goes to the Persian horse traders and chooses from their herd those he likes best. He then holds on to them and is unwilling to sell them at civil prices. One may well think that they will almost have to eat through their fodder, [for] he will have to keep them until the end of the monsoon, or through lack of keep, let them go free. These people are afraid that they have to be accommodating by buying at least two, three or four and as long as he still has some animals; the brokers are not allowed to take buyers elsewhere.

The toll on the sale of horses is paid by the seller and amounts to 2.5 percent for one.

Its brokerage has been farmed out this year for 1,600 *mahmudi*s and its farmer was Chelliel,[94] for which he in turn enjoyed the following:

Rent for the area where the horses are kept, which amounts to two *mahmudi*s per head per month.

Similarly for the preparation of the transportation of each horse, ten *mahmudi*s of which the merchant and the *nakhoda* each pay half.

Freight. The rate of freight to all parts is paid as follows, but there are no fixed rates, for they fluctuate depending on the number of ships or vessels moored.

Sind. During our stay freight was paid in a ship

For each *bahar* of 1,600 lbs.	15	R a/s[95]
Later on another ship	11.5	R a/s
Similarly on barques	25, 30	*lari*s

Mostly it is stipulated to pay there the return voyage:

weighed goods per *candi*	12	*lari*s

---

94. Khalil, who was the special advisor to Abdallah, the Imam's agent.
95. Short for Indian rupee.

piece goods or packs, each pack	36-40	*laris*
Idem, on barques, weighed goods, per *candi*	7	*laris*
each pack . . .	25	*laris*

Kutch. Per *bahar* of dates to be paid there 25, 30 *laris*
Other products per *candi* idem

Vengurla. Each great *bahar* of dates	26	*laris*
each horse . . .	20	*pagodas*[96]
each chest . . .	8	*mahmudis*
on these brokerage has to be paid, *ruinas* etc. per *candi* .	20-25	*laris*

Rajapur. The great *bahar* of dates	33-35	*laris*
ruinas per *candi*	32	*laris*
each horse . . .	idem as above	

If thereafter, another voyage is made 400 *mahmudis*.

Mokha. From here:

each great *bahar* to be paid there	40	*laris*
one pair of chests of loaf sugar	9-12	*mahmudis*
big pack of textiles	20	*mahmudis*
small ditto . . .	14-16	*mahmudis*
The return voyage:		
one *bahar* or *candi* to Muscat	2	Rsd.[97]
to Basra	3	Rsd.

---

96. The *pagoda* or *pardao* was a coin long current in South India, see Hobson-Jobson, s.v.
97. Short for *rijksdaalder* the first coin issued by the Republic of the Seven United Provinces of the Netherlands; it was equal to 48 or 50 *stuivers*.

Basra. each pack of textiles	10	*mahmudis*
weighed goods per candi	10	*mahmudis*
loaf-sugar, pair of chests taken as one	4-5	*mahmudis*
Gamron and **Kong**. textiles, each pack	2.5-3	*mahmudis*
loaf-sugar, pair of chests	2.5	*mahmudis*
weighed products per *candi*	4	*mahmudis*
One pack of cotton of one *bahar* of 680 lbs.	8	*mahmudis*

Ships. All private vessels have to lower their sails (*inkorten*) on arrival in the inner-bay between the water passage-ways. Immediately a guardsman is put on board, who stays on the vessel until it leaves. All goods in it have to be unloaded, unless the ship's crew have stipulated otherwise prior to their entrance into the inner-bay. Nobody is allowed to leave or come aboard after sunset. No ship is allowed to depart before having shown a pass to the western water passageways.

As far as we have been able to learn and observe from the coming and going ships are as follows:

The monsoon from here to **Sind**: the barque usually leaves the first time in mid-May and the second time in mid-September and return again in mid-November until mid-February. Those who want to come from Sind to here after these dates have to sail out of the Gulf to gain the East[ern winds] and may then smoothly run back.

Ships from all other Indian parts come here for the first of December until the end of May. They return home again until 8 to 10 May. Those who have not left by then have to stay until mid-September, when the monsoon to India is good again.

Mokha. From here to Mokha, barques and ships leave from the first of October until the last of February of the next year. They return from there when the monsoon starts at the end of February until the end of April, or at the latest 10 May. Those who have not left by then remain until mid-August, when they can come hither until the end of September.

Patta. From Muscat to Patta one can go from mid-November until 20 February. To return from Patta the first time is from the end of March until mid-April, which is the latest date. Those who have not left by then have to stay until the end of July when they can sail again from there until 20 or 25 August. The Imam's vessel mostly is out at sea for 9 to 10 months.

Annex 3

Prices in Muscat, 1672–1675

Hereunder are prices for some goods offered from the year 1671 until 1674 as they were found in VOC documents.[1] From merchant Georg Wilmson's report (VOC 1304, f. 479vs) it is clear that selling goods in Muscat was a time consuming affair. Apart from having business flair, a merchant needed patience. Goods were both sold in large and small quantities, both by the merchants and shopkeepers. Sales in Muscat depended very much on the information on prices elsewhere in the Persian Gulf and on information of the prices in Surat (this held especially true for the merchants from Mokha). If the level of imports was high this had a downward effect on the price level. This was due to the fact that the absorption capacity of the Muscat market was not considerable. Muscat was a transit port and the prices of the Muscat market, therefore, had to compete with those of other markets in the Persian Gulf. For example, the consumption of cloves and *rompen* in Muscat itself was not more than two to three hundred pounds yearly for each product. Depending on prices elsewhere merchants from Bahrain, al-Hasa, or Mokha would or would not buy the rest. Wilmson observed that for a

---

1 This is a reproduction from Floor, "The Description," pp. 50-53.

great range of goods, prices in Muscat in 1673 (pepper, ginger, sandalwood, sappanwood, *borborrij*, textiles) were lower than in Persia or Basra. Therefore, he advised against VOC trade in Muscat, for its sales there would have a negative impact in sales in Persia and Basra. Because it would be dangerous to draw conlusions from these prices given below other than that what has been said above, I just offer these prices as a piece of tentative information. More such information will be needed before analytical conclusions for the Muscat economy are drawn.

Prices in Muscat (VOC 1279, f. 467vs-468; Harckz report)

500 *bahar* pepper [from Malabar] per *bahar*	38.5	*rijksdaalders*
35 *bahar* Cochin cinnamonper per *bahar* of 400 lbs.	100-115	idem
Kanara rice per *last*	65-70	idem

sold in April-May 1671

Prices in Muscat in 1672 based on Dutch trade information (VOC 1279, f. 1030).

Japanese copper (*staafcoper*) per 24 lbs.	44	*laris*
Rompen (inferior nutmeg) per 8 lbs.	33-35	idem
Japanese camphor per 8 lbs.	30-32	idem

Prices of goods sold by Wilmson in 1762-73 in Muscat (VOC 1304, f. 497vs-480).

Japanese copper (*staafcoper*) per 24 lbs.	42-44.5	*laris*
Tin per 24 lbs.	38-40.5	idem
Japanese camphor per 8 lbs.	29-30	idem
Rompen per 8 lbs.	33-34	*laris*
Cloves per 8 lbs.	93.5-95	idem
retail	120	idem
Radix china per 8 lbs.	2.5-21	idem
Cinnamon per 8 lbs.	52	idem

Goods sold by others

Wild Kanara and Malabar cinnamon per 480 lbs.			*laris*
	ordinary	40-70	idem
	middle	150	idem
	best	320-400	idem

Prices in Muscat (VOC 1285, Wilmson to de Haze, Mascate 10 July 1673, f.418).

Pepper	per *bahar* of 400 lbs.	25		Rupees
Dried ginger	idem	20		idem
Borborry	idem	10		idem
Red areca	idem	12		idem
Benzoïn,	per *farsala* of 24 lbs.	16		idem
Cloves	idem	81		idem
Rompen	idem	20		idem
Cardamom	idem	10		idem
Copper	idem	8		idem
Lead	idem	3.5		idem
Zinc	idem	9		idem
Loaf sugar	idem	5		idem
White Surat sugar	idem	3.5		idem
Tin.	idem	10		idem
Coffee	per *bahar*	45		Rupees

These prices were considered to be high, due to the fact that during the season only eleven vessels came to Muscat: Surat 2; Diu 3; Cambay 3; Daman 1; Malabar 1; Bombay 1.

Some merchants from Mokha wanted to buy cloves at 100 Rs., but did not come, because of lack of money (f. 516).

Prices of goods sold by the VOC trading station mid-1674 (VOC 1297, f. 1014vs).

		Profit in %
200 Ps. *chiadder cangij*[*]	at 100 *mahmudi*s per 40 Ps	25.5
240 Ps. *pancerangijs*[†]	idem	23 13/18
200 Ps. *foppelij*[§]	idem	30
70 lbs. eagle-wood	at 65 *mahmudi*s per 6 lbs.	11 3/8
1,890 lbs. Japanese copper	at 40 *lari*s per 24 lbs.	136 13/16

Prices of goods sold by the VOC trading station in August 1674 (VOC 1304, f. 523).

Vengurla textiles were sold to Arab merchants from the interior (*bovenlandse Arabieren*) at 50 *abbasi*s per corge of 40 Ps. The normal price was 35 to 38 *abbasi*s. The profit was only 20 percent due to the high cost–price and expenses. At a price of 38 *abbasi*s the annual turnover was estimated to be 150 packages, if nobody else imported them.

* I have not been able to identify the term *cangij*.

† Probably *panj rangi* (Persian), meaning 'five colored.

§ I have not been able to identify the term *foppelij*.

ANNEX 4

THE *AMSTELVEEN* SHIPWRECK, 1763

INTRODUCTION

For 136 years, from 1623 to 1759, the *Verenigde Oostindische Compagnie* (V.O.C., United East Indies Company) was the most important single foreign trading firm of Persia. During that period it had factories (trading stations) in Isfahan (1623-1745), Kerman (1659-1725), Bushehr (1737-1753) and Bandar Abbas (1623-1759) as well as a house in Shiraz for its wine maker. Since 1645, the VOC also had a factory in Basra, but it was intermittently occupied during the 17th century, depending on trade and political conditions. Ships coming from Batavia usually sailed via Colombo (Sri Lanka) or Cochin (Malabar Coast) to Bandar Abbas and the same way back. VOC ships only called on Muscat, either coming from Bandar Abbas or Batavia, to take in fresh water, food supplies and firewood. In was only between 1672-75 that the VOC had a small factory in Muscat. The VOC's main export product from Persia was raw silk (until 1696), goat hair, and cash. The VOC imported a wide range of products such as spices, pepper, sugar, textiles and metals.[1] Until 1722 trade with Persia was profitable. However in that year the country was invaded and occupied by the Ghilzay Afghans (1722-30). Trade was insignificant during that period and, therefore, in 1724 the VOC factory in Basra was re-opened. The years after the Afghan occupation, dominated by Nader's Shah's rule (1736-1747) were characterized by constant war with the Ottomans, Moghuls, Uzbeks, as well as internal uprisings. Consequently, VOC trade results after 1722 were disappointing and, in fact, negative. Therefore, in 1748, the Gentlemen XVII considered withdrawing from Persia and the Persian Gulf altogether, with which, in 1752, Jacob Mossel, the governor-general in Batavia, the headquarters of the VOC in Asia, agreed.[2]

When in 1751, Tido von Kniphausen, the VOC chief in Basra, was accused of having relations with a Moslem woman and was forced to pay a large sum to obtain his freedom, on his return to Batavia, he was able to convince Mossel of the advantage of a reform plan for VOC trade in the Persian Gulf. Von Kniphausen suggested to close down the factories in Basra and Bushehr, and eventually also in Bandar Abbas, and to build a factory on the island of Khark. The Supreme Government or chief executive body of the VOC in Asia, based in Batavia, hoped to sell large quantities of Java sugar to the Persian and Turkish markets via Khark. This was especially important for the well-being of Batavia, which had trouble selling its ever-growing sugar production.[3] Its other

---

1. On the activities of the VOC until 1722, see Willem Floor, *The Persian Gulf 1500-1730. The Political Economy of Five Port Cities*; Idem, *The Commercial Conflict between Persia and the Netherlands, 1712-1718*, Durham University, Occasional Papers no. 37. (1988); Idem, *The Economy of Safavid Persia* (Wiesbaden: Reichert, 2000); Willem Floor and Mohammad Faghfoory, *The First Dutch-Iranian Commercial Conflict* (Costa Mesa: Mazda, 2004); and Rudi Matthee, *The Politics of Trade in Safavid Iran*. Cambridge UP, 1999.
2. On the period of the Afghan occupation and Nader Shah, see Willem Floor, *The Afghan Occupation of Persia, 1722-1730* (Paris- Cahiers Studia Iranica, 1998); Idem, *The Rise and Fall Nader Shah* (Washington DC: Mage, 2009).
3. On the problems of the sugar production of Batavia, see J. J. Reese, *De suikerhandel van Amsterdam van het begin der 17e eeuw tot 1813* (Haarlem, 1908), pp. 178-84.

main commodities, spices and pepper, the VOC could sell anywhere. The new factory held out promise of increased sales, especially of sugar and manufactured goods, while overhead would be reduced. Being on an island would guarantee that the Khark factory would free the VOC of the obnoxious 'borrowing' practices by local rulers to which its staff had been exposed in recent years. The factory's garrison would be small, and the construction costs would be low. Moreover, the factories in Basra and Bushehr would be closed down, and Khark would eventually become the only VOC factory in the Persian Gulf. Once the new factory had begun to perform well, the Bandar Abbas factory would also be closed.

Despite the promise of profitable trade, low overhead, and no 'present's to local chiefs, on the contrary, none of these objectives were realized,. The fact that the Khark factory was a commercial failure and never really got off the ground was due to a number of factors beyond the VOC's control. The anarchy that prevailed in Persia, and sometimes in Iraq, made trade routes insecure, which especially hurt VOC trade, for an increasing part of its trade consisted of bulk or heavy goods. These were more difficult to sell and transport than piece goods, when pack-animals were scarce and roads insecure. The general instability of the area also decreased the production capacity of the population, leading to a lower standard of living and less demand for imported goods, such as Java sugar. Formerly Persia had bought about 35 percent of Batavia's sugar production, but now the VOC was having trouble with the sale of sugar in the Persian Gulf and in other parts of Asia as well. The Supreme Government was desperate and ordered its staff to try and increase sugar sales. The pressure was so high that the Supreme Government even decided to make 'sugar voyages' to Muscat and Sind in 1756 and 1757, markets that it had not traded with for about one century.[4] Finally, the VOC was obliged to maintain an expensive establishment on Khark, for the hoped for low overhead did not materialize. This was mainly

---

4. Floor, *The Rise of the Gulf Arabs*, chapter six; "Dutch East India Company's Trade with Sind in the 17th and 18th centuries," *Moyen-Orient & Ocean Indien*, vol. 3 (1986), pp. 111-144.

because the owner of the island, Mir Muhanna, chief of the port of Rig situated opposite the island, claimed payment of the rent, which the VOC had never paid. He unsuccessfully attacked the Dutch fort on Khark in 1762 and infested the Persian Gulf with his acts of maritime violence. Because of the insecurity in the area and the prevailing piracy, the military expenditures absorbed a considerable part of Khark's profits. Although the conditions prevailing in the Persian Gulf also held for the VOC's competitors, they appear to have been less hurt by them, for the time being, probably because the EIC was in a better financial and management position and its pattern of trade was more suited to Persian Gulf market conditions.

On 11 March 1762, the High Government finally decided to discontinue its activities in the Persian Gulf. It had already closed down the Bandar Abbas factory in 1758, where until 1765 a Dutch caretaker remained. However, Governor-General van der Parra had second thoughts about this decision. On 6 April 1762, he proposed that an effort be made to show that Khark really could make a profit, by cutting overhead and increasing sales and profit margins, on condition that the XVII would agree to the continuation of the Khark operation.[5] Trade results for 1764-65 were no better than in the previous year, while the volume of unsold goods was considerable. The Supreme Government's "reform" policy clearly had failed. The Gentlemen XVII had enough of Batavia's indecisiveness and gave orders to close Khark and withdraw from the Persian Gulf area. These orders arrived in June 1766, but when on 20 August 1765 the Supreme Government finally decided to implement them it was too late, because in late December 1765 Mir Muhanna attacked the Dutch factory on Khark, which surrendered on 3 January 1766. Although he kept the goods that he found there as booty Mir Muhanna allowed the Dutch staff to depart and even gave them a few small boats to reach Bushehr. The Gentlemen XVII mistakenly assumed that Batavia had already carried out its earlier orders to close down the

---

5. National Archives at The Hague (NA), 1.04.02, VOC 792, Nadere bedenkingen (Batavia; 06/04/1762), f. 265-82. The sugar surplus problem of Java played an important role in van der Parra's change of mind.

Khark factory.[6] Thus ended 143 years of permanent Dutch presence in the Persian Gulf. Although letters were received from local governors (Hormuz, Bandar Abbas, Bushehr, and Basra) inviting the Dutch to come and trade again at those ports, the VOC had decided that trading in the Persian Gulf was too risky and not profitable enough. It could sell the goods it would sell there in the market of Surat, whence they would taken by so-called country-traders into the Persian Gulf.[7] However, it did not mean that the Dutch no longer went to the Persian Gulf. Each year, between 1777 and 1796, one ship or sometimes two, mostly privately-owned, sailed from Batavia directly to Muscat to sell its cargo, mostly consisting in sugar and some cloves.

One of the ships that was used on the Khark route was the *Amstelveen*. It was built in 1746 in Amsterdam and was one of the largest trading ships of its kind (50 m long, 13 m wide, 1,150 ton capacity). Its first voyage began on 27 October 1747. On 5 May 1762 it sailed for the fifth time from the Netherlands to Batavia, arriving there on 28 November 1762. After some local trips in the Indonesian archipelago, hauling new coins, rice and cotton yarn,[8] it was decided on 17 May 1763 to dispatch the *Amstelveen* to Khark Island in the Persian Gulf.[9] It was not the first time the ship had made this voyage as it had sailed to Khark already on 21 May 1757, returning on 19 January 1758 to Batavia.[10] The *Amstelveen* left Batavia on 16 June 1673, after having been inspected and considered to be seaworthy for the planned voyage.[11] It had a crew of 105 men and a cargo mostly of sugar as well as tin and spices for the Khark trading station. This was a well-known route which VOC ships had been sailing regularly. During the period 1753-62 a total of thirteen ships had made the voyage to Khark. As of 1754, usually two ships sailed

---

6. NA, 1.04.02, VOC 335, XVII to Batavia (05/10/1765), section Karreek, not foliated.
7. On the Khark factory, see Floor, *The Rise*, chapters four and five.
8. Arsip Nasional RI (ANRI), Jakarta, VOC 266a (Hoge Regeering), Daghregisters van Kasteel Batavia 2594, 08/01/1674 and 30/04/1764, pp. 3, 42-43; and Idem, *Minuut-generale notulen Hoge Regeering (HR) 74 Minuut-generale notulen Hoge Regeering*, 07/02/1763, fol. 15.
9. ANRI *HR 74 Minuut-generale notulen Hoge Regeering*, 17/05/1763, fol. 523.
10. ANRI, Daghregisters, 2587, 21/05/1757, p. 87 and 2588, 19/01/1758, p. 13
11. ANRI, *Minuut-generale notulen*, 77, 14/06/1763, fols. 729-730

each year from Batavia, via Colombo or Cochin, to Khark, calling on Muscat to take in water, food and firewood, because often the crews were in need of recuperation after a bad sea voyage. After an uneventful Indian Ocean crossing things went wrong on 5 August 1763 in foggy weather when the *Amstelveen* came too close to the coast of Oman. The ship sailed into the Gulf of Sawqirah, which is as shallow as the Gulf of Masirah, but this was not indicated on the map and, as a result, the ship was wrecked at Capa Mataraca. Of the 105 men crew 75 drowned. Of the 30 survivors only 22 reached Muscat after a trek of more than 500 km as the crow flies through desolate Eastern Hajar suffering hunger and thirst and not always friendly encounters with some of the local population.[12] However, the closer the men came to the inhabited world the more compassion, water and food, they were given. On 11 September, eight survivors, after a hellish journey of 31 days, finally reached Muscat, where they found assistance from Narrotam, the Gujarati Indian VOC broker and from there they continued to Khark and then to Batavia. The other 13 survivors trickled in later or arrived earlier.

Fortunately, one of the survivors, Cornelis Eyks, wrote a short diary about the shipwreck and its aftermath.[13] This diary is very important as it gives us a view of the people of the interior of Oman, Muscat and the Persian Gulf in general for a period when very little information is available about these places. In particular, it is important because it is the first known and very fascinating description of this hitherto totally unknown part of Oman through which Eyks and his surviving crew mates walked. Therefore, his observations about Muscat and of the situation of the Persian Gulf are of great historical importance. Eyks' account concerning the shipwreck and his harrowing trek from the site of the disaster to Muscat and beyond speaks for itself and, therefore, the reader is referred to the footnotes for an explanation of unfamiliar terms and events as well as to more detailed studies.

---

12. For an attempt to identify the route taken by the survivors, see Doornbos, *Shipwreck*, pp. 68, 80.
13. On Eyks's career, see Doornbos, *Shipwreck*, pp. 122-28.

The news of the shipwreck reached Batavia on 7 April 1764 from Malabar and further on 19 May 1674 from Coromandel, the latter accompanied by two sailors who had survived the trek through Oman.[14] Eyks and five other survivors arrived in Batavia on 22 May 1674. On 5 June 1764, Nicolaas Houting, the chief of the VOC naval forces in Batavia was charged with the task to investigate the cause of the shipwreck based on the reports received from Cochim and Cormandel (including the two survivors who had returned via Paliacatte) as well as through interrogation of 7 survivors, namely: Eyks, Daalberg, the boatswain, and five sailors.[15] The investigation committee interrogated the two groups of survivors separately, whose stories agreed on the essential points. On 15 June 1764 the committee concluded that the shipwreck was due to 'negligence' by the ship's authorities (meaning the Captain and first mate, although they were not named). They had not used the sounding lead nor sailed away from the coast or dropped anchor when the weather became foggy again. There may have been discussion about the deviation from the route taken and other technical aspects, but the committee's resolution was short and terse. There was no discussion apparently about the seaworthiness of the *Amstelveen*, because the chairman of the committee was the official who inspected all ships for seaworthiness prior to their departure. It is no surprise that the condition of the ship was never part of his investigation. The authorities in Batavia wanted no embarrassing questions and the matter was shelved and therefore, the case was closed as quickly as possible. The committee further decided that the wages of the "the said mate and boatswain and of the five sailors, who likewise had arrived here would be started on the day that they would be employed again in [VOC] service."[16]

---

14. ANRI, 266a, *Daghregisters*, 2594, 07/041764, fols. 34-35: Idem, 19/05/1764.
15. ANRI, *Minuut-generale notulen*, 77, 05/06/1764, fols. 252-253.
16. ANRI, *Minuut-generale notulen*, 77, 15/06/1764, fols. 313-314; Idem, 05/06/1764, fols. 252-253.

Fateful Vicissitudes

Of the saved crew of the Hon. East Indies Company's ship *AMSTELVEEN* after its shipwreck on 5 August 1763 during the voyage from Batavia to Persia that they experienced during their trek through Arabia; all in accordance with the concise and true notes made by *CORNELIS EYKS*, at that time third mate[1] on the abovementioned ship.

The royal prophet in *Psalms* CVII: 25-30 speaking about "those who sail the seas to trade went floating on the great waters,"[2] concludes his story of the fears that they usually have to suffer by announcing their duty with verses 31 and 32, saying: "Let them give thanks to the Lord for his kindness, and His wondrous works for the sons of men; let them extol Him in the assembly of the people, and praise Him in the conclave of elders." To acquit myself of this common duty, I had resolved to communicate to the world the following particular circumstances that happened to me and the saved crew members as a separate printed report, as glorification of the Lord's kindness towards me. However, realizing that it

---

1. *Derde waak* or third mate is the third person responsible for the navigation; it was possible that more than person could have the rank of third mate; in fact, there were four persons of this rank on board the *Amstelveen* during its fateful voyage, see Doornbos, *Shipwreck*, p. 139.
2 This is a paraphrased version of the intent of the verses referred to.

was too short in length to do so, at the advice of good friends, I have preferred to submit that Notification to the publisher of a Monthly[3] to submit it to his readers, in the hope that others, who may end up in similar sad circumstances, will find it of use. But to avoid boring the dear reader with a long introduction, I will proceed to the story of this unfortunate voyage.

After I had taken service with the Hon. Chartered E.I. Company of the United Netherlands,[4] on behalf of the Zeeland Chamber, I departed with the ship *Nieuw Nieuwerkerk* commanded by Captain *Adriaan van den Boer*, as third mate, on 5 August in the year 1671 and arrived safely in *Batavia* in April 1762. Then, with the same ship I made several voyages to the Coast of Coromandel and returned safely with it to the roads of *Batavia*, where I was transferred to the Hon. Comp's ship *Amstelveen*, which ship, commanded by Captain *Nicolaas Pietersen* and a crew of 105 men, was directed to make a voyage to Persia. To that end, we departed from the roads of *Batavia* on 16 June 1673, hoping for God's merciful aid and help and took our course for the Gulf of Persia. Although soon after our departure we had much bad weather, our voyage however, proceeded rather auspiciously. One month and 19 days after having weighed our anchor, namely on *Friday* 5 August, or, during the day watch,[5] the wind being south to S.S.W. we experienced a dreadful weak wind[6] with foggy air so that at sunrise we could not see the topmast. We changed our N.E. to north course to north to get sight of land. When at 3 bells[7]

---

3. *Maandstukje*; this term refers to a magazine that was published monthly. Eyks' report was published by Jeroen van de Sande in his hometown of Middelburg in 1766 in the monthly *Tydkorting of Magazyn der Heeren*, pp. 365-418. A copy of this very rare magazine is kept in the library of the University of Nijmegen.
4. On the history of the VOC, see Femme Gaastra, *The Dutch East India Company: expansion and decline*. Zutphen: Walburg Pers, 2003.
5. *Dagwacht* or day watch is the first watch after the night (4 to 8 in the morning).
6. The Dutch term '*braamzeilkoelte*' means that the wind was so weak that the ship sailed with its topsail (*braamzeil*).
7 Striking the ship's bell is the traditional method of marking time and regulating the crew's watches. Each bell (from one to eight) represents a 30-minute period since the beginning of a four-hour watch. For example, "Three bells in the

during the fore watch,[8] the air having cleared up somewhat, we saw land and gauged it west-south-west, estimating it to be 6 to 6.5 miles (45-50 km)[9] to the nearest shore, and we presumed it to be the land of Cape *Mataraca* (in the Description of the Coast of Arabia known under the name of *Cape Matakna*).[10] Without fear, we then sailed north-east to the north; on that day we were at the estimated northern longitude of 18 degrees, 41 minutes and latitude, 72 degrees, 55 minutes. According to the octant we were at N. width 18 degrees, 40 minutes.[11]

At the evening measurement of our position (*avondpijl*) we had the wind from south and S.S.W with a common cool weak wind, a misty air and high waves coming from the south-west and south-south-west. We saw then a group of black divers (these are black birds that live at sea, the size of a duck; they were here in such large numbers that none of the crew had ever seen the likes before)[12] and at 3 bells we could no longer see land. We then loosened the ropes [*theuy*] and dropped the

---

morning watch" represents 90 minutes since the beginning of the morning watch, or 5:30 am. "Eight bells" indicates the end of a watch.
8. *Voorwacht*, the watch before midnight.
9. The German mile (7.4 km) is meant here and throughout Eyks' report.
10. Cape or Ras Madraka is a peninsula south of Duqm. From there, now one may reach Muscat in 7 hours by car. The prevailing SW monsoon causes a regular dense fog along its shore, while strong winds beat the unexposed coast and are responsible for the many wrecks that may be seen on the rocky headlands and beaches. For a detailed description, see United States. Hydrographic Office. *Red Sea and Gulf of Aden Pilot*. Washington DC., 1922, p. 534.
11. According to the official sailing instructions, ships had to reach Oman at 20 degrees northern latitude. Presumably the Captain had opted for a different route that offered better winds. Although navigational charts showed shallow areas in the bay north of Mataraca, it did not with regard to the Sawqirah Bay south to it, which also was shallow. In fact, the chart showed that it was easy navigable and therefore, the Captain maintained his chosen course. Because of various errors, the ship ran aground on the south side of Cape Mataraca. Doornbos, *Shipwreck*, pp. 37, 53, 129-32.
12. These *duikers* or divers were so-called Socotra or Arabian cormorants (*Phalacocrorax nigrogularis*). Since they dive in shallow coastal waters this should have been a signal to the crew of the *Amstelveen* that they were too close to the coast.

daily anchor; at sunset we could not see our topmast at all. Based on our afternoon bearing we calculated to have kept a course of north-east to north for 6.5 miles. According to our daily measurement of our position [*bestek*], we were 8 miles offshore and 49 minutes from the island of *Mazerica* (in the map of that coast it is called *Maziera*).[13] We put double lookouts at the helm. At the end of the watch the Captain told me that he had not as yet measured the depth by swinging the lead. I then asked him whether I should make preparations to so, as this seems to be useful. However, he replied, that it was very dangerous to take in sail to swing the lead, because the newly nailed exterior cover to prevent leakage,[14] had totally gone to pieces, also that the molding of the stern was very damaged. Under these conditions, when already we had to bail with buckets the rising water from the gun room[15] and had to continuously pump to keep it dry,[16] it was feared that if we took in sail the high incoming waves from the south south-west would smash the inner protective cover,[17] which was also in quite a bad condition. In that case, the entire gun room would be flooded and, therefore, it was best to head for north-east. On that date, since sunset we had moved another 3 miles on a course of north-east to the north.

During the first watch, we had the wind and weather as mentioned above, with a strong mist; after 8 bells the Captain transferred the watch to the first mate, saying to head to north-east so as to calmly sail onwards. The reason we had not yet been swinging lead was out of fear that the gun room would be flooded, in which case we would be

---

13. Masirah is an island off the East coast of Oman, The shallow ocean bottom environment surrounding Masirah Island is hostile as the majority of the area is covered in either sand or hard rock. During summer there is normally a constant strong wind resulting in a swift current and choppy surface conditions.
14. *Buitenbroeking* or wales, i.e. strakes of thick, broad outside planking on the sides of a wooden ship.
15. *Constabelskamer*, space at the most hind part of the in-between deck (*tussendek*) to store all ammunition and other military supplies.
16. The term used, *lens houden*, is not found in the dictionaries.
17. *Binnenmaking* or thick wooden planks on the inside of a wooden ship.

unable to remain on course, also it was a good opportunity to reach the Gulf of Persia. However, if the sea became calm, then it offered a better opportunity to begin swinging the lead. When during the second bell of that watch the wind and calmed down, the ship no longer reacted to steering and during the 6th glass (which was about 11 o'clock in the evening) the ship hit something. Therefore, we dropped the depth sounding line and we found that we were at 4 fathoms (7 meters) on sandy soil, also that the current pushed north and north-north-west. Immediately, it was decided to lower the longboat [*barcas*] (in Holland these are also called *barkassen*, but in Zeeland they are better known under the name of *large boats* [*groote booten*]); but while preparing this, the soft wind became stronger from the south, and increased into a brisk wind,[18] causing heavy breakers, so that the ship suffered two heavy impacts. Because of the breakers and the stamping of the ship the doors of the cargo room [*lastkamer*] and the gun room burst open, and astern the carved work and windows of the Captain's room, the cabin, and the escutcheon [*galderij*][19] were totally smashed, and the ship keeled over at least 6 times to starboard, so that immediately the breakers gushed into the space between the upper and the second deck [*kuil*], which prevented us from lowering the long boat. Seeing that all human aid and means to save the ship and our lives were thwarted, we cut the masts to prevent other disasters and we threw everything overboard what we could so that the ship would rise up somewhat; in this manner the entire night was spent in miserable confusion.

On *Saturday* the 6th, in the morning, we had wind and weather as above, but during the day the wind became somewhat stronger, we saw that the land was low lying, wherefore we guessed that we were in the Hook of *Enzaädades Baixos*.[20] We then prepared the longboat

---

18. Wind strong enough to propel the ship using only top-gallant and topsail (*braamzeil en marszeilskoelte*).
19. *Galderij* or the outside carpentry of the stern [*spiegel*] towards the sides of the ship, which form a separate space and externally serves to broaden and decorate the stern.
20. The Portuguese name, written Enseada das baxas (baixos) on Portuguese maps, means 'inlet of shallows' for the Gulf of Masirah.

and dinghy, loading them with water and biscuits, and we also placed the Hon. Comp's papers in them, in addition to other necessities, and awaited God's mercy, to, if it might please the Lord, make the breakers such that they would eject the longboat from the ship, to flee with it and to look for a good result; furthermore, we jointly prayed a *Prayer to the Lord, the God of Israel, with whom there are solutions to death*. Towards the evening, while cutting the thick rope of the daily anchor, to which was attached the debris of the tackling of the foresail, was a sailor standing next to me; his head was split into two by a breaker, so that he dropped dead immediately.

Sunday, the 7th we had a south wind, with a cool soft wind, and heavy high-rising breakers as well as a misty air. At 6 o'clock the ship's deck and then the half deck were shattered, on which 8 men were seated, of who only 4 were unscathed; also the under part of the dinghy, which was to the windward side, was smashed by the breakers. At 7 o'clock the boatswain and a sailor drove ashore with the lower spar of the yardarm[21] and safely arrived there. Shortly thereafter, the breakers threw the longboat overboard, which became full of water, and the dinghy cut to pieces against the upper foredeck [*bak*], and with the next breakers the longboat was turned upside down, so that all men in it drowned, except two men. Then the entire port side was smashed away as far as the end of the *bak*, with 4 pieces of 8-pounder cannons. We were still sitting on a piece of the forepart of the ship and still had the bowsprit and the spritsail yard,[22] so that we all fled there, and we cut the woolings[23] and the bobstays[24] and all that we thought might cause us problems as much as we could reach them. At 9 o'clock it fell into the sea, full with people, but it could not get free from the ship as it was still attached to something, so that we were twice pushed under water, and emerging the second time, I took hold of the rope that was hanging down from

---

21. *Onderlijzeilspier*, a spar by which a yard is extended.
22. *Blinde ra*, also *fokkera*.
23. *Woeling*, winding or wrapping anything with a rope, as a mast, using a piece of wood to tighten the woolding.
24. *Waterstag*, rope used to hold down and stabilize the bowsprit of a ship.

the piece of the ship's forepart and with it, I climbed that part of the ship with the aid of the boatswain's mate[25] and a sailor. I asked them to cut my overcoat from my body, because it pulled me down due to the weight of the water, which they did, and looking around, I noticed that the bowsprit with all sails attached to it had gone. Thereafter, again heavy breakers came that totally smashed to pieces the remaining part of the forepart of the ship and we were floating in the water in between its pieces. With God's help and guidance, the breakers smashed us towards the shore. We then were pushed from one wood piece to the other and I had 6 different pieces of wood before I reached the shore, but then I still had great difficulty on the beach, because 3 heavy rollers hit me against the land and pulled me towards the sea again and threw me again against the timber of the wreck that had been smashed ashore. Because of this my body was beaten such that collapsing from pain, I called for help, and in response 3 men came and dragged me across the masts, topmasts, and other pieces of timber and put me down on the sand. I was lying unconscious, because I had a cut on top of my head and one above my left eye, while my legs and arms looked like they had been flayed, while other body parts were in an even worse condition. The surgeon[26] and boatswain came ashore and asked whether any other officers, such as the Captain or the Mates had come ashore, to which they received the answer that I was there, but they did not think that I would live. The said boatswain and surgeon then came to me, the latter bound me up with a piece of plaster that he had in his pocket. The boatswain put me with my back against a small sand hill, where the crew took off my

---

25. *Schieman* or boatswain's mate was in charge of the fore-mast and bowsprite. During loading and unloading he had to be present in the hold and make sure that the merchandise was properly stowed away. He also had to see to it that the heavy ropes in the cable-tier ran smoothly, in Dutch '*schieten*,' hence the name of his title. The *schiemansmaat* was the helper of the boatswain's mate and was especially responsible for the bowsprit.
26. In the Dutch text he is referred to as *meester*, and later it becomes clear that he was the third *meester*, i.e. he served under the ship's chief surgeon, while usually there also was a second surgeon. However, according to the muster-roll, he was the only surgeon on board, see Doornbos, *Shipwreck*, pp. 134-36.

wet clothes and dressed me in their dry clothes. Next, the boatswain with some men went to fetch some planks with which they, as well as they could, erected a shelter as protection against the wind and mist. In the evening he mustered the crew and found that of 105 souls,[27] who had made the voyage with this ship, through the Lord's providence and mercy, 30 of us were still alive, to wit:

I, *Cornelis Eyks*, third mate.

1. *Jonas Daalberg*, boatswain.

1. *Pieter Coene*, third surgeon.

1. *Pieter van Holland*, boatswain's mate helper.

1. *Hans Lutjes*, cook's helper.

21 sailors.

3 soldiers.

1 little black boy.[28]

Thus, 30 heads survived. The Captain, other officers and the other crew members had all died, and of the dead nobody was identifiable, because most of them had lost their arms, legs, head, etc. Therefore, it was painful to look at those who had suffered this wretched fate; among us survivors there also were several wounded. During the night, watch was kept; I believed that the Lord would have ended my life in that night, because I suffered such heavy thrusts in my side that sometimes I could not breathe.

---

27. For the names of ship's crew, their place of origin, position, and fate, see Doornbos, *Shipwreck*, pp. 134-36.
28. He probably was a Javanese slave-boy who served as cabin-boy for Captain Pietersen and his very important passenger, Jan van Oorschot, a member of the VOC Council of Justice in Batavia. The remaining archival documents don't report why he was on board, but it is likely that he was sent to investigate the operation of the Khark trading station with the objective to increase its profits under Jan van der Hulst, who in October 1762 had been dismissed as chief of Khark under suspicion of fraud and who deserted.

Monday, 8 ditto. In the morning, wind and weather like yesterday, and as there was a heavy surf, I, the boatswain and another 6 men went along the beach to see whether we might find some goods. However, we only found mostly empty casks, as well as half-empty vats[29] with arak and wine, full half *aums*[30] with coconut oil and sweet oil, a barrel with meat, a small barrel with French beans, a similar one with sauerkraut, and two of them with sausages, also a small barrel with some flour. We also found roundabout some chests with spices, but these had burst open because of the water, and we also found coils of rope. We rolled all of that as much as possible onto the shore. We then saw 9 of our pigs and 1 cow, of which we caught one and butchered it. Then, because as yet we had no fire, we tried successfully to make that in the manner of the Indians, by rubbing two pieces of wood against each other for as long until it kindled due to the heat produced by the rubbing. We fetched water from a vat that we had found on the beach. We also found the port side with 4 pieces of 8-pounder cannons and other pieces of timber. Further, during the night we kept guard.

On *Tuesday*, 9th ditto. The wind and weather being like yesterday, I, the boatswain and 5 sailors made a trip inland, but we did not meet anybody. We only noticed that other people had been there, and traces thereof one had seen on the beach against the sand dunes, where several vessels were lying, sewn together in the same manner as the *slengen*[31] off the Coast of Coromandel, as well as masts and cordage, fishing nets, pieces of straw sacks, hats and pots. Therefore, we returned, because inland we only saw rocks and sand, and then heard from our men that they had seen 5 *camels* and 2 *pariassen* (these are a kind of large thin dogs, known to us as greyhounds)[32] moving to the west. We kept a good guard.

Wednesday, the 10th ditto. The wind and weather was as before, the boatswain's mate's helper accompanied by 7 sailors made a trip inland

---

29. *Legger*, a barrel with a capacity of 400 or 563 liters.
30. Barrel of 153.6 liters.
31. *Slengen*, a type of vessel found on the Coast of Coromandel.
32. With the term *pariassen* so-called pariah or ownerless dogs are meant.

and on his return he brought news that he had been on a path that led towards the west, and had found clear signs that more people had been there. Because our food had run out we looked for the pigs and the cow, but did not find them, but towards noon the pigs came to us of their own accord, of which we caught one, which we butchered and prepared the whole pig to be able to eat during the planned journey; we also filled our small barrels and jars, and prepared everything to depart the next morning. According to our judgment, we had food for 2 to 3 days. We also saw 2 *pariassen*; and during the night we again kept good guard.

On *Thursday*, the 11th August. At sunrise we began our journey, in the hope of Jehovah's blessing, aid and help. We were 29 Europeans and 1 black boy, according to the abovementioned list; we took with us food and water for 2 to 3 days as well as a change of clothes. We marched that day until sunset and only saw sandy and rocky land with some thorny trees.[33] We laid ourselves to rest, kept good guard during the night and beat the drum,[34] which had washed ashore.

Friday, the 12th ditto. We again marched the entire day, and saw nothing else than what we had seen the previous day. After sunset we again went to sleep, and kept good guard.

Saturday, the 13th ditto. At sunrise we continued our march. On that day many began complaining about stiffness in their joints, saying that they could not continue. We did not eat that day, because we only had food for one day more; here we saw nothing but rocks and some sand. After sunset we went to sleep, and kept a close guard.

Sunday, the 14th ditto. Again we continued the day's march; and then one of our sailors remained lying in the road saying that he'd rather die where he was, because he saw no hope and could not live without eating or drinking. We then continued with 29 persons, and about 10 o'clock in the forenoon we saw two people crossing

---

33. Probably trees such as *Acacia tortilis, Acacia Senegalensis, Tamarix aphylla, Acacia laeta, Ziziphus leucodermis, Salvadora persica,* and *Salvadora* spp.
34. On board the drum was used in foggy weather to alert other ships of one's presence, here, we may assume, the drum was beaten to attract the attention of local inhabitants in the hope that these would provide relief and assistance.

our path; we walked towards them, but because they ran away, we continued our course and about 11 or 12 o'clock we discovered a camel, and therefore, we went to it and saw that its front legs had been tethered; we then immediately saw 4 people coming towards us. The camel belonged to them, but because it seemed that they did not dare to come closer, we remained standing with the rest, and send 2 of our men to them, for whom they waited and then came to us. However, we could not understand them, and therefore, we asked them where is *Muskette*. They also did not understand this and all of them yelled *Arabia, Arabia*! They indicated to us, if we would continue that our necks would be cut and we would be eaten, which for us was a meager consolation. They asked from where we came? We pointed to them that our ship was in pieces and that we had swam ashore; we asked for food and water, but they showed that they did not have it themselves; finally they gave us a little water from a leather bag, which was totally reddish. The 4 persons consisted of 2 women and 2 youths; the latter only had a fabric around their privy parts, and piece of goatskin on their head, carrying *assegais* and a *buiksnijder* (assegais are a kind of spear, and *buiksnijders* are a kind a big and broad curved-knives)[35]; the dress of the women was a large robe that reached from their head to toe, long trousers and with braided hair. While we were standing there and asked them for help, they started plucking at our clothes and tried to plunder us, but we on seeing this left them and continued our road. They then yelled after us, took up stones and threw them at us. At about 3 o'clock we saw 3 men with 1 camel coming towards us; they acted very friendly, but we did not trust them; one of our men asked them about *Muskette*, but they also yelled nothing else but *Arabia, Arabia*! They also made gestures that our heads we be cut off if we continued; with signs we asked them for food and water, but we received nothing. One of the

---

35. Referring to so-called Omani *khanjars*, which are curved daggers and sharpened on both edges. The wooden spear, called *rumh*, was 2.5 meter long with steel tips or a blade at the end, see Neil Richardson and Marcia Dorr, *The Craft Heritage of Oman*, 2 vols. Dubai, 2003.

said 3 men, an old fellow, sent the camel with the other 2 men to fetch water, and stayed with us, behaving very friendly. After sunset we went to sleep, looking at each other with sad eyes, complaining about hunger, thirst and stiffness of the joints, and lamented to the Lord for deliverance. Then we saw 7 camels on which 9 men were seated, who while singing threw their assegais high and caught them again, coming towards us with bare swords in their fists, pretending as if they wanted to eat us alive; they finally jumped off their camels and came to us, but the old fellow went to them and acted as is he wanted to calm them down; but they made furious slashing movements and threw stones, whereupon we also took up stones and threw these as hard as we could at them; as a result, they were driven away, but returning again they threw a stone that caused a wound to the side of my eye, and one of the sailors at that time received a sword cut on his neck; we bound it with a piece of fabric and due the Lord's kindness we put them to flight again, so that night, they left us in peace. The said old fellow laughed about it and was putting things together to light a fire, but we did not allow it, because we mistrusted his game, and kept a sharp watch. That night we dressed the old fellow in a red coat; during the night we heard the murmur of the sea, reason why we guessed that we were close to the coast.

Monday, the 15th ditto. We again started the day with our march; one of our soldiers remained lying here; he said he could not go on and therefore, preferred awaiting his death. We then reached a high rocky mountain range, which extended along the coast, but due to its steepness we could not climb down anywhere. Here the two men with 2 camels, who had been sent the previous day to fetch water, came to us, bringing 6 jugs of water, in a leather bag, so that we moistened our tongues. After the said 2 men had spoken to the old man, they gestured that they would give us more water as well as food, if we put everything we had on their camels, which we did, while we also put one European and the black boy on them. But then they started plucking at our clothes and touched us allover our bodies; also two women came to us with a child in a cradle lying on their back, (this cradle was made of pieces of wood that had been tied together, and was hanging with a rope form their neck) these women also frisked and plucked at us, which annoyed us and we did not want to allow it; then they wanted to leave with their camels, but the old fellow did not allow that. However, it appeared as if the women wore the trousers, because they took the camels away, and we put our things again on our backs and continued towards the coast. They seemed to be willing to make another attack,[36] but seemed to be afraid that we might be too strong for them, and therefore, they were content with staring for a long times after us. We then reached one of the most suitable places in the mountains to look for water, but at first we did not find it. However, after having walked over the rocks for a long time, we found, close to the shore, a well with brackish water, as well as a black cormorant, for which we all thanked the Lord. We killed the cormorant, skinned and ate it and drank with relish what we had, and when we had filled our empty small barrels and jugs, as many as 6 of our men wanted to remain lying here; but through encouraging words they were brought around and continued with us.

Tuesday, the 16th ditto. At sunrise we again continued our journey going up and down the mountains, because we were unable to get to the shore at all. At about 11 or 12 o'clock we saw a thorny tree in whose shadow we sat, because the sun was terribly hot, such that due to its burning heat we almost all felt like fainting. At about 2 o'clock or 2.30 we saw 9 camels with people coming towards us, who while singing threw their assegais into the air and acted as if they wanted to eat us alive. On their approach they gesticulated that they would cut off our heads and threw an assegai at us, but we picked up stones and threw these at them so that we drove them off several times. Then some of us decided to go to their camels and to take these away from them, but one of them who was guarding these animals, chased them away. However, one of the animals was captured, whose throat we wanted to cut, but it escaped. Among this band we found that there were a number of those men, who the previous day had tried to seize us with the camels, and these were

---

36. The Dutch text has *flagje*, which does not occur in the dictionaries with a meaning that makes sense in this context. It is possible that it is a misprint for *slagje*, which does make sense here.

the ones who fought most bitterly against us, because they had fought with us from 2.30 until sunset, and even then they did not want to give up. Because our water had run out in the afternoon, we became faint and could not any longer keep going. Therefore, we decided to try and find out what they wanted; to that end we took one pair of pants, a shirt and other pieces of clothing, put all of it in a pillow case and threw it at them, and then they indicated to us that we might go. Because of the skirmish we had suffered 4 wounded, who as soon as we could, were bound up; most of the night we continued marching. Meanwhile, many complained about thirst and hunger, stiffness in the loins etc., because during the day it was scorching hot, and at night bitterly cold.

Wednesday, the 17th ditto. After having rested for a while, at sunrise we continued our journey again. The entire day we looked for water, but did not find it; therefore, we were forced to drink our own water [urine] and salt water. On that day two sailors remained lying on the road because of thirst. Because we had seen nothing but high rocky terrain and dry valleys the entire day, we looked at each other dejectedly, each of us praying in his heart to the Lord for deliverance, whether, if it might please him, to release us from this miserable life through death. After sunset, still being a group of 26 men, we went to sleep until the next day.

Thursday, the 18th ditto. At sunrise we continued again, and looked for water, but could only find salt water, with which we slaked our thirst as best as we could, and ate a kind of green herbs, in the shape of saltworts,[37] of a salty and bitter taste, which gave most of us diarrhea, making us even weaker. Then the boatswain's mate's helper *Pieter van Holland* and one sailor, *Carsten Pietersze* remained behind in the mountains, and we, still being 24 strong, at 3 o'clock arrived at a flat beach with swampy soil, where we found a boat that had been smashed to pieces against the beach, as well as a fishing net knitted from cotton and a large empty jar. At about 5 o'clock we again saw the previously mentioned camels coming towards us, with the same band. We were unable

---

37. *Zeekralen* is a kind of succulent plant (Salicornia) in the shape of a duck foot, which in Zeeland were eaten as salad; in English variously known as saltwort, glasswort, and even chicken feet.

or hardly able to offer any resistance, both because we were on swampy soil where there were no rocks and because we were exhausted and it was almost indifferent to us whether they would take our lives, because it was more attractive to us to die than continue living, if this was the Lord's will. However, while walking we still picked up some rocks that we found there to put up some resistance and not yield immediately to this band of robbers. At first we resisted as much as possible, but when we had run out of rocks we had to give up. Then they came running at us furiously, putting their naked swords to our bellies or breast and their daggers [*buiksnijder*] to our throats, and made us take off our clothes except for a pair of trousers, when the clothes did not come off fast enough they cut them off our bodies. We looked at each other with tears in our eyes and started to weep, but they just laughed. However, it pleased the Lord to move their heart somewhat to pity and so they returned the empty small casks and jars to us as well as to one a smock, to another an undershirt, to a third a short jacket without sleeves, etc. They gestured us that we could leave, but as a farewell they threw 6 stones or so at us. Continuing our journey we came to large streams that stretched inland, which we crossed while having water up to our throat, but fortunately we all reached the other side, except for the little slave boy, who was carried by the current towards the sea, so that he almost drowned.[38] We continued until, I guess, about 10 o'clock, when we lay down on the sand, and covered ourselves with it. So far we had not been able to observe that the said band lived inland in houses, or exercised some religion, or were engaged in a craft other than stealing and robbing, which is a cursed occupation.

Friday, the 19th ditto. At sunrise we again resumed our march, although many of our company said that they were unable to go with us, and that they would rather die where they were because they would have to die of thirst anyway. However, by cajoling them I and the boatswain were able to persuade them to accompany us, but not for long, because at about 10 o'clock the cook's helper, *Hans Lutges* and a sailor remained lying because of thirst. We, being 22 persons strong, continued until

---

38. This probably is a forked riverbed near Duqm, see Doornbos, *Shipwreck*, p. 68.

about 11 o'clock, when all of us fell down, because of the unbearable heat and faintness due to thirst. After having sat there we stood up again and continued and looked for water. However, the third surgeon, *Pieter Coene*, and an apprentice sailor,[39] named *Bronkhorst* were not willing to go with us and because of thirst remained behind. It apparently would have also been all our turn that day, if the Lord, who knows relief from death, had not saved us, because he showed us his mercy and gave us water to comfort us with which we could quench the thirst of our intestines. At about 12 o'clock we found a small pool of 4 to 5 feet long and 1 to 5 inches deep and saw to our astonishment that water continued to well up continuously from the soil. Here it came to me what is read Isaiah XLI:17.18:

> The poor and needy search for water,
>   but there is none;
>   their tongues are parched with thirst.
> But I the Lord will answer them;
>   I, the God of Israel, will not forsake them.
> I will make rivers flow on barren heights,
>   and springs within the valleys.
> I will turn the desert into pools of water,
>   and the parched ground into springs.

Then we went down on our knees and drank so much that the salt water that we had drank the two previous days we spat out again. Next, we found another pool that was bigger, where a big thorny tree stood, and we thanked the Lord for his mercy and that day we rested there. Then we looked for food, but only found some thin rushes, whose roots we sucked dry. Finally we filled our small casks and jars and send

---

39. In Dutch *jong matroos* to be distinguished from a *matroos* or able seaman or sailor.

a soldier with a stoup full of water[40] to the surgeon and the ordinary sailor, who had remained lying at a distance of about 1 mile. He found them and returned with them, and thus, we were again 22 persons. We also found here some graves,[41] and on each one stood a small jar on a piece of wood, or a fishing net; here we remained until the next day.

Saturday, the 20th ditto. At sunrise we resumed our march, but it did not last long before we were attacked again by some men and women, who took our casks and jars and took our clothes leaving us buck-naked, threatening to cut our throats. We gestured that they could go ahead, because they had stripped us naked and had taken our water, and therefore, we would die of thirst anyway, or the heat of the sun would burn our bodies; however, they laughed at this. We looked dejectedly at each other and some of us started to weep. When they saw this, they gave us a drink from our own vessels and gestured that we could go. However, we asked for our clothes back, and then an old crippled man joined them and looking at us he returned some vessels in which we had kept water, although they were mostly empty; he also gave one of us a pair of trousers, to another a jacket, and again to a third one a pair of trousers or a shirt [*baaitje*], to put over our naked body. However, some had to continue naked, whereupon we divided these among each other to cover our genitals. I received a pair of very bad pants to wear,[42] and half a leg of a seaman's trousers to cover my shoulders. During that day we all were seriously burnt by the scorching sun; underway we saw goats [*bokken*] for the first time; because of walking on rocks, we also developed wounds to the soles of our feet, so that we could barely walk. After sunset we went to sleep.

---

40. A *stoopskruik* or a stoup in English is a drinking vessel of a capacity of one *stoop* or about 2 liters.
41. The text has *begraafplaatsen*, i.e. cemeteries; this does not make sense here.
42. *Zielsverkopersbroek*. A so-called *zielverkoper*, or in English crimp, often a woman, lured men who were unemployed or down on their luck to serve on ships; he/she supplied them with clothes and other needs, but all of bad quality and overpriced. The men signed an IOU, which was known as *ceel*. Because the crimped men were only paid after having served on a ship, the crimp sold their *ceel*, usually to the VOC. Hence they were known as *ceelverkopers*, which term was bastardized to *zielverkopers*, or sellers of *ceels*.

Sunday, the 21st ditto. At sunrise we continued on our road arriving that day at a high mountain range with deep valleys, but we did not find water. Finally we came back to the beach, where we found crabs and periwinkles; we ate them as well as some kind of roots that have the shape of the pineapple crown, which at first has a sweet taste, but a bitter aftertaste. We also found small boats standing on the beach, made in the manner of *slengen* on the Coast of Coromandel and found there shark heads and fins which we gnawed. Many of us were severely burnt by the sun at that time and we all got blisters on our soles because of walking on rocks so that many complained and wanted to lie down. After sunset we went to sleep again, but due to the cold, which we felt, we only slept a little.

Monday, the 22nd ditto. The boatswain and I had much trouble convincing many of our men to continue, but finally we were able to bring them around. The road was very painful, because we had to go up and down crags, some of which were hit by breakers, and because of the steepness of the mountains we could not go up. Thus, we continued on that miserable route with much pain. However, one of us remained lying, a sailor named *Jan Drevan*, whose members had become stiff, having lockjaw and terrible pain in his two amputated fingers and the apprentice sailor named *Bronkhorst*. We continued and arrived on a sandy beach, where we found the boatswain's mate's helper *Peter van Holland* sitting, whom we had lost in the mountains on the 18th of this month, only dressed in a small jacket to cover his body as well as the sailor *Jacob Kleyn*, who had remained lying on the road due to thirst on the 17th of this month, who was buck-naked and had only a small fabric to cover his genitals. They told us that they had been robbed and left naked and that sailor *Carsten Pietersze* had gone ahead. We then saw two men who had fishing-gear with them, and when they saw us, they came to us and asked where we came from? We gestured that we had swam ashore; then they asked how come that your bodies are in such a bad condition? We showed them that we had been burnt by the sun, whereupon they asked whether we had not brought clothes ashore and whether we had no *floes*? (*Floes* is among these people the way to say money of gold and silver.)⁴³ Finally, they gestured that we should come with them and we followed them and arrived at their dwelling, which was a thorn bush in the level field, where they had women, children, camels, donkeys, goats and dogs; their household effects consisted of a pot, *lokjes* (being a kind of wooden trays) and oyster shells. Their women watched us with compassion, and showed that they pitied us, lamenting that we looked so bad. They asked us many questions and it pleased the Lord to turn their heart to our benefit to make them share their poverty with us. Thus, they gave us a piece of shark fin that had been roasted in hot embers, a piece of dried shark, to each of us a piece of *tammer*,⁴⁴ (which is a kind of fruit that grows there, and in taste and size like a fig, however, being elongated, having on the inside a pit the size of a coffee bean.) This was the first food we had since the 15th of this month. They milked the goats and gave us milk mixed with water to drink; they also gave two of our men a piece of fabric to cover their genitals. They greatly desired to have the young slave, but we did not want to give him away. Then they told us that we had to leave, and we asked them where *Mascate* was; they replied: Far! We then continued until sunset when we went to sleep.

Tuesday, the 23rd ditto. Early in the morning we resumed our march and then a man, seated on a camel, who yesterday had also been at the thorn bush, came after us. Having reached us he wanted to take the black boy, but we refused, but he did not leave us alone, gesturing that if we would continue without giving the boy they would cut off our heads. To which we replied that he could take him if the boy agreed to go with him. However, he took the boy against his will and rode away. After he had handed him over to the other two he again came to us bringing us a small basket with *tammer*. We continued on our path, but 4 sailors in our company remained lying on the road, and we finally came again to a bush, where we received a swig of water, but because we had to drink

---

43. From the Arabic *fals* (pl. *folus*) meaning copper or bronze coin; derived from the Greek word *follis*, the name of a Byzantine copper coin.
44. *Tamar* is the generic Arabic term for dates that are ripe or sun-dried, at which time they are mostly harvested (July-August). As dates are stored in tightly pressed form they were given a piece of such tightly packed fruits containing quite many dates.

from our hands we dropped much of that greatly valued water, which we sorely lacked; this was a great grief to us. The more so, since many started to mutter, not knowing when we would find deliverance, also, as if they wanted to set bounds for God, which is innate to human nature. I then asked them whether they knew a shorter route than me and the boatswain? If so they might as well take it, because I was unable to stop them, as I was so weak that I was barely able to carry my own body. The boatswain and I were no longer of a mind to so often beg them to leave in the morning somewhat earlier and in the evening to continue a hour longer, which had happened several times so far. Then I and the boatswain decided to continue our route and that those who wanted could come with us. This entire journey was mere guess-work, because we had no other compass and beacon by which we could hold to our course other than the sun remaining to our right side. At sunset we laid down to sleep, but due to the cold at night we slept little.

Wednesday, 24th ditto. In the morning we resumed our march and that day we met blacks,[45] from whom we received some water to drink and some *tammer* to eat, and we filled our casks and jars with water. They asked us, like the others for *floes* and *groosie* (silver and gold),[46] also from where we came and how come that our bodies looked that way? We could only reply by gesturing, and concerning the last question we pointed to the sun, and then we learnt that the sun in their language is called *shemes*.[47] They further asked us how it came that our feet looked so miserable? We showed them that this was caused by the hot sand and rocks, which they seemed not to understand pointing at their bodies and feet, as if they wanted to ask, why they were not in the same condition? However, they appeared to pity us because they gave us a gift of 3 big raw shark fins. We continued and reached a large plain, which I, with the boatswain and the surgeon, crossed to avoid a big sand bar;

---

45 Due to miscegenation with Africans, the local people were rather swarthy or even black.

46. *Ghurush* (Ottoman Turkish) from the German word *Groschen* was an Ottoman Turkish silver coin.

47. *Shemes* or *shams*, meaning 'sun' in Arabic.

contrariwise the others of our company walked along the beach. After sunset, we had crossed the plain and laid ourselves to rest under a crag, where some time later the other men arrived. Then we heard two blacks, whom we asked for some fire, whereupon they gestured that some of us should go with them to their dwelling. This they did, but learnt that this dwelling was also a crag, just like our resting place, and they did not find any fire so that we had to gnaw these shark fins raw. We also found out that sailor *Kersten Pietersze*, who had abandoned us on the 18th and whom we barely recognized, because he was terribly burnt by the sun, told us that it would be better to travel in groups of 2 to 4 men rather than with many in one group. We slept that night on that spot.

Thursday, the 25th ditto. The boatswain, the surgeon and I each took one stoup of water on our shoulders and continued our route; we met two inhabitants of the country who took us to their dwelling, which was under a crag, and asked us the same questions as the previous ones, and finally gave us a draught of water and a piece of dried fish. Here we were joined by boatswain's mate's helper *de Geus*, *Andries Kolstrop*, and *Janus Balthazar*, both sailors. Thus, we continued with 6 in our company and met another 4 men, who had 5 loaded camels. We asked them about *Maskate*, and they made signs to show us that is was still at a distance of 7 days travel, and that we should keep to these routes, which were 3 to 4 well trodden paths. We then continued, in the hope that the Lord would bring deliverance, if it pleased him. Towards the evening we came to a fresh water *tang* (creek) where we refreshed ourselves as well as filled our 2 jars again. Continuing from there we reached a wood that was totally sandy, which encouraged us, however, in the sand we lost our paths, but we kept going for a while to the wood, where at sunset we laid down to rest. However, due to the cold and pain, which we felt in our burnt bodies, our rest was very little.

Friday, the 26th ditto. At sunrise we continued and passed through the said wood, which was about an estimated 2 to 3 [German] miles [15 - 23 km] long, in high sand dunes, like high mountains, and having to go through the loose sand with our wounded feet was very painful. In the evening, at about 10 o'clock we rested, buried ourselves in the sand, so that only our faces were uncovered, but we could not rest due to the cold; also our water had run out again.

Saturday, the 27th ditto. At sunrise we resumed our journey; underway we dug for water, but we only found salt water. That day we believed that we would be parched with thirst, because of the awful heat in the said high sand dunes. At sunset we again laid down to rest like the previous evening.

Sunday, the 28th ditto. In the morning we continued again, but had much trouble to make surgeon *Pieter Koene* come with us, because he, of all of us, was the most burnt by the sun. Underway we dug a well and found fresh water, where we slaked our thirst and filled our jars. At about 4 o'clock we arrived at the beach and we sat down in the wet sand to rest a while. Here 3 men with a loaded camel came to us (the load of said camel consisted of bags filled with small fish like sardines, also others with *tammer*, and again others with dried limes (where they were taking the load we could not guess, because we did not understand them; the accompanying people were dressed the same, they had a goatskin around their body and otherwise were completely naked.) We asked them for some food and they give as a piece of *tammer*, asked us where we came from etc. Then, they frisked us and touched our trouser belt and asked whether we had no money, but finding nothing they let us go. Then we encountered two others; these took us to near their dwelling which was built in the form of a half moon against the wind and made from thorny branches. This was the first building that we saw in this country. We also received here a piece of *tammer*. We continued our journey until after sunset, when we laid down on the beach to rest. That night 2 jackals came which frightened us, but they fled from us.

Monday, the 29th ditto. At daybreak we resumed our march, but had much trouble to make the surgeon come with us. When the sun rose we came upon two small boats and found at least 7 blacks sitting there, who questioned us several times like the previous ones. Here, we also found two of our sailors, *Matthys Janszen* and *Jan Theunisze*, the latter had a large wound at the back of his heel so that he had to walk with a stick. We learnt from them that they met at the wood, mentioned above on the

25th, where they had separated from the others. We parted company and continued on our route, but the sailor in our party, *Jacob Johan Balthazar*, remained behind and went with them. Meanwhile, the surgeon and the boatswain complained continuously, because they had terrible sun burn, but in particular the surgeon. That day we arrived at huts made of branches and covered with sacks made of goat hair, and next to it a stone building, which was made roughly into a square, but it was as if they had put cobble stones and rocks on top of another. However, this kind of dwelling was the first of its kind that we encountered in this desolate and uninhabited land. We also found a few trees, i.e. here and there some thorny ones. These people as before asked the same questions, and frisked us and even took the cloth buttons from my trousers to see whether there was money in it. Finally, a whole group of men and women gathered and asked us whether we were *Biaans*?[48] When we did not understand they came to us and opened our pants, took a small stick and checked whether we were circumcised. They did this several times and spit in our face, which gave us the idea that they either must be of the Jewish or the Turkish nation, as both these people practice circumcision. We then hurried away and after sunset rested.

Tuesday, the 30th ditto. At daybreak we resumed our journey, but frequently we were stopped, frisked and spit at; finally we met 4 men, who had caught a fine catch of fish; we asked them for something to eat. They gestured that we should come with them, which we complied with and arrived at their huts, where their women took great pity on us and promised us some food, yes they gave us as much roasted fish, *tammer* and water as we wanted. They took great pleasure in seeing us eat, because we ate with such relish, as they so generously gave us this food. In the evening we once again found compassionate people, who regaled us in the same manner. However, the surgeon did not eat anything, because

---

48. *Banya*, a Gujarati word meaning 'trader'. The Portuguese used this word, in the form of Banyan, to refer to any Indian trader, and this appellation was later adopted by other Europeans as well as the Omanis, because during the Portuguese control over Muscat and other Omani ports, Banyans were also living there, as they continued to do after the Portuguese ouster from Oman in 1650.

he was in so much pain, although we encouraged him. Next they put down a large net (being a drag or trawl net) on which we should lie down, which we did. I then said to the surgeon, that if I was in his place, I would stay here a day or more with such people, who had shown so much compassion, however, I did not receive an answer.

Wednesday, the 31st ditto. In the morning we departed to resume our journey, but at 7 o'clock the surgeon took his leave and said that he would try to return and follow the advice I had given him. We then continued and arrived at huts (these were simply made with 4 poles in the ground, about 4 to 5 feet high, and covered with a cloth made from camel hair). They asked whether we were circumcised? They frisked us and further asked whether we wanted to stay there and wanted to have women?[49] (This had happened many times before by others), but we did not reply and continued until the evening when again we laid down to rest.

Thursday, the 1st September. In the morning we resumed our march and underway we received a piece of *tammer* and some water. In the afternoon we came across two sailors, *Willem Nicolson* and *Karsten Pietersze* who were sitting on the beach eating a crab. We first thought they were blacks, but coming closer we saw that they were of our crew, and we learnt from them that on the 25th of last month they had separated from the others. Also, that a soldier, who had been with them on the said 25th, had returned to the *tang*, saying that he wanted to die there. Again, that last night they had been with our surgeon, but he was in a very bad condition and apparently it was unlikely that he was going to make it. Each of us then went his way and in the evening we arrived at a group of huts, where we asked its inhabitants for some food and water, which we received. They questioned us like the previous ones and seem to feel great pity for us. Seeing that my lips and those of the boatswain

---

49. This reminds me of a remark made by Mr. J.P. Bannerman, at a conference at Durham University in 1986, who in the 1950s, when working in rural Oman, was offered women as well. When he asked why, the villagers told him that they looked too swarthy and black and having a white man in the gene pool would make the color of the future generation somewhat less swarthy, or so they hoped. He also showed photos of Omani rural families living under a crag or a thorny tree, just as Eyks described.

were totally raw and skinless they took a piece of black substance which moistened with some water they rubbed on a piece of rock and then smeared our lips with a wood chip.[50] The first two mentioned sailors then joined us and we stayed together. In the evening we gathered some branches and bushes behind which we slept that night.

Friday, the 2nd September. At sunrise we started walking and arriving at some huts where we begged for some food and water, but we did not get any. An old woman said that she would take us to a well, and therefore, we accompanied here. While going there the boatswain said that he could not go on any longer, and he therefore, wanted to remain here for 3 days to see whether his burnt body would heal somewhat. We accompanied the said woman to the well, which was very hard going for us, because it was rather far away and we had to go through hot sand. However, the worst part was that boys and girls followed us who threw rocks and harassed us. At 11 or 12 o'clock we arrived at the said well where a man was seated to whom the boys and girls indicated that he should cut off our head. However, after having questioned and searched us, he did not do so, but gave us a swig of water. We then intended to go to the boatswain, but because it was scorching hot, we feared to take that road again, the more so because of the burning sand, apart from the fact that we had been maltreated here. Therefore, we looked for the beach and went though the wet sand, where halfway along the beach we found an iron piece of an 8-pounder cannon, from which we could concluded that ships had been wrecked here. The more so, because we found in the huts Dutch cargo knives,[51] a copper grease ladle,[52] a leading block[53] and Moorish clothes.[54] We asked the occupants from where

---

50. The substance may have been made with frankincense, a local plant, derived from the resin of *Boswellia spp*.
51. *Cargasoenmessen*.
52. *Smeerlepel*.
53. *Voetblok*, a single block, frequently a snatch block, used as a fairlead to bring the hauling part of a rope or the fall of a tackle into a more convenient direction, or to lead it onto a winch. In the case of a tackle, the fall is known, after it has been led through a leading block, as the leading part.
54. In the original the word used is *kleeden*, which may mean both rugs and clothes.

these items came? They replied that they had obtained from *Musquette*. We then asked them how far away is this place from *Musquette*? In reply some said 15, others 10, and again others 7 and then others 3 days, which told us that we could not rely on this, but had to remain steady and trust only for positive relief in the hand of the Supreme Ruler. We received some *tammer* and water, and they took our jars. In exchange they gave us a leather sack and they told us that a Moorish vessel from Bengal had shipwrecked here, from which they had salvaged the aforementioned goods. In the evening we laid down to rest.

Saturday, the 3rd ditto and *Sunday*, the 4th ditto. We resumed our journey and had the abovementioned daily encounters.

Monday, the 6th ditto. We again went on our way and reached some huts where we only found women, whom we asked for fire to roast some fish, which we had received on the 4th. They supplied us with that and after we roasted our fish, we ate it with much gusto. The said women, seeing that we ate that fish so eagerly, gave us as much *tammer* as we liked as well as butter milk, which they churned in a small leather bag in front of us. We then continued and reached a large tree, though with a low trunk under which was a family. We went and sat in its shadow to rest somewhat, whereupon the said women came to us laughing and making fun of us. We stood up and although they gestured that we could stay, we continued our journey. In the afternoon at about 3 o'clock we encountered 4 women who were gathering firewood. They had shoes on their feet. We asked them for food and water, but they gestured that we should go on until we arrived at *Cagies* (that is what they called their dwellings).[55] We then arrived at 4 paths, which daily were trodden by

---

55. *Cagie*, properly *kargeen*, a local term that was used to denote the common traditional *barasti* huts (communication from Dawn Chatty on 08/08/2013). There were three different types of traditional houses in Oman. The usual term is *arish* for the *barasti* huts. These were made from local wood and filled in with palm fronds and covered with palm leaves. Dionisius A. Agius, *Seafaring in the Arabian Gulf and Oman: People of the Dhow*, New York, 2009, p. 66. The other one is called round house, *beyt al-dawwar*. These were made of stones and the roof was made of local wood, palm leaves and grass. The last one is called *beyt al-qufl*. These were strong houses built of large stones and their walls were thick.

camels and we met several camels on that path that were loaded with fish, which looked like anchovies, but dried. We begged the camel drivers to give us some to eat, but we received nothing, and we therefore, asked them where are you coming from? They replied that they came from the village of *Eet*. We then continued until about 7 or 7.30 and then saw fires burning, which appeared to us as something very odd there. This was the reason why we went there and then we arrived at a *cagie* made from *tammer* sticks, where a man and a woman were seated, while a camel was lying in front of the *cagie*. These people seeing us indicated that we could sit down and they gave us some cooked fish and a swig of water. Then they pointed to a path that we should take, where we should find *tammer* palms. Again we then went towards the light and arrived at a similar *cagie*, which looked reasonably well made, in which 2 women were seated. Seeing us they started to scream loudly, and immediately some men with drawn swords came toward us. We stretched our hands as a sign of friendship and so they shook hands with me and questioned us like all the previous ones and seeing that we were shivering from the cold they gestured that we had to come out of the wind and shelter behind the *cagie*, where they gave us water and *tammer*, which we ate. We then asked them whether we might sleep behind the *cagie* that night, but they had so much pity on us that they took us into a *cagie*, which was open above, where we slept that night.

Tuesday, the 6th ditto. In the morning we saw that it was an entire village where we were, viz. the village of *Eet*, with at least 100 huts, and also stone store-houses.[56] We also saw there *patiels*[57] and *markaps*, which are vessels made in the Persian manner. We continued going through the

---

56. Hadd a village standing in a sandy plain and situated at the foot of the Khor al-Hajar, about 1.6 km inland from Ras al-Hadd. It is 25 km east by south from Sur.
57. *Battil* is a vessel with a long bow; on the Persian coast with one mast and on the Arabian coast with two masts. Depending on its size, it is propelled by oars and sails; the larger ones only by oars when pearling. It was used both for trading and pearling and had a crew of 10 to 20 men, and carried 15 to 60 tons of cargo. *Markab* in medieval Arabic meant 'vehicle, carriage.' In maritime usage it refers to any kind of merchant or transport ship. For more information, see Agius, *In the wake*, p. 38.

entire village and the people seeing us there called: *Portugees*! *Englees*! *Hollandees*! They stopped us and gave us water and *tammer* and questioned us carefully. But we gestured to them that we swam ashore, finally we met a slave boy, who indicated that we should accompany him, which we did. En route he told me that there had come another white man here, who used a stick. He took us to a merchant and skipper,[58] and we found there sailor *Jan Theunissen*, but the other 2 had been unable to follow. He told us that this skipper had a vessel with which he intended to sail to *Musquette* or *Maskat* and from there to *Bassora*. The captain told me the same thing and asked me whether I wanted to accompany him to *Musquette* or *Maskat* (as it is mentioned on the map) and then he took me with him to his vessel, showing me there bags of coffee beans and raw cow hides as well as his pieces of cannon. He asked me whether I could fire those, to which I replied Yes! Hearing this he wanted to employ me as master gunner, if I wanted to sail with him, and pay me 20 *ropijen*, yes he would hire us all. He further asked on what ship I had served? But for some time we had been unable to properly understand one another, but after long gesticulating he understood me and said, *Mallem*,[59] which among them is called a mate. It then appeared to me as if he did not want to detain us, because he asked me when I was at *Maskat*, whether I then would go to *Kareek*?[60] To which I replied, yes! In the afternoon he again came to me with his son and told me that he would send me with his son to *Zoar* (which is also a village, but not as big as the previous one),[61] who would take me there to a skipper, who went to *Maskat* and from there to *Kareek*. He then gave his son some money for our fare and gave us a small basket with *tammer*. In the afternoon at 2 o'clock we went to the vessel, but because the captain was not yet ready, we did

---

58. The Dutch word *schipper*, meaning skipper or ship's captain, was used as the equivalent for the term Captain. Wherever Eyks uses this word I translate it as skipper, not as captain.
59. Properly *mu`allim*, meaning 'teacher, guide, master (of a trade)'.
60. Kareek or Khark, an island opposite Bandar-e Rig, and the location of a VOC trading station.
61. Sur, an important town on the coast of the Eastern Hajar of Oman, situated 28 km west of Ras al-Hadd and 156 km south-east of Muscat.

not depart on that day. Meanwhile, our guide returned to the village to look for the skipper, while we remained sitting under a crag near the roads. But both the skipper and our guide did not come and the father of the said guide sent his slave boy with the message that I, with those who were best able to do so, return to his warehouse. Therefore, we three returned and received *tammer* and water from him, and later slept in the said warehouse.

Wednesday, the 7th ditto. At sunrise, we again went with our guide, the said skipper's son to the vessel and in the morning at 9 o'clock we departed for *Zoar*, where we arrived the next day, being *Thursday*, the 8th ditto. With our guide we went to a merchant and skipper, who was about to leave for *Maskat*, and from there to *Kareek*. During the night we stayed ashore, and received some fish, *tammer* and water.

Friday, the 9th ditto. In the evening at sunset we arrived at *Matra*,[62] which is a fishing village, at about one hour's distance from *Maskat*, situated to the west of the said place, and slept in the vessel, but on *Sunday*, the 11th ditto, the skipper put us ashore with the *chambok*,[63] and we went on foot to *Maskat*, where on arrival we at first found no one who could talk to us; the inhabitants calling us *Englis!*, *Portugees! Hollandees! Francees!* Meanwhile, we saw 4 ships lying there to which we wanted to go, but on the way we met a black man, who spoke to us in Dutch, and asked where we came from. We replied that we had lost our ship, and he then asked, whether we had already been at the Hon. Comp's broker. After I replied that we were strangers here and could not understand the people, he told me that yesterday 2 sailors of my crew had arrived there. He then took us to the broker, who questioned me about where I had lost the ship; after I had given him my report he pointed that I should go upstairs, and coming there, I found 2 of my sailors, viz. *Matthys Jansse* and *Jacobus Johannes Balthazar*. We received food, which consisted of fish, *tammer*,

---

62. Matrah, about 3.3 km from Muscat.
63. *Sambuk* is a local mid-sized vessel that carried a crew of 15 to 20 men and carried 15 to 60 tons of cargo.

rice, onion, and water. After having eaten, he gave us fabric so each of us could make pants, an overcoat and cap. God the Lord be praised and thanked for his guidance so far! He was surprised that we had crossed the country, where only murderers, robbers, and brigands lived. We then learnt that in the previous year 35 vessels from *Zoar* had shipwrecked there, and although each vessel had a crew of 25 to 30 men, nevertheless most of the people had been killed. Moreover, because our bodies were in such a bad condition, we received plasters for our wounds which we dressed. The said broker wanted to keep us there for about 10 days so that our bodies could recuperate, and then send us onwards to *Kareek*. I also would have preferred this and therefore, I wrote two letters to Mr. *Buschman*,[64] which would leave for *Kareek* on the 12th ditto. However, meanwhile we learnt that two English ships from *Bassora* were about to arrive here, and I then said to the broker, I would prefer to depart the next day to prevent other troubles.[65] He approved and prepared some provisions for us, consisting in rice, *tammer*, fish, cakes, onion, limes,[66] salt, and tobacco as well as a cooking pot and a water jar.

Monday, the 12th ditto. In the morning I asked the broker whether there were no vessels that dared to go there, because on the 20th of this month the monsoon was good there, while an easterly wind blew away from the shore, so that there were no breakers. He replied that he would ready a vessel for 1,000 *ropys*. I then asked whether I, or one of my crew, or all of us might go with it, but he told me: No! However, at sunset we went on board to depart for *Kareek* and were in the company of at least 20 vessels.

Monday, the 19th ditto. We saw two three-masters, which were the English ships, which went to Bengal. I then asked our skipper where I might go aboard one of them, whereupon he had me and one of the sailors who could speak English sail to one of these

---

64. Wilhelmus Buschman was the chief of VOC trade on Khark from 21 December 1755 to 19 August 1765.
65. It is not known what kind of troubles Eyks refers to.
66. *Lemmetje* or *limoen* (*Citrus aurantifolia*).

ships. Arriving the Captain asked why we wanted to come aboard? We then yelled that we were Dutchmen who had lost their ship. He then said we could come aboard. Having done so, he asked me where we had lost our ship, as well as whether we wanted to have some rice? Then he gave me half a bag of rice, 6 bottles of arak, 1 bottle filled with tea, and 6 loaves of bread. I asked the Captain to be so good as to orally inform the Hon. Director in Bengal, Mr. *N. Taillefert*,[67] because I had no paper, and the people of the vessel I was on, did not give me enough time to write. The Captain then asked whether we wanted to go with him to Bengal, telling us that he would not charge us the fare, but we thanked him for his kindness, because we were so close to the Comp's trading office, where our vessel was headed, and therefore, we returned to our vessel.

Friday, the 25th ditto. We anchored between *Cabo Bardestant-*[68] and *Congo*,[69] in the Bight of *Deyer*,[70] having remained there for 3 days with a three-mast and a two-mast *goerap*,[71] as well as about 75 *Zoari* and *Maarcaaps patiels*,[72] I asked the skipper, why he did not depart for *Kareek*? But because we did not understand each other very well, he gestured that *Baljoosje*[73] and *Miermannie*[74] were brothers and

---

67. Louis Taillefert was director of VOC trade in Bengal from 1760 to 1763.
68. Cape Bardestan.
69. Although Congo normally refers to Kong, here it refers to Kangan, which is a small port situated on the eastern shore of a deep bay near Cape Bardistan.
70. Dayer, a small port, is situated to the west of Cape Bardestan.
71. *Ghurab* had a low and a sharp projecting prow and a square stern like that of a galley with two or three masts; it weighed from 150 to 300 tons.
72. Meaning, *battil*s and *markab*s belonging to people of Sur (Zoar).
73. The term *bailo* probably comes from the Latin word *baiulus* which originally meant 'porter'. In the Ottoman Empire it was the title of the Venetian resident or consul, who oversaw his community of compatriots and had to promote his country's trade; later it was used for all other European consuls. Here the term refers to the Dutch chief of the VOC trading station on Khark Island.
74. Miermanie or properly Mir Muhanna was a pirate and the chief of Bandar-e Rig, a port situated opposite Khark Island. After having tried to take the island in March 1762, peace was concluded between the Dutch and Mir Muhanna. The Dutch broke the peace in 1765, when they were forced by Karim Khan

together seized *Zoari* vessels. I then shook my head, signifying 'no,' and gestured that if it came to that we would help him fight. Every day they were engaged in small talk[75] on board of our vessel and they wanted me and my men to move to the three- and two-mast *goeraps* as master gunners, for which they would give us *ropys* when we arrived at *Bassora*. However, we had no knowledge with whom they were at war, and that it might be against our own nation. But they put the front finger as hooks into one another and said: *Kareek* and *Boesher zamzammä poe poe grab*![76] implying that that *Kareek* and *Boesher* were collaborating and would shoot at the *goeraps*. We gestured 'no'! And therefore, they wanted to return to *Maskat*.

Thursday, the 29th ditto. We saw 3 vessels approach the Bight of *Dyer*, which they believed to be *gallowets* of *Miermanie*, (*Gallowets* are galleys)[77] and therefore, we all made ready for battle. The *gallowets* that were outside the bay fired 3 salutes as a sign of friendship, but as we did not understand it that way 75 vessels set sail and formed a half moon to surround the three mentioned vessels. Then one of the three, being a *Kareek bagaar*, sailed right into the middle of the fleet to the *goeraps* with a letter from *Kareek* (these have the shape of an ordinary sea-going ship, but without a lion and sprit in front, some have two and some have three masts). They hailed many of the *Zoari* vessels, saying that the two *gallowets* in their company belonged to the *baljoostje* (*Gallowets of the baljoostje* means as much as the mer-

---

Zand, the ruler of Persia, to assist the Bushehr fleet against Mir Muhanna, as a result of which the Dutch lost Khark, see Willem Floor, *The Rise of the Gulf Arabs*. Washington DC: MAGE, 2007.

75. The term used is *passiaaren*, which does not occur in the dictionaries.

76. Khark and Bushehr had indeed friendly relations and operated together to protect the shipping lanes. *Zamzameh* means here 'there was a rumor,' *poe poe* is an onomatopoeia, imitating the sound of shooting, and *grap* refers to a type of local vessel, viz., a *ghurab*, an armed galley. Thus, the sentence means, [The chiefs of] Khark and Bushehr are rumored to shoot at [hostile] *ghurabs*.

77. *Gallivat*, an armed vessel, with sails and oars and small draught of water; the term may be a bastardization of the Portuguese term *galeota*, i.e. galiot or galley in English, which in Arabic became *qaliyat*.

chant's galleys, because they call a merchant *baljoost,*)⁷⁸ who had come to escort them, because the Hon. Comp. sold much merchandise to them every year. Now it was feared that they dare not come to *Kareek*, because they had been made to believe that the *baljoost*, which were we Dutchmen, were collaborating with *Miermannie*, but now they saw us and knew better. The galowets came toward us and seeing that they flew the Prince's flag,⁷⁹ I told the skipper: they are Dutchmen. He then asked, *baljoost?* And then I understood what they meant by *baljoost*. We went and stood with all the others and when the *gallowet de Verfisch* passed close by, we were asked where we came from? I yelled from the wrecked ship *Amstelveen*, which they passed on to the *gallowet de Revengie*, which was commanded by Joseph Rama. Immediately, he had his yawl rowed to me and asked me to come on board where he received me warmly. He had the other men fetched, of whom 4 were taken to the other *gallowet*. Then the entire fleet set sail.

Monday, the 3rd October. At sunset we anchored in the roads on *Kareek*. I then went ashore to see the chief, Mr. *Buschman*, to whom I gave the report of my journey. Also, in the roads came the *snow*⁸⁰ the *Courier*, skippered by *Lasboom*, from Bassora. God the Lord be praised for our arrival, so far!

Tuesday, the 4th ditto. The following men were signed on, to wit: in accordance with the orders for the *Westerveld*,

At Dfl. 14   Carsten Pieters, from *Heir*, gunner, 1763
Dfl.   14   Willem Nicholsoon, from *'sHertogenbosch*, gunner, 1763

---

78. The author is in error, the proper translation would be the *gallivat* of the *balyuz*, i.e. of the Dutch chief of the Khark station. The latter indeed owned such a vessel and traded with it for his own account, see Floor, *The Rise*, p. 197.
79. The flag of the Prince of Orange (orange, white, blue), which was used during the so-called Eighty Years War (1568-1648) and was often used as an alternative for the Dutch national red, white and blue flag.
80. A *snaauw schip* was a long, low small ship used for coastal navigation.

Dfl.	9	*Matthys Janszen*, from *Dantzig*, young unskilled sailor,[81] 1763
Dfl.	9	*Jan Theunissen*, from *Luxemburg*, *oplooper*, 1763
Dfl.	11	*Jansz Andreas* Kolstrop, from *Dronthem*, gunner on the *Oud Carspel*, according to the orders Anno 1762.
Dfl.	7	*Jacobus Johannes*

Balthazar, from *Wetteren*, young unskilled sailor on *'t Huis de Boede*, according to the orders Anno 1762.

The chief, Mr. *Buschman*, told me that it would be better for me and the boatswain's mate's helper to go with the free trader's *snow*, the *Courier*, to *Mallabaar* or *Ceilon*, because there was no employment here, and that we only would be an expense to the Hon. Comp.'s trading station. I told Mr. *Buschman* that I would do as he thought was best, and thus I left without an assigned task.

After having stayed for 15 days at *Kareek*, I took my leave of Mr. *Buschman* on *Wednesday*, the 19th ditto, and embarked with Captain *N. Lasboom* and the same day we set sail to *Banderbasië* or *Bandar-Abbasi*, also known as *Gamrun* or *Gamron*, situated in the Straits of *Ormuz*, where in the past there had been a East Indies Comp's trading station.[82] There, we still found a Company's factory with one European.[83] Because that port is situated at the mouth of the Gulf of Persia, Europeans used it to engage in great commerce.

Friday, the 28th ditto. We arrived in the roads of *Bandar Abbasi*, where we took in salt. Two hours inland we found a mountain on which

---

81. *Oploper* or *hooploper* was an unskilled sailor (12-16 years old) used for all kinds of jobs.
82. On Bandar Abbas and the Dutch trading station there, see Floor, *Five Port Cities*, chapter 5.
83. The factory at Bandar Abbas was closed down in 1758, although until 1766 a Dutch caretaker, remained, see Floor, *The Rise*, pp. 73, 78, 84.

one saw 4 rarities, viz., First, *salt*, which flowed down from the top of the mountain like glass, and where one finds more of those mountains from which salt flows down. Second, one found growing on the mountain *Persian red*. Third, one found there *sulfur*,[84] and Fourth, *black glistening sand*,[85] and all of that on one mountain. Near that mountain we found a well with water that was so hot that one hardly could put one's hand into it. We also discovered that here Indians make sacrifices.[86] We remained until 2 December, when 9 galleys from the island of *Ormuz*, which is quite close by, came toward us to seize us, because we had refused to load salt from them, and they even had to hire men to fetch salt. We made preparations and readied for battle, but because the winds did not favor us, we upped anchor, and sailed away during the night.

Saturday, the 4th December.[87] We departed from the roads of *Bandar Abbasie* to *Maskatte* and arrived in their roads on *Saturday* the 11th ditto, where the Hon. Comp's broker *Nariton* came aboard.[88] On that occasion, I asked him whether the vessel that he had sent to where our ship had been stranded had yet returned? He replied that of the two vessels sent one had returned with goods, bringing 19 pieces of balks and planks, 106 pigs of tin, 13 baskets with various spices, and other goods. I asked him whether he would be so kind to allow me to write these down, which he promised, when I came ashore. After having been twice ashore and having asked him 3 times to let me note down the goods I did not receive a reply and therefore, I returned to

---

84. Sulfur, red oxide (red lead, Indian red), and salt were produced near Bandar Abbas and on the island of Hormuz and sometimes exported by the VOC – it also served as ballast, see Willem Floor, *The Economy of Safavid Persia*. Wiesbaden: Reichert, 2000, pp. 306-07.
85. Bitumen.
86. On the Indians in Bandar Abbas as well as the hot springs there, see Floor, *Five Port Cities*, pp. 251, 266, 269-271.
87. If the day is correct then the date is 2 December 1674.
88. In VOC documents he is variously referred to as Nariton, Naraitoen, Narrottam, and Naraitun. The most likely form of the name is Narottam (from Sanskrit Nara, man, and Uttama, the best), a very common name among Gujarati Jains.

the vessel having achieved nothing.[89] I also learnt from him that there was still yet another of the sailors of the wrecked ship, who was blind; also in that location where our ship had stranded, the Arabs were killing each other over the goods and that some 400 of them had lost their lives. All the drowned Europeans had been washed ashore, and that they also had seen the anchors and ropes as well as other goods lying on the ground. The 13th December sailor *Steven Hillekens* from *Deventer* came on board; he was the one whom we lost on 17 August. He told us that he had made the journey to *Maskat* on foot in 3 months less 2 days; also that he been miserably ailing, yes, sometimes he had not had anything to drink or eat for 7 days and that his entire body had been burnt from top to bottom. Also, he had been in the mountains that we had passed on 22 August and found *Jan Drevens* lying dead among the crags, and ordinary sailor *Bronkhorst* lay next to him as if dead from hunger and thirst, but he was still conscious and had told him that the said sailor had died the previous day. He said that he would like to go with him, but because of hunger and thirst was unable to do so. He also reported that meester *Pieter Koene* allegedly had died.[90] The said sailor is the 22nd man who has shown up, but one of them died at *Maskat*, and the others were distributed over Dutch and English ships and vessels.[91] Here, I saw that *Maskat* is situated between mountains on which 4 castles with guard-houses were built; it had a beautiful harbor or bay. Said *Maskat*, which we Dutch generally call *Musquette*, is a rather big and well-known merchant town situated on the Gulf of *Ormuz* on the Arabian Coast and is inhabited by *Arabs*, *Indians*, and *Jews*. It is considered to be the most powerful of the Arab principalities, and is situated east of *Arabia Felix*, which is so named, because of its fertility in comparison with *stony* and

---

89. The author clearly implies that Narrotam was not going to report these finds and sell them for his benefit.
90. Eyks later learnt that he indeed had died in the village where he had returned to recuperate, Doornbos, Shipwreck, p. 118.
91. Two sailors of the *Amstelveen*, Jan Brinkhoud (Amsterdam) and Hendrik Poolman (Hamburg) arrived 6 February in Paliacatta (Pulicat) in South Coromandel (east coast of India) via Gale (Sri Lanka). They related that they kept themselves alive by eating locusts and leafs and by drinking salt water. Arsip Nasional RI, Jakarta, Bataviasch Daghregisters, 19/05/1764.

desolate *Arabia*.[92] However, while we were walking along the shoreline we had to cross the most desolate and sandiest parts and despite this we found the shortest way by God's grace, because one year after this one of my colleagues, who is also mentioned in this report, had wandered about for more than a year and in the middle of the lands of the fierce and rapacious Arabs, who only lead a life rovers and acknowledge their chiefs and leaders as their only sovereign, but nevertheless he was saved.

Saturday, the 18th December.[93] We departed from *Maskat* to *Cochim*,[94] where we dropped anchor in the roads on *Sunday* 22 December 1764. We also found in the roads the Hon. Comp's ship *De Erf-Prins*, commanded by Captain-Lieutenant *Pieter Schooneman*, as well as *Vredestein*, skipper *Johan Hendrik Doodendorp*.

Tuesday, the 24th ditto.[95] Captain *Lasboom* came on board and told me that on the orders of the Hon. Commander *Weyermans* I had to come ashore. That same day I went ashore and at about 5 o'clock and went to the Hon. Commander *Weyermans*, who asked me for an extract account of the perishing of the ship. In reply, I gave the said gentleman my *Journal*. He then told me that I would go with one of the ships to *Batavia*, and arranged that I was given board.

Friday, the 27th ditto.[96] I as well as the *schiemansmaat* and sailor received our orders for the Hon. Comp's ship *De Erf-Prins* to go to *Batavia*, as follows:

> The authorities of the Hon. Comp.'s ship *De Erf-Prins* enroll 3 persons with their belongings, *Cornelis Eyks* from *Middelburg*, Third Watch, *Peter van Holland* from *Rotterdam*,

---

92. Referring to Arabia Petraea and Arabia Deserta.
93. 18 December 1673 was on a Monday.
94. Cochin (now Kochi) a port in Western India (Kerala State); at that time Fort Cochin was ruled by the Dutch.
95. 24 December 1673 was on a Sunday.
96. 27 December 1673 was on a Saturday.

boatswain's mate's helper, *Steven Hillekens*, sailor, to be transported to *Batavia* and serve for board.[97]

Saturday, the 28th ditto.[98] Three of us from the perished ship *Amstelveen* came aboard of the said Comp's ship *De Erf-Prins*, commanded by the Hon. Manly Captain-Lieutenant *Pieter Schooneman*, to go from *Cochim* to *Batavia*, crewed by:

64 European sailors
23 Moorish ditto
27 European soldiers
8   Passengers

Thus, in all 122 there were men. The said ship had 18 cannons, 6-pounders, 4 ditto 3-pounders and 6 swivels. The ship's aft drew 17 feet of water, and in front 16 feet, therefore, 1 foot rake of keel.

Wednesday, the 22nd February.[99] We received information that the *Martasch* pirates[100] had been sighted off *Crangenoor*,[101] wherefore we made all preparations to give battle on their arrival and had lookouts posted to watch for them.

Thursday, the 23rd ditto.[102] In the morning the Captain came on board and the topsails were set with thin yarns[103] (fastened in this way so that the yarns could be cut and the ship would be under sail at once) so that on arrival of the said pirates we could immediately

---

97. Meaning that they received no wages, which was intended as punishment, although they were not responsible for the shipwreck, see Doornbos, *Shipwreck*, p. 112.
98. 28 December 1673 was on a Thursday.
99. 22 February 1674 was on a Thursday.
100. The Mahratta pirates of Mallabar.
101. Cranganore Fort, north of Cochin, built by the Portuguese, but since 1661 in hands of the Dutch.
102. 23 February 1674 was on a Friday.
103. *De zeilen werden op stootgaren gezet.*

head for sea, and everything that might serve to defend ourselves was made ready. However, at 11 o'clock at night we received news that that they were still seen near *Calicut*. We were also asked whether we still needed munitions. If so, the narrow lighter,[104] the *Susanna*, under the official in charge of ships' supplies,[105] *Laurens Beys* would come outside the harbor with the necessarysupplies to await our orders. We sent a letter in reply and asked for 2 additional pieces of 6-pounder cannon.

Friday, the 24th ditto.[106] We did not see anything during the day, but received another 24 soldiers under the command of an ensign as reinforcement as well as the 2 pieces of 6-pounder cannons that we had requested. The former we placed in the hut, and the two 6-pounders in the front-cabin at the galley as hunters. The narrow lighter also came outside and dropped anchor close behind us. We received a letter from shore to remain lying at anchor, to keep good watch, and in case the said pirates fled to call on the roads of *Coulang*[107] to received further orders. We then gave a flag-signal to the lighter, raised our yard anchor, and shortened our daily anchor, raised the yard anchor to the lower yard and also asked for another 2 three-pounders. We received a master gunner from shore, because our master gunner was sick. *Saturday*, the 25th ditto, we placed it on the half-deck, keeping watch that day as well as on *Sunday*, the 26th ditto, but did not learn anything.

Monday, the 27th ditto.[108] We heard rumors that the pirates were slowly moving down towards the south. Therefore, we sent a Company's letter to shore in which we asked whether it would not be advisable to depart for *Coulang* until the pirates had turned towards the north? However, we received reply that on shore they knew

---

104. *Smal-scheepje*.
105. *Equipagemeester*.
106. 24 February 1674 was on a Saturday.
107 The fort of Kollam, Kerala, on India's Malabar Coast, also known as Coulang, Quilon or Coylan, lies roughly 71 km north of Trivandrum, India. Kollam Fort was originally built by the Portuguese, and was captured by the Dutch in 1671.
108. 27 February 1674 was on a Tuesday.

nothing about these rumors, and therefore, we would have to wait until further news arrived from shore. We kept good watch.

Tuesday, the 28th ditto.[109] We received a Company's letter from the shore reporting that the pirates numbered 8 *goeraps* and 30 *Gallowets* and were still cruising off *Calicut*,[110] and there kept busy 3 *Portuguese* ships under the protection of one of their men-of-war. Therefore, it was not likely that they would come down this far south, the more so since the monsoon was mostly over. However, it was left to us whether we wanted to stay or depart, in accordance with what we believed was the most appropriate. We then held ship's council and in return sent a Company's letter in reply that we would remain waiting till the last moment, because we, like the council onshore, were unable to decde one way or the other. Nevertheless, we kept good watch, but did not see anything that day or the following day, when a large ship came from the north without showing colors.

Thursday, the 1st March. In the afternoon we received news from the shore by way of a Company's letter that the pirates were seen at *January*,[111] and as a result, they sometimes come further down to the south. Therefore, first, we should set sail and head for the *Coulang* roadstead. The lighter left for the river, and we left under sail with a variable wind from south-west to W.N.W and a weak cool air. On *Friday*, the 2nd ditto, we went to and fro, and at sunset, having gauged *Porce*[112] in the East W.S. northerly and the southern coast S.E. to the S, we were forced to come to anchor by the current and contrary wind. But at 6 bells during the graveyard shift on *Saturday*, the 3rd ditto, we raised anchor and went under sail again and we came to anchor in the *Coulang* Roads at sunset. Here, on *Monday* the 5th ditto, in the afternoon at 4 o'clock the Comp' ship *Damzight*, Captained by *Lodewyk Thomassen*, coming from *Ceilon*, also came into the roads.

---

109. 28 February 1674 was on a Wednesday.
110. Calicut or Kozhikode, was the capital of Mallabar during the reign of the Zamorins (12th century-1795).
111. I have not been able to identify this location.
112. Porce perhaps is Purakkad factory on the Malabar coast.

Tuesday, the 6th ditto. We received a Company's letter from *Cochim*, reporting that the pirates had turned towards the north, further containing orders to return to *Cochim*. Therefore, at 3 o'clock we as well as the ship *Damzigt* went under sail and both arrived on Saturday the 10th ditto in the roads of *Cochim*, where we found 3 Portuguese and 1 English ship.

Saturday, 31st March. At 10 o'clock in the morning the Hon. Captain came aboard with the Hon. Comp's papers as well as the passengers and at 10.30 we raised anchor to sail for *Batavia*, the Hon. Comp's ship *Damzigt* remained lying in the roads.

Friday, the 6th April. At 2 bells in the forenoon the schiemansmaat *Peter van Holland*, from *Rotterdam*, died who was a member of the crew of the perished Comp's ship *Amstelveen* as related above. There were no further particular events.

Tuesday, 22nd May. At 3 o'clock in the afternoon we arrived safely in the roads of Batavia and dropped anchor there. *The Lord be praised and thanked for a safe journey, so far!*

On 18 June 1774, again in the Comp's service, I was ordered to depart with the ship *Lekkerland*, under the command of Captain *Christiaan Blom*, to *Kareek* in *Persia*. Therefore, on 24th ditto, I went on board. On the 29th ditto, at 7 o'clock in the morning the Hon. *Fiscaal*[113] came on board and held muster; no absentees were found.

Saturday, the 30 June. At 6.30 in the morning the Hon. Captain came on aboard with the Hon. Comp's papers and we immediately raised anchor and went under sail, saluting the roads with 11 cannon salvos and were thanked by the Admiral's ship with 3 salvos.

Saturday, 7 July at noon we were off the harbor and were at southern latitude of 6 degrees, 40 minutes and longitude of 120 degrees of the median from where our compass [reading] began.

Saturday, 25 August. At the beginning of the day watch, we saw the eastern castle of *Maskat*, and because of the weak condition of the crew, - we already suffered 10 dead during the voyage as well as some

---

113. VOC official in charge of law and order as well as public prosecutor.

sick, – and as well as to fill our empty barrels, we decided to call on the bay of *Maskat*. Due to a weak wind and the current that drew us to the north, we arrived at the bay at 9 o'clock at 0.25 mile from the nearest shore, and we lowered the barque and boat.

Sunday, 26 ditto. We raised anchor, but seeing that the strong current pushed us downwards, we again dropped anchor at a depth of 25 fathoms and remained lying there. Then the apprentice sailor *Barend Bronkhorst*, being one of my old crew of the ship *Amstelveen* that had perished on 5 *August* 1673, came on board. On 11 *December* it had already been reported that *Steven Hillekens* had found him almost dead next to the deceased *Jan Drevens*. He told me that Arabs had taken him in and they looked after him with food and water and thus had kept him alive and that he only arrived 7 days ago at *Maskat*. The vicissitudes of the said person were as follows. He had had to live for some month with the Arabs, who, willy-nilly circumcised him. He hid himself under a fishing-net in a vessel that was ready to depart without knowing where it was going. After 4 to 6 days without much food having kept hidden under there he heard that they sailed for *Maskat*, When they safely arrived, he, as soon as he saw a clear chance (because the skipper and crew were ashore) left the vessel and went to the Hon. Comp's broker there, Mr. *Narriton*, who has been mentioned above several times. The latter gave him food and dressed him in Turkish clothes, and on our arrival he sent him aboard our ship. We took in water and stayed in the roads, until *Friday*, 31 August when at 5 o'clock towards evening we raised anchor and went under sail. We saw an English ship, which came from *Bombay* and wanted to go to *Bassora*, and had likewise arrived in the roads of Maskat on *Tuesday*, 28 ditto. It then also set sail and followed us.

Thursday, 11 October ditto. We arrived in the roads of *Kareek* and Captain *Blom* went ashore, while meanwhile we made preparations to unload. On Saturday, 13 ditto, we saw the native fleet arrive there, coming from *Meccha*;[114] and on *Sunday*, 14 ditto, a fleet of 14 vessels, which the next day left for *Bassora*. Then we unloaded and then loaded goods and

---

114. Meccha or al-Mokha was the main port of Yemen at that time, and exported coffee among other things.

fresh provisions, staying in the roads until *Monday*, 3 November, when at 10 o'clock in the morning Captain *Blom* came aboard with the Comp's papers accompanied by the chief and other colleagues from *Kareek* to sent us on our way. In the afternoon, at 3 o'clock, when the said gentlemen returned to shore, we raised anchor and went under sail to return to *Batavia*. During the voyage nothing unusual happened and we safely arrived on Tuesday, 2 April 1765 just after sunset in the roads of *Batavia*, within the *Mantle*.[115] *God be praised for a safe voyage*, so far!

>NB. With the said ship I served in my abovementioned capacity and under the command of the said captain on another voyage from there to Cheribon,[116] and back to Batavia, leaving the roads on Saturday, 4 May 1675 and returning on the same vessel on Wednesday, 12 June of that same year.

In October, I received my orders to repatriate with the Homebound Fleet to the Fatherland and I was appointed as third mate on the Hon. Comp's ship *Zuid-Beveland*, commanded by Captain *Huibregt van der Kneu*; this ship was 150 feet in length across the prow, aft depth 22.25 feet, fore 20.50 feet, therefore, 1.25 [sic; properly 1.75] rake of keel and was crewed by 104 sailors, 11 soldiers, 2 craftsmen, 8 passengers, 4 unfit for sailing [*onbekwaam*], together 120 persons, and armed with 22 pieces of 4-pounder cannons and 8 metal 1-pound swivels.

Monday, 28 ditto. At 9 o'clock the Hon. *Fiscaal* came on board as well as the inspection committee and held muster and found no absentees, whereupon we made ready to sail.

Tuesday, 29 ditto. At 9 o'clock in the morning, the Captain *Huibregt van der Kneu* came on board with the Comp's paper, after which we raised anchor and together with the other ships and the yacht went under sail, but due to the lack of wind we could not get from the roads

---

115. The defensive barrier spanning the harbor.
116. Cirebon, a port city in West Java.

and thus, we had to drop anchor again. However, *Wednesday*, 30 ditto, at daybreak we raised anchor and together with our colleagues we set sail and after having experienced nothing unusual we came to anchor on *Monday*, 6 January 1766, at 2 o'clock in the afternoon in the roads of *Cabo de Goede Hoop*, where, after having taken in fresh provisions and having laid there until 3 February, at 3 o'clock in the afternoon the Commander gave orders to get under sail, and therefore, we immediately raised anchor and continued our voyage to the Fatherland in the company of the entire Homebound Fleet and without having experienced anything noteworthy, on *Friday*, 16 May we arrived safely and came to anchor at *de Vlakke* before *Rammekens*[117] our destination harbor. For this we praise the Lord and thank him for his custody and guidance onto this safe harbor our desire!

---

117. The harbor of Arnemuiden, a town on the island of Walcheren (Zeeland), was deep and safe and de Vlakke, the name of the southern part of the natural harbor, was situated before Rammekens, which is the name of a sea fort there. De Vlakke served as the roadstead of Vlissingen.

Annex 5

Letters from Muscat to Batavia, 1798-1806

LIST OF RULERS AND GOVERNORS-GENERAL

Ya`ariba Dynasty

Naser b. Morshed al-Ya`ariba	1625-1640
Sultan b. Seyf	1640-1680 (October 4)
Bel`arab b. Sultan b. Seyf	1680-1692
Seyf I b. Sultan	1692-1711 (October 15)
Sultan II b. Seyf	1711-1719
Seyf II b. Sultan (1st time)	1719-1724 (September)
al-Mohanna b. Sultan b. Majid	1719-1720
Ya`rob b. Bel`arab	1722-1723 (March 16)
Mohammad b. Naser (Banu Ghafir)	1724-1728 (March)

Seyf II b. Sultan (2nd time)	1728-1743 (coastal area)
Sultan b. Morshed	1742-1743 (coastal area)
Bel`arab b. Himyar	1728-1749 (in the interior)

AL BU SA`ID DYNASTY

Ahmad b. Sa`id	1749-1783
Sa`id b. Ahmad	1783-1784
Hamad b. Sa`id	1784-1792
Sultan b. Ahmad	1792-1804
Salem b. Sultan	1804-1806 co-rulers
Sa`id b. Sultan	1804-1806 co-rulers
Sa`id II b. Sultan	1806-1856

GOVERNORS-GENERAL OF THE VOC (1610-1796)

Pieter Both	1610-1614
Gerard Reynst	1614-1615
Laurens Reael	1615-1619
Jan Pieterszoon Coen	1619-1623
Pieter de Carpentier	1623-1627
Jan Pieterszoon Coen	1627-1629
Jacques Specx	1629-1632
Hendrik Brouwer	1632-1636
Anthony van Diemen	1636-1645
Cornelis van der Lijn	1645-1650
Carel Reyniersz	1650-1653
Joan Maatsuycker	1653-1678
Rijckloff van Goens	1678-1681
Cornelis Speelman	1681-1684

Johannes Camphuys	1684-1691
Willem van Outhoorn	1691-1704
Joan van Hoorn	1704-1709
Abraham van Riebeeck	1709-1713
Christoffel van Swoll	1713-1718
Hendrick Zwaardecroon	1718-1725
Mattheus de Haan	1725-1729
Diederik Durven	1729-1732
Dirck van Cloon	1732-1735
Abraham Patras	1735-1737
Adriaan Valckenier	1737-1741
Johannes Thedens	1741-1743
Gustaaf Willem van Imhoff	1743-1750
Jacob Mossel	1750-1761
Petrus Albertus van der Parra	1761-1775
Jeremias van Riemsdijk	1775-1777
Reinier de Klerk	1777-1780
Willem Arnold Alting	1780-1796

GOVERNORS-GENERAL OF THE DUTCH EAST-INDIES (1796-1811)

Pieter Gerardus van Overstraten	1796-1801
Johannes Siberg	1801-1805
Albertus Henricus Wiese	1805-1808
Herman Willem Daendels	1808-1811
Jan Willem Janssens	1811-1811

VOC Directors in the Persian Gulf (based at Bandar Abbas)

Directors

Huybert Visnich	1623-1630
Antonio Del Court	1630-1632
Hendrik Hagenaar (pro tem)	1632-1633
Nicolaas Jacobsz Overschie	1633-38
Adriaan van Oostende (pro tem)	1638
Adam Westerwolt	1639
Adriaan van Oostende (pro tem)	1640
Wollebrant G(h)eleynsen de Jong(h)	1640-1643
Carel Constant	1643-1645
Wollebrant G(h)eleynsen de Jong(h)	1645-1647
Nicolaes Verburg	1647-1649
Dirck Sarcerius	1649-1653
Joan Berkhout	1654-1655
Jacob Willemsen	1656-1661
Hendrik van Wijk	1661-1666
Huybert de Lairesse	1666-1667
IJsbrand Godske	1667-1671
Lucas van der Dussen	1670-1671
François de Haze	1671-1673
Frederik Lambertsz Bent	1673-1679
Reynier Casembroot	1679-1683
Justus van den Heuvel (pro tem 1683-84)	1685-1688
Joannes Keyts	1689-1690
Adriaan Verdonk	1693-1695
Alexander Bergainje	1695-1697
Jacobus Hoogkamer	1698-1701

Magnus Wichelmans 1700-1705
Frans Castelyn 1705-1708
Willem Backer Jacobszn. 1708-1715
Hendrik Grousius 1715-1717
Johan Josua Ketelaar 1717-1718
Jan Oets 1718-1721
Johannes de Croeze November 1722- June 1723
Hermannus de Backer June-September 1723

Gezaghebbers (Head)

Pieter 't Lam 1723-1729
Leendert de Cleen (de Kleene) 1729-1734
Dames Hey (2 months only) 1734
Carel Coenad 1734-1741
George Gutchi October 1741-December 1741
Simon Clement 1741-1743
Emmanuel de Poorter (pro tem) October 1742-July 1744
Abraham van der Welle 1744-1745
Jacob van Schoonderwoerd 1745-1755

Resident

Gerrit Aansorg 1755-1758

Chiefs of Khark Island

Tido Frederik von Kniphausen 1755-1759
Jan van der Hulst 1759-1762
Wilhelmus Johannes Buschman 1762-1765
Pieter Houtingh 1765-1766

ANNEX 6

Wood, Horses and Friendship.
The Arabic Letters from Muscat to the Dutch in Kochi (1779) and Batavia (1798–1806)

Jan Just Witkam*

Introduction[1]

The direct relationship between Oman and the Dutch began in 1665 after hesitating overtures on either side. In 1650 the Omanis had chased away the Portuguese from Muscat, and a year later the first reconnaissance trip by a vessel of the Dutch, who had already established factories in the Gulf, came to Oman. This mission was organized from the Dutch factory in Bandar ʿAbbās on the Persian shore of the Gulf. The first surveys of the Omani coast were in fact conducted by Dutch ships and date from that period.[2] The Dutch establishment in Bandar ʿAbbās fell under the authority of the Governor-General of the Dutch East India Company in Batavia (Jakarta). Commercial prospects in Oman were never great, and maybe that is why the relationship between the two nations always remained friendly. It was maintained via Bandar ʿAbbās, Kochi and eventually Batavia, the headquarters of the Dutch East India Company in South-East Asia, but not directly from the Netherlands in Europe. Muscat's strategic position on the Arabian Sea, and also the power wielded by the Omanis over the eastern part of the Indian Ocean, especially their footholds in Zanzibar and the East African mainland, ensured that Oman could not be ignored or neglected. However, the direct importance of Oman for the Dutch East India Company, which was officially dissolved in 1795 and whose overseas possessions were then taken over by the Dutch government, did not go much further than a certain interest in the pearl trade. In the late 19th century, an interest in Oman, Zanzibar and their dependencies was once more articulated by the Dutch from the East. That all came to an end, when, in 1942, the Japanese quickly overran what is now Indonesia. But already long before 1942, the Dutch had ceased to play a role of importance in the Gulf region. From 1958 onwards, Shell, a Dutch-British consortium, established an operation in Oman and between then and now the relations between the two countries have further developed and greatly diversified.[3]

The early history of the relationship between the Omanis and the Dutch can be reconstructed from the archives of the Dutch East India Company and from the reports written by captains of Dutch ships. These archives abound with information of all sorts. The reports in travelogues often contain striking – sometimes even endearing – personal observations. Whenever documents in exotic languages would arrive at one of the Company's factories, these were translated into Dutch.[4] The translations and originals were usually kept together in the archive of the factory itself. The Journal (*Dagh-Register*) of the factories eventually would arrive in the Netherlands as well, as would copies of letters and enclosures. There is a wealth of documents in the National State Archive in The Hague, more than 1.5 km on the shelf, but papers of the Dutch factory in Muscat, including the Journal for the years 1778–1786, have ended up in the archive of Chennai as part of the archives of the Dutch rule on the Malabar coast.[5] All in all, these constitute an enormous amount of paper with a great richness of economical and geopolitical information. The only handicap for foreign researchers is that the documents in these archives are almost without exception written in 17th- and 18th-century Dutch.

I am aware neither of the existence of Omani historical sources on the Dutch nor of archives in Oman where documents relevant to the contacts with the Dutch could have been preserved. This means that the Dutch archival collections are the only source available for a history of the early relations between the two countries.

A small number of original Omani documents, however, has been preserved. These are the ten documents that are presented here. Eight are in Arabic (Nos. 1–3, 6–10) and are edited and translated in the present article, the other two (Nos. 4, 5) are in Persian, and will

· 274 ·

only be summarily mentioned. They may in due course become the object of a separate study. In contrast to the great quantity of documents that are available in Dutch, these are the only authentic Omani sources on relations with the Dutch that seem to have been preserved. Many more of such documents must have existed, but, for the moment, they must be considered lost. In the National Archive in The Hague there is not a special 'Oman Collection', but documents about Oman are dispersed over different related files, and there is only one document in Arabic, a letter from the *wālī* of Muscat, Khalfān, which is here edited and translated for the first time (No. 1, below). B.J. Slot has searched in the Arsip Nasional in Jakarta for more original letters from Oman, but did not discover any. He was also unable to find Arabic originals in Colombo, where the only original correspondence available comes from the Maldives, written in a remarkable type of local calligraphy which resembles Arabic. As a parallel document Slot once mentioned to me a letter from the Sultan of the Comoros which is preserved in Cape Town. The oldest original documents come from French archives (Paris, Caen, Réunion) and have been published by Sheikh Sulṭān Muḥammad al-Qāsimī, the learned ruler of Sharjah.[6] The oldest Arabic letter from Oman (a copy, not the original document), which dates from around 1700, is preserved in the archive of the English East India Company in London.[7] From Slot's exhaustive research it is clear that Omani documents in European archives are very rare indeed.

The Omani Documents

The documents presented here are nothing more than a few letters that have accidentally been preserved, and only because they were *not* kept in an archive. They are preserved precisely *because* they were taken away from the archival collection in which they were once kept. Two groups of documents can be distinguished. First there is the single letter (No. 1) that was sent from Muscat by Khalfān b. Muḥammad to the Dutch ruler of Kochi and concerns the purchase of wood for ship building. The document may have been removed from the factory's archive in Kochi by Adriaan Moens who, from 1770–1781, was the Dutch commander of the Malabar Coast. This letter is now kept in the Dutch National Archives in The Hague, because, in 1894, it was purchased from the Moens family. At a later stage the entire Moens archive was acquired by the National Archives. It was not uncommon that commanders or governors would take such original documents out of their official archive and privately keep them to themselves as curiosities.[8]

The second group, letters Nos. 2–10, are part of the diplomatic correspondence between Muscat and Batavia and they cover the period 1798–1806. Eight letters are from two rulers of Oman, seven from the Sultan Sulṭān b. al-Imām Aḥmad b. Saʿīd (ruled 1792–1804) and one from his successor, the Sultan al-Sayyid Badr b. al-Sayyid Sayf (ruled 1804–1806). The recurrent theme in the correspondence is the maintenance of the good relationship between the Omanis and the Dutch. The letters are not very long and, in fact, serve no more than as an introduction and expression of feelings of friendship. The actual messages were to be given orally by the Omani captains. The expression 'the rest of our message is on the tongue of those who arrive at your place' occurs in several letters.

This little cache of letters was preserved by accident. From the numerous letters which in course of time arrived in Batavia from all over the Indonesian archipelago and from the Western Quarters of the Dutch East India Company, many must have been stored in archives and should, ideally speaking, now still be kept in the Indonesian Arsip Nasional in Jakarta. This is not the case, however. A considerable number of these documents seems to be lost, yet there is a small number of letters and documents that at some stage, around the middle of the 19th century, were sent from Batavia to Holland, not to be kept in any archive, but in order to serve as educational material for the training of Dutch civil servants in the colony, and that is how the letters Nos. 2–10, which are herewith presented, have survived. In 1891 these originals were incorporated in the Oriental collections of Leiden's University Library, where they still are.[9]

In 1998 a large collection of original letters from South-East Asia, mostly in Malay, has for the first time been individually described.[10] Most of these documents date from the periods of office of Governors-General Willem Alting (1780–1796), Pieter Gerardus van Overstraten (1796–1801), Johannes Siberg (1801–1805), and Albertus Henricus Wiese (1805–1808). How and by whom the documents were selected for educational use is not known, but so much is evident that they cover almost all areas which were under control of the Dutch East India Company or with which the Company had a regular relationship, including some regions which are now part of Malaysia. They range from very simply made letters in Latin script, e.g. from the Moluccas and from Kupang (West Timor) and surrounding environs, to evidently royal documents written in Malay in impressive Arabic calligraphy and provided with magnificent ornamentation, truly golden letters.[11] Apart from a wide selection by area, this collection of Indonesian documents must have been brought together in a haphazard way. It may have been a private collection of one of the members of the Indian Council,[12] but all concrete information about the selection process is lacking. Probably part of the static archive in Batavia was just raided at the request of a professor of the Delft or Leiden academies, the former Governmental Training College for Indian Civil Servants,[13] by a former student. For the use of students of these Training Colleges, lithographed editions were produced of selections of such letters and several generations of aspiring colonial civil servants may have ruined their eyes in their attempts to decipher them.

Among all these letters there are a few which did not come from the Archipelago. Some Arabic and Persian documents from Oman and the Gulf were somehow included.[14] Because of this educational purpose, this collection of documents and letters can not, in any way, be considered as a complete source for the history of the relationship between the Western Quarters of the Dutch East India Company and the central government in Batavia. It is not my purpose to write such a history, only to have a close look at the few documents that by chance have survived. The documents only randomly capture a few short moments in that history, but it is all the original material that we have.

Historical Context of Documents Nos. 2–10 (1798–1806)

On either side of the correspondence there was, politically speaking, a highly volatile situation, as both in Europe and South-East Asia the consequences of the French conquest of large parts of the European continent made themselves felt. The war between France and England cannot have been particularly favorable for trade, the quick succession of constitutions of the former Dutch Republic (which from 1795 onwards had become a satellite state of France), the dissolution of the Dutch East India Company, the French expedition to Egypt in 1799–1801, and the increasing English expansion in South and South-East Asia, all these events did not fail to have an impact on the relationship between Batavia and the Western Quarters.

Nor was the situation on the Omani side very stable. The Wahhābī threat up North in the Arabian Peninsula was very real. In 1804 Medina had been conquered and sacked by them. In his letters of 1801 to Batavia (Nos. 8, 9), the Sultan Sulṭān b. Aḥmad refers to a ǧihād, a holy war, which he is going to embark upon, and which may have been directed against the Wahhābīs. A 'people that have spread disorder in the land and who have rejected the way of right guidance', he calls his adversaries.

But the Sultan had also something to conceal from the Dutch. As a precaution against the Wahhābī threat he was, quite wisely, developing a special relationship with the British and in 1798, the very year of his first two documents in the present collection (Nos. 2, 3), he concluded his first treaty with the English East India Company.[15] Part of the deal was that he promised not to allow the French and their Dutch allies to establish factories in his territory as long as they were at war with the English.[16] Hence he must have been eager to know about the Dutch or Dutch-Indian reaction to this. Their continuous absence from Muscat, apparently for years, may have been worrying him.

One wonders whether the calling of Omani ships at the port of Calcutta, as is mentioned in Sulṭān's letters (Nos. 8 and 9), was really for necessary repairs. The Dutch were sure to learn about the appearance of Omani ships in Indian ports, and this should be explained before awkward questions could be asked or lame excuses found. The intended trade, the buying of sugar, does not seem to be very impressive or urgent. The detour via Calcutta, the Asian headquarters of the English East India Company, does indeed explain the long period between the dispatch of the letters from Muscat (August, 27 1801) and their arrival in Batavia (October, 14 1802).

The dynamics of disruption within the Bū Saʿīd ruling family of Oman were yet another source of instability. The last letter in the collection completely changes the discourse. The new Sultan, al-Sayyid Badr b. al-Sayyid Sayf, who had gained the ascendancy with Wahhābī support after the death of Sulṭān b. Aḥmad in a sea battle in 1804, did not live long to enjoy his good fortunes. In 1806 he was killed by Sulṭān's son Saʿīd. He did send a letter to Batavia, however (No. 10). It is a document entirely different from the diplomatic letters which were sent by Sulṭān b. Aḥmad. The ideological shift is clear from both form and contents.

A few general remarks should be made about the making of the letters. To judge from the script, they were evidently written by professional secretaries, but it is at once clear that these were people without a classical education. The language of the letters is full of formulaic niceties, but the overall grammar is weak, especially in syntax. All sorts of faults are made against the rules of classical Arabic, to such an extent even that the conclusion that the scribes were not local scholars with a traditional education seems inevitable. These secretaries may have been Indians, a fact which could explain why two of the letters are in Persian (Nos. 4 and 5), which was, till 1857, the *lingua franca* of the Indian subcontinent. It is not well conceivable that a lettered Arab would write Masgad (for Masqaṭ, Muscat), as we can see in letter No. 6, line 7.[17]

The use of the plural in letter No. 9 (lines 6, 10 and 11) which refers to one person (as becomes clear from the parallel texts in letter No. 8, lines 5, 9 and 10 respectively) might be interpreted as a persianism. The script of two of the letters (Nos. 8 and 9) makes an Indian impression as well. Letter No. 10 is written in a remarkable chancery hand and in an impeccable and straightforward Arabic. It may have been composed by a secretary with good or primary knowledge of Arabic.

The seals on the documents are modest in size and ornament. The three senders, Khalfān b. Muḥammad, Sulṭān b. Aḥmad and Sayf b. Badr, all contain a Qur'ānic reference. For the two seals of Sulṭān (with dates 1211 and 1212) and the seal of Badr clever use was made of the fact that either word occurs in the Qur'ān, though not as a proper name.

Edition and Translation

I have arranged the ten documents which I present here in chronological order. The documents kept in MS Leiden Or. 2141 IV, can be found here under the following numbers:[18]

Or. 2141 IV (1)	Persian letter from the Pāshā of Baghdād (1793), not included here
Or. 2141 IV (2)	=> No. 3, in Arabic.
Or. 2141 IV (3)	=> No. 4, in Persian.
Or. 2141 IV (4)	=> No. 5, in Persian.
Or. 2141 IV (5a, 5b)	Persian letter from several people in Surat (1800) with old Dutch translation, not included here.
Or. 2141 IV (6)	=> No. 7, in Arabic.
Or. 2141 IV (7)	=> No. 6, in Arabic.
Or. 2141 IV (8)	=> No. 8, in Arabic.
Or. 2141 IV (9)	=> No. 9, in Arabic.
Or. 2141 IV (10)	=> No. 10, in Arabic.
Or. 2141 IV (11)	=> No. 2, in Arabic.

I have fully transcribed the Arabic texts of each of the documents precisely as they are but I have added punctuation whenever a correct understanding makes that necessary and possible. I have not added vowels or reading signs, even if they are there in the original documents. For easy reference I have added line numbers. My translation is rather literal, and I realize that the internal rhyming and some of the other stylistic niceties employed by the secretaries which make the Arabic texts euphonious and elegant, are thereby lost. That I have only edited and translated the Arabic texts is for practical reasons only. At a later stage I intend to work more thoroughly on the Persian texts from the Gulf region to Batavia and edit and translate these as well. Four of the eight letters from Sultan Sulṭān b. Aḥmad come in fact in two pairs (Nos. 6–7, 8–9). The texts in either pair are either largely identical or closely related, or they complement one another. If one letter is addressed to the Governor-General, a similar letter is addressed to Batavia's harbormaster. All Omani documents are given here in facsimile. Relevant details of each document are shown in separate images. An index of proper names must facilitate reference to the letters.

Apart from No. 10 all letters have an empty space where the name of the addressee should be written. Mention of the name of Governor-General Wiese in No. 10 ('Ġandarāl Pīsī') was possibly done after the letter had been written, as the script seems larger and might be in a hand, different from the secretary's. This may have been the idea for the empty spaces in the other documents as well. It is also possible that the Omanis did not know the names of the addressees. These addressees are indicated by their function, usually the Governor-General or the harbormaster of Batavia. Neither Sultan (letters Nos. 2–10) refers to himself as Imām, hence I refer to them as Sultan.[19] From the Leiden documents it is evident that they were once bound together, possibly with other documents. Further information on this is lacking.

« 1 »

Letter in Arabic from Khalfān b. Muḥammad b. ʿAbdallāh al-Būsaʿīdī, the *wālī*, governor, of Muscat,[20] to the Dutch governor of Kūtshī. The letter contains the request for permission for the non-commercial export of wood from Cochin to Muscat, for the purpose of ship repair. The Journal of Malabar in the East India Company archives contains a number of Dutch translations of documents from the same period that concern repairs of Arab ships in Malabar or the export of wood from there.[21]

On the verso side the letter contains the name and the seal of the sender and also the date: 22 Shaʿbān 1193 (September 3, 1779). Also on the verso is the addressee. The original document is kept in the Dutch National Archives, The Hague, as 1.11.01.01,659 (formerly as 'Aanwinsten 1e afd. 1894 23'). A remnant of a red wax seal can be seen on top of the verso side. Notes made in 1894 by the Leiden Professor M.J. de Goeje (1836–1909) on the contents of the document are kept together with the document.

The letter is addressed to *Bālyūz al-Wulandīn* (line 1). The word *bālyūz* is an Arabic loanword from Italian *balio*, governor, the title of the heads of the Venetian colonies which hence developed to 'ambassador'. The Venetian representative in Constantinople was called so. In Persian documents the title *bālyūz* is used in addressing the director of the East India Company's trade in the Persian Gulf.[22]

The city of Kūtshī of the document is present-day Kochi (colonial spelling: Cochim or Cochin), on the south western coast of the Indian subcontinent, the so-called Malabar Coast, which had been in hands of the Dutch East India Company since its conquest in 1663 from the Portuguese. The economic relationship between the Omanis and the Dutch in Cochin is known to have been good and this also becomes clear from this letter.[23]

I have guessed that the word شبارنا (line 6) would mean something like 'our ship'.

The reading of the word السركار (line 7) is a guess, as is my interpretation as the head of the wharf, 'the supervisor of the work'.|

1| حضرت باليوز الولندين حاكم كوتشي سلمه الله تعالى
2| اهدي اطيب كلام فاح عبيره وتأرجت ازاهيره وفاح مسكا ذكيا وهب له النسيم نديا الى المحب
3| الصافي الناصح الودود المحتشم المراد بذلك وسلمه وكفاه وعافاه آمين انا ولله الحمد بمحمد من فضل الله ثم من فضل سيدنا
4| الامام اعزه الله جعلكم الله بحال السرور الدايم ارضى الله غبّ الدعاء ونشر بجميل الثنا ان المدعي سحة ذاتكم العلية واعتدال اوقاتكم السنية
5| التي هي القصد والمراد كفانا الله واياكم كيد الحساد والاضداد وثم لا يخفاكم اطال الله بقاكم انا هذه السنة ارسلنا
6| اليكم شبارنا المنصور الي بندركم المعمور وفيه تابعنا سلطان الحبشي ومن معه من الاصحاب فالمرجو من عميم
7| احسانكم ان تلخصوهم بعين الشفقة وتراعوهم في تحميل ما يريدوه من حطب والواح لان اكثر حاجة السركار
8| الي ذلك لاجل اصلاح المراكب وما دبرناهم الا لاجل ذلك لا للتجارة بل لاصلاح بندركم والاتصال بكم حيث
9| ان الحال والمال واحد والبنادر واحدة والقلوب بذلك شاهدة وكلما تفعلوا معهم من
10| الاحسان محسوب علينا والله بحالهم لا تجعلوهم مثل خشب ساير الناس ومحسنون بكم
11| الظن اولا وثاليا وبقية الاعلام علي لسان الواصلين اليكم كفاية وان بدا جنابكم العالي حاجة
12| ام عرض فانا للقيام
13| به نتعرض ولا تقطع المكاتبات
14| لانها نصف الملاقات ودم سالما سلم الله علي
15| المشايخ الاولاد والاصحاب ومن حضر مقامكم الشريف ويسلم عليكم
16| سيدنا الامام واولاده الكرام واولادنا سليمان ومحمد

17| واخوتهما والجماعة والاصحاب باتم السلام ||

Sender and his seal on the verso:

المحب المخلص | خلفان بن محمد بن عبدالله | البوسعيدي | يخصكم باتم السلام بتاريخ | ٢٢ شعبان سنه ١١٩٣ |

Text in the seal:

| خلفان بن محمد | عبده | افوض امري الى الله |

Addressee on the verso:

محروس بندر كوتشي | يتشرف الكتاب بمطالعة الاكرم | المكرم | المحتشم حضرت الصديق الناصح | باليوز الولندين حاكم كوتشي | سلمه الله تعالى ان شا الله | امين امين | آمين

To His Excellency the *Bālyūz* of the Dutch, the ruler of Kūtshī, may God, the Exalted, grant him peace.

I give my best word – may its odor spread and may its flowers be fragrant; may it spread the odor of tasty musk, and may it make the air around like dew – to the pure friend, who gives good advice, who is friendly, who is honored and respected, with whom is meant,[24] and may God give him peace, may God spare him trouble and protect him. Amen.

Praise be to God, with praise by the grace of God, and then by the grace of our Lord, the Imām, may God make him strong, may God bring you in a state of permanent joy, may God grant the outcome of the prayer and may He spread the beautiful praise, whereas the object of the prayer is the excellent health of your good selves and the harmony of your elevated times, which is the purpose and what is desired, may God be sufficient to us and to you [in the struggle] against the deceit of the envious and the enemies.

Well then, it may not have escaped you, may God lengthen your life, that in this year we have sent to you our ship al-Manṣūr to your prosperous harbor, and aboard of it was our subject, Sulṭān al-Ḥabashī, and those companions who were together with him. We request from your all-encompassing goodness that you view them with sincere compassion and that you give them your consideration in the loading of the wood and the planks that they want, because the head of the wharf is very much in need of this for the repair of the ships, and we had nothing else in mind with these materials, no commerce but only the improvement of your harbor, and in order to be in contact with you, since the situation and the money are one, and the harbors are one, and the hearts are witness of this, and whenever you do this goodness to them, we will be under your obligation. By God, may God be in their situation, and do not treat them as with the wood of other people, as we appreciate you now and later, and the rest of the message is on the tongue of those who arrive at your place. So far [our message], and if your good selves are in need of anything or if you want to offer something, then we will undertake to do that. And do not cut off the correspondence because correspondence is next best to [actual] meeting. May you have a long life in good health, and may God bless the young Sheikhs and the friends, and whoever is present in your noble abode. Our Lord the Imam greets you with his most perfect greetings, and so do his noble sons, and so do our sons Sulaymān and Muḥammad and their brothers, and the whole community [here] and the friends.

Sender (on the verso): 'The sincere friend Khalfān b. Muḥammad b. 'Abdallāh al-Būsa'īdī conveys to you the most perfect greeting. On the date of 22 Sha'bān of the year 1193'. This is followed by a print of the sender's seal (not well legible): 'Khalfān b. Muḥammad [...] 'Abduh. I commit my case to God.'[25]

Addressee (on the verso): 'To the harbor of Kūtshī, may God preserve it. May this letter have the honor to be read by the most noble and revered friend and adviser, the Bālyūz of the Dutch, the ruler of Kūtshī, may God, the Exalted, protect him, if God wishes. Amen, amen, amen.'

« 2 »

Presentation note in Arabic from Sulṭān b. al-Imām Ahmad b. Sa'īd for the gift of two horses, possibly addressed to the Governor-General in Batavia, dated 17 Rabī' I 1213 (August 29, 1798). Leiden University Library Or. 2241-IV (11) No. 216 (Klinkert No. 11), Wieringa (a.o.), *Catalogue* (1998), pp. 408–409.

One sheet of paper, 19.5 x 13 cm, *naskh* script, text on one side only, dated 17 Rabī' I 1213 (August 29, 1798). Verso is blank. The text in the seal refers to Qur'ān 44:19, the seal contains the date 1211.

The ship Sīb-i Bādam is mentioned in several letters, as is its captain 'Abd al-Raḥmān. The other names of ships in the documents all have an evident meaning, but this particular name I could not well understand. I maintain it here because I have no better guess. Another reading could be Sīb bā Dam, but that is as unclear to me as the first one.

|1| هو
|2| الصادر على سبيل الصداقة والهدية
|3| في المركب المزبور سيب بادم صحبة القبطان
|4| عبد الرحمن راسين خيل تفضلوا
|5| بقبول ذالك والسلام حرر فى 17
|6| شهر ربيع الاول سنه 1213 ||

Text in the seal: بسم الله القوي المتين انى آتيكم بسلطان مبين 1211

'*Huwa*'
Coming out, by way of friendship and present on the ship named Sīb-i Bādam with captain 'Abd al-Raḥmān, two stallions. Please, accept that. Greetings. Thus done on 17 of the month Rabī' I of the year 1213.'

The text in the seal reads: 'In the name of God, the Almighty, the Strong One. I come to you with clear authority. 1211'.[26]

« 3 »

Letter in Arabic from Sulṭān b. al-Imām Aḥmad b. Sa'īd, to *Ǧandarāl Batāwa*, the Governor-General in Batavia, dated 17 Rabī' I 1213 (August 29, 1798). Received at Batavia on October, 12 1798. Leiden University Library Or. 2241-IV (2) No. 220 (Klinkert No. 2). Wieringa (a.o.), *Catalogue* (1998), p. 408.

One sheet of paper, 55.5 x 39 cm, folded once, *naskh* script with features of *ta'līq*, text in Arabic on one side only, Dutch explanations on the verso side.

Text in the seal which is placed over the text:
بسم الله القوي المتين انى آتيكم بسلطان مبين 1211

|1| الحمد لله وحده
|2| حضرت الصديق الناصح جندرال بتاوه سلمه الله تعالى
|3| بعد اهداءآ جزيل لوازم التسليم وابلاغ لواحق التعظيم يفضح دقيق المسك نشورا ويفوق الاقحوان زهورا
|4| الصديق الصدوق المشار اليه حرسه الملك الديان من طوارق الحدثان بحق من اجرا دالنون فى بطون الحيتان
|5| بعد ان تحرك ظاهر السوال والتفحص عن هذا الحال فانا وله الحمد فى احسن حال وانعم بال واخبار اطرافنا ساكنة الحركات
|6| نامية البركات وبعد فمن هذه ستتين لم نرا احدا منكم تردد الى اطرافنا كعادتكم سابقا فاحبينا ان نكشف خبركم
|7| وسبب انقطاعكم هذه المده على سبيل الصداقه والمحبه بين الطرفين وجهنا مركبنا سيب بادم وبه نوخدا رجالنا
|8| عبد الرحمن والمعلم وزير وجهنا ذالك لكشف حقيقه حال انقطاعكم كعادتكم سابقا من الله تعالى وصوله اليكم بالسلامة
|9| واتصاله بكم على حسب المطلب والمراد فعلى سبيل الصداقة والاتحاد نرجوا لهم الحشمة والمراعاة كما جرت به العادة
|10| بين الطرفين المودة بين الجانبين فعلى ذالك حررنا كتاب الصداقة وارسلناه بمنه تعالى وقد حملنا فى المركب المزبور
|11| بعض وكذالك امرناهم بشراء سكر وغيره من البضايع المستحسنة لهم مرجوا لهم من تراعوهم فى المشترا وان
|12| تجعلوا لنا المسامحه والمراعاه دون غيرنا حيث نحن واياكم اخص الاصدقآ وكذالك انشآء الله متى ساعرت
|13| مراكبكم بندرنا ليروا منا المراعاة دون غيرهم ولا ترفعوا نظركم عنهم وما تعملوه من معروف عليهم محسوب علينا

|14| ونرجوا وصولكم ولا تقطعوا العاده الجاريه في المساعره والتردد الى
اطرافنا والمرجوا ان ترتيق المركب يرجع
|15| الينا عاجلا لا يكون يتاخر وانّ لا تخرجونا من الخاطر العاطر على
الدوام والسلام خير ختام وان سنح لكم غرض
|16| من هذا الطرف فهو يقفى بحسب التعريف حرر فى ١٧
شهر ربيع الاول سنه ١٢١٣
|17| المخلص سلطان
|18| بن الامام احمد بن سعيد ||

Text in the seal: 'In the name of God, the Almighty, the Strong One. I come to you with clear authority. 1211'

To the Excellency, the friend, the giver of good counsel, *Ǧandarāl Batāwa*, may God, the Exalted, keep him safe.

After presenting all formalities of greeting and after conveying the accessories of glorification, comes about the spread of delicate musk and rises the flowery scent of daisies. [To] the above-mentioned true friend,[27] may the King, the Judge, protect him against the vicissitudes of misfortune, by the right of the One who placed Dhū al-Nūn in the stomachs of the fishes. After thinking to ask [after you] and to enquire after this well-being, [we can inform you that] we are, praise be to God, doing very fine and that we are very well. The news of our regions is stable, and their blessings are increasing.

Well then, it has been two years now that we have not seen anyone of you visiting these parts as it used to be your habit. We would therefore like to have news from you and to know the reason why we have been separated during this period. We have sent out, by way of mutual friendship and love, our ship Sīb-i Bādam, with on board two captains of our men, ʿAbd al-Raḥmān and al-Muʿallim Wazīr. We sent that [ship] out in order to find out the true reason why you have become cut off from our harbor. We pray God, the Exalted, that it reaches you safely, and that it arrives with you according what is wished and meant [to be]. Therefore, by way of friendship and union we request that they are given respect and consideration, as was customary between the two parties, according to the love between the two sides. That is why we have composed a letter of friendship, which we have sent by the grace of God, the Exalted, and we have loaded the aforementioned ship with some [goods], and we have also ordered them to purchase sugar and other things that they wish to have. We request on their behalf that you will be considerate towards them concerning the goods to be purchased and that you will give us permissiveness and consideration, more than to other people, since we and you, we are very special friends. Equally, when, God willing, your ships trade in our harbor, may they see from us a consideration that we do not give to others, and please, do not look away from them. You will oblige us by whatever good treatment you will give to them. We hope to be in connection with you, and that you do not interrupt the current custom between us in trading and in visiting our parts. We hope that [news of] the repair[28] of the ship returns to us quickly and without delay, and that you will never place us outside your fragrant thoughts. And saying a greeting is the best way to conclude [a letter]. And if it occurs to you to decide to come here, please let us know.

Thus done on 17 of the month Rabīʿ I of the year 1213.

Sincerely, Sulṭān b. al-Imām Aḥmad b. Saʿīd.

Dutch texts on the verso of the document:
| Musquette | Van Sulthaan Ebnoe Jmam Ah | med Ebnoe Said, | Aan Zijn hoogEdel | heid. ontv. batavia | den 12. 8ber. 1798. | = 'Muscat, from Sulṭān b. al-Imām Aḥmad b. Saʿīd to His Excellency. Received in Batavia on 12 October 1798.'

On top of this is written: | den 16. 8ber 1798 | = 'the 16th of October 1798'.

On the side one can read: | de Translaat Van deze Briev bevind | Zich onder de Bijlagen van den 16 octb. 1798. | = 'The translation of this letter can be found among the enclosures of the 16th of October 1798.'

« 4 »

Letter in Persian from Sulṭān b. al-Imām Aḥmad b. Saʿīd (because of the seal and the note of receipt on the verse), addressed to the Governor-General (*Sar Gawnar Ǧanrāl Ṣāḥib*, end of line 1) in Batavia. There is a date on the verso, in an inexpert hand (the captain's?), in Persian, saying 'on 10/15 Ramaḍān 1214' (February 5/10, 1800).[29] Received in Batavia on May 23, 1800.

Leiden University Library, Or. 2241-IV (3). No. 262 / Klinkert No. 3. Wieringa (a.o.), *Catalogue* (1998), p. 408. One sheet of paper, folded once, 42 x 30 cm, *nastaʿlīq* script (*shekaste-amīz*). Text written on one side only.

Text in the seal which is placed on the verso:
بسم الله القوي المتين اني آتيكم بسلطان مبين ١٢١٢

Text in the seal: 'In the name of God, the Almighty, the Strong One. I come to you with clear authority. 1212'

Dutch text on the verso of the document: | Musquette | Van den Jmam | Aan Zijn Hoog | Edelheid. ontvangen | bat. den 23. Maij | 1800 | = 'Muscat. From the Imām. To His Excellency. Received in Batavia on the 23rd May 1800'.

« 5 »

Letter in Persian from Sulṭān b. al-Imām Aḥmad b. Saʿīd (because of the seal over the text, and the text of receipt on the verso side), addressed to the Governor-General (*Ǧandarāl Ṣāḥib*), according to the text of the letter. Dated at the end of the text 12 Shawwāl 1214 (March 9, 1800). On the reverse the addressee is mentioned, also in Persian, with numerous titles, but here referred to as *Shāhbandar Ṣāḥib*, 'the harbormaster' in Banda Baṭāwiya, the harbor of Batavia. Also on the verso is a note in a different hand (the captain's?) of a few words in Malay, and a note in Dutch on the receipt of the letter in Batavia on 21 July 1800.
Leiden University Library, Or. 2241-IV (4). No. 270 / Klinkert No. 4. Wieringa (a.o.), *Catalogue* (1998), p. 408. One sheet of paper, folded once, 42 x 30 cm, *nastaʿlīq* script (*shekaste-amīz*). Text written on one side only.

Text in the seal which is placed over the text:

بسم الله القوي المتين اني آتيكم بسلطان مبين ١٢١٢

Text in the seal: 'In the name of God, the Almighty, the Strong One. I come to you with clear authority. 1212'

Addressee in Persian on the verso side, in fact a somewhat shortened version of line 1 of the text of the letter:

انشاء الله تعالى | شانه العزيز اين مراسله محبت ترقيم در بند بطاويه بنظر عاليشان رفيع مكان بمواقفه والامتنان دوست عقيدنشان عمده الاعاظم زينة الافاخم العبوديه اعتضاد دوستان شاه بندر صاحب مد ظله العالي | موصول باد

'May, with the wish of God, may He be exalted and may His status be honoured, this letter written in friendship arrive in Banda Baṭāwiya [and come] under the eyes of the elevated and highplaced person, [the one] with love and gratitude, the trustworthy friend, the pillar of the great, the ornament of the mighty, the friend of the helper of the humble, the *Shāhbandar Ṣāḥib*, may the Highest One elongate his shadow.'

On the left, over the address, a few words in Malay are written, possibly by the captain or someone on behalf of the receiving party: سود كاسه سام جندر ... , *suda kasa sama jandar*... The last word is partly covered by a paste-on. This phrase may mean 'already the same fine muslin for the [Governor-]General'. If the word *kāsa* is of Arabo-Persian origin, it might mean 'bowl', 'cup' or the like.

Dutch text on the verso of the document: | Musquette | Van den Jmam | Aan zijn Hoog | Edelheid. ontvangen | bat. den 21. Julij | 1800 | = 'Muscat. From the Imām to His Excellency. Received in Batavia the 21st of July 1800'.

« 6 »

Letter in Arabic from Sulṭān b. al-Imām Aḥmad b. Saʿīd (because of the seal and the note of receipt on the verso side) from the port of Muscat (line 7) to the *Shābandar Batāwa*, 'the harbormaster of Batavia'. On the reverse the sender is mentioned in Arabic, with a date, 23 Rabīʿ I 1215 (August 14, 1800) and his seal. Received in Batavia on 21 October 1800.
Leiden University Library, Or. 2241-IV (7). No. 273 / Klinkert No. 6. Wieringa (a.o.), *Catalogue* (1998), p. 408. One sheet of paper, folded once, 41.5 x 30 cm, *naskh* script with *taʿlīq* features. Text written on one side only.

1 | الحمد لله وحده
2 | حضرت الاكرم الاحشم صديقنا الناصح شابندر بتاوه سلمه الله تعالى
3 | سلام الله الاتم ورضوانه الشامل الاعم وثناءه الاسنى وتحيته الوافرة الحسنى يهدى
4 | ويزف الى جناب عالى الجناب الصديق الناصح والصفى المود المناصح اعنى به
5 | سلمه الله تعالى وابقاه ومن المكاره وقاه ووفقه لما فيه رضاه بمحمد وآله وصحبه التقاه وبعد ان تحرك الخاطر
6 | بالسؤال عنا فانا ولله الحمد والمنة فى احسن الاحوال لا زلتم فى خير وعافيه وسرور مدة الايام والشهور
7 | وقد صدرت الاحرف من المحروس بندر مسكد واعلامنا من فضل الله تعالى ساره وحركات اطرافنا قارة
8 | وبيننا نترقب اخبار سلامتكم اذا فى ابرك الساعات واشرف الاوقات ورد كتابكم الكريم صحبة عبد الرحمان
9 | قبطان سيب بادم فاسر الخاطر واقر الناظر حيث اشعر بسلامتكم التى هى القصد والمراد وكافه ما ذكرتم
10 | صار معلوم وما تفضلتم به على رسم الهديه السنيه وصل بموجب التفضيل والتقرير انعم الله عليكم وازادكم
11 | من واسع فضله ولا زلتم آخذين بيد الفضل وفى العام الماضى ارسلنا مركب احد اصحابنا الذى هو سيب بادم
12 | على سبيل المحبه والصداقه حيث وجدناكم انقطعتم من بندرنا ونحب ان تكون المواصله غير منقطعة
13 | فيما بيننا واياكم وعلى رسم الاتحاد والصداقه السابقه ارسلنا مركبنا جنجاور ويه رجالنا الحاجى
14 | محمود بن مشكور اولا الغايه فى ارساله على سبيل
15 | الاتصال والخلطه وثانيا لشرا بعض السكر من بندركم المعمور فالمرجوا
16 | والمأمول لهم العزه والحشمه والمراعاه كما هو المعتاد منا ومنكم فى السابق والاحق
17 | وذالك فيما بين الطرفين لا يحتاج الى ابدا حيث انتم اصدقانا من قديم الزمان وبسبب عدم اتصالكم
18 | بنا ارسلنا مركبنا المشار اليه لتجديد الصحبه والصداقه القديمه وكل معروف تعمل معه محسوب
19 | علينا والله بالالتفات وعدم رفع النظر عنه وجنابكم لا تحتاج الى توصيه فيمن هو من طرفنا

|20| ونتيقن ان المركب مركبكم والمال مالكم وياقى اعلامنا على السنة الواصلين اليكم
|21| والسلام عليكم ورحمة الله وبركاته والسلام خير ختام ||

On the verso is the sender with the date, and a print of his seal:

المحب المخلص سلطان بن الامام احمد بن سعيد | حرر فى ٢٣ شهر ربيع الاول سنة ١٢١٥

Text in the seal: ١٢١٢ بسم الله القوى المتين انى آتيكم بسلطان مبين

Praise be to God alone.

To the most noble and respected Excellency, our friend with good advice, the *Shābandar Batāwa*, may God, the Exalted, keep him safe.

May God's most complete greeting, His most comprehensive and general favor, His highest praise and His abundant and best salutation be given en be transmitted to the most respected friend, the giver of counsel, the pure one, the loving one, the giver of sincere advice, with whom I mean,[30] may God, the Exalted, keep him safe and give him a long life, may He protect him against mishap and may He grant him success by the contentment that He has of him, and may he encounter [the Prophet] Muḥammad, his family and his companions.

Well then, if your mind moves to enquiring after us, we are, praise be to God, and by His grace, in the best of circumstances. May you remain well, safe and joyous as long as the days and the months last. This writing comes from the harbor of Masgad, may God protect it, where our good people, by the grace of God, the Exalted, are cheerful, and where what moves in our parts is stable. While we were looking out for news about your well-being, there came, on the most blessed of hours and the noblest of times, your esteemed letter together with ʿAbd al-Raḥmān, the captain of the Sīb-i Bādam, and it gave joy to our minds and rest to our opinions when we learnt that you are doing fine, which is the purpose and the intention. Everything that you mentioned has become understood and everything that it pleased you to send by way of a splendid present has arrived according to your preference and your resolve, may God bestow His favors upon you, and may He give you even more of the largesse of His grace, and may you keep receiving His bounty. Last year we sent the ship of one of our friends, namely the Sīb-i Bādam, by way of love and friendship, as we had the impression that you had become cut off from our harbor. We would like that the connection between us and you is uninterrupted. Therefore, in view of the union and the friendship that used to be between us we sent our ship Ğanğāwar, with on board our man al-Ḥāğğī Maḥmūd b. Mashkūr. Firstly the intention for sending the ship was to establish the connection with you and to meet with you, and secondly to buy some sugar from your prosperous harbor. We wish and we hope that they are received with honor, respect and consideration, as is customary with us and with you, both in the past and in the present. As this is mutual it is not necessary to make a display of it since you are our friends from a long time ago, and because of the lack of connection between you and us we have sent the above-mentioned ship, in order to renew the old companionship and friendship. You will oblige us with all the good treatment you give to it. And by God, may God give you attention to it and that you do not turn your eyes away from it. You do not need further information about who the man from our side is, as we are convinced that the ship is your ship, and the money is your money. And the rest of our message is on the tongues of those who arrive at you. Enough! Peace be upon you, and the grace of God and His blessings, and saying a greeting is the best way to conclude [a letter].

On the verso is the sender with the date, and a print of his seal: 'The sincere friend Sulṭān b. al-Imām Aḥmad b. Saʿīd. Thus done on 23 of the month Rabīʿ I of the year 1215'.

Text in the seal: 'In the name of God, the Almighty, the Strong One, I come to you with clear authority, 1212'.

Dutch text on the verso of the document: | Musquette | Van den Imam, | Aan den Saban | daar. ontv. | bat. den 21. 8ber. | 1800. – | = 'Muscat. From the Imām to the Shābandar. Received in Batavia, the 21st of October 1800.'

« 7 »

Letter in Arabic from Sulṭān b. al-Imām Aḥmad Saʿīd to *Ğandarāl Batāwa*, the Governor-General in Batavia, dated 23 Rabīʿ I 1215 (August 14, 1800). The text on the reverse mentions both sender and date.

Leiden University Library, Or. 2241-IV (6). No. 275 / Klinkert No. 5. Wieringa (a.o.), *Catalogue* (1998), p. 408. One sheet of paper, folded once, 41.5 x 30 cm, *naskh* script with *taʿlīq* features. Text written on one side only.

|١| الحمد لله وحده
|٢| حضرت الاجل الاكمل الصديق الناصح جندرآل بتاوه سلمه الله تعالى
|٣| احسن ما يتهاداه اهل الوداد واكمل ما يتعاطاه اهل الشفقه والاتحاد هو من الله سلام عديد ودعاء
|٤| ليس عليه فريد يهدى ويزف ويحلى ويتحف الى جناب عالى

الجناب عمدة الكرام الانجاب المحروس بعين
[5] عناية الملك الوهاب المشار اليه سلمه الله تعالى وابقاه ومن المكاره والمخاوف
[6] وقاه ووفقه لما فيه رضاه والباعث لتحرير ذريعة الوداد وصحيفة الاتحاد هو السوال
[7] عن صحة ذاتكم واعتدال اوقاتكم اللتان هما غاية القصد والمراد وبينما نترقب اخبار سلامتكم
[8] اذ فى ابرك الساعات واشرف الاوقات ورد كتابكم الكريم صحبة قبطان مركب سيب بادم محبنا عبد الرحمان
[9] وجميع ما ارسلتموه من الهديه السنيه بموجب التقرير والتفضيل فضل وانعم الله عليكم وازادكم
[10] من واسع فضله ونحن فى العام الماضى ارسلنا ذالك المركب لاحد من اصحابنا على طريق الصداقة
[11] والمحبه حيث وجدنكم انقطعتم من بندرنا ونحب ان تكون المواصلة غير منقطعة بيننا وايكم
[12] وعلى رسم الاتحاد والصداقة السابقة الآن ارسلنا مركبنا جنجاور وبه رجالنا الحاجى
[13] محمود بن مشكور اولا على سبيل الاتصال والخلطة وثانيا لشراء بعض السكر من بندركم
[14] فالمرجو والمأمول لهم العزة والحشمه والمراعاه كما هو المعتاد منا ومنكم فى السابق واللاحق
[15] ونرجوا ونأمل ما هو مذكور بدون الاباآ حيث انتم اصدقانا من قديم الزمان ويسبب عدم
[16] اتصالكم بنا ارسلنا مركبنا المشار اليه لتجديد الصحبه والصداقة القديمه ولا ترفعوا
[17] نظركم العالى عن رجالنا المشار اليه صدر الكتاب وكل معروف تعملوه معه
[18] محسوب علينا والله الله بالالتفات وعدم رفع النظر عن المشار اليه فيما يبدوا والواصل
[19] على يده بعض الهدية راسين خيل عنا هم يكونوا قدم مبارك وباقى اعلامنا على
[20] الالسنه الواصلين اليكم كفايه والسلام عليكم ورحمة الله وبركاته ||

In the corner follows here a short text in Malay, in a different, much smaller hand, evidently a later addition:

سود اين دان | ساتو كشد شاه بندر | سام ارتيث دغن اين كود | ساج | تياد دسان سبوة

On the verso is the sender and the date of sending:

[1] المحب المخلص سلطان بن الامام احمد بن سعيد
[2] حرر فى ٢٣ شهر ربيع الاول سنة ١٢١٥ ||

Text in the seal: ١٢١٢

بسم الله القوى المتين انى آتيكم بسلطان مبين

Praise be to God alone.

To the most elevated and perfect friend, the one with the good advice, the *Ğandarāl Batāwa*, may God, the Exalted, keep him safe.

The best exchange of presents between people of lo and the most perfect bestowing of gifts between peop of compassion and union is the ample peace greeting from God and the prayer to Him. There is no other ind vidual like Him Who gives guidance, Who brings go tiding, Who provides and Who presents. [This is ad dressed] to the excellent friend, the support of the en nent and the distinguished people, may he be protect by the eye of the Munificent King, with which frienc mean,[31] may God, the Exalted, keep him safe and g him a long life. May He protect him against mishap a adversities. May He grant him success by the content ment that He has of him. The reason for composing this message of love and for writing this leaf of uni is to enquire after your good health and the harmony your times, and these two are the ultimate intent a purpose. While we were looking out for news about yo well-being, there came, on the most blessed of hours and the noblest of times, your esteemed letter togetl with the captain of the ship Sīb-i Bādam, our belov friend 'Abd al-Raḥmān. Everything that you sent by way of the sublime present, according to your preference a your resolve, is a bounty and may God give even mo of the largesse of His grace, and may you keep receivi His grace. Last year we sent that ship, which belongs one of our friends, by way of friendship and love, as had the impression that you had become cut off fro our harbor. We would like that the connection is n interrupted between us and you. In view of the uni and the friendship that was between us we sent our sh Ğangāwar, with on board our man al-Ḥāğğī Maḥmūd Mashkūr. Firstly the intention for sending the ship w to establish the connection and to meet you, and sec ondly to buy some sugar from your harbor. We wish a we hope that he is received with honor, respect and co sideration, as is customary with us and with you, both the past and in the present. And we wish and hope [tl happens] what is mentioned, without making a disp of it, since you are our friends from a long time ago, a because of the lack of connection between you and us we sent our above-mentioned ship, in order to renew the c companionship and friendship. Do not take your hi regards away from our man who is mentioned earlier the letter. You will oblige us by all the good treatme that you give to him. And by God, may God give y attention to it and that you do not turn your eyes aw from the said person in what he shows. In his hand come as a present two horses from us, may they be a propitic step forward. The rest of our message is on the tongu of those who arrive at you. Enough! Peace be upon yo and the grace of God and His blessings.

Here, directly next to the end of the text of the letter, in the lower right corner of the page follows a short text in Malay: | suda ini dan | satu kepada syah bandar | sama artinya dengan ini kuda saja | tiada di sana sebut | = 'Indeed and one for the harbour master, meaning this horse is not mentioned there [in the letter].'³²

On the verso is the sender and the date of sending: 'The sincere friend Sulṭān b. al-Imām Aḥmad b. Saʿīd. Thus done on 23 of the month Rabīʿ I of the year 1215'.

Text in the seal: 'In the name of God, the Almighty, the Strong One. I come to you with clear authority. 1212'.

Dutch text on the verso of the document: | Musquette | Van den Imam | Aan Zijn Hoog | Edelheid. ontvan | gen bat. den 21. 8ber. | 1800. – | = 'Muscat. From the Imām to His Excellency. Received in Batavia on the 21st October 1800.'

« 8 »

Letter in Arabic from Sulṭān b. al-Imām Aḥmad b. Saʿīd b. al-Imām Saʿīd al-Būsaʿīdī to al-Qāʾim Maqām Qupanī al-Dawla al-Wulandīziyya Ǧandarār Batāw, the Governor-General in Batavia, dated 17 Rabīʿ II 1216 (August 27, 1801), received in Batavia on October 14, 1802.

Leiden University Library, Or. 2241-IV (8). No. 244 / Klinkert No. 8. Wieringa (a.o.), *Catalogue* (1998), p. 408. One sheet of paper, folded once, 37.5 x 28 cm, Indian-style *naskh* script. Text written on one side only. Addition in Malay.

|1| نهدي جزيل الاشواق والتحيات على ممر الازمنة والاوقات لجناب القائم مقام قـپـنـي الدولة الولنديزية جندرار بتاو سلمه الله تعالى

|2| اما بعد فانا بحمد الله تعالى بخير وعافيه ونعمه وافيه لا زلتم كذلك سالمين مدة الدهور والسنين وقد وصلنا

|3| كتابكم المرسول في المركب المبارك كنجاور فسرنا حيث اخبر عن صحه سلامتكم والاتحاد المحبه بيننا وبينكم وجميع ما عرفتم به

|4| فقد صار عندنا معلوم ولدينا مفهوم وكذلك وصل محبنا الحاج محمود في المركب المذكور بالسلام فوجدناه يثني

|5| عليكم بالجميل والاحسان ويشكر حسن صنيع ما عملتم معه من الرعاية والمحبة وذلك هو المأمول من جنابكم فسعيكم عندنا

|6| مشكور وصنيعكم لدينا مقبول وقد عزمنا ان نوجهه لخدمتكم ايضا في هذا الموسم في مركبنا الموسوم بفتح اسلام

|7| لكنا رأينا المركب يحتاج لبعض الأصلاح وفهمنا بان الأشياء التي يحتاج لها تتعذر في طرفكم في بعض الأحيان فلذلك وجهناه

|8| اولا الى بندر كلكته لأجل اصلاح المركب ثم من بعد ذلك امرنا ان يتوجه من هناك الى خدمتكم فالمأمول منكم

|9| بعد وصوله الى تلك الناحيه ان تبدوا لهم المحبة والرعايه والمساعده في كل ما يحتاجون اليه كما وفيتم بذلك كله

|10| اولا وكلما تعاملون معهم من الجميل والاحسان فهو راجع لنا ومحسوب علينا وقد بدا لنا في هذه الأيام التوجه لناحية

|11| الشمال لجهاد قوم اظهروا في الارض الفساد وصدوا عن طريق الرشاد نرجو النصر عليهم والظفر من رب العباد فانه قادر

|12| على ما اراد وهو حسبنا ونعم الوكيل نعم المولى ونعم النصير والمأمول اتصال المكاتبة و

|13| التعريف لتجديد المحبة والاتحاد والباقي دوام سلامتكم في خير وعافية وسرور

|14| على ممر الازمنة والدهور

|15| من المحب سلطان بن الامام احمد بن سعيد البوسعيدي

|16| بتاريخ ۱۷ من شهر ربيع الأخر

|17| سنة ۱۲۱٦ ||

Text in the seal: ۱۲۱۱ بسم الله القوي المتين اني آتيكم بسلطان مبين

We present abundant feelings of love and greetings over the course of time to the honorable representative of the *Qupanī* of the Dutch government, the *Ǧandarār Batāwī*, may God, the Exalted, protect him.

Well then, we are, praise be to God, the Exalted, doing fine and we are well-guarded and we enjoy abundant favors, may you also be all the time in that same situation, over the times and the years. Your letter that was sent on board the blessed ship Gangāwar has arrived with us, and we were glad when we learned that you are doing fine and that there is the union of love between us and between you. Everything that you told in it became known and understood by us. Also our friend al-Ḥāǧǧ Maḥmūd arrived safely with us on board the above-mentioned ship and we found that he spoke out his praise about you with beauty and goodness, and that he was thankful because of the good treatment that you had given to him, which consisted of consideration and love. That was what we had hoped for from you, we thank you for your effort towards us and we gladly accept your favors to us. We had decided that we would direct him to your service, also in this season, on our ship named Fatḥ-i Islām, but we thought that the ship was in need of some repair, and we understood that the necessary materials were not always available in your land. Therefore we have directed him first to the harbor of Kolkata (Calcutta) in view of the repair of the ship, and after that we have ordered [him] to go from there [in your direction] in order to be at your service. We hope from you that after he has arrived in this region that you show him love, consideration and assistance in all that he needs, in the same way as you have done before. All good and beautiful with which you will treat him will mean our profit and our obligation [towards you]. It seemed a good thing to us, these days, that we direct us towards the region of the North in order to wage war on the people who have spread disorder in the land[33] and who have rejected the way of right guidance. We pray [God] that we triumph over them, and victory comes from the Lord of the Believers, because He is capable to do whatever He wants. He suffices to us and what a perfect Caretaker, what a perfect Lord and what a perfect Victor He is. It is hoped that the letter arrives [at your place] and [serves as] the acknowledgment of the renewal of love and union, and further we also wish that you will continue to do well, in prosperity, safety and joy, as long as the times and ages pass by.

From the friend Sulṭān b. al-Imām Aḥmad b. Sa'īd al-Būsa'īdī, on 17 of the month Rabī' II of the year 1216.

Then follows the seal which contains the following text: 'In the name of God, the Almighty, the Strong One. I come to you with clear authority. 1211'.

Dutch text on the verso of the document: | Musquette | Van den Jmam | Aan zijn | HoogEdelh. | ontv. bat. den | 14. 8ber. 1802 | = 'Muscat. From the Imām to His Excellency. Received in Batavia the 14th October 1802.'

« 9 »

Letter in Arabic from Sulṭān b. al-Imām Aḥmad b. Sa'īd al-Būsa'īdī to the *Dariktūr*, the director, of the harbor of Batavia', dated 17 Rabī' II 1216 (August 27, 1801). Received in Batavia on October 14, 1802.

Leiden University Library, Or. 2241-IV (9). No. 245 / Klinkert No. 9. Wieringa (a.o.), *Catalogue* (1998), p. 408. One sheet of paper, folded once, 37 x 26.5 cm, Indian-style *naskh* script. Text written on one side only.

| ١ | نهدي جزيل الاشواق والتحيات على ممر الازمنة والاوقات لجناب محبنا وصديقنا دريكتور بندر المعمور بتاو سلمه الله تعالى
| ٢ | اما بعد فانا بحمد الله تعالى في خير عميم وحال مستقيم لا زلتم كذلك سالمين ومما نكرهون آمين آمين
| ٣ | مدة الدهور والسنين وبعد فقد وصلنا كتابكم المرسول في المركب المبارك كنجاور فسرنا حيث اخبر عن صحة
| ٤ | سلامتكم التي هي غاية قصدنا ومرادنا وجميع ما عرفتم فيه فقد صح عندنا معلوم ولدينا مفهوم لا سيما عن اتحاد
| ٥ | المحبه والصداقة بيننا وبينكم وكذلك وصل محبنا الحاج محمود بن محمد بن مشكور في المركب المذكور بالسلام
| ٦ | فوجدناه يثني على جنابكم بالجميل والاحسان ويشكر حسن صنيع ما عملتم معهم من الرعاية والمحبة وذلك هو المأمول
| ٧ | من جنابكم فسعيكم عندنا مشكور وصنيعكم لدينا مقبول وقد عزمنا على ان نوجهه لخدمتكم ايضا في هذا

| ٨ | الموسم في مركبنا الموسوم بفتح اسلام لكنا رأينا المركب يحتاج لبعض الاصلاح وفهمنا بان الأشياء التي تحتاج
| ٩ | لها لا تتعذر في طرفكم في بعض الأوقات فلذلك وجهناه اولا الى بندر كلكته لأجل أصلاح المركب ثم من
| ١٠ | بعده امرناه ان يتوجه من هناك الى خدمتكم فالمأمول منكم بعد وصولهم الى تلك الناحيه ان تبدوا
| ١١ | لهم المحبه والأحسان اليهم والمساعدة في كل ما يحتاجون اليه كما وفيتم بذلك اولا
| ١٢ | وكلما تعاملون معهم من الأحسان والجميل فهو راجع لنا ومحسوب علينا وقد بدا لنا في هذه
| ١٣ | الايام التوجه لناحية قوم اظهروا في الارض الفساد وصدوا عن طريق الرشاد نرجوا
| ١٤ | النصر عليهم والظفر من رب العباد فانه قادر على ما اراد وهو حسبنا ونعم الوكيل
| ١٥ | من المحب سلطان بن الامام احمد بن سعيد البوسعيدي
| ١٦ | بتاريخ ١٧ شهر ربيع الاخر
| ١٧ | سنة ١٢١٦ ||

Text in the seal: بسم الله القوي المتين اني آتيكم بسلطان مبين ١٢١١

We present abundant feelings of love and greetings over the course of time to our respected confidant and friend, the *Dariktūr* of the prosperous harbor, the harbor of Batāwi, may God, the Exalted, protect him.

Well then, we are, praise to God, the Exalted, doing very fine and [we are] in excellent condition. May you also be all the time in that same situation, and may you be safe against what you adversities, amen, over the times and the years.

Further: Your letter that was sent on board the blessed ship Gangāwar has arrived with us, and we were glad when we learned that you are doing fine, which is our ultimate aim and intent. Everything that you told in it has become well known and understood by us, especially what you wrote about the union of love and friendship between us and between you. Also our friend al-Ḥāǧǧ Maḥmūd b. Muḥammad b. Mashkūr has arrived safely with us on board the above-mentioned ship and we found that he spoke out his praise about you with beauty and goodness, and that he was thankful because of the good treatment that you had given to him, which consisted of consideration and love. That was what we had hoped from you, we thank you for your effort towards us and we gladly accept your favors to us. We had decided that we would direct him to your service, also in this season, on our ship named Fatḥ-i Islām, but we thought that the ship was in need of some repair, and we understood that the necessary materials were not always available in your land. Therefore we have directed him first to the harbor of Kolkata (Calcutta) in view of the repair of the ship, and we have ordered to go from there in your direction in order to be at your service.

We hope from you that after he has arrived in this [your] country that you show him love, consideration and assistance in all that he needs, in the same way as you have done before. All good and beautiful with which you will treat them is our profit and our obligation [towards you]. It seemed a good thing to us, these days, that we direct us towards the region of the people who have spread disorder in the land and who have rejected the way of right guidance. We pray [God] that we triumph over them, and victory comes from the Lord of the Believers, because He is capable to do whatever He wants. He suffices to us and what a perfect Caretaker He is.

From the friend Sulṭān b. al-Imām Aḥmad b. Saʿīd al-Būsaʿīdī, on 17 of the month Rabīʿ II of the year 1216.

Then follows the seal which contains the following text: 'In the name of God, the Almighty, the Strong One. I come to you with clear authority. 1211'

Dutch text on the verso of the document: | Musquette | Van den Jmam, | Aan den wel Ed. | Groot Agtb. heer | Directeur Gene | raal. ontvangen | bat. den 14. 8ber. 1802 | = 'Muscat. From the Imam to the Much Respected Gentleman, the Director General. Received in Batavia on the 14th October 1802.'

« 10 »

Letter in Arabic from al-Sayyid Badr b. al-Sayyid Sayf b. al-Imām Aḥmad b. Saʿīd al-Būsaʿīdī to Ǵandarāl Pīsī, Governor-General A.H. Wiese (in office 1805–1808), dated 15 Ṣafar 1221 (May 4, 1806). Received in Batavia on December 6, 1806.
Leiden University Library, Or. 2241-IV (10). No. 516 / Klinkert No. 10. Wieringa (a.o.), *Catalogue* (1998), p. 408. One sheet of paper, folded once, 37.5 x 28 cm, *naskh* script. Text written on one side only.

|1| الحمد لله كافي المهمات

Text in seal: نصركم الله ببدر ١٢١٥

|2| من المعتصم بالله المنتصر به السيد بدر بن السيد سيف بن الامام المرحوم احمد بن سعيد البوسعيدي لطف الله تعالى به آمين
|3| الى اخينا ومحبنا وسبق من اباءنا وبينه المودة والصحبة والعقد المولف والعمل المشرف الاكمل الاحشم المحب
|4| جندرال پيسي سلمه الله من الاسواء وحماه من كل بلوى ووفقه لمراده في السير والمأوى واصلكم انشآء الله مركب الحاجي عنبر داوود خليل
|5| المسمى الخليلي نوخذه ابراهيم بن حسن وهو مركب لنا يخص احد رعايانا فالمرجو منكم له الحشمة التامة والفعل الجميل كما قد سبق بين اباءنا وبين اباءكم

|6| وبينكم وما عملتموه معه من جميل القول والعمل فكما عملتموه معنا هذا ونرجوا الله ان تجديد الصحبة والموده بيننا وبينكم
|7| ثابته كما سبق من اباءنا معكم لان مودة الابا صلة فى الابنا ونحن كما علمتم مما اجرى الله على الامام السيد سلطان
|8| بعد وفاته متولين منزلته فى العقد والعهد والامان فالمرجو منا ومنكم تمام ذلك في كل حال واوان والذي ارسلتموه للسيد سلطان
|9| وصل الينا كما هو مذكور والاخبار ان شآء الله تعالى تصل اليكم في غير هذ المركب حتى لا يخفى حرر في ١٥
|10| من شهر صفر من سنه ١٢٢١ ||

Praise be to God, Who performs the tasks.

Text in seal: 'God helped you at Badr.[34] 1215'.

From the one who takes shelter with God, and who is victorious through God, from al-Sayyid Badr b. al-Sayyid Sayf, son of the late Imām Aḥmad b. Saʿīd al-Būsaʿīdī. May God, the Exalted, treat him with kindness. Amen.

To our brother and friend – there existed in the past love, friendship, a well-made bond and a perfect conduct of respect and decency between our fathers and between him – [that is] to the friend *Ǵandarāl Pīsī*, may God protect him against evil and may God defend him against all misfortune, and may He grant him success in where he wants to go and where he wants to take his refuge.

There is arriving, God willing, at your place the ship of al-Ḥāǧǧī ʿAnbar Dāwūd Khalīl, named al-Khalīlī, under captain Ibrāhīm b. Ḥasan. This is a ship of us and it belongs to one of our subjects. You are requested to grant him full respect and to act well towards him, as used to be the case between our fathers and your fathers and yourselves. If you speak well to him and treat him in a good way, it is as if you did that to us personally. Furthermore we pray that God grants the renewal of the friendship and the love between us and between you, in the same permanent way as this used to be the case with our fathers and with you, because the love between the fathers implies a bond between the sons. We are, as you know, after what God let happen to the Imām al-Sayyid Sulṭān, after his demise, in charge of his position is as far as bonds, treaties and safety are concerned. It is requested from us and from you to fulfill this in every situation and at every moment in time. What you have sent to al-Sayyid Sulṭān has arrived with us, as was mentioned. The news will come to you, God willing, by way of another ship, so that it will not remain unknown to you. Thus done on 15 Ṣafar of the year 1221.

Dutch text on the verso of the document: | Musquette | Van den Jmam Aan | Zijn hoogEdelheid. ontv. | bat. den 6. dec. 1806. – | = 'Muscat. From the Imam to His Excellency. Received in Batavia the 6th of December 1806.'

WOOD, HORSES AND FRIENDSHIP • ANNEX 6 • 287

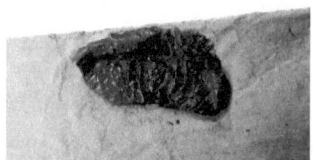

1b. Detail from 1a. Remnant of red wax seal, on top of the document. The Hague, National Archive, 1.11.01.01, 659, verso. Photograph by B.J. Slot, April 2011.

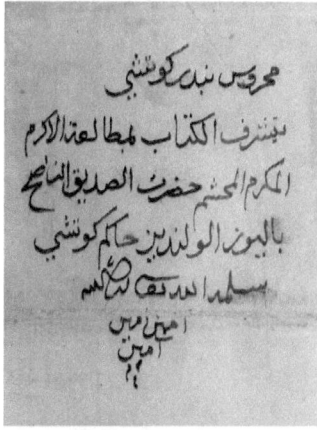

1c. Address on the letter from Khalfān b. Muḥammad, the wālī of Muscat, to Bāliyūz al-Wulandin, the Dutch governor of Kochi, dated 22 Sha'bān 1193 (September 3, 1779). The Hague, National Archive, 1.11.01.01, 659, verso. Photograph by B.J. Slot, April 2011.

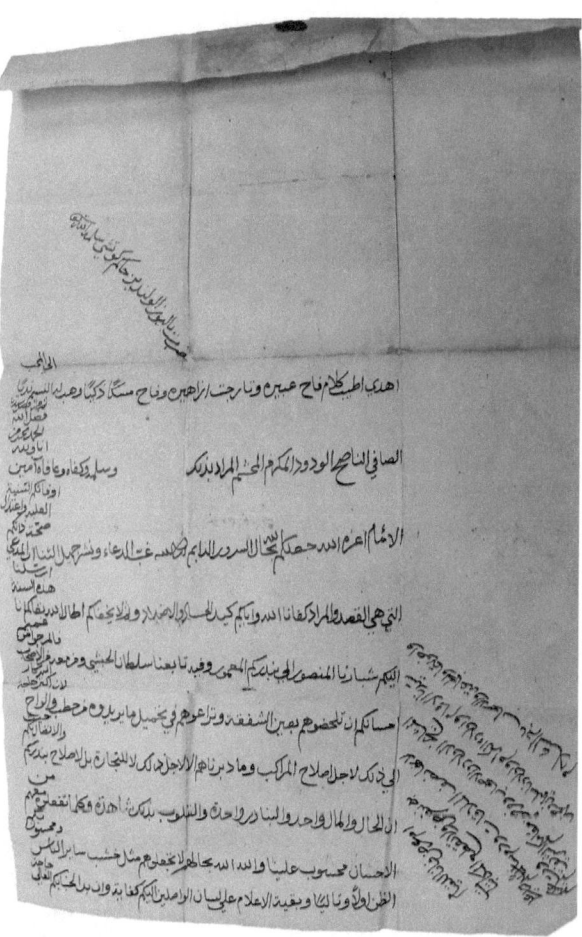

1a. Letter in Arabic from Khalfān b. Muḥammad b. 'Abdallāh al-Būsa'īdī, the wālī of Muscat, to Bāliyūz al-Wulandin, the Dutch governor of Kochi (Cochin, Kerala), dated 22 Sha'bān 1193 (September 3, 1779). The Hague, National Archive, 1.11.01.01, 659 (formerly known as 'Aanwinsten 1e afd. 1894 23'), recto. Photograph by B.J. Slot, April 2011.

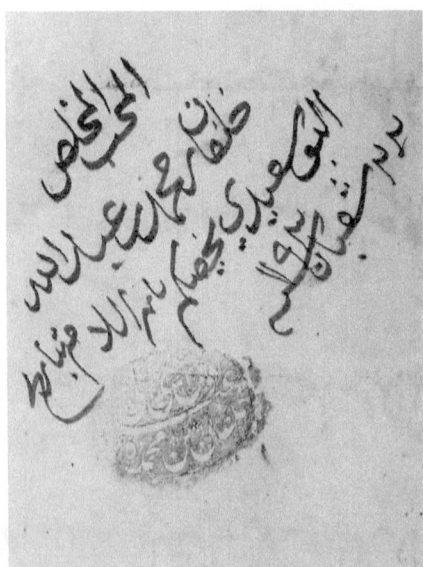

1c. Detail from 1a. The sender's name and a print of his seal. The Hague, National Archive, 1.11.01.01,659, verso. Photograph by B.J. Slot, April 2011.

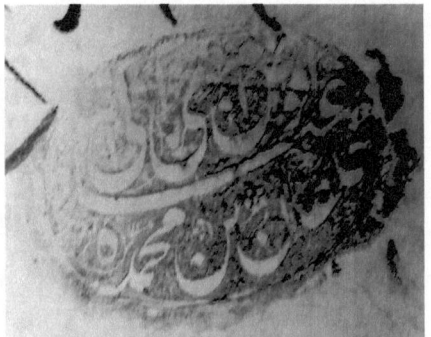

1d. Detail from 1c. Print of sender's seal with his name with a quotation from Qur'ān 40:44. Photograph by B.J. Slot, April 2011.

2b. Detail of 2a: Seal of Sulṭān b. al-Imām Aḥmad b. Saʿīd, with a quotation from Qur'ān 44:19, and the date 1211. Leiden University Library Or. 2241-IV (11), recto (detail).

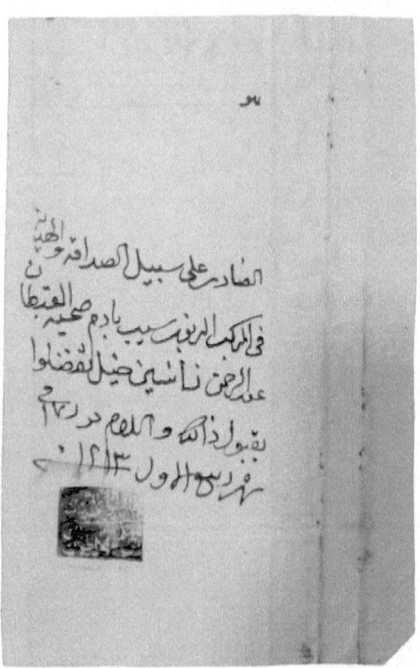

2a. Presentation note in Arabic from Sulṭān b. al-Imām Aḥmad b. Saʿīd for the gift of two horses, possibly to the Governor-General in Batavia, dated 17 Rabīʿ I 1213 (August 29, 1798). Leiden University Library Or. 2241-IV (11), recto.

WOOD, HORSES AND FRIENDSHIP · ANNEX 6 · 289

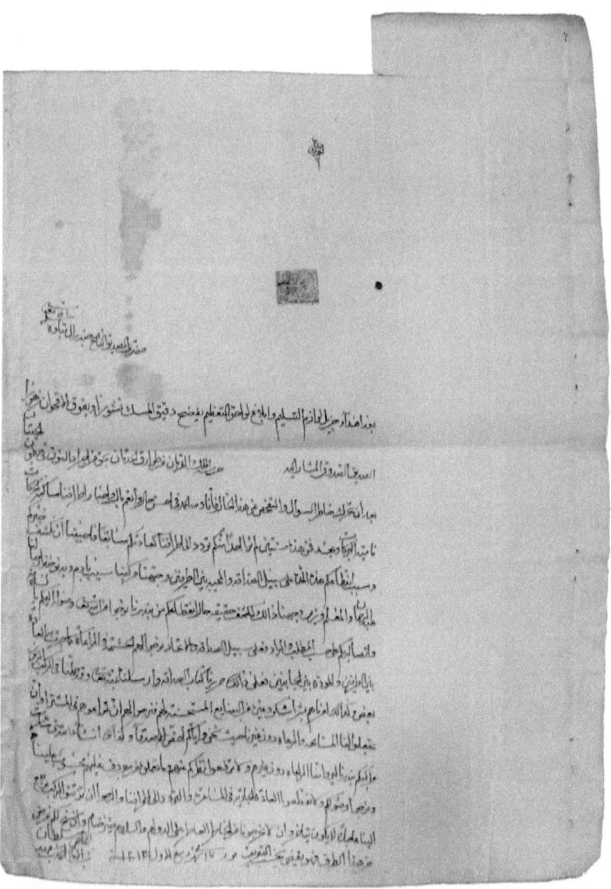

3a. Letter in Arabic from Sulṭān b. al-Imām Aḥmad b. Saʿīd, to Ğandarāl Batāwa, the Governor-General in Batavia, dated 17 Rabīʿ I 1213 (August 29, 1798). Leiden University Library Or. 2241-IV (2), recto.

3b. Detail of 3a. Invocation over the text: al-Ḥamdu lillāh waḥdahu. Leiden University Library Or. 2241-IV (2), recto (detail).

3c. Detail of 3a: print of sender's seal with his name and a quotation from Qurʾān 44:19, and date 1211. Leiden University Library Or. 2241-IV (2), recto (detail).

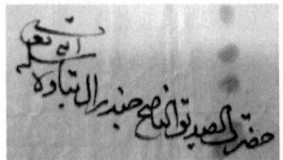

3d. Detail of 3a. Addressee Ğandarāl Batāwā.
Leiden University Library Or. 2241-IV (2), recto (detail).

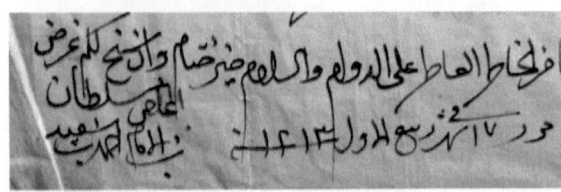

3e. Detail of 3a. Sender Sulṭān b. al-Imām Aḥmad b. Saʿīd, and date 17 Rabīʿ I
1213 (August 29, 1798). Leiden University Library Or. 2241-IV (2), recto (detail).

of the letter from Sulṭān b. al-Imām Aḥmad b. Saʿīd, to the
~General in Batavia, dated 17 Rabīʿ I 1213 (August 29, 1798).
'niversity Library Or. 2241-IV (2), verso.

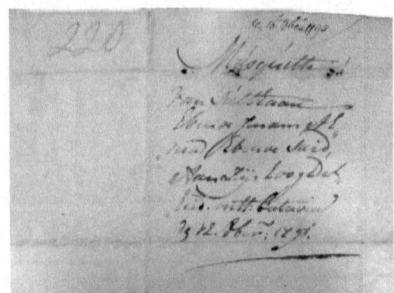

3h. Detail of 3f. Note in Dutch of receipt in Batavia, dated 12 and
16 October 1798. Leiden University Library Or. 2241-IV (2),
verso (detail).

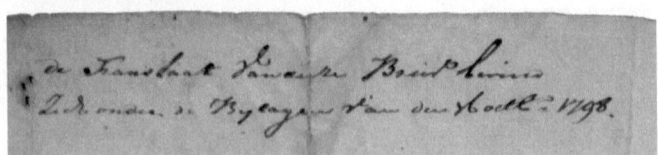

l of 3f. Reference to the Dutch translation, kept in Batavia, dated 1798.
'niversity Library Or. 2241-IV (2), verso (detail).

WOOD, HORSES AND FRIENDSHIP · ANNEX 6 · 291

4b. Detail of 4a. Opening line with mention of the addressee, Ḥaḍrat Sar Gawnar Ǧanrāl Ṣāḥib. Leiden University Library Or. 2241-IV (3), recto (detail).

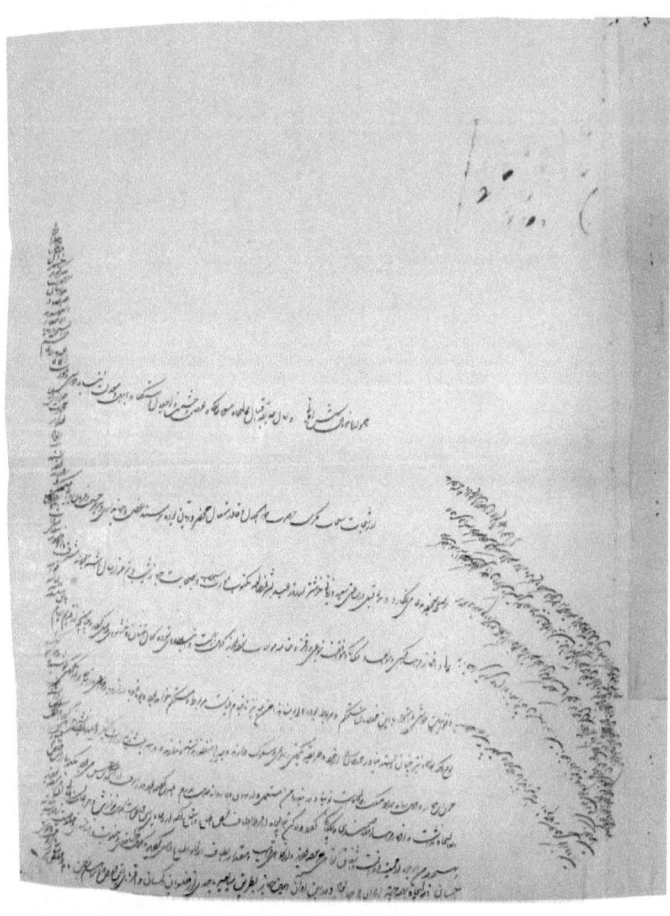

4a. Letter in Persian from Sulṭān b. al-Imām Aḥmad b. Saʿīd, to Sar Gawnar Ǧanrāl Ṣāḥib, the Governor-General in Batavia. Undated but possibly sent on 10 Ramaḍān 1214 (February 5, 1800). Received in Batavia on May 23, 1800. Leiden University Library Or. 2241-IV (3), recto.

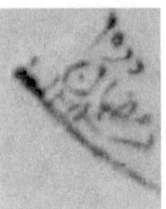

4e. Detail of 4c. Note in Persian (by the captain?) with date 10 or 15 Ramaḍān 1214 (February 5/10, 1800). Leiden University Library Or. 2241-IV (3), verso (detail).

4c. Verso side of the Persian letter from Sulṭān b. al-Imām Aḥmad b. Saʿīd, to the Governor-General in Batavia, possibly sent on 10/15 Ramaḍān 1214 (February 5/10, 1800), received in Batavia on May 23, 1800. Leiden University Library Or. 2241-IV (3), verso.

4d. Detail of 4c. Seal of Sulṭān b. al-Imām Aḥmad b. Saʿīd with date 1212. Leiden University Library Or. 2241-IV (3), verso (detail).

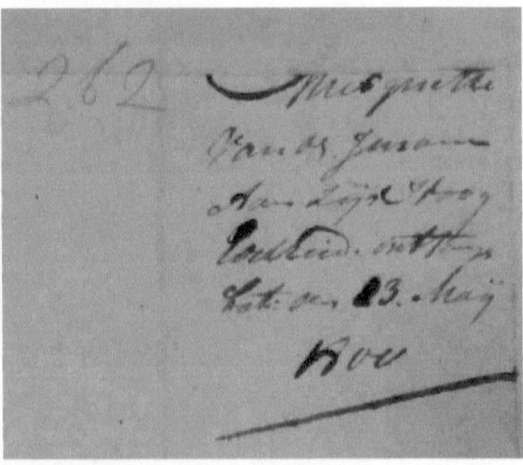

4f. Detail of 4c. Note in Dutch of receipt in Batavia, May 23, 1800. Leiden University Library Or. 2241-IV (3), verso (detail).

Detail of 5a. Invocation over the
In shā'a Allāh ta'ālā. Leiden
versity Library Or. 2241-IV (4),
(detail).

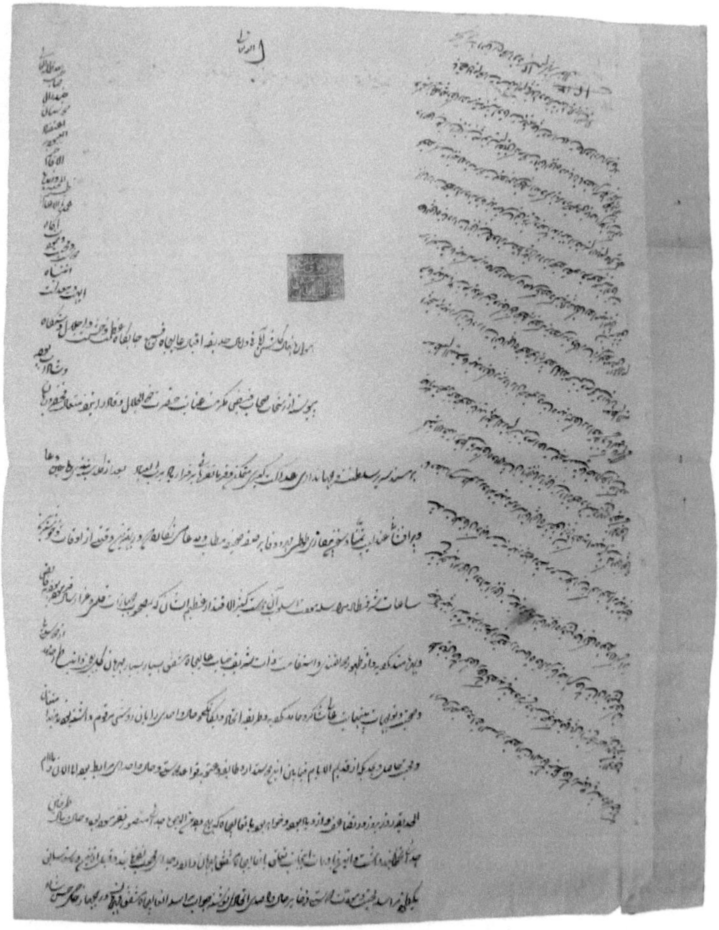

5a. Letter in Persian from Sulṭān b. al-Imām Aḥmad b. Sa'īd, addressed to Ġandarāl Ṣāḥib, the Governor-General in Batavia, according to the text of the letter (but on the reverse the addressee is mentioned as Shāhbandar Ṣāḥib, the harbormaster of Batavia), dated 12 Shawwāl 1214 (March 8, 1800), received in Batavia July 21, 1800. Leiden University Library Or. 2241-IV (4), recto.

5d. Detail of 5a. Seal of Sulṭān b. al-Imām Aḥmad b. Sa'īd with date 1212. Leiden University Library Or. 2241-IV (4), recto (detail).

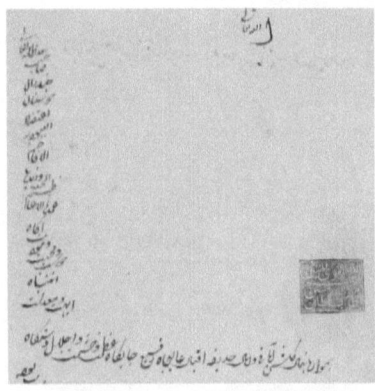

5b. Fragment of 5a. Invocation, seal and opening line with the addressee Ġandarāl Ṣāḥib. Leiden University Library Or. 2241-IV (4), recto (detail).

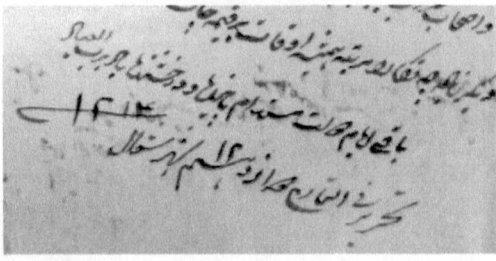

5f. Texts on the verso side of the letter from Sulṭān b. al-Imām Aḥmad b. Sa'īd to the harbormaster (Shāh Bandar Ṣāḥib) in Bandar Baṭāwia, dated 12 Shawwāl 1214 (March 8, 1800), with a note in Malay, and a note on the receipt in Batavia on July 21, 1800. Leiden University Library Or. 2241-IV (4), verso (detail).

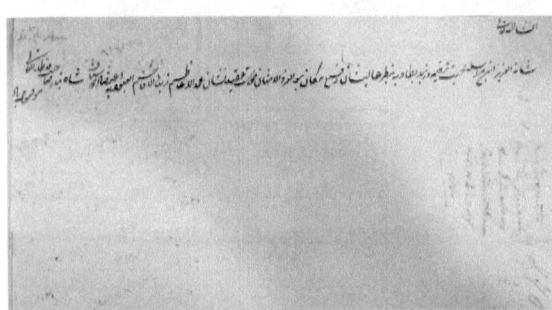

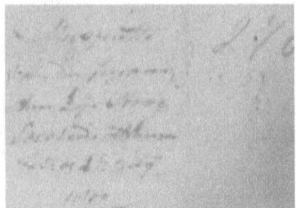

5h. Detail of 5f. Note of reception in Batavia, July 21, 1800. Leiden University Library Or. 2241-IV (4), verso (detail).

5e. Detail of 5a. Date of the letter 12 Shawwāl 1214 (March 8, 1800). Leiden University Library Or. 2241-IV (4), recto (detail).

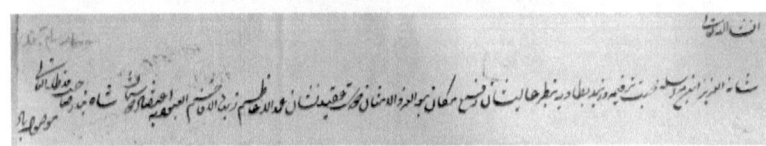

5g. Detail of 5f. Addressee of the letter and address Banda Baṭāwiya, with a later addition in Malay. Leiden University Library Or. 2241-IV (4), verso (detail).

WOOD, HORSES AND FRIENDSHIP • ANNEX 6 • 295

6b. Detail of 6a. Invocation over the text: al-Ḥamdu lillāh Waḥdahu. Leiden University Library, Or. 2241-IV (7), recto (detail).

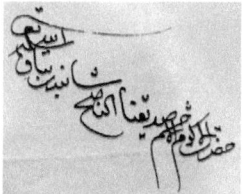

6c. Detail of 6a. Addressee: Shābandar Batāwa, *the harbormaster of Batavia.* Leiden University Library, Or. 2241-IV (7), recto (detail).

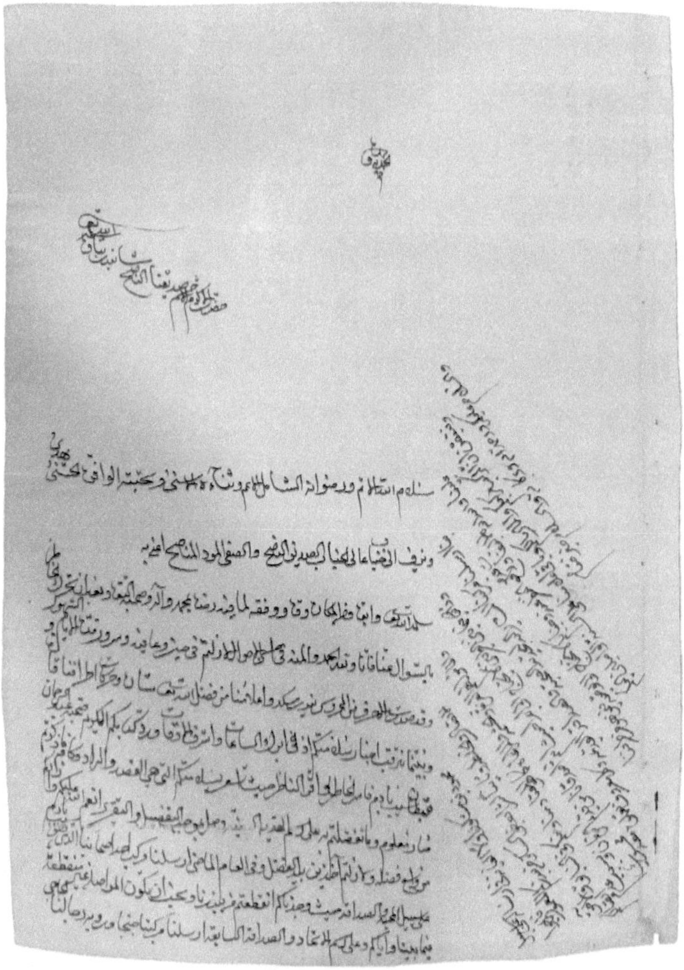

6a. Letter in Arabic from Sulṭān b. al-Imām Aḥmad b. Saʿīd to Shābandar Batāwa, *the harbormaster of Batavia. Dated (on the verso side) 23 Rabīʿ I 1215 (August 14, 1800). Leiden University Library, Or. 2241-IV (7), recto.*

6d. Verso of the letter from Sulṭān b. al-Imām Saʿīd to 'the harbormaster of Batavia'. Dated 23 Rabīʿ I 1215 (August 14, 1800), with sender and seal. Note of receipt at Batavia October 21, 1800. Leiden University Library, Or. 2241-IV (7), verso.

6e. Detail of 6d. Sender: Sulṭān b. al-Imām Aḥmad b. Saʿīd, and date 23 Rabīʿ I 1215 (August 14, 1800). Leiden University Library, Or. 2241-IV (7), verso (detail).

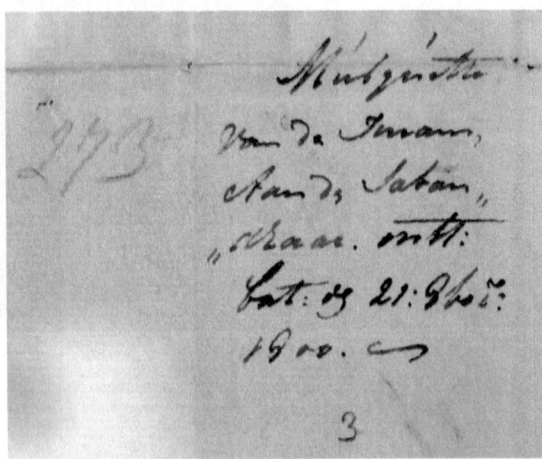

6f. Detail of 6d. Seal of Sulṭān b. al-Imām Saʿīd, and date 1212. Leiden University Library, Or. 2241-IV (7), verso (detail).

6g. Detail of 6d. Note of receipt in Batavia, October 21, 1800. Leiden University Library, Or. 2241-IV (7), verso (detail).

7b. *Detail of 7a. Invocation over the text:* al-Ḥamdu lillāh Waḥdahu. *Leiden University Library, Or. 2241-IV (6), recto (detail).*

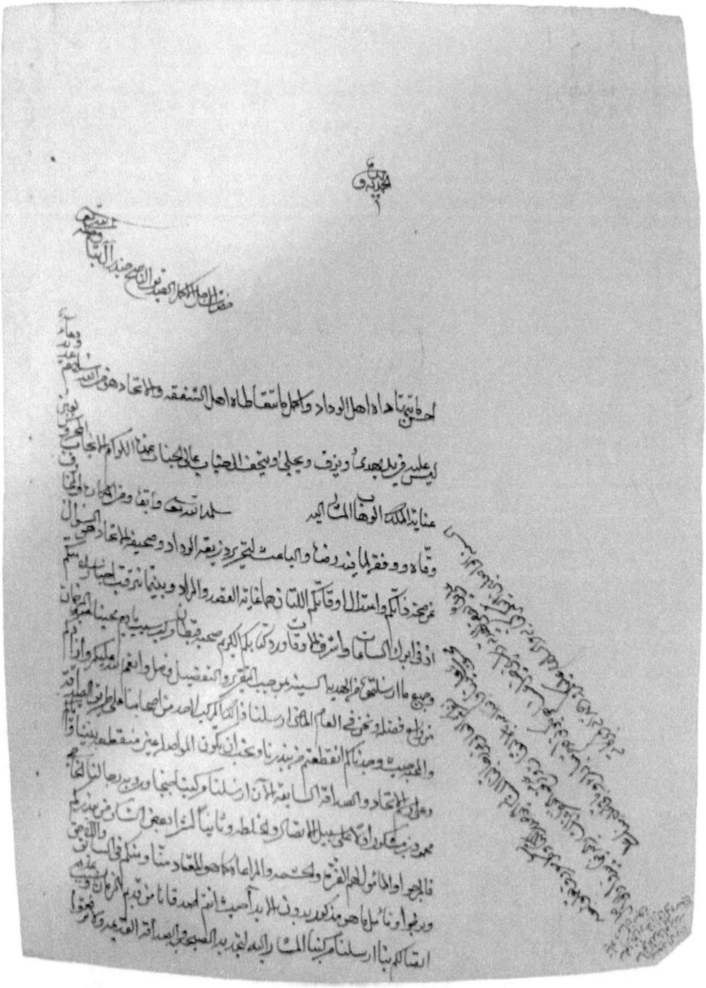

7a. *Letter in Arabic from Sulṭān b. al-Imām Aḥmad b. Saʿīd to Ğandarāl Batāwa, the Dutch Governor-General in Batavia. Dated (on the reverse) 23 Rabīʿ I 1215 (August 14, 1800). Leiden University Library, Or. 2241-IV (6), recto.*

7c. Detail of 7a. Addressee: Ğandarāl Batāwa, the Governor-General in Batavia. Leiden University Library, Or. 2241-IV (6), recto (detail).

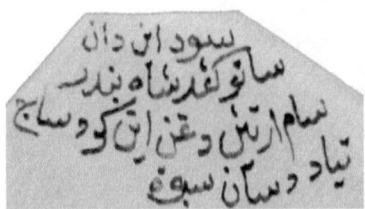

7d. Detail of 7a. Note in Malay, at lower right corner. Leiden University Library, Or. 2241-IV (6), recto (detail).

7e. Verso of the letter from Sulṭān b. al-Imām Saʿīd to Ğandarāl Batāwa, the Governor-General in Batavia. Dated 23 Rabīʿ I 1215 (August 14, 1800), received in Batavia, October 21, 1800. Leiden University Library, Or. 2241-IV (6), verso.

7g. Detail of 7e. Seal of Sulṭān b. al-Imām Saʿīd, and date 1212. Leiden University Library, Or. 2241-IV (6), verso (detail).

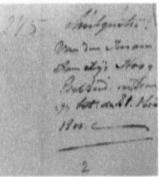

7h. Detail of 7e. Note of receipt in Batavia, October 21, 1800. Leiden University Library, Or. 2241-IV (6), verso (detail).

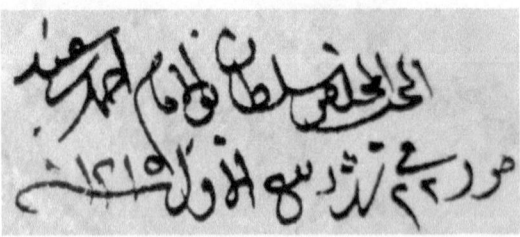

7f. Detail of 7e. Sender: Sulṭān b. al-Imām Aḥmad b. Saʿīd, and date: 23 Rabīʿ I 1215 (August 14, 1800). Leiden University Library, Or. 2241-IV (6), verso (detail).

WOOD, HORSES AND FRIENDSHIP · ANNEX 6 · 299

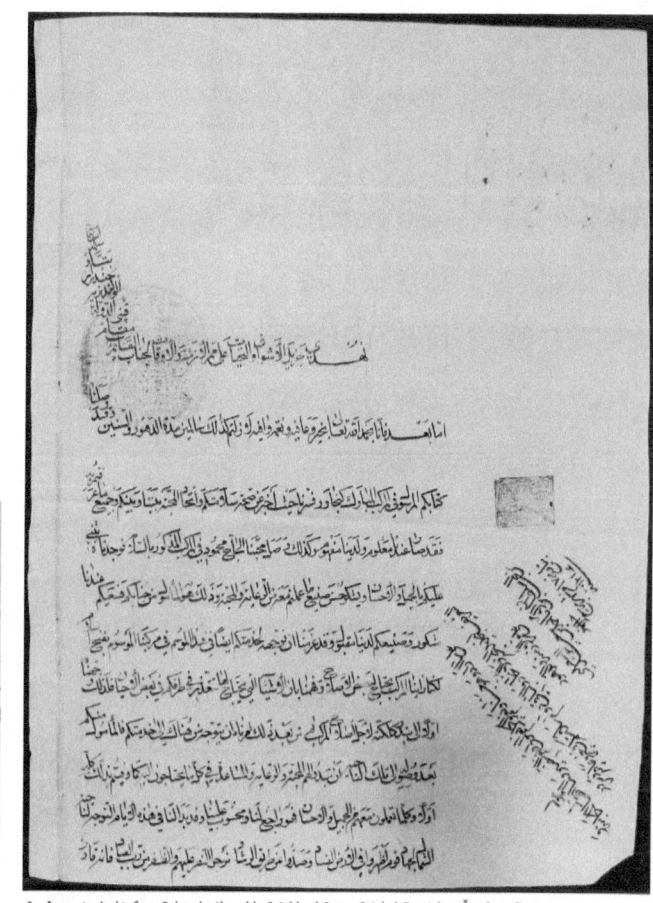

8b. Detail of 8a. Addressee: 'the Qā'im Maqām of the Company of the Dutch government, Ġandarār Batāw'. The seal (or is it the offset of a seal from another document?) could not be read. Leiden University Library, Or. 2241-IV (8) recto (detail).

8a. Letter in Arabic from Sulṭān b. Aḥmad b. Sa'īd b. al-Imām Sa'īd al-Būsa'īdī to Ġandarār Batāwī, the Governor-General in Batavia, dated 17 Rabī' II 1216 (August 27, 1801). Leiden University Library, Or. 2241-IV (8) recto.

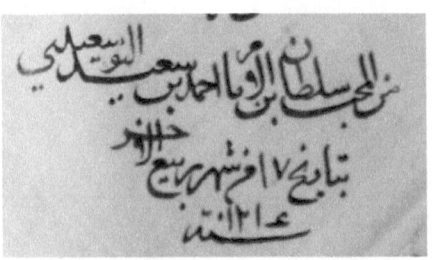

8d. *Detail of 8a. Sender: Sulṭān b. al-Imām Aḥmad b. Saʿīd al-Būsaʿīdī, and date 17 Rabīʿ II 1216 (August 27, 1801). Leiden University Library, Or. 2241-IV (8), recto (detail).*

8c. *Detail of 8a. Seal of Sulṭān b. al-Imām Aḥmad b. Saʿīd al-Būsaʿīdī, and date 1211. Leiden University Library, Or. 2241-IV (8), recto (detail).*

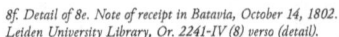

8f. *Detail of 8e. Note of receipt in Batavia, October 14, 1802. Leiden University Library, Or. 2241-IV (8) verso (detail).*

8e. *Verso of the letter from Sulṭān b. al-Imām Aḥmad b. Saʿīd al-Būsaʿīdī to the Governor-General in Batavia, dated 17 Rabīʿ II 1216 (August 27, 1801), received on October 14, 1802. Leiden University Library, Or. 2241-IV (8) verso.*

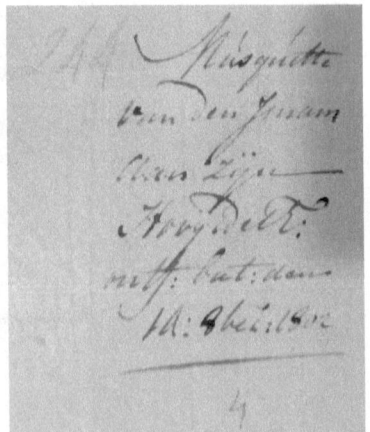

WOOD, HORSES AND FRIENDSHIP • ANNEX 6 • 301

9b. Detail of 9a. Addressee: 'our friend the Dāriktūr of the prosperous harbor, the harbor of Batavia', dated 17 Rabīʿ II 1216 (August 27, 1801). Leiden University Library, Or. 2241-IV (9), recto (detail).

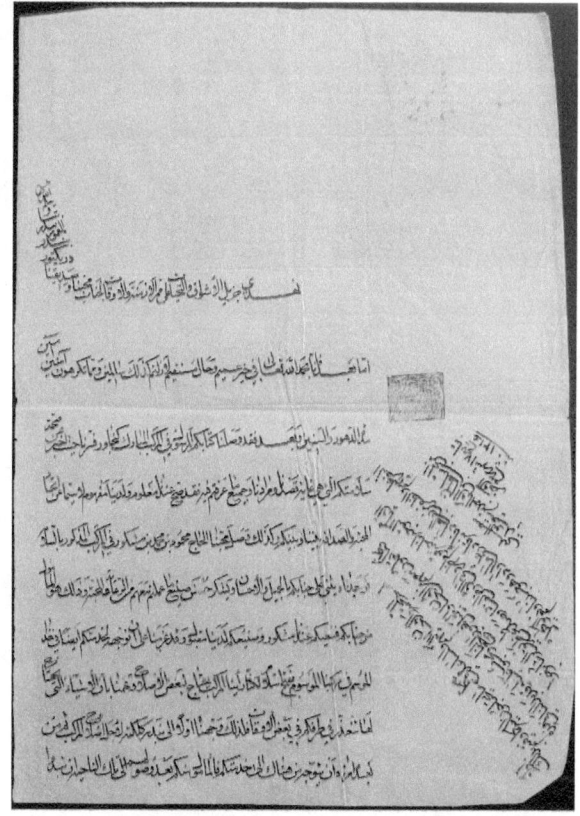

9a. Letter in Arabic from Sulṭān b. al-Imām Aḥmad b. Saʿīd al-Būsaʿīdī to the Dāriktūr, the director of the harbor of Batavia', dated 17 Rabīʿ II 1216 (August 27, 1801). Leiden University Library, Or. 2241-IV (9), recto.

302 • DUTCH – OMANI RELATIONS

9c. Detail of 9a. Seal of Sulṭān b. al-Imām Aḥmad b. Saʿīd al-Būsaʿīdī, and date 1211. Leiden University Library, Or. 2241-IV (9), recto (detail).

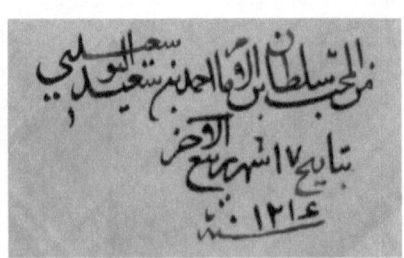

9d. Detail of 9a. Sender: Sulṭān b. al-Imām Aḥmad b. Saʿīd b. al-Būsaʿīdī, and date: 17 Rabīʿ II 1216 (August 27, 1801). Leiden University Library, Or. 2241-IV (9), recto (detail).

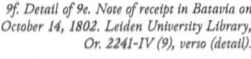

9f. Detail of 9e. Note of receipt in Batavia on October 14, 1802. Leiden University Library, Or. 2241-IV (9), verso (detail).

9e. Verso of the letter from Sulṭān b. Aḥmad b. Saʿīd b. al-Imām Saʿīd al-Būsaʿīdī to 'the director of the harbor of Batavia', dated 17 Rabīʿ II 1216 (August 27, 1801), received on October 14, 1802. Leiden University Library, Or. 2241-IV (9), verso.

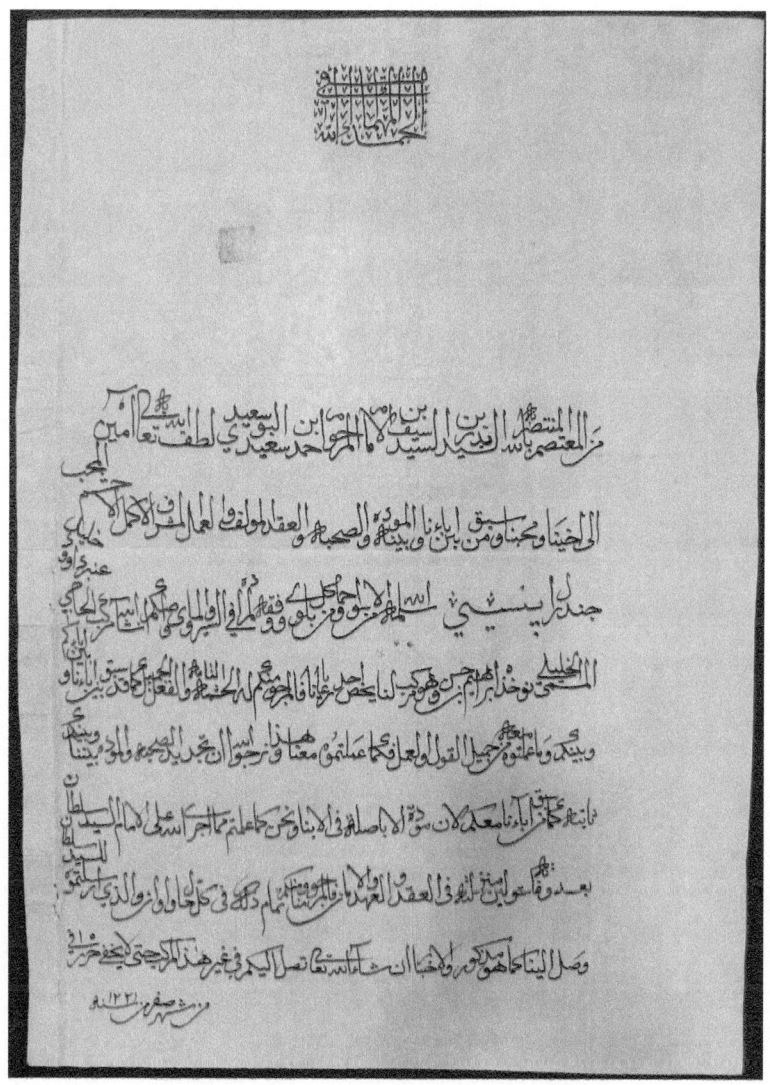

10a. Letter in Arabic from al-Sayyid Badr b. al-Sayyid Sayf b. al-Imām Aḥmad b. Saʿīd al-Būsaʿīdī to Ğandarāl Pisī (Governor-General Wiese), dated 15 Ṣafar 1221 (May 4, 1806). Received in Batavia, December 6, 1806. Leiden University Library, Or. 2241-IV (10), recto.

10c. Detail from 10a. Seal of al-Sayyid Badr b. al-Sayyid Sayf b. al-Imām Aḥmad b. Saʿīd al-Būsaʿīdī, with date 1215. Leiden University Library, Or. 2241-IV (10), recto (detail).

. Detail from 10a. Invocation over the text: al-Ḥamdu lillāh Kāfī al-ihimmāt. Leiden University Library, Or. 2241-IV (10), recto (detail).

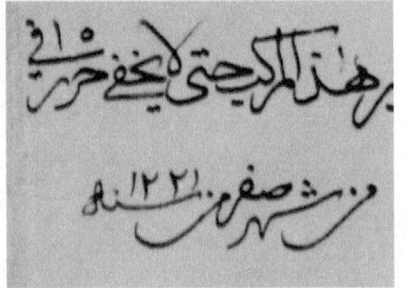

10d. Detail from 10a. Dated 15 Ṣafar 1221 (May 4, 1806). Leiden University Library, Or. 2241-IV (10), recto (detail).

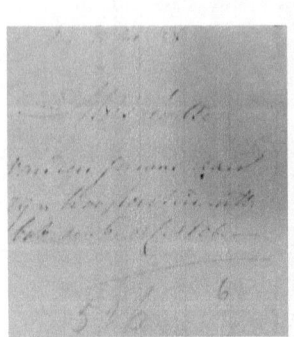

*. Detail from 10e. Note of receipt in Batavia, ed December 6 and 12, 1806. Leiden University Library, Or. 2241-IV (10), verso (detail).

10e. Verso of the letter in Arabic from al-Sayyid Badr b. al-Sayyid Sayf b. al-Imām Aḥmad b. Saʿīd al-Būsaʿīdī to Governor-General Wiese, dated 15 Ṣafar 1221 (May 4, 1806). Leiden University Library, Or. 2241-IV (10), verso.

Notes

* Emeritus Professor of the Chair of Paleography and Codicology of the Islamic World, Faculty of Humanities, Leiden University (j.j.witkam@hum.leidenuniv.nl), now attached to the Leiden Institute of Area Studies (LIAS).

1 An earlier and lesser version of this study was privately published under the title "News from the West: Letters from Oman to Batavia, 1798–1806" at the occasion of the visit to Leiden University Library on July 11, 2003, by Shaikh Abdullah bin Mohammed bin Abdullah al Salimi, the minister of Awqaf and Religious Affairs of the Sultanate of Oman.

2 See on the common history between Oman and the Netherlands B.J. Slot, *Nederlanders aan de kusten van Oman*. Den Haag (Museon) 1991. The historical context of the activities of the Dutch in the Gulf region till the late 18th century, including Oman, is described in B.J. Slot, The Arabs of the Gulf, 1602–1784. An alternative approach to the early history of the Arab Gulf states and their relations with the European powers, mainly based on sources of the Dutch East India Company. Leidschendam (published by the author) 1995. That work more or less ends where the documents described here begin.

3 Since a few years the Sultan has financed a chair of Oriental studies in the University of Leiden (as he does in Cambridge and other places for that matter), to name but one example. On May 2, 2011, the two countries agreed on the exploration of common maritime heritage by searching together for the East India Company's ship Amstelveen which in 1763 sunk at Cape Mataraqa on the Omani coast on its way to Muscat (Slot, *The Arabs of the Gulf*, 1602–1784, p. 365). A castaway of the shipwreck, Cornelis Eyks, wrote an account of his difficult journey through the Omani desert (*Noodlottige gevallen aan het gesalveerde volk van het Ed. Oost-Indisch Compagnies Schip Amstelveen, na deszelfs verongelukken in dato 5. Augustus 1763., op de Tocht van Batavia na Persiën, op hun weg door Arabiën overgekomen*, which was published in 1766).

4 The Dutch translations were often made with the assistance of a dragoman, e.g. MS Leiden Or. 2241 IV (5), where the translation by P. Kool of a Persian letter from three people in Surat to Governor-General van P.G. Overstraten in Batavia (in office 1796–1801) was made with the help of the interpreter Amīn Ḥasan.

5 All specific information on the Dutch East India Company I owe to Dr. B.J. Slot, who informed me at several instances in the past years of details which I would not easily have found myself (if at all), and who provided me with photographs of document No. 1 of the present collection. When it turned out that his book *The Arabs of the Gulf, 1602–1784* was not available in the Leiden library he kindly presented me with a copy. A survey of the specific Dutch archival sources is given by Slot in his *The Arabs of the Gulf*, 1602–1784, pp. 403–407.

6 Sulṭān Muḥammad Al-Qāsimī, *al-Wathāʾiq al-ʿArabiyya al-ʿUmāniyya fī Marāhia al-Arbif al-Faransiyya ʿGam' wa-taḥqīq Sulṭān b. Muḥammad al-Qāsimī*. al-Shāriqa 1993. There exists a French translation by Abdeljelil & Mireille Temimi, *Les relations entre Oman et la France (1715–1905)*. Paris (L'Harmattan) 1995.

7 This information on other original documents comes from a personal letter from B.J. Slot to me, dated February 2, 2002.

8 Personal information from B.J. Slot, April 11, 2011.

9 See for the different Dutch educational institutions for civil servants for the Indies and their curriculums C. Fasseur, *De indologen. Ambtenaren voor de Oost 1825–1950*. Amsterdam (Bakker) 1993.

10 In E.P. Wieringa, *Catalogue of Malay and Minangkabau manuscripts in the Library of Leiden University and other collections in the Netherlands*. Edited by Joan de Lijster-Streef & Jan Just Witkam. Volume 1, comprising the acquisitions of Malay manuscripts in Leiden University Library up to the year 1896. Leiden (Legatum Warnerianum) 1998, pp. 407–409. All descriptions of the individual documents in Arabic script in this catalogue were made by me.

11 The genre of 'golden letters' from South-East Asia has been extensively described and illustrated by Annabel Teh Gallop, with Bernard Arps, *Golden letters. Writing traditions of Indonesia. Surat emas. Budaya tulis di Indonesia*. London (British Library) / Jakarta (Lontar Foundation) 1991.

12 'Raad van Indië', the highest governing body in the colony, presided over by the Governor-General.

13 'Rijks-Instelling tot Opleiding van Indische Ambtenaren', founded in 1864 in Leiden. In 1877 it was replaced by a municipal college, but otherwise with the same purpose, and in 1891 it ceased to exist altogether.

14 They have been summarily described by H.C. Klinkert, 'Verzamelingen van Maleische brieven, voorhanden in de Rijksbibliotheek te Leiden', in *Tijdschrift voor Nederlandsch Indië*, August 1882, pp. 81–103. The documents here under discussion are described by Klinkert on p. 101.

15 See C.E. Bosworth, *The Islamic Dynasties*. Edinburgh (Edinburgh UP) 1967, pp. 78–80.

16 C.F. Beckingham, art. Bū Saʿīd, in *EI*, new edition, vol. 1. Leiden (Brill) 1960, pp. 1281–1283.

17 I am told, however, that Masgad is an older and equally correct spelling.

18 Taken from Wieringa (a.o.), *Catalogue* (1998), pp. 407–409.

19 I owe this observation to Prof. Abdul Sheriff of the Zanzibar Indian Ocean Research Institute (ZIORI) in Zanzibar. There is one exception. In letter 10, line 7, Sultan Badr b. Sayf refers to Sultan Sulṭān b. Aḥmad as imām. On the 'empty space' see also Annabel Teh Gallop, 'Elevatio in Malay Diplomatics', in: *Annales Islamologiques* 41 (2007), pp. 41–57.

20 See his place in the Omani royal genealogy by Christopher Buyers in: http://www.royalark.net/Oman/oman2.htm (accessed on 8 April 2011), where it is said of him: '[...] An early adherent of his cousin Aḥmad, who successfully aided him in his bid for the Imamate by taking Nizwa and Izki on his behalf. Wakīl of Muscat 1744–1749, Wali of Muscat 1749–1786. [...]' This 'cousin Aḥmad' was Aḥmad b. Saʿīd (d. 1783), who from 1744–1783 reigned as the first elected imām of the Bū Saʿīd dynasty over Oman.

21 References in Slot, *The Arabs of the Gulf*, 1602–1784, p. 370, note 15.

22 Personal information from B.J. Slot, 12 April 2011.

23 Slot, *The Arabs of the Gulf*, 1602–1784, p. 218.

24 Blank space in the original.

25 The second half comes from Qurʾān 40:44. Translation M.A.S. Abdul Haleem (Oxford 2004).

26 The second part comes from Qurʾān 44:19. Translation M.A.S. Abdul Haleem (Oxford 2004).

27 Blank space in the original.

28 My reading (and interpretation) of the word ترتيب in the original is doubtful.

29 Instead of 15 Ramaḍān one could also read 10 Ramaḍān 1214 (and February 5, 1800 therefore).

30 Blank space in the original.

31 Blank space in the original.

32 Dr. Roger Tol in Jakarta kindly provided me with this interpretation. It may mean that there was yet another horse, which was not mentioned in the letter, and which was meant to be given to the Shāhbandar.

33 The expression 'to spread disorder in the land' is Qurʾānic, e.g. 40:26. The next following expression 'to reject the way....' has also a Qurʾānic connotation (e.g. 16:94; the expression is in fact quite common in the Qurʾān).

34 Text in the seal from Qurʾān 3:123. Translation M.A.S. Abdul Haleem (Oxford 2004).

Index of names and titles

References are to the serial number of the letter, then to the line numbers in the Arabic text

ʿAbd al-Raḥmān: captain of the ship Sīb-i Bādam, No. 2, line 4; No. 3, line 7; No. 6, line 8; No. 7, line 8
[al-Sayyid] Badr b. al-Sayyid Sayf, son of the late Imām Aḥmad b. Saʿīd al-Būsaʿīdī, No. 10, line 2
Bālyūz al-Wulandīn: the governor of the Dutch, addressee of No. 1, line 1
Batāwa: Batavia, No. 3, line 2; No. 6, line 2; No. 7, line 2
Batāwī: Batavia, No. 8, line 2; No. 9, line 1
Batāwiya: Batavia, No. 5, verso
Dariktūr: the director (Batavia's harbormaster), No. 9, line 1
Dhū al-Nūn: the prophet Jonah, No. 3, line 3
Fatḥ-i Islām: 'The Conquest of Islam', name of a ship, No. 8, line 6; No. 9, line 8
Ǧandarāl Batāwa: the Governor-General in Batavia, addressee of No. 3, line 1
Ǧandarāl Pīsī: Governor-General A.H. Wiese, No 10, line 4
Ǧandarāl Ṣāḥib: the Governor-General in Batavia, addressee of No. 5, line 2
Ǧanǧāwar: 'The Bringer of Treasure', name of a ship, No. 6, line 13; No. 7, line 12; No. 8, line 3 written Ganǧāwar; No. 9, line 3 written Ganǧāwar
Gawnar Ǧanrāl Ṣāḥib: the Governor-General in Batavia, addressee of No. 4, line 1
al-Ḥāǧǧī ʿAnbar Dāwūd Khalīl, named al-Khalīlī: owner of a ship, No. 10, lines 4–5
al-Ḥāǧǧī Maḥmūd b. Mashkūr: captain of the ship Ǧanǧāwar/Ganǧāwar, No. 6, line 13–14; No. 7, lines 12–13; No. 8, line 4, al-Ḥāǧǧ Maḥmūd; No. 9, line 5, al-Ḥāǧǧ Maḥmūd b. Muḥammad b. Mashkūr
Ibrāhīm b. Ḥasan: captain of a ship, No. 10, line 5
Khalfān b. Muḥammad b. ʿAbdallāh al-Būsaʿīd: sender of No. 1, with his seal
Kolkata: Calcutta, No. 8, line 8; No. 9, line 9
Kūtshī: the town of Kochi, No. 1, line 1
al-Manṣūr: 'The Victorious', name of a ship, No. 1, line 6
Masgad: Muscat, No. 6, line 7
al-Muʿallim Wazīr: captain of or passenger on the ship Sīb-i Bādam, No. 3, line 7
Muḥammad: son of Khalfān b. Muḥammad b. ʿAbdallāh al-Būsaʿīd, No. 1, line 16
Qupanī al-Dawla al-Wulandīziyya: 'the Company of the Dutch government', No. 8, line 1
Sar Gawnar Ǧanrāl Ṣāḥib: the Governor-General in Batavia, addressee of No. 4, line 1

Shābandar Batāwa: the harbor master of Batavia, addressee of No. 6, line 2
Shāhbandar Ṣāḥib: the harbor master of Batavia, addressee of No. 5, verso
Sīb-i Bādam: name of a ship, No. 2, line 3; No. 3, line 6; No. 6, lines 9, 11, No. 7, line 8
Sulaymān: son of Khalfān b. Muḥammad b. ʿAbdallāh al-Būsaʿīd, No. 1, line 16
Sulṭān al-Ḥabashī: an envoy, No. 1, line 6
Sulṭān b. al-Imām Aḥmad b. Saʿīd: sender of No. 2, seal; No. 3, lines 17–18; No. 4, seal; No. 5, seal; No. 6, verso; No. 7, verso; No. 8, line 15, with the *nisba* al-Būsaʿīdī; No. 9, line 15, with the *nisba* al-Būsaʿīdī; No. 10, line 7, mentioned as al-Imām al-Sayyid Sulṭān; No. 10, line 8, mentioned as al-Sayyid Sulṭān

Bibliography

Archives

AHU	– Arquivo Histórico Ultramarino, Lisbon
	C.I.: Caixas da India
ANNT	– Arquivo Nacional da Torre do Tombo, Lisbon
HAG	– Historical Archives, Panaji, Goa [see *BFUP*]
NA	– Nationaal Archief, The Hague
	Collectie Geleynssen de Jonghe
	Collectie Sweers
	Collectie Leupe nr. 865
	KA = old classification for VOC, be it with different numbers

VOC - Records of the Verenigde Oostindische Compagnie (VOC) (Dutch East-India Company)
Hooge Regeering Batavia

Books and Articles

Allen, C.H. "The Indian Merchant Community of Muscat," *BSOAS* XLIV/1 (1981), pp. 39-53.

Amin, A.A. *British Interests in the Persian Gulf 1747-1780* (Leiden, 1976).

Anonymous. *Relãçao das plantas e descripções de todas as fortelezas, cidades e povoações que os Portugueses têm no Estado da India* ed. A. Botelho da Cousa Velga (Lisbon, 1936).

al-Ashban, A.A. "The Foundation of the Omani Trading Empire under the Ya`arubah Dynasty 1642-1719," *Arab Studies Quarterly* I/4 (1979), 354-71.

Assentos do Conselho do Estado 1618-1750 (Proceedings of the State Council at Goa), edited by Panduronga S. S. Pissurlencar/ Vithal T. Gune, 5 vols. (Bastorá/Goa: Rangel, 1953-57).

Aubin, Jean ed. *L'Ambassade de Gregório Fidalgo à la cour du Châh Soltân-Hoseyn* (Lisbon, 1971).

As Gavetas da Torre do Tombo, Gavetas I-XXIII (henceforth *Gavetas*) 12 vols., edited by A. Silva Rego (Lisbon: Centro de Estudos Históricos Ultramarinos, 1960-77).

Badger, G.P. tr. *History of the Imams and Seyyids of `Oman by Salil Ibn Razik from AD 661-1856* 2 vols. (London, 1871).

Baladouni, Vahe and Makepeace, Margaret. *Armenian Merchants of the Seventeenth and Early Eighteenth Centuries. English East India Company Sources* (Philadelphia 1998).

Barendse, R.J. *The Arabian Seas. The Indian ocean World of the seventeenth century* (Armonk/London, 2002).

Bathhurst, R.D. *The Ya`rubi Dynasty of Oman* (unpublished dissertation University of Oxford, 1967).

___, "Maritime Trade and Imamite Government: Two Principal Themes in the History of Oman to 1729," in: D. Hopwood, *The Arab Peninsula. Society and Politics* (London, 1972), pp. 89-106.

Biker, Júlio Firmino Júdice ed. *Collecção de tratados e concertos de pazes que o Estado da India Portuguesa fez com os reis e senhores com que teve relações nas partes da Asia e Africa Oriental.* 14 vols. (Lisbon, 1881-87).

Boletim da Filmoteca Ultramarina Portuguesa 50 vols. (Lisbon, Centro de Estudos Históricos Ultramarinos, 1955-1989).

Bocarro, António. *Livro das plantas de todas as fortalezas, cidades e povoações do estado da India Oriental.* 3 vols, (Lisbon, 1992).

Boxer, C.R. tr. *Commentaries of Ruy Freyre de Andrada* (London, 1930).

___, "Anglo-Portuguese rivalry in the Persian Gulf," in E. Prestage ed. *Chapters in Anglo-Portuguese Relations* (Watford, 1935), pp. 46-129.

Bruce, J. *Annals of the Honorable East India Company* 3 vols. (London, 1810).

Carré, Abbé. *The travels of Abbé Carré in India and the Near East (1672-74)*, 3 vols. (London: Hakluyt, 1947).

Colenbrander, H. T. & Coolhaas, W. Ph. eds. *Jan Pietersz. Coen. Bescheiden omtrent zijn bedrijf in Indië* 8 vols. (The Hague, 1919-53).

Coolhaas, W. Ph. *Generale Missieven van Gouverneurs-Generaal en Raden aan Heren XVII der Verenigde Oostindische Compagnie*, 6 vols. (The Hague, 1960-1980).

Cordeiro, Luciano. *Questões Histórico-Colonais* 3 vols. (Lisbon, 1936).

Della Valle, Pietro. *Les Fameux Voyages* 4 vols. (Paris: Gervais Clouzier, 1664).

Dam, P. van. *Beschrijvinge van de Oost Indische Compagnie*, ed. F. W. Stapel, Rijks Geschied-kundige Publicatiën 83, The Hague, 1939.

Doornbos, Klaas. *Shipwreck & Survival in Oman, 1763*. Amsterdam: Pallas, 2012.

Dunlop, H. *Bronnen tot de geschiedenis der Oostindische Compagnie in Perzië* (The Hague, 1930).

Ferrier, R.W. *British-Persian Relations in the 17th Century*, unpublished dissertation (Cambridge University 1970).

Floor, Willem. "First Contacts between the Netherlands and Muscat," *ZDMG* 132 (1982), pp. 289-307.

____, "Dutch trade with Muscat in the second half of the 18th century," *African and Asian Studies* 16 (1982), pp. 197-213.

____, "A Description of Muscat and Oman Anno 1673/1084 H," *Moyen Orient & Océan Indien* 2 (1985), pp. 1-69.

____, "Dutch East India Company's Trade with Sind in the 17th and 18th centuries," *Moyen-Orient & Ocean Indien* 3 (1986), pp. 111-144.

____, *Commercial Conflict between Persia and the Netherlands 1712-1718*, University of Durham Occasional Paper Series no. 37 (1988).

____, *Afghan Occupation of Persia, 1722-1730* (Paris/Louvain: Cahiers Studia Iranica, 1998).

____, *The Persian Textile Industry, Its Products and Their Use 1500-1925* (Paris: Harmattan: 1999).

____, *A Fiscal History of Iran in the Safavid and Qajar Period* (New York: Bibliotheca Persica, 1999).

____, *The Economy of Safavid Persia* (Wiesbaden: Reichert, 2000).

____, "The Lost Files of Jean Billon of Cancerilles and French-Persian Relations during the beginning of the eighteenth century," *Eurasian Studies* 2 (2003), pp. 43-94.

____, and Faghfoory, Mohammad, *The First Dutch-Iranian Commercial Conflict* (Costa Mesa: Mazda, 2004).

____, *The Persian Gulf 1500-1730. The Political Economy of Five Port Cities*. Washington DC, 2006.

____, *The Rise of the Gulf Arabs*. Washington DC: MAGE, 2007.

Foster, William ed. *The English Factories in India 1618-1669*. 13 vols. (London, 1906-27).

Fryer, John. *A New Account of East India and Persia Being Nine Years' Travels, 1672-1681*, 3 vols. (London, 1909-15).

Gemelli-Careri, Gio Francesco. *Giro del Mondo* 6 vols. (Napoli: Giuseppe Roselli, 1699).

Godinho, Manuel. *Relação do novo caminho que fêz por terra e mar vindo da Índia para Portugal, no ano de 1663 o Padre Manuel Godingo* (Lisbon, 1944).

Hagenaer, Hendrick. "Scheep-vaert naar Oost-Indien," in Izaäk Commelin, *Begin ende Voortgangh* 2 vols. (Amsterdam, 1645).

Hamilton, Alexander. *A New Account of the East Indies* 2 vols. (London, 1930).

Kaempfer, Engelbert. *Die Reisetagebücher* ed. K. Meier-Lemgo. (Wiesbaden, 1968).

Klein, Rüdiger. *Trade in the Safavid Port City Bandar Abbas and the Persian Gulf Area (ca. 1600-1680). A Study of Selected Aspects* (School of Oriental and African Studies, 1993/94).

Kroell, Anne, "Billon de Cancerille et les rélations Franco-Persanes au début du XVIIIe siècle," *Le Monde Iranien et l'Islam* II (1974), pp. 127-56.

___, "Louis XIV, la Perse et Mascate," *Le Monde Iranien et l'Islam* 4 (1976-1977), pp. 1-78.

___, *Nouvelles d'Ispahan 1665-1695* (Paris, 1979).

Lockhart, L. *Nadir Shah* (London, 1938).

___, *The Fall of the Safavi Dynasty* (Cambridge, 1956).

Lockyer, Charles. *An Account of British Trade in India* (London, 1711)

Lorimer, J. G. *Gazetteer of the Persian Gulf* (Calcutta, 1915 [1970]).

Mandelslo, J.A. von. *Journal und Observation (1637-1640)* ed. M. Refslund-Klemann (Copenhagen, 1942).

Mar`ashi, Mohammad Khalil. *Majma` al-Tavarikh*. ed. Abbas Eqbal (Tehran, 1328/1949).

Martin, François. *Mémoires de -, fondateur de Pondicherry*, 3 vols. ed. A. Martineau (Paris 1931-34), of which vol. 1 and part of vol. 2 have been translated into English by Aniruddha Ray as *François Martin Mémoires Travels to Africa, Persia & India* (Calcutta, 1990) [cited as Martin, *Travels*] and the remainder of vol. 2 and vol. 3 by Lotika Varadarajan as *India in the 17*[th] *Century. Social, Economic and Political (memoirs of François Martin)* 2 vols. in 4 parts (New Delhi, 1981), cited as Martin, *India*.

Matos, Luís ed. *Das relações entre Portugal e a Pérsia 1500-1758. Catálogo bibliográfico da exposição comemorativa do XXV centenário da monarquia no Irão* (Lisbon: Fundação Calouste Gulbenkian, 1972) translated into Persian by Mehdi Aqa Mohammad Zanjani as *Asnad va Ravabet-e Tarikhi-ye Iran va Portughal* (Tehran, 1383/2003).

___, *Imagens do Oriente no século XVI: reprodução do códice português da Biblioteca casanatense* (Lisbon, 1985).

Meier-Lemgo, K. *Die Briefe E. Kaempfers* (Mainz, 1965).

Miles, S.B. *The Countries and Tribes of the Persian Gulf* (London, 1969).

Nasiri, Mohammad Ebrahim b. Zeyn al-`Abedin, *Dastur-e Shahriyan*. ed. Mohammad Nader Nasiri Moqaddam (Tehran, 1373/1995).

Niebuhr, Carsten. *Beschreibung von Arabien, aus eigenen beobachtungen und in lande selbst gesammleten nachrichten abgefasset nachrichten* (Copenhagen: N. Möller, 1772).

___, *Reisebeschreibung nach Arabien und andern umliegenden Ländern*. 3 vols. in one (Zürich, 1997).

Ovington, J. *A voyage to Surat in the year 1689* ed. H. G. Rawlinson (London, 1929).

Risso, Patricia. *Oman & Muscat an early modern history* (New York, 1986).

Ross. E.C. ed. *Annals of Oman from Early Times to the Year 1728 AD* (Cambridge: Oleander Press, 1984).

Serjeant, R.B, "Omani Naval Activities off the Southern Arabian Coast in the late 11th/17th Century from Yemeni Chronicles," *Journal of Omani Studies* 6/1 (1983), pp. 77-80.

Slot, B. J. *The Arabs of the Gulf, 1602-1784: an alternative approach to the early history of the Arab Gulf States and the Arab peoples of the Gulf mainly based on sources of the Dutch East India Company* (Leidschendam, 1993) translated into Arabic by `Ayidah Khuri muraja`at Mohammad Mursi Abdollah as `*Arab al-Khalij, 1602-1784: fi daw` masadir Sharikat al-Hind al-Sharqiyah al-Hulandiyah* (Abu Dhabi, 1995).

Steensgaard, Neils. *Carracks, Caravans and Companies. The structural crisis in the European-Asian trade in the early 17th century* (Copenhaguen, 1973).

Subrahmanyam, Sanjay. *The Portuguese Empire in Asia 1500-1700* (London, 1993).

Tavernier, Jean-Baptiste. *The Six Voyages* translated by John Phillips 2 vols. (London: R.L. and M. Pitt, 1678).

___, *Voyages en Perse et description de ce royaume* (Paris, 1930).

Teles y Cunha, João Manuel de Almeida. *Economia de um império. Economia política do Estado da Índia em torno do mar Arábico e golfo Pérsico. Elementos conjuncturais: 1595-1635*. (Universidade Nova de Lisboa, 1995).

Terpstra, H. *De Opkomst der Westerkwartieren der Oost-Indische Compagnie (Suratte, Arabië, Perzië* (The Hague, 1918).

Thevenot, J. de. *The Travels of M. de Thevenot into the Levant* (London, 1686 [1971]).

Wilkinson, J. *Water and Tribal Settlement in South-East Arabia* (Oxford, 1977).

___, *The Imamate Tradition of Oman* (Cambridge, 1987).

Yule, H. and Burnell, A. C. eds. *Hobson-Jobson, a glossary of colloquial anglo-indian words and phases, and of kindred terms, etymological, historical, geographical and discursive* (London, 1903).

Ziolkowski, Michele C. *The historical archaeology of the coast of Fujairah, United Arab Emirates: From the eve of Islam to the early twentieth century*, 2 vols. (University of Sydney, 2002).

INDEX

A

Aatsjerek 190
Abbas I 2, 6, 8, 10, 14, 79
Abbas II 30, 31
Abbas Qoli Khan 83
Abdol-Rahman 167
Aden xxii, 127, 194
agriculture 117
aguilwood 192
Ahmad b. Sa'id xxiii, 144
Al Abu Moheyr 83
Alaur Aga 194
al-Hasa 117
Ali Jamal 9
Ali Mardan Khan 83, 84, 86
Ali Reza Khan 92
Alledzja kalberga 197
Alledzja mioneh 197
Alledzja molla abrahunnij 197
Alledzja zjome shah 198
Alledzja zjome waar 197
al-Mokha 38, 266
al-Mu`allim Wazir 167
Aloe 152
Alphen, the 47, 53
al-Sha`am 174
Al Zo`ab 83
amber 195
ambergris 200
Amir Mehin 83
Amq 182
Amstelveen, the xxiv, 217, 221, 223, 226, 227, 257, 262, 265, 266

Anbar Dawud Khalil 168
anchorage 43
anchors 203, 260
arak xxv, 162
areca 191, 192, 193, 200, 201, 215
Armenians 7, 24, 28, 78, 80, 88, 134, 169, 308
arms 123
arsenal 112
Asafetida 152
assegais 235
aureum pigmentum 164
avondpijl 227

B

baaitje 241
Badr b. al-Sayyid Sayf 168
baftas 159, 196, 197, 202
Bahlah 116
Bahrain 94, 95, 96, 97, 98, 99, 117, 127, 134, 139, 142, 143, 196, 197, 198, 202, 213
Bai`ah 180
bailo 255
bait al-qufl 177
bak 230
Balthazar, Jacob Johan 247
Balthazar, Jacobus Johannes 253, 258
Balthazar, Janus 245
Baluchis 22, 66, 104, 124, 125, 137
bamboo 145, 194
Bandar Abbas xxi, 6, 31, 33, 35, 48, 61, 79, 134, 147

Bandar-e Deylam 83
Bandar-e Kong 11, 16, 19, 24, 26, 27, 31, 38, 56, 58, 60, 78, 80, 81, 82, 83, 84, 86, 89, 92, 93, 94, 96, 99, 135, 136, 138, 139, 196
Bandar-e Rig 31, 142
bangsar 129
bankshall 195
Bantam 164
Banyan xxii, 20, 22, 24, 33, 67, 104, 105, 114, 129, 133, 148, 151, 204, 205, 206, 247
Banyans 18, 23, 60, 69, 72, 104, 110, 113, 118, 119, 121, 126, 130, 132, 137, 185, 202, 204, 205
barasti huts 176, 250
Barbara Theodora, the xxiv, 150, 154, 155, 160
Barkah 115
barkassen 229
Barkeh 183
Baron van der Capellen 169
Basra xxi, xxii, xxiii, 6, 7, 9, 11, 23, 25, 27, 31, 35, 38, 41, 42, 44, 51, 58, 70, 94, 100, 101, 112, 117, 127, 132, 134, 136, 142, 143, 153, 161, 165, 196, 197, 198, 199, 200, 205, 209, 210, 214, 217, 218, 221
Basrur 132, 192, 204, 205
Bassein 66, 67, 68, 70
Batavian Republic 166
Batinah 8
Battil 251
Bazaars 113, 127
beglerbegi 83, 96
Bengal 145, 158
Bent, Frederik Lambertsz 71, 73, 74
benzoïn 156, 194
bestek 228
Beurs van Amsterdam, the 47, 51
Beys, Laurens 263
beyt al-dawwar 250
beyt al-mal 120
Bhatkal 132, 192, 205
Bidyah 180
Bil`arab b. Sultan 76

Billon, Jean 88
Binnenmaking 228
Blinde ra, 230
Blom, Christiaan 265
borborrij 190, 214
borborry 187, 193
Botelho, Nuno Àlvares 12
Boudaens, Elias xxi, 21, 22, 105
bovenlandse Arabieren 216
braamzeilkoelte 226
Brahé 146
Brahmin 204
Brangwin 79
breede raad 6
brimstone 158, 164
Brinkhoud, Jan 260
Broach 191
brokerage 129, 130, 156, 206, 208, 209
Bronkhorst 240, 242, 260, 266
Brouwershaven 33
Bruijn, Gerrit 164
Buginese 153
buiksnijder 235
Buitenbroeking 228
Buschman, Wilhelmus 254, 257, 258
Bushehr 7, 142

C

Cabo de Goede Hoop 268
Cagie 250
cahonie 199
Calcutta 168
Calicut 155, 193, 263, 264
camelins 22
camphor 32, 159, 194, 214
Cananore 22
Canara 61, 93
Canarese xxii, 67, 71, 127, 192
Cannanore 193, 205
cannekijns 202
cannons 24, 46, 66, 90, 123, 125, 184, 203, 267
Capa Mataraca 222
Cape Bardestan 255
Cape Mataraca 227
Cape Mataraqa xxiv

captives 105
cardamom 158, 190, 193, 194, 200, 201, 205
Cargasoenmessen 249
cash 68, 98, 126, 127, 145, 146, 147, 155, 164, 200, 201, 202, 217
Cassia fistula 191, 198
Ceylon xxii, 27, 32, 36, 45
chador 188
chador cambatij 202
chador daboelij 201
chadors 199
chanks 195
Chaul 135
cherik 83
chiadder cangij 216
chickens 180
chillas 199
chintzes 202
Chitsware 198
church 108, 112, 113, 114
cinnamon 32, 146, 150, 185, 207, 214, 215
circumcision 247
cisterns 85
civet 195
cleeden 128, 187, 195, 199, 202, 203
clockspijs 118
cloves xxv, 32, 146, 159, 162, 163, 164, 201, 206, 213, 216, 221
Cochin 217, 261
Cochineal 159
coconut palms 28
coconuts 27, 132, 191, 194, 195
Coene, Pieter 232, 240
Coen, Jan Pieterszoon 10, 308
coetlij 191
coffee 22, 24, 121, 127, 145, 153, 194, 243, 252, 266
Coffee 200, 215
Coin, Jan 87
coins 135
coir 132, 191, 194, 195, 203, 205
Colombo xxi, xxii, 47, 50, 217, 222
Colville Cove 176
commercial treaty xxii, xxiii, 46, 50, 51, 53, 55, 56, 61, 62, 64, 65, 69, 72, 96

Concordia xxi, 21, 162
conifers 194, 200
Constabelskamer 228
construction wood 132
copper 169, 214
copperware 152, 158
copra 193, 200, 201
Cornelis, Dutch mate 27
Cornelis Eyks 232
Coromandel 33, 202, 223, 226, 233, 242
Correia de Sá, João 59, 60
cost of ship 148, 154
cotton 123, 188, 189, 192, 197, 198, 199, 207, 210, 221
cotton yarn 188, 189, 221
country traders 153, 158, 169
Courier, the 257, 258
cows 180, 233
cradle 236
crafts 118, 119, 137
craftsmen 105, 118
Crangenoor 262
credit 152
Crouch 166
cultivation 116, 117
cumin 188
curcuma 27, 158, 159, 185, 187
customs duties 23, 29, 31, 35, 37, 43, 44, 52, 54, 56, 60, 62, 63, 64, 65, 69, 71, 72, 74, 99, 130, 133, 149, 205
customs duty 26
customs-house 31, 129, 132
customs rate 149

D

Daalberg, Jonas 232
Dagwacht 226
Daman 135
Damzight 264
Danish pirates 88
Dantzig 258
Dashtestan 95
date palm fronds 179
dates 127, 130, 145, 153, 158, 175, 200, 206

Dayer 255
Dedel, Jacob 5
De Erf-Prins 261
de Geus 245
de Haze, François 47, 51, 56, 60, 66, 69, 74, 215
de Jager, Herbert 34
de Keyser, Cornelis 164
de Leest 177
de Mardeville, Michiel 74, 75
de Mello de Castro, Antonio 57
de Meneses, António 86
de Nijsz 146, 147, 149, 160
de Noronha de Albuquerque, Pedro António 80
de Silveira, Gonçalo 13
Deventer 260
de Vlakke 268
de Vos Jobsz, Cornelis 74, 75
Dharmapatam 193
Diba 8, 9, 179
Dikkah 147
Dimaniyat 184
dissatisfaction, population 58
Diu 66, 105, 108, 118, 138, 216
D. Manoel, Portuguese admiral 40
Doggebay 175
dongrys 199
Doodendorp, Johan Hendrik 261
Doodkist 177
Drevan, Jan 242
Drevens, Jan 260, 266
Dronthem 258
ducats 147, 154, 158
Duhat Qabal 178
Duhat Shaishah 178
duikers 227
dungarees 27
Dutch 41, 144
Dutch mission 53

E

eagle-wood 192, 216
earthenware 201
East Africa 82, 127, 134
Eastern Hajar 222, 252
East India Company 2

elephants tusks 153, 207
Emam Qoli Khan 15, 16
Emir of Vodona 25
English 149, 158
English deserters 73
Esma`il al-Basri 134
Esma`il Bandari 112, 134
exchange rates 147
Eyks, Cornelis 222

F

Fahal 184
famine 58
Father António de Jesus 82
Fath Islam 168
Fattaa Remam 101
Film 177
fire making 233
firewood 90, 128
Fiscaal 265
fish 115, 247
fishing 175
Floes 242
Florens, Johannes 165
flour 18, 233
fokkera 230
food supplies xxi, xxiii, 18, 29, 58, 85, 97, 115, 217
foppelij 216
forwarding of letters 161
Frederik Hendrik, Stadtholder 14
freight 208
French 38, 42, 44, 48, 57, 63, 79, 88, 91, 138, 149, 166, 167, 309
French beans 233
fruits 181, 201

G

Galderij 229
galeotas 9
Gallivat 256
Gambia 55
Gamron xxi, 11, 13, 156, 174, 184, 205, 210, 258
Gaudereau 88
Geleynsen, Wollebrandt 17

INDEX • 317

Ghabbi 116
Ghubb Ali 176
Ghubbat Shabus 178
Ghurab 255
ginger 27, 159, 185, 191, 192, 193, 194, 200, 205, 214, 215
glass beads 191
glop 109
Goa 1, 5, 11, 12, 13, 15, 16, 17, 23, 27, 38, 56, 61, 71, 80, 82, 84, 90, 96, 190, 307, 308
goat hair 217, 247
goats 180
Godske, IJsbrand 108
goeries 196, 197
goony 191, 192
Gotsche 147, 150
Graaf Bensdorff 166
grains 115, 198
groosie 244
groote booten 229
groundnut 188
ground-nuts 189
Gujarat xxii, 66, 134, 185, 188
Gulbarga 197
Gulf of Masirah 222
Gulf of Sawqirah 222
Gum Arabica 152
gum-lac 159
Gum myrrh 152
Gum olibanum 152
gums 145, 158

H

Hadd 251
Hajji Khalil 49, 52, 53
Hajji Qasem 42
hamelslagen 118
Harapatnam 190
Harckz, Jacobus 41, 42, 43, 45, 46, 47, 48, 50, 54, 65, 214
Hardtsjerie 190
Hartman, Jacob 50, 61
Hartsing, Georgius xxii, 42, 43, 44, 45
Hasa 127, 198, 202
Heeren XVII 18, 76, 160

Heeren Zeventien 6
Heir 257
helileh 191
hemp 191, 192
Herat 30
herbal juice 106
Heusden 5
Heynes 15
hides 185, 188
Hillekens, Steven 260, 262, 266
Hing 152, 201
Hoogcamer, Jacobus 83, 86
Hook of Enzaädades Baixos 229
hooploper 258
Hormuz 2, 4, 5, 7, 8, 9, 11, 12, 15, 17, 18, 82, 86, 96, 97, 99, 136, 139, 221, 259
horses 22, 32, 37, 44, 51, 52, 53, 110, 115, 116, 117, 127, 130, 133, 156, 167, 168, 169, 201, 204, 207, 208, 209
hotels 112
household effects 106
Houting, Nicolaas 223
Hugli 88
Hula 69, 100
huts 178, 179, 247

I

Ibadi sect 19
Ibrahim b. Hasan 168
Imam's soldiers 123
Indian merchants 133, 134, 207
Indians 105
Indigo 198
Indonesia xxv
interpreter 43, 82
Irias 198
iron 118, 123, 124, 128, 132, 135, 145, 146, 158, 169, 174, 178, 179, 185, 193, 203
irrigation works 28

J

Janjawar 168
Janszen, Matthys 246, 258

japancij 201
Japanese 32, 159, 214, 216
Jask 11, 23, 24, 39
Jazirat al-Ghanam 176
Jews 104, 113, 137, 149, 260
jihad 137
Jolfar 8, 32, 61, 124, 127
jong matroos 240
Jupiter 166

K

kad aewasije 189
kad kenaiedaar 196
Kadmiersay 197
kahonie 199
Kalba 182
Kanara 67, 93, 115, 199, 201, 214, 215
Kangan 255
Kaphol Banyans 105
Kapok 153
kargeen 250
Karshah 178
Karwar 192, 198, 205
Kazerun 83
Kerala 105, 134
Kerman 7
Ketelaar, Jan Josua 96
Khalfan b. Mohammad 147, 154
Khalili 168
khanjars 235
Khark xxiii, xxiv, 7, 116, 141, 142, 143, 146, 147, 155, 156, 157, 158, 160, 161, 169, 218, 219, 220, 221, 252, 254, 255, 256
Khasab 8, 171, 174
Khor al-Sham 175
Khor Fakkan 180
Khor Quwai 176
Khur Fakkan 8, 59
Khur Qoway 12
Killiesie 190
Kleyn, Jacob 242
Koene, Pieter 246, 260
Kollam 263
Kolstrop, Andries 245
Kolstrop, Jansz Andreas 258

Konkan 26, 127, 133, 198
Kuhgilu 92
kuil 229
Kumzar 176
Kutch 127, 131, 132, 188, 198, 201, 204, 209

L

lack 188
lamp-oil 188, 189, 191, 192, 198
Lar 7, 29, 30, 83, 206
Larek 10, 93, 96, 97, 99, 139, 174
Lasboom 257, 261
lastkamer 229
lead 119, 136, 158, 198, 201, 207, 261
leather 198
Lekkerland 265
lens houden 228
Lessenaren 177
levies 83
lighters 41, 128
lijwaten 196, 197, 200
Lima 8, 9, 178
Lima Qadimah 179
limes 180, 254
linen 22
Lion 13
Lispensier, Bartholomeus 100
loafsugar 116
Locke, John 91
lokjes 243
longi 189, 196, 201
longijs sabonie 196
longis 189
long loebieij 196
Lotf Ali Khan 96, 97, 98
Lucassen, Philips 15, 16
Lutges, Hans 232, 239
Luxemburg 258

M

Maandstukje 226
mace 146, 162
madder 22
madraseh 114

Mahmud b. Mohammad b. Mashkur 168
Makallah 105
Makran 124
Malabar xxii, 5, 26, 27, 31, 41, 47, 56, 71, 108, 127, 132, 158, 159, 170, 185, 193, 199, 201, 214, 215, 216, 217, 223
Malabari traders 65
Malcolm's Inlet 177
Maldives xxii, 195, 200
Malindi 194
Manah 116
Mangalore 82, 132, 138, 192, 205
Manuel Mensos 38
Mappilas 105
Maratha 37, 190
Marienbosch, the xxiii, xxiv, 146, 147, 148, 153, 156
Markab 251
marszeilskoelte 229
Martin, François 38, 310
Mashhad 30
Masirah 228
masts 132, 195, 200, 203, 229, 251
Masulipatnam xxii, 27, 41, 42
Matrah 147, 153, 155, 253
mawijs 196
Mecca 55, 96, 135
Meerkadt, the 36, 171
meetwaren 207
Mehrab Sultan 95
Melinde xxii, 26, 127
melons 180
metals 158, 218
Michel, French ambassador 91
milij 189
military goods 132
Mir Muhanna 255
Mirza Naser 91
Mirza Rabi`eh, nazer 89
Mirza Rabi`, secretary 82
Mirza Taher, grand vizier 82
Mirza Taqi, grand vizier 17
Mocha 135
Mohammad Sheikh Abdallah 47
Mohammad Sheikh Abdallah Soleyman 42

Mohammad Sheikh Abdallah Soleyman 76
Mohanna` b. Sultan 99
Mokha xxii, 22, 117, 127, 132, 194, 200, 209, 210
Mombasa 26, 80, 82, 86, 87, 90, 138, 153
Mondas Naan 24
monsoon 128, 130, 134, 210
Moqaqah 177
Morteza Qoli Beg 28
Mossel, Jacob 144, 150
Mozambique 5, 40
Mr. George 43
mu`allim 252
Mughab 184
mules 117
Musa Beg 10
Musandam 40, 171, 177
Muscat xxiv, 145, 147, 219
Muscat garrison 77
Muscat navy 94
Muscat trade xxii, 127
Muscat war fleet 66
mustard-seed 179
Muysenbergh, the 47, 53

N

Nabar 182
nails 169
nakhoda 133, 202
Narrotam 151, 222, 260
Narutem 105
nazer-e boyutat 89
Nederhoven 100
negotie raad 6
Neijk 201
Nepthunus, the 164
Nicholsoon, Willem 257
Nicolson, Willem 248
Nieuw Nieuwerkerk 226
Nizwa 19, 27, 33, 48, 49, 50, 53, 73, 116, 117
nutmegs 146, 159, 162, 201

O

Oets, Jan 97, 98
Oman xxiv
Omani levies 77
onbekwaam 267
Onderlijzeilspier 230
onions 180
Oploper 258
Ormus Marsjant 90
Ottomans 2, 17, 70, 218
Otub 95
Overschie, Nicolaes 17, 18

P

paatsjehaer 202
Padbrugge, Robert 46, 49, 51, 52, 53, 54, 55
paleng peosj moltony 197
pancerangijs 216
pariassen 233
parren 207
passiaaren 256
Patan 127, 132, 189, 198, 201, 204
Pate 194
patha 199, 202
Patta 200, 201, 211
pearls 22, 158
peas 188, 189
pepper 22, 27, 41, 132, 146, 158, 185, 193, 194, 200, 201, 205, 214, 218, 219
Pereira Fidalgo, Gregório 82
Persian red 259
Pieters, Carsten 257
Pietersen, Nicolaas 146, 151, 165, 223, 226, 267
Pietersze, Carsten 238, 242
Pietersze, Karsten 248
Pietersze, Kersten 245
pigs 233
pilgrims 90, 135
pilots 51, 67
pirates 27
planks 132, 194, 195, 200, 203, 228
Poeloe Pinang 165

Ponnani 193
Poolman, Hendrik 260
Porce 264
porcelain 201
Portchartrain 88
Portuguese 16, 19, 32, 37, 43, 44, 47, 52, 57, 61, 70, 81, 84, 131, 135, 163, 180, 181, 199, 264, 308, 311
Portuguese buildings 111
Portuguese renegades 73, 104
putchok 188

Q

qadi 120
Qatar 95, 127, 134, 196, 202
Qatif 13, 134, 196
Qavasem 94
Qeshm 92, 96, 97, 99, 100, 139, 174
Quryat 122

R

raad van politie 6
Rajapur 127, 132, 190
Rama, Joseph 257
Rammekens 268
Rams 8
Ras al-Bab 177
Ra's al-Hadd 24, 48, 86, 87, 122
Ras Mukhalif 176
Ras Qabr Hindi 177
Ras Sarkim 178
Ras Sheikh Mas`ud 175
reals called foulerie 201
Red Sea 5, 13, 21, 86, 134, 135, 145
Revengie, the 257
rice 18, 22, 23, 63, 68, 115, 118, 127, 129, 132, 133, 158, 159, 185, 191, 192, 199, 200, 203, 207, 214, 221, 254, 255
right of entrepot 130
Ritsert, Nicolaes 61, 65, 66, 69, 71, 72, 73, 75
rompen 32, 206, 213, 214
Rood, Simon 150, 151, 153, 155

INDEX · 321

Roothals, Wouter 36, 37
rosewater 153, 158, 201
Rui Freire de Andrade 9, 11, 12, 16
ruinas 194, 201, 209
rumh 235
Runas 152
Rustaq 144, 147, 148, 153, 154

S

Safi I 10, 14, 16
Safi Qoli Khan 92
Salamah wa-Banatha 177
Salameth Ras 42
Salameth Surat 43
salammoniac 188, 198
salt 118, 158
saltpeter 165, 188, 201
saltwort 238
Samad 116
Sambuk 253
sandalwood 107, 158, 185, 187, 190, 201, 214
sandalwood oil 107
Sangameshwar 190
Sanganians 198
sappanwood 158, 169, 193, 214
sauerkraut 233
sausages 233
Schieman 231
schiemansmaat 231
Schoonderwoerd, Jacob 143, 145
Schooneman, Pieter 261, 262
Schouten, Jan 41, 42, 43, 64
schuit 207
sesamium 189
Seyf b. Sultan 134
shahbandar 18, 28, 30, 69, 79, 98, 121
Shah Sultan Hoseyn 78, 81, 85, 96, 98, 100
Sharjah 94
Sheikh Abdallah 42, 43, 48, 49, 52, 53, 54, 60, 63, 64, 65, 69, 71, 72, 73, 74, 100, 122, 130, 132, 134, 203
Sheikh Abdallah Soleyman 47
Sheikh Jabbareh 100

Sheikh Khalfan b. Mohammad 151
Sheikh Khamis 83
Sheikh Majd 83
Sheikh Mohammad b. Majed 96
Sheikh Naser 142
Sheikh Naser b. Morshed al-Ya`ariba 19
Sheikh Omar 26, 48
Sheikh Omeyr 26, 41, 48, 76
Sheikh Saleh 90
Sheikh Zuhayr tomb 174
shemes 244
Sherley 2
'sHertogenbosch 257
ship building 94
Shiraz 7, 15, 82, 217
Shivaji 37, 55, 127, 131, 132, 190, 198
Siam 39
Sib 115, 183, 184
Sib Badam 167, 168
Sibi River 176
silk 2, 4, 16, 86, 89, 106, 188, 189, 196, 197, 207, 217
Sind xxii, xxiii, xxiv, 18, 24, 29, 38, 41, 42, 55, 61, 124, 127, 132, 134, 136, 146, 149, 160, 187, 196, 200, 201, 204, 208, 210, 219, 309
Sindis 104, 118, 119, 124, 134, 137
Sirat 180
Sjeklassen 159
sjoerij 189
slaves 23, 28, 63, 67, 90, 104, 115, 127, 194, 195, 200
slengen 233
Smeerlepel 249
Smidt, Jan 10
snaauw schip 257
Socotra 55
Soesjes 159
soetlij 192, 194
Sohar 7, 32, 35, 58, 122, 182
Sultan b. Ahmad 167, 168
Sultan b. Seyf 20, 27, 49, 92, 99, 105, 134
sounding lead 223
Sourath 43

specie 150, 155
spices xxv, 55, 132, 141, 158, 167, 169, 201, 218, 219, 221, 233
spy 49
States-General 10
steel 158, 169
stone store-houses 251
stoopskruik 241
stort rijst 203
sugar xxiii, xxiv, xxv, 22, 23, 28, 67, 116, 126, 127, 130, 133, 141, 145, 146, 150, 152, 155, 157, 158, 160, 162, 163, 164, 167, 169, 191, 201, 206, 209, 210, 215, 218, 219, 221
Sulfur 153, 259
Sur 252
Surat xxiv, 5, 7, 38, 42, 68, 90, 93, 94, 101, 127, 132, 160, 161, 170, 191, 199, 201, 202, 204, 213, 215, 216, 221, 311
Susanna, the 263
Suwadi islands 183
Suwaiq 183
Swally 12
swinging the lead 228
synagogue 114

T

Taenmeter 72
Taheri 100
Tahmurath Beg 97
Taillefert, Louis 255
tamarind 191
tammer 182, 243, 247, 252
tang 245, 248
tebhiel 201
terradas 9, 82
terranquins 9
textiles 18, 22, 127, 128, 132, 134, 158, 159, 185, 187, 190, 192, 195, 198, 199, 201, 202, 203, 209, 210, 214, 216, 218
The Coffin 177
The Consent 42
the Kedrie 145
The Last 177
the Latokinu 166
The Lectern 177
The Quoins 177
Theunissen, Jan 252, 258
Theunisze, Jan 246
theuy = touw 228
Thewil 206
Thomassen, Lodewyk 264
thorny trees 234
't Huis de Boede 258
timber 194, 200
tin 32, 146, 164, 169, 201, 207, 221
Tin 158
tolerance 104
tolls 204
tortoise shell 200
'tPasgeld xxiii, xxiv, 146, 149, 160
traditional houses 176
tRad van Avontuur 41
transit-emporium 44
trehiel 193
tsiadder 'tsjonnie 196

U

Umm al-Faiyarin 178
Uzbegs 30

V

vacht 110
vakil 147
Vali Omar 41
van den Boer, Adriaan 226
van den Broecke 5
van der Dussen, Lucas 43
van der Kneu, Huibregt 267
van der Parra 220
vander Werff, Adriaen 171
van Goens, Rijcklof xxii, 36, 45, 46, 47, 50, 51, 54
van Hogendorp, Wiilem 162
van Hogendorp, Willem xxv
van Holland, Pieter 232, 238, 242, 261, 265
van Linschoten 1

van Oorschot, Jan 232
van Wijck, Hendrick xxii, 27, 28, 29, 30, 31, 32, 33, 35, 36, 37, 171
Vengurla 31, 33, 44, 51, 132, 190, 201, 205, 207, 209, 216
Verenigde Oost-Indische Compagnie 1
Visnich, Huybert 6
Vlietlust, the xxiii, 144
VOC factories 7
VOC ranks 7
Voetblok 249
Vogel, Jacob 171
von Kniphausen, Tido xxiv, 142, 143, 157
voor de loos 109
Voorwacht 227
Vredestein 261

W

war drum 66
water melons 180
waterpassen 108
Waterstag 230
wax 194
weigh-house 73, 114, 121, 128, 129, 133, 195, 203, 206
weights 129, 207
Welke, Godfried 164
Westerveld 257
West India 127
Wetteren 258
Weyermans 261
Wiegerman, J. H. 162, 164
Wiese, Albertus Henricus 168
Wilmson, Georg 44, 50, 55, 58, 60, 61, 63, 64, 65, 104
wine 71, 82
Woeling 230

Y

Ya`qub Sultan 96
Yemen 55

Z

zakat 126, 131
Zanzibar 168
Zeekralen 238
Zetaab [?] 59
Zeyn al-Abedin Khan Beg 2
Zielsverkopersbroek 241
zinc 135, 145, 146, 159, 192
zjoerijsen 189
Zuid-Beveland 267

OTHER MAGE TITLES BY WILLEM FLOOR

THE PERSIAN GULF SERIES

A Political and Economic History of 5 Port Cities, 1500–1750

The Rise of the Gulf Arabs, The Politics of Trade on the Persian Littoral, 1747–1792

The Rise and Fall of Bandar-e Lengeh, The Distribution Center for the Arabian Coast, 1750–1930

Bandar Abbas: The Natural Trade Gateway of Southeast Iran

Links with the Hinterland: Bushehr, Borazjan, Kazerun, Banu Ka'b, & Bandar Abbas

The Hula Arabs of the Shibkuh Coast of Iran

IRANIAN HISTORY

Agriculture in Qajar Iran

Public Health in Qajar Iran

The History of Theater in Iran

A Social History of Sexual Relations in Iran

Guilds, Merchants, and Ulama in Nineteenth-Century Iran

Labor & Industry in Iran 1850-1941

The Rise and Fall of Nader Shah: Dutch East India Company Reports 1730-1747

Games Persians Play: A History of Games and Pastimes in Iran from Hide-and-Seek to Hunting

ANNOTATED TRANSLATIONS

A Man of Two Worlds: Pedros Bedik in Iran, 1670–1675
Pedros Bedik
translated with Colette Ouahes from the Latin

Astrakhan Anno 1770
Samuel Gottlieb Gmelin

Travels Through Northern Persia 1770–1774
Samuel Gottlieb Gmelin

Titles and Emoluments in Safavid Iran: A Third Manual of Safavid Administration
Mirza Naqi Nasiri

IN COLLABORATION WITH HASAN JAVADI

The Heavenly Rose-Garden: A History of Shirvan & Daghestan
Abbas Qoli Aqa Bakikhanov

Travels in Iran and the Caucasus, 1652 and 1655
Evliya Chelebi

SOME OTHER MAGE TITLES

Faces of Love: Hafez and the Poets of Shiraz
Hafez, Jahan Khatun, Obeyd Zakani / Translated by Dick Davis

Garden of the Brave in War
Terence O'Donnell

French Hats in Iran
Heydar Radjavi

Tales of Two Cities: A Persian Memoir
Abbas Milani

Crowning Anguish: Taj al-Saltana
Memoirs of a Persian Princess
Introduction by Abbas Amanat / Translated by Anna Vanzan

Stories from Iran: A Chicago Anthology 1921-1991
Edited by Heshmat Moayyad

Savushun: A Novel about Modern Iran
Simin Daneshvar / Translated by M.R. Ghanoonparvar

Also available as an Audio Book

My Uncle Napoleon
Iraj Pezeshkzad / Translated by Dick Davis

Also available as an Audio Book

Vis and Ramin
Fakhraddin Gorgani / Translated by Dick Davis

Also available as an Audio Book

Shahnameh: the Persian Book of Kings
Abolqasem Ferdowsi / Translated by Dick Davis

Borrowed Ware: Medieval Persian Epigrams
Translated by Dick Davis

From Persia to Napa: Wine at the Persian Table
Najmieh Batmanglij

Silk Road Cooking: A Vegetarian Journey
Najmieh Batmanglij

*Food of Life: Ancient Persian and
Modern Iranian Cooking and Ceremonies*
Najmieh Batmanglij

*Happy Nowruz: Cooking with Children to Celebrate
the Persian New Year*
Najmieh Batmanglij

The Persian Garden: Echoes of Paradise
Mehdi Khansari / M. R. Moghtader / Minouch Yavari

*The Persian Sphinx:
Amir Abbas Hoveyda and the Iranian Revolution*
Abbas Milani

Masters and Masterpieces of Iranian Cinema
Hamid Dabashi

The Strangling of Persia
Morgan Shuster

The Persian Revolution of 1905–1909
Edward G. Browne / Introduction by Abbas Amanat

www.ingramcontent.com/pod-product-compliance
Lightning Source LLC
Chambersburg PA
CBHW021932290426
44108CB00012B/816